CHINESE FILMS IN FOCUS

25 New Takes

Edited by
Chris Berry

bfi Publishing

This edition first published in 2003 by the
British Film Institute
21 Stephen Street
London W1T 1LN

The British Film Institute promotes greater understanding and appreciation of, and
access to, film and moving image culture in the UK.

Cover design: ketchup, London
Cover image: *Chungking Express* (Wong Kar-wai, 1994)

Set by Fakenham Photosetting, Fakenham, Norfolk
Printed by Cromwell Press, Trowbridge, Wiltshire

British Library Cataloguing-in-Publication Data

A catalogue record for this book is available from the British Library
ISBN 0 85170 985 0 (hb)
ISBN 0 85170 986 9 (pb)

Contents

Acknowledgments   v

Notes on Contributors   vi

Introduction: One Film at a Time   1
Chris Berry

1. *Black Cannon Incident*: Countering the Counter-espionage Fantasy   8
   Jason McGrath

2. *Boat People*: Second Thoughts on Text and Context   15
   Julian Stringer

3. *Bullet in the Head*: Trauma, Identity and Violent Spectacle   23
   James Steintrager

4. *Centre Stage*: A Shadow in Reverse   31
   Bérénice Reynaud

5. *A Chinese Ghost Story*: Ghostly Counsel and Innocent Man   39
   John Zou

6. *Chungking Express*: Time and its Displacements   47
   Janice Tong

7. *Crouching Tiger, Hidden Dragon*: Cultural Migrancy and Translatability   56
   Felicia Chan

8. *Crows and Sparrows*: Allegory on a Historical Threshold   65
   Yiman Wang

9. *Ermo*: (Tele)Visualising Urban/Rural Transformation   73
   Ping Fu

10. *Evening Bell*: Wu Ziniu's Visions of History, War and Humanity   81
    Yingjin Zhang

11. *Farewell My Concubine*: National Myth and City Memories   89
    Yomi Braester

12. *Floating Life*: Nostalgia for the Confucian Way in Suburban Sydney   97
    Kam Louie

13. *Flowers of Shanghai*: Visualising Ellipses and (Colonial) Absence   104
    Gang Gary Xu

14. *The Goddess*: Fallen Woman of Shanghai   111
    Kristine Harris

15. *Hibiscus Town*: Revolution, Love and Bean Curd   120
    Charles W. Hayford

16. *In the Mood for Love*: Intersections of Hong Kong Modernity   128
    Audrey Yue

17. *Love Eterne*: Almost a (Heterosexual) Love Story   137
    Tan See Kam and Annette Aw

18. *Not One Less*: The Fable of a Migration   144
    Rey Chow

19. *The Red Detachment of Women*: Resenting, Regendering, Remembering   152
    Robert Chi

20. *A Time to Live, A Time to Die*: A Time to Grow   160
    Corrado Neri

21. *A Touch of Zen*: Action in Martial Arts Movies   167
    Mary Farquhar

22. *Vive L'Amour*: Eloquent Emptiness   175
    Fran Martin

23. *Wedding Banquet*: A Family (Melodrama) Affair   183
    Chris Berry

24. *Yellow Earth*: Hesitant Apprenticeship and Bitter Agency   191
    Helen Hok-Sze Leung

25. *Yi Yi*: Reflections on Reflexive Modernity in Taiwan   198
    David Leiwei Li

Chinese Names   206
Chinese Film Titles   209
Compiled by Wang Dun
Index   211

Acknowledgments

I would like to thank all the authors who have contributed to this anthology not only for their highly original and rigorous analyses, but also for their patience and co-operation. Without their hard work, the volume could not exist. Thank you also to Wang Dun for compiling the Chinese character lists and to the Center for Chinese Studies at the University of California, Berkeley, for funding his diligent work. Last but certainly not least, Andrew Lockett at the British Film Institute has been an incisive and constructive editor, and the Institute's anonymous readers have given powerful and constructive feedback and guidance.

Notes on Contributors

Annette Aw is currently a public relations practitioner. She received her doctoral degree from the University of Oklahoma. She has taught at the School of Communication and Information, Nanyang Technological University, Singapore.

Chris Berry teaches in the Film Studies Division of the Department of Rhetoric and in the Department of Theatre, Dance, and Performance Studies at the University of California, Berkeley. He is the editor of *Perspectives on Chinese Cinema* (BFI, 1991), the author of numerous articles on Chinese film, the co-author of *Cinema and Nation: China on Screen* (Cambridge University Press, forthcoming), and the translator of Ni Zhen's *My Memoirs from the Beijing Film Academy: The Origins of China's Fifth Generation Filmmakers* (Duke University Press, 2003).

Yomi Braester is Associate Professor of Comparative Literature at the University of Washington. His recent and forthcoming publications on cinema include: 'From Real Time to Virtual Reality: Chinese Cinema in the Internet Age', *Journal of Contemporary China*, 2–3 (2002); 'Shanghai's Cinematic Memory and the Forgotten Good Eighth Company Campaign', in a volume edited by Xudong Zhang and Elizabeth Perry (forthcoming); 'Tracing the City's Scars: Demolition and the Documentary Impulse in New Urban Cinema', in a volume edited by Zhen Zhang (forthcoming); and 'The Dream of Flying: Taipei's Cinematic Poetics of Demolition', in a volume edited by Charles Laughlin (forthcoming).

Felicia Chan is a doctoral candidate in the School of Critical Theory and Cultural Studies at the University of Nottingham, researching Chinese and other East Asian cinemas in terms of the cultural translatability and readability of these texts. A previous essay comparing Ang Lee's adaptation of Jane Austen with Douglas McGrath's is forthcoming.

Robert Chi is Assistant Professor of Comparative Literature at the State University of New York at Stony Brook. His articles have appeared in *Cultural Critique* and *Tamkang Review*, as well as in *Wanxiang* (*Panorama*).

Rey Chow is Andrew W. Mellon Professor of the Humanities at Brown University. She is the author of numerous articles and several books, including, most recently, *The Protestant Ethnic and the Spirit of Capitalism* (Columbia University Press, 2002). She has also edited the volume *Modern Chinese Literary and Cultural Studies in the Age of Theory: Reimagining a Field* (Duke University Press, 2000) and the special issue 'Writing in the Realm of the Senses' of the journal *differences*, 11, no. 2 (1999).

Mary Farquhar is Associate Professor at Griffith University, Australia. Her book, *Children's Literature in China: From Lu Xun to Mao Zedong* (ME Sharpe, 1999) won the International Children's Literature Association's annual award for the most distinguished scholarly work in the field. Her current work with Chris Berry is called *Cinema and Nation: China On Screen* (Cambridge University Press, forthcoming).

Ping Fu is Assistant Professor in Asian Languages and Literatures, Asian Studies, and Media Studies at Carleton College, where her courses include Chinese and East Asian Cinema and Women and World Cinema. Her publications include 'Dongxie Xidu *dui Jin Yong jianghu shijie de tiyan he wajie*' ('*Ashes of Time*: Experiencing and Deconstructing Jin Yong's Fictive World'), in *Jin Yong xiaoshuo yu ershi shiji zhongguo wenxue* (*Jin Yong's Writings and Twentieth-century Chinese Literature*) (Minhe Press, 2000).

Kristine Harris is Assistant Professor of History at the State University of New York, New Paltz. Her work has appeared in *Cinema and Urban Culture in Shanghai* (Stanford University Press, 1999) and *Transnational Chinese Cinemas* (Hawaii University Press, 1997). She is currently completing a book on early Chinese cinema to 1937.

Charles W. Hayford, Independent Scholar/Visiting Professor, History Department, Northwestern University. Recent publications in the field of modern Chinese history and US–China relations include *To the People: James Yen and Village China* (Columbia University Press, 1990); *China* (ABC–Clio World Bibliography Series, 1997); 'What's So Bad about *The Good Earth?*', *Education about Asia*, vol. 3 no. 3 (December 1998); 'The Open Door Raj: Chinese–American Cultural Relations, 1900–1945', in *Pacific Passage: The Study of American–East Asian Relations*, ed. W. I. Cohen (Columbia University Press, 1996); and 'The Storm Over the Peasant: Rhetoric and Representation in Modern China', *Contesting the Master Narrative*, ed. S. Stromquist and J. Cox (University of Iowa Press, 1998).

Helen Hok-Sze Leung is Assistant Professor of Women's Studies in Simon Fraser University, Canada. Her publications have appeared in *positions: east asia cultures critique*, *The Journal of Lesbian Studies*, *West Coast Line* and *The Capilano Review*.

David Leiwei Li is Collins Professor of the Humanities in the Department of English at the University of Oregon. He is the author of *Imagining the Nation: Asian American Literature and Cultural Consent* (Stanford University Press, 1998) and editor of *Globalization and the Humanities* (a special double issue of *Comparative Literature*). He is working on a manuscript tentatively entitled *The Thrill and Terror of Choice: Modernity, Globality, and Transnational Chinese Cinema.*

Kam Louie is Professor of Chinese Studies at the Australian National University. Publications include *Theorising Chinese Masculinity* (Cambridge University Press, 2002), *The Politics of Chinese Language and Culture* (with Bob Hodge, Routledge, 1998), *The Literature of China in the Twentieth Century* (with Bonnie McDougall, Columbia University Press, 1997) and *Inheriting Tradition* (Oxford University Press, 1986).

Fran Martin is Lecturer in Cinema Studies at La Trobe University, Australia. She has published on contemporary Taiwan cinema and culture in journals including *Intersections*, *GLQ*, *Communal/Plural*, *Critical InQueeries* and *Chung-wai Literary Monthly* (Taiwan). Her book, *Situating Sexualities: Queer Narratives in 1990s Taiwanese Fiction and Film*, was published by Hong Kong University Press (2003). She is co-editor with Chris Berry and Audrey Yue of *Mobile Cultures: New Media and Queer Asia* (Duke University Press, 2003). Her anthology of literary translations, entitled *Angelwings: Contemporary Queer Fiction from Taiwan* was published by Hawaii University Press (2003).

Jason McGrath is a PhD candidate in the Department of East Asian Languages and Civilizations at the University of Chicago. He is completing a dissertation on trends in Chinese cinema and literature in the 1990s.

Corrado Neri is a doctoral candidate at the University of Venice. He has previously published in *Asiatica Veneziana.*

Bérénice Reynaud teaches Film History and Theory at the California Institute of the Arts. She is the author of *Nouvelles Chines, nouveaux cinémas* (Editions de l'Etoile, 1999) and *Hou Hsiao-hsien's A City of Sadness* (BFI, 2002). She has written extensively on Chinese, Taiwanese and Hong Kong cinema, including the chapters on Chinese cinema since 1978 and Taiwanese cinema since 1945 for *Storia Del Cinema (in quattro volumi)* (Torino: Giulio Einaudi Editore, 2001).

James A. Steintrager is Assistant Professor of Comparative Literature at the University of California, Irvine. He has published on cruelty, violence and moral monstrosity in the European context, and is currently expanding his study to include the international impact of mass media.

Julian Stringer is Lecturer in the Institute of Film Studies at the University of Nottingham. He has published widely on Hong Kong cinema, including articles in *Asian Cinema*, *Cineaction*, *Film Quarterly* and *Screen*.

Tan See Kam is an Assistant Professor who teaches and researches at the School of Communication and Information, Nanyang Technological University, Singapore. He has published his works in *Screen*, *Asian Cinema*, *Cinemaya*, *Social Semiotics*, *The South East Asian Journal of Social Science*, *Media Asia*, *Intermedia*, *Antithesis* and *Queer Asian Cinema: Shadows in the Shade* (Harrington Park Press, 2000). Most recently he has co-edited a special issue entitled *Gender in Asian Cinema* for *Asian Journal of Communication* (with Marchetti). Presently he is co-editing an anthology, *Chinese Connections: Film, Diaspora and Identity* (with Marchetti and Feng, Temple University Press, forthcoming).

Janice Tong is a doctoral candidate in Film Studies at the Department of Art History and Theory at the University of Sydney. Her thesis 'Aporia of Time: The Cinema of Wong Kar-wai', is a full-length study on the films of Wong Kar-wai, and critically examines aspects of Deleuzean philosophy, with a particular focus on his cinema books. She has previously published on Pasolini in the philosophy journal *Contretemps*, Issue 2.

Yiman Wang is a doctoral candidate at Duke University. She has published on Chinese film in *Intersections*.

Gang Gary Xu is Assistant Professor of Chinese and Comparative Literature at University of Illinois at Urbana–Champaign. His most recent article on Chinese film is an interpretation of *Flowers of Shanghai* in Chinese, 'Translated Visuality: *Haishanghua* from Novel to Film', which was published in *Jintian* (*Today*), 52 (Spring 2001): 254–265.

Audrey Yue is Lecturer in Cultural Studies at the University of Melbourne. Her essays on Hong Kong cinema appear in *Inter-Asia Cultural Studies Journal*, *Intersections* and *The Horror Reader* (Routledge, 2000). She is the author of *Preposterous Hong Kong Cinema* (forthcoming), and co-editor of *Mobile Cultures: New Media in Queer Asia* (Duke University Press, 2002).

Yingjin Zhang is Professor of Chinese and Comparative Literature at University of California–San Diego. He is the author of *Screening China* (Michigan University Press, 2002), *The City in Modern Chinese Literature and Film* (Stanford University Press, 1996) and *Encyclopedia of Chinese Film* (with Zhiwei Xiao, Routledge, 1988), and editor of *China in a Polycentric World* (Stanford University Press, 1988), and *Cinema and Urban Culture in Shanghai, 1922–1943* (Stanford University Press, 1999).

John Zou is Assistant Professor of Chinese at Bates College, Maine. His 'English Idiom and Republican China: Repatriated Subject in Wong-Quincey's *Chinese Hunter*' is forthcoming in the journal *World Englishes* from Blackwell.

Introduction: One Film at a Time

Chris Berry

The idea for this anthology came during the Chinese Film Studies conference held at Hong Kong Baptist University in 2000. Listening to panel after panel of groundbreaking papers together with over one hundred other participants, I was impressed by the transformation of the field. Ten years ago, the equivalent event could have been held around my kitchen table, and when I edited the earlier BFI anthology, *Perspectives on Chinese Cinema* (1991), we had to translate material from Chinese to complete the collection. Now, not only does Chinese cinema studies in English have such a close relationship with its Chinese-language counterparts that they are beginning to constitute a transnational and translingual field, but it is also diverse, burgeoning, complex and wide-ranging. However, the keynote speaker of the 2000 conference, David Bordwell, leant over and punctured my reveries by remarking that, great achievement though the event was, there was a dearth of papers on individual films. This volume meets that gap in the field.

Each of the essays in *Chinese Films in Focus: 25 New Takes* has been specially commissioned for the anthology, and each one focuses on an individual film of the author's choice. There was no set list or canon of films to be written on. Rather, fresh angles and excellence of scholarship have determined the selection of essays, in the hope that they will stimulate engagement with individual films and reinvigorate discussion of them. This introduction considers the essays in relation to two questions. First, what do they say about the state of this transformed field? Second, what do they tell us about studying Chinese cinema one film at a time? In other words, why are single-film analyses necessary and what do they contribute?

As already mentioned, the first significant change in Chinese cinema studies in English this volume maps is its growth, and also the depth produced by time. Although the field is young, it is large enough and has been in existence for long enough that there are now well-established debates, and these debates include a variety of different perspectives on individual films. Therefore, most of the pieces in *Chinese Films in Focus* first summarise the existing debate around a well-known film – with references that readers can follow up – and then produce a new angle of their own. For example, at least three essays note the domination of realism and realist aesthetics in the debates around much Chinese cinema, but then go on to challenge that status quo in different ways. Rey Chow's analysis of Zhang Yimou's film, *Not One Less*, notes the consensus that his recent works have been more realist than earlier productions. In contrast, she reads the film as a sly reflection on the strategy of making things appear transparent, obvious and real in the new 'mediatised' economy and culture of the People's Republic. Yiman Wang's essay on Zheng Junli's 1949 classic *Crows and Sparrows* argues that what is usually understood as realism in this particular film and in Chinese film in general needs to be reinterpreted as allegory. And Mary Farquhar's piece on King Hu's 1971 classic *A Touch of Zen* counters the idea of action as purely formal play that suspends realist narrative. Instead, she traces a local Chinese operatic tradition informing Chinese cinematic traditions that is anything but realist yet also makes action a meaningful part of narrative development.

In some cases, the films were so new at the time of the anthology's production that there was no existing scholarly debate on them. Examples include Edward Yang's *Yi Yi*, which David Leiwei Li considers, and Ang Lee's *Crouching Tiger, Hidden Dragon*, discussed by Felicia Chan. In these cases, each essay maps out some terms of debate for the film and produces one of the first sustained and serious interrogations of them. Li reads *Yi Yi* as an argument for the importance of reconfigured ethical engagement in response to the challenges of globalised modernity. Chan examines the variations in *Crouching Tiger, Hidden Dragon*'s reception in different Asian territories as well as the 'West', arguing that the different cultural knowledges audiences bring to the film not only shape their understanding of it but may hinder the film's translatability as much as help it.

However, although Chinese cinema studies in English may be infinitely richer and more diverse than it was only a few years ago, most attention is still paid to quite a narrow range of films. In the early 1990s, Yeh Yueh-Yu and Mark Abe Nornes argued that residual leftist prejudices had led Western film scholars to focus on the cinema of the People's Republic of China at the expense of Taiwan and Hong Kong.[1] Together with Mary Farquhar, I have argued elsewhere that the persistence of the 'national cinema' paradigm and the difficulty of fitting the non-nation-state territories of Hong Kong and Taiwan into that particular box may also have contributed to this neglect.[2] In recent years, anthologies by Esther Yau, and Fu Poshek and David Desser, together with monographs by Stephen Teo, David Bordwell, and Lisa Odham Stokes and Michael Hoover, mark the end of this neglect for Hong Kong cinema, and I believe that the situation for academic work in English on Taiwan cinema is also improving.[3]

In recognition of the need to combat past narrowness, the coverage of *Chinese Films in Focus* is wide, both territorially and historically. The films discussed here are from Republican China, the People's Republic, Taiwan, Hong Kong and the diaspora. Chineseness is not defined politically here. Because foreign languages are used in many diasporic films, even the currently fashionable concept of 'Chinese-language film' (*huayu dianying*) is not broad enough. Rather, a flexible cultural understanding operates here. As for historical scope, the earliest film in the volume, *The Goddess*, was made in 1934, and the most recent ones are from 2000.

As part of this effort to stretch the usual coverage, some essays in the anthology introduce us to less well-known films the authors feel merit more attention. For example, Yingjin Zhang writes on *Evening Bell*, which is well known to scholars in the People's Republic but not outside. Zhang demonstrates how pivotal the film is in the history of Chinese Fifth Generation cinema, standing as a key moment in that movement's engagement with the war-film genre. Kam Louie's essay on *Floating Life* is another example. It introduces Clara Law's reflections on the contemporary Chinese diasporic condition through a film that is well known in Australia, but is not a commercial enough film to have achieved significant international profile yet.

Despite the wide range of films included, no claim can be made for representativeness. This is because many classic Chinese films are simply unavailable, especially outside the VCD and DVD stores of Hong Kong. Even some of the most famous films discussed here are not easy to find there. Furthermore, despite the effort to push the coverage, this has been balanced against the desire to ensure that if these essays stimulate readers to seek out films they have not seen, they will be available. (Ideally, we would have liked to provide a guide to sources, but these vary so much from country to country and change so quickly that it seemed futile.) Therefore, let me hasten to acknowledge the unfortunate absence of films from Hong Kong and Taiwan before the 1960s, or from anywhere during the Japanese-occupation period, for example. If the shape of this volume makes you feel their absence more keenly, then I hope that will stimulate your desire to see them and their re-appearance in formats such as subtitled DVDs, leading in turn to more academic work in the future.

The essays comprising *Chinese Films in Focus* could easily be sorted into various different types of category. To group them according to territory or time would be easy, but would minimise the very connections and comparisons I hope the anthology will promote. But if theme is privileged, various groups stand out that correspond to some of the major areas of debate that are current in Chinese cinema studies in English. For example, sexuality is significant in Bérénice Reynaud's analysis of *Centre Stage*, Tan See Kam and Annette Aw's work on *Love Eterne*, John Zou's reading of *A Chinese Ghost Story*, Fran Martin's work on *Vive L'Amour* and my own essay on *Wedding Banquet*. Another group might be essays on globalisation and the response to it. This would include Ping Fu's essay on *Ermo*, Rey Chow's on *Not One Less*, Kam Louie's on *Floating Life*, David Leiwei Li's on *Yi Yi* and probably Gary Xu's on *Flowers of Shanghai*. But by no means all the essays are particularly concerned with themes. For example,

Janice Tong's essay focuses on the way time is constructed through the deployment of cinema in *Chungking Express*, and Kristine Harris is concerned to understand issues stemming from the precise historical context of *The Goddess*'s production and reception. These also mark important directions in the field: on one hand, towards connecting Chinese cinema studies in English with the theoretical paradigms informing the field of Cinema Studies as a whole and interrogating them; and on the other hand, towards an effort to ground our understanding of Chinese films historically and socially.

To consider the types of work these essays undertake is to move into the second question this introduction addresses: why study Chinese cinema one film at a time? In recent years, the 'textual' emphasis in Film Studies has come under attack. For example, in what he admits is a 'shameless polemic', Toby Miller argues that we should 'acknowledge the policy, distributional, promotional, and exhibitionary protocols of the screen at each site as much as their textual ones'. He continues: 'Enough talk of "economic reductionism" without also problematizing "textual reductionism." Enough valorization of close reading and armchair accounts of human interiority without establishing the political significance of texts and subjectivities within actual social movements and demographic cohorts.'[4] Calls for understanding the cinema as a social, economic and political institution as well as a set of texts are timely. But approaches to the issue like Miller's can be problematic on at least three counts. First, they may exaggerate the degree to which Cinema Studies has neglected the institutional. Second, they risk empiricism, implying a divide between the supposed subjectivity of textual interpretation and objectivity of investigations into the so-called 'real world' – the 'data' of the latter is also interpreted. Third, they risk falsely dividing Cinema Studies between the institutional and the textual. Important though all the areas Miller mentions are, seeing, responding to and making sense of individual films is at the centre of all of them. Policies are made in response to and in anticipation of films, films are bought on the basis of distributor's perceptions of how they will be received by audiences, and so on.

Rather than setting up an opposition between empirical institutional study and textual interpretation, I would argue that Cinema Studies requires a range of approaches to the cinema that understands the singularity of the film and the importance of the cinema as an institution without trying to divide them or set them in opposition to each other. In Stephen Neale's classic study of genre – itself an example that challenges the claim that the institutional side of cinema has always been neglected – he points out that the singularity of the individual film-viewing experience is a primary and defining characteristic of the cinema and the film industry. Filmgoing differs from most other commodities. People go back to McDonald's because they want the product to be standardised and predictable. But film audiences expect a different experience every time. In their efforts to regulate and control the marketplace, film producers have developed genres and stars to balance the consumers' desire for originality with their desire to repeat previously pleasant experiences; the logic is that if you liked this musical or that Jackie Chan film, you'll like another one.[5] Understanding the process of genre formation and change requires attention to both the cinema as a socio-economic institution and to the range of individual film texts and how they both repeat and change existing generic norms in the play of predictability and originality that is built into the cinema as we know it.

With this understanding of cinema and cinema studies in mind, I would argue that the essays in this volume focus on the individual film in a variety of different ways. Some of them place the text at the intersection of institutional and social patterns, helping to answer the concerns of writers like Miller, whereas others place them at the intersection of discursive patterns. But all of them of have an important place within the study of the cinema understood as both textual and institutional. Although I will not use each essay to illustrate more than one tendency, most could be invoked more than once.

Many of the essays included here work precisely to account for the single film as a text by placing it within the historical and social context of its initial production and circulation. In contrast to the temptation to 'apply' theoretical formulas or large ahistorical generalisations about Chinese culture when reading Chinese films, and in the process risk missing telling and particular contextual details that enable a closer and more specific understanding, these essays emphasise the moment and location of their production to enable new insights. Felicia Chan's essay on the different responses to *Crouching Tiger, Hidden Dragon* is exemplary.

Yomi Braester notes that the dominant interpretations of *Farewell My Concubine* 'deplored' the film for its 'emphasis on national narratives … backed by catering to the taste for the exotic of an Orientalising overseas audience'. In contrast, Braester heeds director Chen Kaige's own claim that the film is a personal story. He argues that the emphasis on Beijing as a local city brings out the tension between grand narrative at the national level and personal experience represented by the local culture and cityscape. Carefully tracing *Farewell*'s place among films with a Beijing setting, Braester concludes that it 'signals the beginning of ashift … away from a national grand narrative to the history of specific cities', and the personal memories and traumas they hold.

The 1934 classic *The Goddess* also benefits from Kristine Harris's meticulous mapping of the circumstances surrounding the film's production and reception. Not only does she locate it among the anxieties around the figure of the fallen woman circulating in Shanghai at the time, but she also goes on to question the frequent critique of the film for being too hesitant in its damnation of the exploitation of women and the upholding of Confucian patriarchy. Using the strict censorship codes of the time, she undertakes a subtler search of the text for subversive 'visual cues' beneath its seeming narrative acquiescence with official optimism and traditional values.

Ping Fu's essay, like Harris's, places particular emphasis on visuality, but she investigates a much more recent film and places it in the particular moment of China's integration into the global economy. Zhou Xiaowen's 1994 *Ermo* is a 'vivid depiction of a rural woman in pursuit of the biggest TV in town'. The television set itself, the programmes on it and the way it and Ermo are visually represented all combine in Fu's analysis of the contemporary Chinese experience of globalisation at the intersection of the city and the countryside. While the film visualises the tremendous price Ermo pays for the television set – in blood as well as sweated labour and cash – Fu's awareness of China's tortuous pursuit of the modern as the context of the film's production leads her to note carefully that the film is fundamentally unsure yet about whether these transformations will be worth the price.

Audrey Yue's essay on *In the Mood for Love* locates the film precisely in the intersection marked by Hong Kong's transition not only to but also after 1997. Furthermore, she mobilises the particular regional intersections marked by the histories of migration and cultural movement in the film to counter the common critical tendency to abstract Wong's Hong Kong as just another abstract sign of urban cosmopolitanism. In so doing, she opens up new ways of thinking about the significance of Hong Kong and Hong Kong cinema in the new post-1997 age, as well as prompting us to ponder the politics of our various passions of Chinese cinemas.

A second major tendency in the essays here is to consider the individual film in terms of values. The discussion of values must feature strongly in any focus on a category of films defined by culture. Given the multiple and incompatible value systems from Confucianism to Maoism that have been mobilised in Chinese cultures since the advent of the cinema, this is even more true for Chinese Film Studies, and both David Leiwei Li and Kam Louie's essays pursue these issues.

While Kam Louie detects Confucian values in *Floating Life*, Charles Hayford also uncovers a return to Confucianism in famous melodrama director Xie Jin's 1980s epic, *Hibiscus Town*. However, the setting and circumstances of this Confucian turn are almost diametrically opposite to the diasporic modernity featured in *Floating Life*. *Hibiscus Town* is small-town China after the ravages of the Cultural Revolution, reflecting upon what has gone awry. In this way, unlike both Maoist cinema and Fifth Generation 'modernism', Xie Jin's melodrama 'sets up a space for historical judgment which does not disparage tradition, but builds on enduring, adaptable values as a basis for reform China'.

The legacy of Maoism also informs Helen Hok-Sze Leung's focus in her essay on *Yellow Earth*. Where other authors emphasise this keystone film as emblematic of Chinese Fifth Generation film-makers' stylistic and political rejection of the Maoist legacy, her subtle reading takes us closer to the film. As she argues, *Yellow Earth* 'is at once a critique of Mao's dysfunctional political project and an embodiment of the desire such a project inspires but is unable to fulfil'. As well as offering a new take on *Yellow Earth* itself, she notes how the film-making process echoes the journey of the soldier in the film.

Finally in regard to this second tendency, Robert Chi returns to the Maoist project and its cinema. He examines one of its most rousing and repeatedly filmed political epics, *The Red Detachment of Women*. Focusing on the 1960 version by Xie Jin, who went on to make *Hibiscus Town*, Chi looks beyond established debate on gender issues in the film and extends existing accounts of how these films work to mobilise their audience. He notes that the individual transformation of the main character not only provides a model for the audience, but that this transformation is crucially tied to the production of memory that is not only cognitively known but also felt and inscribed in the body. In this way, he brings us back to and reinvigorates our thinking about a core body of films and issues that has been neglected recently.

A mode of engagement with the single film that is centrally concerned with the cinema as at once institution and text is the attempt to place the film within networks of intertextual connections, such as genre conventions and other geneaologies, themselves inscribed in both industrial and critical practices. Yomi Braester's essay discussed above locates *Farewell My Concubine* within a lineage of films that represent Beijing. Mary Farquhar's essay places *A Touch of Zen* within the generic conventions of martial arts films, and Yingjin Zhang situates *Evening Bell* between the conventions of the war film and the characteristics of early Fifth Generation cinema.

However, not all the intertextual connections are necessarily with other films. Corrado Neri's essay on *A Time to Live, A Time to Die* looks to literature and specifically autobiography to account for some of the unique features of Hou Hsiao-hsien's autobiographical filmmaking. He notes that 'Autobiography (*zizhuan*) is far from the modern western tradition of … romanticism and psychology. It is more a matter of finding a place in society … It is also a way to pay respects to the memory of parents and family.' As well as tracing how these thematic concerns structure Hou's autobiographical films, Neri also suggests that they are a kind of cinematic *biji*, a literary genre that is much more impressionistic, poetic and distanced from state and politics than more conventional forms.

Jason McGrath's essay on the 1980s comic favourite *Black Cannon Incident* also mobilises intertextual connections relatively ignored in the West,

but in this case the spy-film genre. He points out that the production of spy films was a staple of 1950s and 1960s People's Republic cinema. Therefore, audiences for *Black Cannon Incident* would have viewed it in the light of their prior knowledge of the earlier films. By tracing the echoes of the key narrative elements, character types and iconography of the earlier genre, he enhances our comic enjoyment of *Black Cannon Incident* and our appreciation of its social critique, as well as solving the long mystery of why the main character is a Roman Catholic.

Tan See Kam and Annette Aw work on *Love Eterne*, the 1963 classic much loved by Ang Lee, the director of *Crouching Tiger, Hidden Dragon*. Lee's remarks on *Love Eterne* work against the queer dimension of this cross-dressing opera in which two actresses perform as a male and female couple, one of whom cross-dresses as a man. In contrast, Tan and Aw work the intertext to maximise the queer dimensions of the film. Drawing on the literary tradition of scholar-and-beauty (*caizi jiaren*) romances, they highlight how both the film and its heritage depend on a carnivalesque play with gender and sexuality norms in mainstream Chinese culture.

Changing sexual norms are of course at the centre of Ang Lee's own popular gay farce, *Wedding Banquet*. But where other writers have focused heavily on this dimension of the film, I examine its generic intertext at the point where Hollywood and Chinese family melodrama meet. Although it is a hybrid text, *Wedding Banquet*'s ambivalence and ambiguity are mobilised by clear differences between the Chinese and Hollywood family melodrama. Tracing what those differences are helps us not only understand the two textual traditions, but also the different values the film invokes.

Two further types of single-film analysis are undertaken in the essays. These might be seen as the more purely interpretive types of single-film analysis, but I want to argue that they continue to have a central role in Cinema Studies. First, there are those readings that look at a particular film as a site to investigate theoretical paradigms. Given that so much film theory has originated in the study of Hollywood or European films, Chinese films can be exciting to work with precisely because their Chinese origins may challenge existing paradigms.

James Steintrager's essay on John Woo's *Bullet in the Head* not only grounds the film as an allegorical reflection on the trauma of Tiananmen in 1989, but also as an intertextual construction referring to global high – or low – points in cinematic violence. Noting the exhilarating but gruelling experience of viewing the film, Steintrager returns to the core theoretical issue of pleasure in the cinema. He argues that missing from most of existing theory on cinematic violence has been the role of the death drive and the masochistic pleasures it inspires. As he points out in his conclusion, such pleasures are not necessarily destructive: Freud believed the formation of community depended to some degree on the breaching of the individual ego, which the kind of engagement traced here provokes. Therefore, Steintrager's work on *Bullet in the Head* asks us to re-think our assumptions about violence in the cinema in general.

For Janice Tong, time and the cinema and Deleuze's ideas about the relationship between them motivate her work on Wong Kar-wai's *Chungking Express*. As Tong notes, 'It is Wong's rendering of time in his cinematographic images that unhinges our perception of time when viewing *Chungking Express*. But how so?' Just as Steintrager's meditations on violence are enabled by the Hong Kong response to 1989, so Tong's on time are enabled by Hong Kong's complex understanding of how its experience of time is refracted by the anticipation of its 'back to the future' 1997 return to China. It is this particular disruption of the linear time schemes of modern teleology that enables *Chungking Express*'s creativity with cinematic time, which Tong carefully demonstrates to explore 'the substance of Wong's cinematic time'.

Like Wong Kar-wai, Stanley Kwan works at the intersection of art film and popular genres. But the particular aspect of his films that interests Bérénice Reynaud in '*Centre Stage*: A Shadow in Reverse' is the tripartite relationship between his engagement with the genre of the woman's film, his now public homosexuality and feminist theory. Although generated by the particular circumstances of the Chinese history of gender and sexuality, Reynaud's investigation and theorisation of this crucial nexus has broader ramifications, as male homsexuality and femininity are linked in so many patriarchal cultures. In order to maintain an appropriately subtle and yet rigorous ambivalence about Kwan's use of female figures to talk about male homosexuality and at the same time investigate precisely how this closeted tex-

tual operation functions, Reynaud focuses on denial, contradiction and reverse discourse as generative tropes.

John Zou's witty and incisive essay on the division of men in to the 'lovable' and the 'edible' in *A Chinese Ghost Story* is part genre analysis, making it a candidate for the above discussion on intertextuality, and part extension of horror-film theory. Zou draws on Carol Clover's ideas about the cross-gender identification of male audiences in many horror films, where they are asked to identify with the female protagonist who survives monstrous attack – the Final Girl, in Clover's terms. But, as he notes, in *A Chinese Ghost Story*, the survivor is a Final Boy. With this insight, he opens up both a new avenue in our understanding of the complex engagement of gender and subjectivity in horror film, and also questions whether this can ever be regarded as an eternal story about the production of selfhood. With this in mind, Zou pursues a surprising but convincing and original take on the film as a parable about Hong Kong's ambivalent relation to and anticipation of 1997 as both return to the (homogenous identity of the) motherland and arrival of another (heterogenous) colonial force. In this way he also pushes the boundaries of conceptual models for understanding the colonial and postcolonial imagination.

Finally, there are a number of essays that, although they may also engage in some of the directions enumerated above, place a particular emphasis on a direct engagement with the text, emphasising the critical intervention of the interpreter in our understanding of the film. In Cinema Studies, we are frequently reminded that we are examining a piece of discourse, a text, and not a reflection of reality. Yet, as Rey Chow points out her essay on *Not One Less*, 'the study of modern and contemporary China is so dominated by so-called realism that even the most imaginative writings and artworks, however avant-garde they might be, have tended to be read largely for factographic value'. All the essays in this volume are mindful of the dangers of such narrow foreclosure on other possibilities. But those under consideration here place particular emphasis on teasing out the textual specificity of the films as a way of countering attempts to read them as direct reflections of Chinese societies. Both Chow's own essay on *Not One Less* and Yiman Wang's essay on *Crows and Sparrows* are key examples of this tendency.

For Fran Martin in '*Vive L'Amour:* Eloquent Emptiness' the stakes are somewhat different. She finds that most work in English on the film has attended to it as simply a reflection of alienation in modern Taiwan, but that it has neglected the specifically Taiwanese queer dimensions of the film. In her careful working through of elements such as the metaphor of the 'family' in the film and its particular resonance for queer subjects in Taiwan, she counters this. Furthermore, she takes issue with those critics who have attended to the queer dimension of the film but seen it as pessimistic. By going into close detail on not only the representational level but also on the cinematic level of lighting and framing, she produces a very different understanding of *Vive L'Amour*'s trajectory.

Also on Taiwanese cinema, Gang Gary Xu's essay on Hou Hsiao-hsien's *Flowers of Shanghai* may surprise readers, because it is about Taiwan as well as Taiwanese film. Most writers have assumed that because it is set in colonial Shanghai over a century ago, *Flowers of Shanghai* has nothing to do with Taiwan. However, Xu teases out the significance of both the production process and of the film itself as continuing Hou's project of interrogating his homeland, its history and its contemporary condition. As he writes, 'Thematically, although "Taiwan" is no longer relevant to the story of the film, its absence becomes present in *Flowers of Shanghai* because of Hou's increasing awareness of MIT – Made in Taiwan.'

Finally, the second essay in the anthology is by Julian Stringer on Ann Hui's *Boat People*, a 1980 film about the fate of Vietnamese following the arrival of communism throughout the country. For a long time now, writers on the film have assumed that it is an allegory reflecting fearful anticipation of Hong Kong's future return to mainland China, and that there is nothing more to say about it. Stringer notes, 'such arguments are perfectly valid and seemingly "correct." However, the simple repetition of this primary interpretation inevitably overshadows *Boat People*'s other variable and even contradictory meanings.' Attending to the film afresh and to its distri-bution context, Stringer emphasises the analysis of the role of photojournalism as an issue in the film. Placing *Boat People* within an internationally circulating cycle of such films, he argues that its less than heroic depiction of its non-Western main character is both what made it 'difficult' from the point of view of distributors and what makes it interesting.

I hope that readers will be as excited by the variety of the essays and freshness of their perspectives as I am.

NOTES

1. Mark Abe Nornes and Yeh Yueh-Yu, 'Introduction', in *A City of Sadness*, ed. Mark Abe Nornes and Yeh Yueh-Yu, 1994: <http://remarque.berkeley.edu:8001/~xcohen/Papers/CityOfSadness/Intro.htm> (14 November 1996).

2. With Mary Farquhar, 'From National Cinemas to Cinema and the National: Rethinking the National in Transnational Chinese Cinemas', *Journal of Modern Literature in Chinese*, 4, no. 2 (2001): 109–122.

3. Esther Yau, ed., *At Full Speed: Hong Kong Cinema in a Borderless World* (Minneapolis: University of Minnesota Press, 2001); Fu Poshek and David Desser, ed., *The Cinema of Hong Kong: History, Arts, Identity* (New York: Cambridge University Press, 2000); Stephen Teo, *Hong Kong Cinema: The Extra Dimensions* (London: British Film Institute, 1997); David Bordwell, *Planet Hong Kong: Popular Cinema and the Art of Entertainment* (Cambridge: Harvard University Press, 2000); Lisa Odham Stokes and Michael Hoover, *City on Fire: Hong Kong Cinema* (London: Verso, 1999). Regarding Taiwan cinema, Lu Fei-i's history and an anthology are forthcoming from Hong Kong University Press, the former in a joint imprint with Duke University Press.

4. Toby Miller, 'Cinema Studies Doesn't Matter; or, I Know What You Did Last Semester', in *Keyframes: Popular Cinema and Cultural Studies*, ed. Matthew Tinkcom and Amy Villarejo (London: Routledge, 2001), 303, 308.

5. Stephen Neale, *Genre* (London: British Film Institute, 1980), 48–55.

1 *Black Cannon Incident*: Countering the Counter-espionage Fantasy

Jason McGrath

Black Cannon Incident (Huang Jianxin, 1985) is one of the defining works of the 'Fifth Generation' of Chinese film-makers – those who were among the first graduates of the Beijing Film Academy in the post-Mao era. Like other early Fifth Generation films, it reflects many of the dominant intellectual and aesthetic trends of the time, including a strong interest in formal experimentation, a renewed concern for individual subjectivity, an openness to artistic influences from abroad and an increased willingness to test the bounds of ideological control. The film is generally read as a direct comment on the contemporary reform era, exploring the question of whether reform-minded intellectuals would be adequately heeded by the socialist bureaucracy. Without contradicting such a reading, this essay seeks to complement it with a comparative study that looks back to the cinematic history of the Mao era. The Fifth Generation films of the 1980s, despite their stylistic differences from previous mainland Chinese cinema and their debts to international art cinema, served nonetheless as ideological interventions in a cinematic discourse distinctive to the People's Republic of China. In the case of *Black Cannon Incident*, I will argue that both narrative structure and visual rhetoric are used to unmask previous Mao-era spy-genre films as purely performative ideological operations rather than realist representations.

Black Cannon Incident begins with an engineer named Zhao Shuxin sending a mysterious telegram that reads simply: 'Lost Black Cannon. Look 301. Zhao.' A suspicious postal clerk reports the telegram to the police, who launch an investigation into the possibility that Zhao is a spy working for foreigners, engaged perhaps in industrial espionage. Managers and Party representatives from Zhao's own employer, a state-owned mining enterprise, take over the case. In the course of the investigation, Zhao is barred from his usual role as translator for a visiting German engineer, Hans Schmidt, who is helping with the installation of a large and expensive piece of equipment called the 'WD'. After much trouble and intrigue, it turns out Zhao's message was merely about a black cannon Chinese chess piece he had inadvertently left in a hotel room on a business trip. Moreover, in the end it is discovered that the incompetence of Zhao's replacement translator has led to an installation mistake in the WD causing over US$1 million in damage. The message is clear: the Party's lingering distrust of intellectuals seriously cripples the national project of modernisation in the reform era.

In a study of director Huang Jianxin's 1980s films, Paul G. Pickowicz reads *Black Cannon Incident* as a post-socialist critique of the Chinese Communist system, a dystopic 'red' comedy (i.e. a black comedy about Communism) expressing the continued disillusionment of the people with the government even during the reform era.[1] Chris Berry and Mary Ann Farquhar also analyse the film as a post-socialist political satire, but with a more detailed emphasis on artistic form rather than narrative political content. Berry and Farquhar show how the cinematography and set design of the film evoked the aesthetic and thematic concerns of modernist art, including alienation, expressionism/abstractionism and distanciation, which served to 'break the aesthetic stranglehold of socialist realism on the cinema'.[2] Similarly, Jerome Silbergeld relates some of the set designs of *Black Cannon Incident* to the modernist Chinese paintings and installation art that also began appearing in the mid-1980s.[3]

Indeed, the film's stylistic elements reflect a broader modernist or avant-garde aesthetic in much contemporaneous Chinese art and literature. In the case of cinema, the aesthetic experimentation of the 1980s is widely attributed to the very different sort of education the young post-Mao film-makers received in comparison to their elders educated before the Cultural Revolution (1966-76). By the early 1980s, students at the Beijing Film Academy had access both to works of Western film theory in Chinese translation and to previously unavailable foreign art films.[4] Much has been made of the effect such a cosmopolitan education had on the style of the Fifth Generation. Nevertheless, while such genealogies may locate possible sources of various stylistic decisions, to explain how the Fifth Generation films of the 1980s functioned as interventions in an ideological field specific to post-Mao China it is necessary to place the films in the context of the cinematic history of the Mao era itself. Although Western viewers might be better attuned to the Fifth Generation's affinity with international art cinema, contemporary Chinese audiences would have been equally aware of their engagement with, and subversion of, the norms of Maoist realism established during the previous three decades. Beijing film scholar and cultural critic Dai Jinhua places *Black Cannon Incident* in this context by suggesting that 'the discursive forms and contexts' of the Mao-era spy genre are 'deconstructed through comic mimicry' in the film.[5] The remainder of this essay will explore the ideological implications of such a genre deconstruction by reading *Black Cannon Incident* against its antecedent patriotic spy films of the 1950s.

Unsurprisingly, in mainland China in the 1950s, the combination of the Korean War, the threat of attack or subversion from Taiwan and the menace of nuclear-armed America made for an obsession with national security and a strong fear of possible infiltration by spies who would enable the 'imperialist' forces to undermine the new socialist society from within. The typical counter-espionage film (*fante pian*) of the 1950s thus opens with a secret agent from Hong Kong or Taiwan, loyal to Chiang Kai-shek and the American imperialists, who enters China and establishes contacts with reactionary or foreign elements already inside the country. The spy ring then enacts a plan to steal Chinese security secrets or cultural relics, or perhaps to blow up a Chinese building or ship. Working with upstanding regular citizens and newly repentant collaborators, Chinese security forces gradually detect the plan and zero in on the spy ring, and the film ends with a dramatic confrontation and arrest of the spies, along with the unearthing of their secret weapons and other valuable objects.[6]

Despite the reality of its geopolitical context, the 1950s spy genre essentially constitutes an ideological fantasy – that is, an imaginary narrative in which public fears and desires are activated, manipulated and finally negated with a reassuring sense of closure. The imagined 'other' of the typical spy film was not so much a depiction of an actually existing antagonist but a condensation of the traits that needed to be negated by the hegemonic ideology of the Party. The spy's overdetermined position as 'other' is evident from the fact that sexual and even religious layers were often added to his or her political identity to provide elements of mystery, seduction and danger that extended well beyond the threat of military or political subversion. The Catholic Church, for example, was often depicted as the lair of dangerous spies inside China. In *Declawing the Devils* (Shen Fu, 1953), the leader of a spy ring is an Italian Catholic archbishop in China who supervises a spy sent from Hong Kong and manipulates mainland Catholic believers into aiding his subversive scheme to steal military secrets. In *Mysterious Travelling Companions* (Lin Nong and Zhu Wenshun, 1955), a foreign Catholic priest is the intended recipient of a secret shipment of arms being smuggled into China on horseback. Significantly, in both cases the rituals of religious belief are preserved even in the most private consultations among spies, with secret agents routinely making the sign of the cross, kissing the archbishop's ring and so on. Western religion is thus presented as not simply a cover, but rather an essential part of the alien and perverse ethical universe of the spies; their exotic Western superstitions are tied directly to their menace as 'other'. Excessive sexuality was another common means of characterising the subversive element in Mao-era spy films. For example, the priest in *Declawing the Devils* is finally discovered to have photographs of nude women among his hidden secrets; one of the main Chinese collaborationist smugglers in *Mysterious Travelling Companions* is depicted as a lecher who repeatedly tries to sexually molest an innocent young minority woman hired to accompany the horse train; and in *Secret Guards in Canton* (Lu Jue, 1957), the lead female spy is portrayed as a sexually insatiable middle-aged *femme fatale* whose temptations must be overcome by the double-agent Communist hero posing as a fellow spy.

Such portrayals of alien religious belief and transgressive sexual appetite are inseparable aspects of the overall ideological 'othering' of the spy as a threat to Chinese socialist normativity in the 1950s spy genre. Insofar as a villain resists the truth of Party doctrine, he/she must be defined as either profoundly misguided or inherently perverse. In the former case, as with the Chinese Catholic followers who later realise the error of their ways and co-operate with the authorities in *Declawing the Devils*, the collaborators learn the falsity of their position through correct education from concerned Party members. However, in the case of villains who are committed to foreign, imperialist values in a spirit of fully conscious (and therefore purely wicked) opposition to the Party's truth, a final confrontation must be enacted in which the guilty are arrested, their secrets exposed and the threat smashed. As the narrative builds to such a climax, details in characterisation clearly mark the ideological enemy as a subverter of Chinese normativity in general, while the Party line is synonymous with morality and national essence.

Black Cannon Incident skilfully cues the customary expectations of audiences well-versed in the Mao-era spy drama by interspersing key signifying elements of the genre within the narrative. However, by emptying these ideological signifiers of their traditional signifieds, the film effectively 'traverses' the ideological fantasy – revealing its status precisely *as fantasy*, as lacking any real, material support – since, quite simply, it turns out that the foreigner Hans Schmidt is *not* a threat and neither is Zhao a spy or collaborator. The film's key opening scene clearly establishes its generic reference points. As Dai Jinhua has noted, this scene 'employs the stylised appearance of mainland counterespionage films from the "seventeen years" (1949–66): a rainy night, flashing lightning, a suspiciously behaving man sending a suspect cable at the post office'.[7] The scene is reminiscent, for example, of the rainy night scene in *Declawing the Devils* when an ominous-looking American agent in Hong Kong intercepts a letter between two Chinese engineers, or of the stormy scene in *Mysterious Travelling Companions* in which a minority peasant woman surreptitiously observes the horse train of the smugglers in the woods at night and then reports to the authorities, spurring an investigation. In *Black Cannon Incident*, a shot of the postal clerk reading

the strange telegram and then looking inquisitively up at its sender cuts to a shot of Zhao lit in a style characteristic of villains in Maoist spy films, with the top half of his head covered by a dark shadow as lightning flashes and thunder rolls. The next shot is a close-up of the clerk's hand ringing up the police to launch the 'black cannon' case.

In the subsequent investigation, a background check reveals Zhao received his engineering education from China's top science and technology university and has had previous close contact with the German engineer/advisor Schmidt. It is duly noted that Zhao's 'family class background' is that of an 'office worker' (not a proletarian or peasant). He has no history of political involvement, but his parents were both Catholics and he was a believer himself, at least in childhood – a detail of obvious significance considering the generic precedents mentioned above. It is never explicitly asserted that Zhao is a secret agent engaged in deliberate subversion; rather, he may be more like the 1950s engineer Zhou Changmin who works at the defence factory that is the main setting for *Declawing the Devils*. In that film, Zhou is not a spy, but his status as a Westernised intellectual makes his position somewhat suspect, and his lack of vigilance does result in near disaster when a foreign agent posing as his nephew steals the design plans for a new anti-aircraft weapon. Educated in America and still maintaining contacts abroad, Zhou first appears dressed in Western suits, though later he has switched to the 'Mao suit' tunic preferred by Party cadres, thus implicitly indicating his growing identification with the masses. Like Zhou, *Black Cannon Incident*'s Zhao is a highly educated engineer with foreign contacts, not to mention a Catholic background, all of which are enough to reinforce the suspicions raised by the mysterious 'black cannon' telegram.

Other details periodically surface to play on the conventions established by the Mao-era spy drama. Many spy films of the 1950s, for instance, involve the smuggling of ammunition into China to arm counter-revolutionaries. *Declawing the Devils* and *Mysterious Travelling Companions* both include close-ups of stashes of pistols or bullets discovered when the spy ring is finally broken, while *Secret Guards in Canton* and *Ten O'Clock on the National Holiday* (Wu Tian, 1956) both revolve around the planned use of explosives by the spies. *Black Cannon Incident* also associates the foreigner with ammunition, but in a way that ironically subverts the narrative structure of the earlier films. The incompetent translator who replaces Zhao in working with Schmidt mistranslates the German *Kugel* as 'bullet' rather than its intended 'ball-bearing' when Schmidt requests the item during installation of the WD equipment. After a short while, the translator presents actual rifle bullets to the German engineer, who responds, dumbfounded, 'What am I supposed to do with these?' In effect, then, the foreign 'other' in the film is presented with the objects with which he would customarily be concerned in the generic Maoist spy drama, only to reject them as incomprehensible, underlining the apparent irrelevance of the former ideological fantasy to the present reform era.

Of course, the most essential element of the generic spy film referenced in *Black Cannon Incident* is the mysterious *object* of intrigue itself.[8] In the Mao-era spy drama, the fears and desires of all the characters, whether patriotic or subversive, centre upon some object of fascination, generally a technological tool such as communication equipment, firearms or explosives, or perhaps culturally significant archaeological treasures that apparently signify a Chinese essence in jeopardy of being stolen by foreigners. (Thus, it is far from irrelevant that the recipient of Zhao's mysterious cable about the black cannon happens to be the director of the 'Suzhou Antiques Office', or that Schmidt is said to have asked Zhao for help in procuring antiques during a previous visit.) Often in Mao-era spy films antique cultural objects are linked to objects of military use, as for example in *Secret Guards in Canton*, in which a spy ring based in an antiques shop hides a bomb intended to blow up a boat inside an ornate antique Chinese box. In *Ten O'Clock on the National Holiday*, the object is a bomb concealed in a child's clock. In every such case, the object of fear and desire sets much of the plot in motion, even though its real nature may only be revealed at the end of the film. In *Declawing the Devils*, as if the film-makers were afraid of leaving something out, besides the main plot element of stolen design plans for Chinese military equipment, the archbishop is ultimately found to be hiding guns, ammunition, communications equipment, dynamite, liquid explosives hidden among Chinese antiques *and* the aforementioned dirty photographs of nude women.

In *Black Cannon Incident*, the mysterious object of intrigue is of course the 'black cannon' itself, which brings us to the ultimate subversion of ideological fantasy in the film: the revelation that 'the other does not exist' – the supposed agent motivating everyone's desires and identifications turns out to be a mere phantasm, a figment of the ideological imagination left over from the Mao era. The non-existence of the 'black cannon' *qua* object of fascination and fear is vividly illustrated in two crucial scenes that destroy any semblance of generic consistency between *Black Cannon Incident* and its Mao-era antecedents. The first is the scene in which Schmidt visits Zhao in his apartment, where his chess set is laid out with a small black canister replacing the lost black-cannon piece. Zhao's plant manager shows up unannounced and inquires about the canister. When Zhao explains that it is a substitute for a lost black cannon, his boss realises for the first time the true nature of the whole 'black cannon' case and soon departs. Schmidt, meanwhile, has noticed the intrigue surrounding the previous conversation (in Chinese) about the black-cannon substitute:

> Schmidt: What's this box?
> Zhao: It's just a box.
> Schmidt: What's inside?
> Zhao: Nothing.
> Schmidt: [suspiciously shakes box next to ear, opens it, sees nothing inside] Nothing? What was that about then? What was all that? [smiles in disbelief] I don't understand the Chinese.

In the span of a brief conversation ending with a shot of the mysterious object opened and displayed as containing nothing, the ideological fantasy of subversion from abroad is completely traversed; the object itself is revealed as insubstantial while the threatening foreign 'other' is depicted as not only ignorant of the entire intrigue, but honestly perplexed as to the discursive context of his Chinese counterparts. The message is reinforced when the authorities finally intercept the package sent back to Zhao in response to his original telegram. The parcel is unwrapped to reveal the absurdly literal nature of the mysterious 'black cannon' that had set the entire narrative in motion: it turns out to be merely a black chunk of wood with the character for 'cannon' written on it – a simple Chinese chess piece with no industrial or military implications whatso-ever. In combination with the previous scene reveal-ing the 'black cannon' substitute as an empty lack, this scene exposes the ideological fantasy of indus-trial or military subversion precisely *as fantasy*, sug-gesting that the Mao-era spy paranoia lacks the real-world referent of any actually existing threat but nevertheless continues to disfunctionally run its ideological course of its own accord. The 'black cannon' in *Black Cannon Incident* is a Hitchcockian McGuffin – an object imbued with great signifi-cance by the characters in the story, but which in fact is merely a pretext for setting the plot in motion – but it is a McGuffin exposed *as such* to both the audience and the characters.

The black-humour value of such a genre decon-struction is reinforced by the woefully inadequate responses of the characters to the revelation regard-ing the 'black cannon' case and the resulting expens-ive damage to a real piece of valuable equipment. Rather than criticising herself for her paranoid sus-picions, the company's Party vice-secretary castigates Zhao for his irrationality in sending a telegram to recover something as cheap and inconsequential as a chess piece. For his part, Zhao pathetically vows that he will never play chess again, as if his hobby is to blame for the entire fiasco. This exchange humor-ously mimics the obligatory moment in 1950s spy films when the Chinese citizens who have mistak-enly aided the foreign agents must tearfully admit their mistakes and express their remorse before the authorities. It is as if the characters in *Black Cannon Incident* are determined to cling to their faith in the power of the phantasmic McGuffin rather than acknowledge that what caused all the damage was the ideological fantasy itself.

Up to now, the parallels I have drawn between *Black Cannon Incident* and its 1950s antecedents have been mainly at the level of characterisation and plot, largely eliding the question of cinematic style. In fact, despite the generic visual cues parodied in the open-ing scene of the film as analysed earlier, *Black Cannon Incident* is profoundly different stylistically from the counter-espionage films of the Mao era. In the 1950s spy films referenced here, the aesthetic of socialist realism, largely imported from the Soviet Union, was the formal standard in mainland Chinese film-making. Such an aesthetic, which actually owed

much to the classical Hollywood style, aims at maxi-mum narrative legibility and favours the story itself over any experimentation that might distract the audience or introduce ambiguity to the narrative. In contrast, as mentioned previously, *Black Cannon Inci-dent* has been noted precisely for its modernist visual aesthetic, which is in fact the dialectical opposite of socialist realism in the context of 1980s China. Its stylistic oddities include the use of striking set designs, unusual formal compositions achieved with telephoto lenses, several scenes that seem superfluous to the narrative and a complicated temporal structure using multiple flashbacks.

These stylistic features have been analysed at greater length elsewhere,[9] but here I argue that the modernist visual style of the film can also be read, at least in part, as an element of the film's rhetorical undermining of the spy genre. We should first note that the point of *Black Cannon Incident* is not simply that the authorities mistakenly launched a counter-espionage investigation into the activities of a man who was in fact innocent – that is, some overzealous ideologues just went too far this time (particularly in the new era of opening to the West and so on). Rather, the true subversion of the film lies in its depiction of this investigation precisely *as a formal operation*; the film points not just to a gap between (past) ideology and (present) reality, but also to the very illusory nature of the ideological fantasy itself. That is, the counter-espionage effort is highlighted as a *performative* operation rather than a *descriptive* one: the dangerous spy is generated *by* the perform-ance of the ideological ritual, instead of entering the social space as a presence from *out there* to be dealt with through ideological opposition.[10]

This essentially formal nature of the ideological ritual is illustrated in the film's most formalised, modernist scenes, which are precisely the ones most associated with the assertion of Party authority: the two scenes in a formal conference room where company officials and Party ideologues debate Zhao's fate in his absence. As a point of comparison, we can note the *mise en scène* of the meeting room in the defence plant of *Declawing the Devils*: in typical socialist realist style, a group of people are loosely gathered, as if spontaneously drawn to the spot, around a speaker/leader who stands slightly above them. The arrangement of figures suggests both the naturalness of the authority of the Party representa-

Factory meeting room in *Declawing the Devils* (left); conference room in *Black Cannon Incident* (right).

tive and the solidarity of this authority with the masses themselves. In contrast, in *Black Cannon Incident*, Party ideologues and company managers meet not in a space formally defined by socialist realism – the presumed aesthetic and ideological support that would point to an objective reality they share and convey – but rather in a space of solipsistic modernist formalism reminiscent of cinematic fantasy-scapes from Lang's *Metropolis* to Kubrick's *2001: A Space Odyssey*. Their meeting room is completely white, arranged in perfect symmetry, and dominated by an absurdly gigantic stylised black clock that looms in the centre of the frame above the conference table. The stifling sense of formality conveyed by the set and composition is the exact opposite of the naturalness characteristic of socialist-realist representations of group gatherings. In this way, the ideological underpinnings of authority are themselves denaturalised and revealed as consisting of a purely ritualistic performative operation rather than being a reflection of objective reality. In the first scene in the room, the establishing shot drags on for over two and a half minutes while those gathered chat aimlessly before finally getting around to Zhao's case. More remarkably, this long take is stretched further by the fact that the minute hand of the massive clock actually traces four minutes. Both scenes in the conference room last just over five minutes, with no obvious ellipses in the editing, but by reference to the clock the viewer realises each meeting actually has lasted well over an hour, thus emphasising the sense of the authorities' inertia and detachment from reality.

Perhaps the single most striking formal choice in *Black Cannon Incident* is the 360-degree pan shot

near the end of the film, when the principal characters at the company contemplate the disastrous mistake in the WD installation that their paranoia has caused. As the group sits in a loose circle in a bright, airy room, the camera pans across the characters from the centre of the room until its rotation has made a full circle – a daring shot that becomes a synecdoche for the entire film. By smoothly and methodically exposing all lateral offscreen space, the shot vividly illustrates the message to the company and Party bosses that there is no hidden and mysterious 'other' who can be blamed; there are only themselves. The full arc made by the camera echoes earlier images such as the circular face of the oscillating fan in the same room, the circle traced by the hands of the giant black clock in the company boardroom, the close-up of a spinning ball-bearing that ends the 'bullet' sequence and the circular forms of the empty 'black cannon' substitute as well as the harmless chess piece itself. Most particularly, the 360-degree pan shot epitomises a certain circular logic of the ideological spy fantasy in general. Director Huang Jianxin has said that inspiration for the film came from both *Catch-22* and computer scientist Douglas R. Hofstadter's idea of the 'Strange Loop' – any structure that, when its elements are traced in succession, paradoxically ends in the same place it began.[11] Hofstadter applies this concept to many phenomena, from M. C. Escher's drawings to conundrums of mathematical set theory such as Russell's paradox of 'the set of all sets that do not contain themselves'. The most simple visualisation of a Strange Loop is the Möbius strip, a favourite image of Lacan's which illustrates the fundamental interdependence of such binary oppositions as *self* and *other* while also exemplifying a system in which movement never ultimately gets anywhere but just continually turns in on itself. According to Huang, *Black Cannon Incident* depicts just such a movement: 'From the loss of the black cannon to its return, we have precisely the completion of a Strange Loop.'[12] The 360-degree pan and Strange Loop metaphor satirise the futility of the ideological spy fantasy's circular logic, which redundantly conjures and defeats its own threatening 'other' as a necessary element of its performance in the public sphere. Again, we have ideology as what Slavoj Žižek calls 'the pure performative, the tautology of pure self-reference'.[13]

The 360-degree pan shot ends with a view of a doorway; but does the film as a whole point to a way out? According to set theory, Russell's paradox can be resolved only by introducing a meta-proposition that can logically refigure a set containing its own contradiction. In the structure of *Black Cannon Incident*, an analogous meta-viewpoint is provided by none other than the visiting German engineer, whose function in the narrative is indicated by his simple conclusion, 'I don't understand the Chinese'. By reference to the scientific knowledge and earnest friendship of the foreigner, the spy fantasy of the authorities is revealed as paranoid and irrational, as incomprehensible to the 'objective' perspective of the Western visitor. In other words, in the process of debunking the Maoist ideological fantasy, *Black Cannon Incident* invokes its own foreign *other* to suit the ideology of the pro-reform 1980s intellectual. This 'other', now benign and rational rather than wicked and perverse, is depicted as an ally of the Chinese intellectual, the latter being invested in an ideology of liberalism and openness to the West and a teleology of technological and social progress that seeks to break out of the perceived circular futility of the inherited political culture.

In sum, in the context of the early reform era, the real subversion of *Black Cannon Incident* lay in its subversion *of* subversion. The point was not to oppose the Party with some dissident political plan, but rather to expose dissidence as being in some sense generated *by* the Party itself – or, more broadly, by the entrenched ideological fantasies of a public discourse that the young film-makers, with an ideological agenda of their own, wished to portray as inadequate to the task of modernisation.

NOTES

1. Paul G. Pickowicz, 'Huang Jianxin and the Notion of Postsocialism', in *New Chinese Cinemas: Forms, Identities, Politics*, ed. Nick Browne, Paul G. Pickowicz, Vivian Sobchack and Esther Yau (Cambridge: Cambridge University Press, 1994), 57–87.
2. Chris Berry and Mary Ann Farquhar, 'Post-socialist Strategies: An Analysis of *Yellow Earth* and *Black Cannon Incident*', in *Cinematic Landscapes: Observations on the Visual Arts and Cinema of China and Japan*, ed. Linda C. Ehrlich and David Desser (Austin: University of Texas Press, 1994), 110.
3. Jerome Silbergeld, *China into Film: Frames of Reference in Contemporary Chinese Cinema* (London: Reaktion, 1999), 245–249.
4. See Hu Ke, 'Contemporary Film Theory in China', *Dangdai dianying*, 2 (1995): 65–73. Trans. Ted Wang, Chris Berry and Chen Mei at: <www.latrobe.edu.au/www/screeningthepast/reruns/hkrr2b.html>
5. Dai Jinhua, *Wuzhong fengjing: Zhongguo dianying wenhua, 1978–1998* (Beijing: Peking University Press, 2000), 195.
6. This sketch of a model narrative is distilled from the plot structures of the 1950s counter-espionage films discussed later in this essay; its basic elements can also be found in many other films of the Mao era.
7. Dai, *Wuzhong fengjing*, 195.
8. For a suggestive reading of the 'black cannon' and technology itself as the twin Lacanian object-causes of desire in the film, see Kwai-cheung Lo, 'Feminizing Technology: The *objet a* in *Black Cannon Incident*', in *Significant Others: Gender and Culture in Film and Literature East and West*, ed. William Burgwinkle, Glenn Man and Valerie Wayne (Honolulu: University of Hawaii Press, 1993), 88–95.
9. See Berry and Farquhar, 'Post-socialist Strategies', 100-110; Silbergeld, *China into Film*, 245–249.
10. On ideology as a pure performative rather than descriptive operation, see Slavoj Žižek, *The Sublime Object of Ideology* (London: Verso, 1989), 98–100.
11. Hofstadter's *Gödel, Escher, Bach: an Eternal Golden Braid* (New York: Vintage, 1979) had been translated into Chinese in 1984. See the director's comments in 'Cu ren shensi de *Heipao shijian*', *Dianying yishu*, 4 (1986): 10.
12. Ibid., 10.
13. See Slavoj Žižek, 'The Fetish of the Party', in *Lacan, Politics, Aesthetics*, ed. Willy Apollon and Richard Feldstein (Albany: State University of New York Press, 1996), 12.

2 *Boat People*: Second Thoughts on Text and Context

Julian Stringer

Following a television drama (*The Boy From Vietnam*, 1978) and prequel feature film (*The Story of Woo Viet*, 1981), *Boat People* is the third instalment of Ann Hui's 'Vietnamese Trilogy.' Shot on location on Hainan Island, the film sparked an international controversy over its politically incendiary subject matter. The movie opens with Akutagawa (George Lam), a Japanese photojournalist, covering the liberation of Da Nang, Vietnam, in 1975. Three years later he returns to the country as a guest of the government's Cultural Bureau.

As well as spending time with communist officials, Akutagawa strikes up a friendship with Cam Nuong (Season Ma), a teenage street urchin, and her two young brothers. One of them, Ah Nhac, is later killed by a land mine. After witnessing the youngsters scavenge from the bodies of execution victims at the nearby 'chicken farm,' Akutagawa tries to help them. The journalist had been impressed by the organisation of a new economic zone (NEZ) he had been invited to visit. However, he is told by To Minh (Andy Lau), an ex-translator for the American army who now plans to escape from Vietnam by boat, that the zone he toured, number 16, is a show model designed to impress visitors: the other zones are much more inhumane. After witnessing further examples of social injustice, Akutagawa resolves to help Cam and her brother escape. Akutagawa is killed in the attempt, but the two young Vietnamese succeed in reaching the boat and put out to sea. A final freeze-frame depicts the two of them looking out across the ocean, an uncertain future ahead.

A commercial and critical event in Hong Kong, *Boat People* was the subject of intense political debate and the precursor of other similarly-themed allegorical narratives. It remains a powerful, if suppressed, document of its time.

Entry on *Boat People* in *Encyclopedia of Chinese Film*.[1]

Barbara Klinger has outlined the limitations of the 'single-discourse' approach often taken in Film Studies to the text–context relation. All too frequently a neat correspondence is posited between these two terms, resulting in the production of critical work that imposes 'a unity between a film and its historical moment at the expense of considering the intricate untidiness of this relationship'. In Klinger's view, scholars seeking to account for the diverse meanings particular films may be ascribed in specific historical circumstances should work to provide a sense

> not of *the* ideology the text had in a historical context, but its *many* ideologies. By placing a film within multifarious intertextual and historical frames – the elements that define its situation in a complex discursive and social milieu – the film's variable, even contradictory, ideological meanings come into focus.[2]

As the above entry from *Encyclopedia of Chinese Film* implies but never quite spells out, *Boat People* (Ann Hui, 1982) – in common with many films produced in Hong Kong throughout the 1980s and 1990s – has often been assessed in terms of an overarching single discourse, namely, the '1997 factor'. A key text of the post-1979 'New Wave', *Boat People* is ostensibly concerned with the contemporary Vietnamese refugee 'problem'. However, the movie has been widely interpreted as an allegory concerning the then-British colony's possible future fate under Chinese sovereign rule. For example, Derek Elley suggested in 1984 that Hui's film demonstrates how the 'shadow of 1997 is already making itself shown in Hongkong cinema as the colony reasserts its ties with the Mainland'; and Tony Rayns wrote in the same year that while 'Western critics have tended to see the film as a lurid exposé of Communist brutalities and hypocrisies, Hong Kong audiences, less naively, took it as a troubled commentary on the tensions within *China*'s Communist Party – and, consequently, on their own prospective future after 1997'.[3]

Subsequent academic scholarship has consolidated this dominant viewpoint. In a particularly influential formulation, Li Cheuk-To claims that the 'importance of the film lies in the remarkable way in which today's Vietnam is used as a metaphor for tomorrow's Hong Kong. ... When the film was released in Hong Kong, the local audience had no trouble in equating the Vietnamese Communist characters with their Chinese counterparts. Postliberation Vietnam was tantamount to post-1997 Hong Kong.' (Li further claims, however, that 'in *Boat People* there is a sense of hope as signified in the [final] freeze-frame shot of the young girl hugging her brother, both staring into the distance at dawn.') Stephen Teo, too, regards Hui's film as 'the most allegorical treatment up to that time of the China syndrome haunting Hong Kong people in the early 80s', while Patricia Brett Erens and Leung Ping-kwan both reproduce the view that the film was received 'as an intended allegory of the future condition in Hong Kong after 1997'. In a recent Hong Kong filmography published in the USA, John Charles reiterates that Hui's film must be 'an obvious metaphor for the trepidations over Communist rule that many HK citizens were starting to experience around this time'.[4]

It is important to point out that such arguments are perfectly valid and seemingly 'correct'. However, the simple repetition of this primary interpretation inevitably overshadows *Boat People*'s other variable and even contradictory meanings. To be sure, work does exist which has adopted a different take on the film or framed analysis from an alternative perspective. This work includes recent articles by both Erens and Elaine Yee-lin Ho on the place the movie occupies in the context of Hui's overall artistic career, and in particular her identity as a 'woman director'; and Law Kar's discussion of the importance of the social-realist aesthetic *Boat People* and other New Wave titles injected into Hong Kong's cinema in the early 1980s.[5] Yet such pieces only underline the need to be more aware of the variety of elements that define the film's situation in a complex discursive and social milieu.

One of the historical frames largely unexamined by the existing critical literature is the crucial role played by international film festivals in the transnational circulation and reception of *Boat People*. By adopting a perspective that considers the significance of overseas distribution practices, it becomes possible to raise issues largely overlooked in previous accounts of the film's importance. My argument in this essay, then, is that in order to grasp more clearly the intricate untidiness of the text–context relation, it is necessary to consider *Boat People* in terms of the art world of the international festival circuit. The 'second thoughts' I want to explore are these. First, that *Boat People* proved a difficult movie for this art world to position. Second, that this contextual situation mirrors with uncanny appropriateness the film's thematic focus on travelling political 'problems' (i.e. refugees).

As a way of illustrating the latter of these two points, it is helpful to bear in mind that Klinger discusses the key role played at moments of historical reception by areas 'closely affiliated with a film's appearance ("intertextual zones")': these include other media and arts, review journalism and fan cultures, but also exhibition circumstances such as art-museum and film-festival screenings and revivals.[6] Similarly, in their introduction to the excellent *Traffic in Culture: Refiguring Art and Anthropology*, George E. Marcus and Fred R. Myers differentiate more specifically between key spaces of the contemporary art world's various 'intertextual zones'. For Marcus and Myers, there exists on the one hand a 'zone of speculation', wherein the international art market – its dealers, gallery owners and art writers – recognises and registers interest in avant-garde or emergent forms, in new work or newsworthy material. On the other hand, there is the 'zone of legitimation', wherein art works play their privileged role in the formation of canons and take up their privileged place in the memory work of cultural narratives. For Marcus and Myers, 'the crucial point of intersection' is the 'interzone': this is where art works move, or do not move, from speculation to recognition; it is the in-between space that determines whether or not art works 'breakthrough'. The interzone is where 'particular contemporary artists and works of art move from the location of speculation and recognition, registered by a small world of dealers, gallery owners, curators, collectors (private and corporate), and art writers (journalists, critics, scholars), into the legitimated art world which is the world of art history'.[7] In short, the interzone is where art works sink or swim.

In 1983, as it sailed into the festival interzone, *Boat People* might have been expected to make quite a splash. After all, contemporary reports make clear that when first released in Hong Kong in 1982 Hui's movie constituted a social 'event'. Mel Tobias writes that it was

> by far the most popular, much written-up and talked about contemporary Hong Kong film since King Hu's heralded *A Touch of Zen* in Cannes … *Boat People* had a good 'hype' even before the final sequence was envisioned by respected femme director [*sic*] Ann Hui. . . . *Boat People* was both a financial (grossed HK\$15 million) and a critical success.[8]

Unfortunately, though, such words now sound rather ironic, because it has been relatively difficult to actually get to see *Boat People* outside Hong Kong since its original theatrical release. The simple reason for this regrettable situation is that despite its initial status as a highly controversial and contested 'must-see' attraction, Hui's movie experienced a reversal of fortune once it entered international waters. The globalised festival circuit presented Ann Hui with the same question it habitually poses other film-makers seeking overseas distribution and exhibition rights for their work: will this movie stay afloat? However, unlike *A Touch of Zen*, *Boat People* was not exactly 'heralded' at Cannes when screened there in 1983. Sure, it had its throng of vocal supporters. Yet, as Harlan Kennedy documents, this Official Selection was protested by the Vietnamese government, and attacked on grounds of political naivety and opportunism as well as aesthetic superficiality and crude melodrama (the virulence of these attacks were enough to force the film out of competition). Patricia Brett Erens further reports that 'critics at the New York International Film Festival [1983] objected to the rather one-sided representation of the Vietnam government and the film's lack of historical perspective. Others found the work politically simplistic and sentimental'.[9]

As a result of negative reactions such as these, *Boat People* did not secure widespread international distribution and became for all intents and purposes a canonical unseen film. This inability to 'break through' internationally created the curious situation that exists today, whereby a body of English-language critical writing exists on a movie much talked-about but apparently seldom viewed. I have not undertaken a full study of how many prints or copies of *Boat People* exist in libraries or archives in the Western world. However, I do know that New Yorker Films in the USA distribute a subtitled 16mm copy (this is the version I have had access to) and, according to John Charles, a Star Entertainment (Hong Kong) unsubtitled laser disc is available for import, as is a China Star (Hong Kong) unsubtitled DVD. The point to make here, though, is that whereas subtitled versions of other Ann Hui feature films are readily available through such exhibition 'windows' as VCD and DVD, *Boat People* – her event movie – is much harder to track down.

By a curious twist of fate, then, the narrative drama of *Boat People* accurately parallels the chilly reception the film itself received on the globalised festival and distribution circuits circa 1983. The film's international exhibition fate mimics its thematic dynamics. To repeat, the story concerns a small group of characters caught up in a web of political turmoil and ultimately cast out onto the open seas (literally or metaphorically). On its initial overseas festival screening at Cannes in 1983 (in September 2001 *Variety* is still referring to Ann Hui as a director of so-called 'festival films'), the movie generated political controversy but subsequently failed to achieve widespread international distribution. The film remained stuck in a 'no-man's land', waiting to arrive.

By positing the international festival circuit as a key part of the contemporary art world broadly conceived, a new text–context relation has now come into view. *Boat People* revolves diegetically around displaced persons seeking a place of safety, a new legal 'home'. The film's own reception history testifies to the occupation of a similar in-between liminal status. The movie made waves within the international film world's zone of speculation, but failed to move into the zone of legitimation. It became stuck in the interzone, cast adrift in the limbo it regrettably remains in to this very day. Moreover, one result of this unavailability is that critical writing has had a virtually free hand in embalming *the* ideology this text had in a particular historical context over the *many* meanings it may have in diverse contexts. In short, in the absence of regular screenings and opportunities for reassessment, it has proved hard for international film culture to 'remember' much about *Boat People* outside the '1997 factor'.

So, why exactly was this movie difficult for this art world to position? The critics cited above raise a number of observations concerning the perceived limitations of *Boat People* as a text – namely, that it is naive, opportunistic, deficient in matters of historical perspective and melodramatic or sentimental (all readings largely swept aside by the force of the 1997 discourse). Yet two further contextual considerations are also worth suggesting.

To begin with, Hui's movie had a troublesome relationship to a then-current international genre. *Boat People* is a rare Asian entry in what Claudia Springer has identified as a cycle of 1980s 'third-world investigation films'.[10] Produced most frequently by the US movie industry, such films combine 'two established genres: the action-adventure genre set in the third world and the reporter-film genre' (167). The result of this 'generic hybrid is a narrative pattern that combines adventure with investigation, all revolving around an outsider who interprets an unfamiliar location' (168). Across the various examples cited by Springer – including *The Year of Living Dangerously* (Peter Weir, 1982), *Last Plane Out* (David Nelson, 1983), *Under Fire* (Roger Spottiswoode, 1983), *The Killing Fields* (Roland Joffe, 1984) and *Salvador* (Oliver Stone, 1985) – the spectator is 'typically' positioned 'in the role of cultural outsider by virtue of techniques that encourage identification with the reporter protagonist ... but more importantly, they are concerned with constructing white Western male subjectivity' (168).

Boat People shares many of the dominant generic features of this cycle, including the following key elements: a preoccupation with 'a journalist who investigates a situation, typically increasing his or her knowledge as the narrative progresses' (167); a specific narrative movement, whereby an initially uncommitted journalist-protagonist gradually invents a new self through aligning himself with an individual and a cause (174); the equation of vision with understanding ('the more he sees, the better he is able to achieve what the film presents as the correct interpretation' (178)); and the utilisation of 'a seamless representational style of realism' (187) – albeit tempered with melodrama in *Boat People*'s case. All of this is achieved through the central dramatic focus on Akutagawa's awakening to the truth concerning the communist regime's brutal activities in Vietnam.

Just as importantly, however, *Boat People* deviates from this generic 'model' in a number of important ways. Clearly, its central character is Japanese, not a white Westerner, and while the plot creates a vivid sense of Akutagawa's 'helplessness in the face of unpredictable violence' (171), it nevertheless denies him the kind of optical point-of-view shots granted central characters throughout other entries in the cycle. Indeed, Akutagawa's position as adventurer-hero is consistently undercut. This particular photo-journalist may well investigate and report, but he is relatively ineffectual when it comes to action and derring-do. (Compare this with the hunky physicality of the Nick Nolte character in *Under Fire* or lithe James Woods in *Salvador*.) At the most extreme, it is difficult to imagine the Third World investigation films' white Western male subjects – Sydney Schanberg (Sam Waterston) in *The Killing Fields*, say – immolated in flames, as Akutagawa is at the end of *Boat People*. That would just be too much of a 'downer'.

The 'problem' of Akutagawa has been argued before by Tony Rayns in terms of casting.[11] However, in the context of this specific film cycle, the character as written is already a problematic figure of audience identification. Symptomatically, in *Boat People* the hero-function of the 'typical' reporter film becomes split between a range of subsidiary characters, all of whom are revealed as unable fully to take control of their own destinies. In refusing to offer a simplistic foregrounding of any one central character, Hui's film devotes narrative interest to Cam and her family, To Minh (the ex-translator for the American army who is killed trying to escape on a refugee boat) and his best friend An Tranh (who is killed by a land mine), Comrade Vu (the party official who accompanies Akutagawa) and Commander Nyugen (the melancholy military officer who cannot get over his earlier life experiences in France), as well as the restaurant owner, played by Cora Miao, who ultimately resolves to help Akutagawa help others.

Devoting screen time to a variety of secondary characters works to deny the subjectivity and narrative stability of the reporter-protagonist. Moreover, Akutagawa's status as hero and adventurer is further undermined by the absence of what Springer terms a 'recuperative switch' (180), wherein stock narrative tropes are introduced at opportune moments to bolster the foreign reporter's normative masculinity (for example, matey banter and rivalry between journal-

Boat People: George Lam as Akutagawa.

ists, derring-do and a heterosexual romance). As Springer further elaborates, to 'heighten the aura of seductive danger, the films consistently introduce a character who individually embodies the culture as a whole and evokes the reporter's simultaneous attraction and confusion. The object of the reporter's fascination is usually a woman' (171).

Like the photojournalist Billy Kwan (Linda Hunt), in *The Year of Living Dangerously* – along with *Boat People*, by far the most distinguished entry in the cycle – Akutagawa tries his best to help save a woman and a child. However, Hui's film presents no story line comparable to the relationship between *The Year of Living Dangerously*'s hero (played by Mel Gibson) and love interest (Sigourney Weaver). Such refusal of easy romantic pleasure is only exacerbated by *Boat People*'s non-exploitative presentation of Cam Nuong. (Springer claims that 'the camera participates in the narrative investigation by scrutinizing both [the woman's body] and the setting' (173).)

In the particular context of the other films in the Third World investigation cycle, the result of all this undermining of Akutagawa is that as a central pro-

tagonist he comes across as a severely compromised figure – a loner, ineffectual, a walking funeral pyre. *Boat People* ends up resembling what *The Year of Living Dangerously* might have been like had the Gibson and Weaver characters been written out and Billy Kwan taken centre stage.

A second reason why Hui's film was difficult to position, or may have generated discomfort internationally in 1983, is because of its internal critique of cross-cultural looking relations. One of the most intriguing aspects of *Boat People*'s plot is its ability to indicate or anticipate the very reading positions through which the art world of the international festival circuit would comprehend it. This occurs through a narrative foregrounding of the processes through which cultural institutions frame or interpret new work or newsworthy material.

As my point of embarkation for analysis of this particular argument, I want to start at the end of the journey, with that final freeze-frame shot of the two young refugees looking out across the sea. The reproduction of this still as accompaniment to Li Cheuk-To's article in the groundbreaking 1994 anthology

New Chinese Cinemas: Forms, Identities, Politics makes clear that this is an iconic moment in contemporary Hong Kong cinema. It is also a powerfully haunting image, one that in the seven years since I first viewed *Boat People* I have been unable to banish from my own mind's eye. In terms of sheer dramatic power it is comparable to (and more than a little reminiscent of) the stunning freeze-frame that ends *Les Quatre Cents Coups/The Four Hundred Blows* (Francois Truffaut, 1959) – another classic social-problem drama and 'controversial' Cannes festival title, concerning an orphan child who ends up gazing out across an endless ocean, an uncertain future ahead.

Boat People's freeze-frame image – presented as the final climactic shot of the entire film – captures and suspends a moment in time. It 'arrests' one fleeting second and offers it up for the viewer's contemplation, if not interrogation. What does this moment mean? What does it represent? However, the shot also has the simultaneous effect of suggesting the very limitations of photography as a medium. Consider the fact that just as folk wisdom is doubtless correct to claim that 'every picture tells a story', it is also true that a picture cannot tell every story. Certainly, this particular still image does not exist in isolation: it carries much cultural and historical baggage – namely, the context provided by the rest of *Boat People*'s narrative – which viewers who have watched the entire film will already be aware of.[12] Given this, one of the ways in which this freeze-frame works is as evidence of the static image's inadequacy fully to account for the tragic life and situation of two young Vietnamese refugees (much as the '1997 factor' is unable fully to account for the text–context relation).

Another way of putting this is to say that after being presented with one hundred minutes of dramatic and compelling narrative information, viewers of *Boat People* are now confronted with the 'story' as it will appear in the global media – that is, as a single discourse depicting anonymous 'boat people' as a newsworthy 'social problem'. Ironically, then, at the very moment Akutagawa – the 'world famous' Japanese photojournalist who sacrifices himself in order to save Cam and her young brother – is killed, the film takes upon itself the task of fulfilling the professional and personal goal that drove his actions throughout each prior narrative development. Akutagawa had sought to capture, with a single click of his Nikon camera, the one symbolic image that would sum up the significance of what he saw around him in Vietnam. (His images are destined, in the words of a party cadre from the Cultural Bureau, for 'foreign magazines'.) It turns out in the end that Akutagawa himself never gets to take that picture, but the film does still provide it. The final freeze-frame supplies the solitary captivating image Akutagawa had all along hoped would enable the story to travel. The paradoxical nature of this situation is clear. The photograph eventually revealed in the final scene denies the background story of the individual boat people's lives, at the same time as it finally makes their predicament known to the outside world.

By such means, *Boat People* reveals itself to be centrally concerned with the processes through which international journalism frames and presents topical or newsworthy social dramas for overseas consumption. Indeed, this issue is raised explicitly in the very first scene. The re-creation of the liberation of Da Nang in 1975 is achieved through what John Gillett describes as 'a superbly shot victory parade', characteristic of Hui's direction as a whole in that 'the staging is confident and expert with a highly mobile camera'.[13] Camera mobility is the antithesis of the photographic freeze-frame. One represents motion, the other stasis. Here and elsewhere in her work, the means by which Hui's graceful tracking and craning movements are used so as to foreground social and political themes has perhaps been under-appreciated.

Through the lens of Hui's ever-mobile camera, we see Akutagawa taking snapshots of tanks as they roll down the street and crowds of onlookers cheering military muscle as it parades in front of their eyes. What *Boat People* therefore presents, and explores, in this powerful opening scene is an official public spectacle. Moreover, due to Akutagawa's presence as a photojournalist documenting this event for the foreign media, a connection is forged between text and context. The spectacular political display depicted through the staging of this victory parade corresponds to the moment *Boat People* announces itself to be an art work self-conscious of – and ultimately self-questioning about – its own event status.

On both textual and contextual levels, then, we might say that the story is now able to develop in ways that expose the single discourse, or 'big picture', as insufficient. On the one hand, Akutagawa comes to realise that the NEZ he had been so impressed by is in reality a showpiece constructed for the benefit of foreign onlookers enlisted in the staging of the government's political spectacle. On the other hand, *Boat People*'s own self-critique of its exploration of issues of cross-cultural looking relations provides some indication of why the film may have been an uncomfortable viewing experience for some outside observers.

As a further indication of the interweaving of textual and contextual levels, it is useful to consider what happens at the end of the movie's first scene. Akutagawa walks away from the street where the victory parade is taking place in order to go in search of the one key iconic image he is looking for. His attention is before long drawn to the sight of a small child hobbling pitifully on crutches down a side street. The photojournalist pursues him, perhaps thinking that the boy's maimed physical condition might provide a 'human interest' angle, or could be made to function as a symbol that sums up the 'state of the nation'. Either way, Akutagawa follows the boy. The next scene then cuts to 1978, three years later, when Akutagawa returns to Vietnam and will eventually meet up with Cam and her family. These individuals come to represent the 'reality' Akutagawa searches for behind all the falsehoods he is confronted with by the *apparatchiks* of the state-propaganda machine.

An important theme has been introduced at this point. As we have already seen, Akutagawa, with his desire to snap that one iconic image, may provide the film's requisite narrative drive, but he is far from being the only point of narrative interest. While the young child on crutches depicted early on turns out to be 'unimportant' to the unravelling of the rest of the plot, various other characters will soon be introduced as 'more important'. The development of all of these characters, in turn, allows the film to take a multi-dimensional approach to the subject of the 'boat people'. Tellingly, these separate individuals all represent lives whose existence is not captured in the single discourse of the final freeze-frame image. And because these people are not actually photographed by Akutagawa as he pursues the 'real' story lying beneath the surface of the staged public spectacle, *Boat People* complicates Akutagawa's 'heroic' status by implicitly questioning some of his own motives and actions. Once again, audiences have been invited to identify with a character they may end up having a problematic investment in.

In conclusion, it is worth picking up on the film's awareness of itself as a self-aware political spectacle and public event so as to consider more closely international distribution practices. The narrative of *Boat People* foregrounds the workings of cultural institutions whose job it is to provide discursive frames around 'difficult' media material. Specifically, aside from the phenomenon of international photojournalism, there are the activities of the Vietnam government's Cultural Bureau, which regulates the potentially incendiary symbols created by the foreign photojournalist's Nikon camera. As one party official puts it, the Cultural Bureau's role is to ensure that Akutagawa's photographs cannot be 'misused' once circulated internationally.

Both the structuring centrality of the role cultural institutions play in the framing of 'difficult' visual representations, and the suggestion that the meaning of such representations are contested, and open to 'misuse', suggest an appropriate analogy to the importance of international film festivals. Akutagawa seeks to publish his images of Vietnam overseas; festivals activate multifarious intertextual and historical frames as they project local subject matter for international consumption. However, in this particular case, Cannes, New York and other similar events were in 1983 unwilling to keep afloat a troublesome movie highly self-aware of its own existence as a public political spectacle. This drama was played out against the backdrop of the emergence of a cycle of (mostly) Western films that took a more distanced view on the investigation of the Third World and offered a variety of more standard recuperative pleasures.

To say all of this is not to try to impose a neat sense of closure on the matter at hand. I have sought in this essay to offer a number of claims about why Hui's film was a relative failure at its original sites of overseas exhibition. These claims draw upon issues both internal and external to the 'text' of *Boat People* itself. Yet other ways of reading the film, and other ways of accounting for the significance of its moments(s) of international reception, are no doubt available. In order to further explore the inherent untidiness of the text–context relation, a variety of – variable, even contradictory – critical perspectives need to be advanced. Renewed attention to the interest and importance of *Boat People* should undermine the force of the single discourse, or the 1997 factor, and will hopefully shed new light on the historical relevance of what remains an impressive cinematic achievement.

NOTES

1. Julian Stringer, '*Boat People*', in *Encyclopedia of Chinese Film*, ed. Yingjin Zhang and Zhiwei Xiao (London: Routledge, 1988), 99.

2. Barbara Klinger, 'Film History Terminable and Interminable: Recovering the Past in Reception Studies', *Screen*, 38, no. 1 (1997): 110.

3. Derek Elley, 'Hongkong', in *International Film Guide 1984*, ed. Peter Cowie (London: The Tantivy Press, 1984), 154; Tony Rayns, 'Chinese Changes', *Sight and Sound*, 54, no. 1 (1984/5): 27.

4. Li Cheuk-To, 'The Return of the Father: Hong Kong New Wave and its Chinese Context in the 1980s', in *New Chinese Cinemas: Forms, Identities, Politics*, ed. Nick Browne, Paul G. Pickowicz, Vivian Sobchack and Esther Yau (Cambridge: Cambridge University Press, 1994), 166, 167, 168. Li's article includes a frame-grab of the movie's final frozen image together with the caption, 'Today's Vietnam as a metaphor for tomorrow's Hong Kong', 168; Stephen Teo, *Hong Kong Cinema: The Extra Dimensions* (London: British Film Institute, 1997), 150–151; Patricia Brett Erens, 'The Film Work of Ann Hui', in *The Cinema of Hong Kong: History, Arts, Identity*, ed. Poshek Fu and David Desser (Cambridge: Cambridge University Press, 2000), 176–195; Leung Ping-kwan, 'Urban Cinema and the Cultural Identity of Hong Kong,' in Fu and Desser, *The Cinema of Hong Kong*, 242; John Charles, *The Hong Kong Filmography 1977–1997* (North Carolina: McFarland and Company, 2000), 100.

5. Erens, 'Film Work of Ann Hui'; Elaine Yee-lin Ho, 'Women on the Edges of Hong Kong Modernity: The Films of Ann Hui', in *At Full Speed: Hong Kong Cinema in a Borderless World*, ed. Esther C. M. Yau (Minneapolis: University of Minnesota Press, 2001), 177–206; Law Kar, 'An Overview of Hong Kong's New Wave Cinema', in Fu and Desser, *The Cinema of Hong Kong*, 31–52;

6. Klinger, 'Film History', 113.

7. George E. Marcus and Fred R. Myers, 'The Traffic in Art and Culture: An Introduction', in *The Traffic in Culture: Refiguring Art and Anthropology*, Marcus and Myers (Berkeley: University of California Press, 1995), 31.

8. Mel Tobias, 'Two Views of *T'ou-Pen Nu-Hai* (*Boat People*)', in Cowie, *International Film Guide 1984*, 156.

9. Harlan Kennedy, '*Boat People*', *Film Comment*, 19, no. 5 (1983), 41–43, 47; Erens, 'Film Work of Ann Hui', 184.

10. Claudia Springer, 'Comprehension and Crisis: Reporter Films and the Third World', in *Unspeakable Images: Ethnicity and the American Cinema*, ed. Lester D. Friedman (Urbana: University of Chicago Press, 1991), 168. Hereafter cited in text.

11. 'The major weakness is the central casting: Lam is hopelessly unconvincing as both a Japanese and a professional photographer.' Tony Rayns, '*Boat People*', in *Time Out Film Guide*, tenth edition, ed. John Pym (London: Penguin, 2002), 128.

12. The opposite effect is achieved at the very start of *A Fishy Story* (Anthony Chan, 1991). Here, still photographs of the 1960s anti-colonial riots in Hong Kong – accompanied with great poignancy (especially when we see images of police firing tear gas into the crowd) by the The Platters' classic ballad 'Smoke Gets in Your Eyes' – are juxtaposed with still images of the film's heroine on a shopping spree. These two levels – the political and personal – will be kept in tandem throughout the film, albeit in uneasy combination.

13. John Gillett, 'Two Views of *T'ou-Pen Nu-Hai* (*Boat People*)', in Cowie, *International Film Guide 1984*, 156.

3 *Bullet in the Head*: Trauma, Identity, and Violent Spectacle

James Steintrager

Contemplating the manifold and often unexpected relations that define experience today, Édouard Glissant asks: 'Is it meaningful, pathetic, or ridiculous that Chinese students have been massacred in front of a cardboard reproduction of the Statue of Liberty?'[1] According to Glissant, theorist and poet of post-colonial diversity, to consider a question of this sort is to acknowledge a world that can no longer be described in terms of stability, dialectical progress or clear geo-political divisions. Rather, when we contemplate the improbable scenario of Tiananmen, the language of chaos theory offers a far more promising way to grasp a state of affairs in which order – contingent, unlikely and inevitably doomed – springs from disordered and turbulent relations. Glissant's query and his concerns are entirely fitting for an examination of John Woo's *Bullet in the Head* (1990), an unlikely allegory of the student uprising, its brutal ending and the psychic sequelae for Hong Kong's populace, faced at the time with the impending return to mainland sovereignty. Certainly we might find something of the ridiculous in a director best known for over-the-top action films using the format to address topical and deadly serious issues. There is also something pathetic – no doubt in both senses of the term – about a creator of popular cinema working through such issues on screen. Woo's attempt at a critical use of the very system of media that has been criticised for indulging its consumer-spectators in the worst sort of ideological entertainment does appear both poignant and perhaps misguided. But what of the meaningful, the third term that Glissant places alongside the ridiculous and pathetic in his characterisation of the scene at Tiananmen?

What I will try to show in this essay is that one meaningful aspect of *Bullet in the Head* lies in the ways that the film brings complexity to our understanding of the relations between identity and violent spectacle. To this end, I first examine how an analysis of the film's content affords us insight into geographically and temporally specific constructions of identity. I then complicate the notion that the film can be understood solely as a function of milieu. For one thing, *Bullet in the Head* openly recalls other films from across the globe, indulging at times in well-worn sadistic fantasies. Likewise, Woo, dazzling with virtuoso yet familiar gunplay, relies on the repertoire of techniques of the action director. Yet more importantly, *Bullet in the Head* does not simply reflect constructions of identity. It also forces the viewer into a disturbing – yet potentially masochistically enjoyable – encounter with identification and its disintegration. Indeed, because of the violence to which Woo subjects us, some have suggested that *Bullet in the Head* is a film about which we cannot 'remain neutral' and must therefore 'love' or 'hate'.[2] Certainly, neutrality does not seem an option. Nonetheless, we might precisely experience the film as both attractive *and* repulsive. If we take this ambivalence as an occasion for reflection, we may discover in *Bullet in the Head* not only a heuristic but also an ethical dimension.

IDENTITY CRISIS: HONG KONG, 1990

Woo himself has acknowledged making *Bullet in the Head* as comment on and reaction to the political events of the previous year.[3] In relation to the looming presence of Tiananmen, moreover, the narrative continually calls up a longing for a lost past and anxiety about an uncertain future. The story starts in the 1950s, with the Monkees' anodyne 'I'm a Believer' playing on the soundtrack as bobby-soxed teens practise ballroom dancing. The entire opening-credit sequence, replete with photographs of Elvis and JFK, reveals a nostalgia that is real but mitigated, self-aware and ironic. For example, it features a gang fight strongly reminiscent of *West Side Story* (Robert Wise and Jerome Robbins, 1961), but which is too brutal to be taken as pure homage. The first time that we see the three friends around whom the story revolves – Ben (Tony Leung), Frank (Jacky Cheung) and Paul (Waise Lee) – they are happily riding bicycles through the streets of their city. They are a sort of microcosm of imagined Hong Kong community at the time: at the brink of manhood and in innocent solidarity (although there are inklings of the trouble to come). I should underline that Woo's vision of this community values certain locales (seedier districts over the financial centre of Hong Kong Island) and certain types (scrappy, resilient and more than a touch sentimental). That is, the trio is not so much a fractal of Hong Kong as it is a privileged facet – and one all the more attractive for its flaws.[4]

As the scene shifts to the late 1960s, this nostalgia is increasingly tempered. Ben and Frank have taken revenge on a petty gangster, the fight accidentally escalating into murder. At Paul's instigation, the trio decamps to Vietnam to escape the heat and take advantage of the war for quick financial gain. The departure occurs against the ominous backdrop of the anti-British riots. The quashing of student protests overtly recalls Tiananmen. An attempted defusing of a time bomb – clock shown ticking away – that explodes and leaves a policemen writhing, limbless, grimly forecasts the city's fate after handover. While we might jump to conclude that Woo is re-creating an era where a specific Hong Kong identity congealed in relation to the colonial situation, the riot scenes are actually doubly ambiguous. On the one hand, the students' endorsement of the People's Republic seems strikingly naïve in relation to the concerns of 1990 over the neo-colonial relation of the mainland government to the future Hong Kong Special Administrative Region (SAR). On the other, the three friends' lack of engagement in the riots as they flee to make money suggests frequent self-criticisms levelled by and at Hong Kong's citizens: uninterested in politics and obsessed with gain. At the outset of the film, Paul's father asserts that those without money are nothing, and it is Paul's increasingly money-hungry behaviour that eventually tears the small group apart. Freewheeling capitalism and economic success are portrayed as crucial to the identity of Hong Kong, but also as a sort of corruption at the origin.[5]

The voyage to Vietnam further plays out anxieties over the fate of a Hong Kong identity that,

however imperfect, is now threatened with coerced assimilation into 'Chineseness'. The Vietnamese are in fact a primitivist caricature of a backward and brutal mainland.[6] When the trio first arrives in Vietnam, they are suspected of being involved in a terrorist bombing. Threatened at gunpoint and prostrate, they hold up their second-class British passports and declare in English: 'We're Hong Kong people! We're Chinese Hong Kong people!' Another moment that is symptomatic of this identity problem occurs when Ben first encounters Sally, a heroin-addicted Hong Kong singer kept against her will in Vietnam. When Ben asks whether he can help her, she questions why he would aid a stranger. In the English subtitles, Ben's reply is 'Because we are Chinese'. In the Chinese subtitles: 'We are both Chinese people.' In the Cantonese dialogue: 'We are both Hong Kong people.' There is thus a fear of violent misrecognition that raises the spectre of Cantonese speakers forced to adapt to rulers who employ 'common speech'.[7] In relation to such anxieties we can understand the role of Luke (Simon Yam), a suave hit man who helps the friends shoot their way out of trouble. Tough and aloof, Luke is a Eurasian who speaks French and English as well as Cantonese and who is a paragon of cosmopolitanism. His character represents a sort of paradoxical essential hybridity: a supposedly biological mixture of East and West who thus solves Hong Kong's neither/nor identity problem. Yet the insufficiency of such an imaginary solution is brought home as the film progresses and the friendship is torn apart: Frank takes a bullet in the head from Paul and is left a quasi-vegetable; Paul returns to Hong Kong and rises to prominence in the Triads; Ben eventually tracks down his childhood companion and exacts revenge in a fiery denouement. By this point, the fear for Hong Kong's future as a community is unmistakable.

MEDIATING TRAUMA: CINEMA HISTORY AND CINEMATIC TECHNIQUE

The specific anxieties about identity and community vis-à-vis the People's Republic and in the wake of Tiananmen come to a head in a particularly difficult scene that lies at the heart of *Bullet in the Head*. The companions first witness malevolent Vietcong forcing one American captive to shoot other captives in the face at point blank range. Frank is then compelled to do the same. When he becomes deranged and unable to carry through any longer, Ben takes over the slaughter of the supplicating victims. This violent turning of fellowman on fellowman by a sadistic power clearly echoes the spectacle of soldiers turning on students under government orders. Yet precisely scenes such as this remind the informed viewer that understanding *Bullet in the Head* only through synchrony, socio-political reference and geographical specificity is reductive. This is because Woo here borrows his shots openly from Michael Cimino's harrowing Vietnam War epic *The Deer Hunter* (1978). A good deal of Woo's story-line is lifted from the same. Similarly, Woo's work in *Bullet in the Head* frequently recalls the stylised violence of Sam Peckinpah's bloody sagas. The plot too is reminiscent of Peckinpah's allegorical use of the Mexican Revolution in *The Wild Bunch* (1969) to address the Vietnam War and the possibilities of moral action in an increasingly technological, late capitalist society.[8] More broadly speaking, *Bullet in the Head*, *The Wild Bunch* and *The Deer Hunter* are all entries in the 'buddy' genre of films, respecting and tweaking its guidelines. These are not criticisms, but rather reminders that *Bullet in the Head* is a part of film history, and it makes ample use of techniques and citation of shots from previous Hong Kong productions, Japanese martial arts movies, American Westerns, war pictures, and even musicals.[9] In this respect, to even speak of Hong Kong cinema falsely imposes boundaries that the global reach of mass media renders largely irrelevant.[10] Our understanding of *Bullet in the Head* depends not only on how the film refers to political events and anxieties but also how it refers to and reworks previous mediations of violence. Crucially, these cinematic references remind us that the violence of *Bullet in the Head* is mediated and that this has consequences. Succinctly put, meaning is not just a matter of *what* the film shows us, but also a matter of *how* what we are shown affects us.

To arrive at an understanding of how *Bullet in the Head* functions as mediation, we might first ask how the cinematic violence of Hong Kong action films in general has been approached. We will then be in a better position to consider what Woo's production shares with other films and in what respects it is different. David Bordwell, for example, argues in *Planet Hong Kong: Popular Cinema and the Art of Entertainment* that the ways in which Woo and like-minded directors put together their action sequences unite the traditionally high and the low. Indeed, two terms frequently applied in assessments of such Hong Kong fare are 'acrobatics' and 'ballet', the latter pointing us in the direction of the *art* of bodily performance and the former suggesting skilful physical *entertainment*. Of course, these epithets are also used in an extended sense to suggest that the best action directors call upon all the powers of *mise en scène* and editing to deliver complex and visually compelling objects for their viewers. The very pace of action films – not to mention the frantic pace of production that has been traditional in Hong Kong – has apparently further fuelled the quest for stylistic innovation. In *Planet Hong Kong*, Bordwell provides frame-by-frame analysis of the techniques of the action director, and certainly, the scene in which the trio with the help of Luke shoot their way out of the Bolero nightclub or the scene of the final showdown between Ben and Paul easily stand up to this manner of scrutiny.[11] But the insistence on performance and technique tends to abstract violence out of the picture, when it is clear that bloodshed is part of the thrill of watching. The very sophistication of analysis in this case tends to intellectualise the fan's unreflective pleasure.

In fact, much of what has been written in English about action films and the work of Woo has taken the form of amateur enthusiasm. In such appraisals, speed, bloodshed and transgression of Hollywood boundaries are treated to panegyrics that demonstrate little desire consciously to analyse the nature of these spectacular indulgences. Tom Weisser in *Asian Trash Cinema* coos about Woo's *The Killer* (1989): 'The violence is unexpected and extraordinarily brutal, a constant swirl of gunblasts and bloody mayhem … This movie is an absolutely remarkable accomplishment. If you see only one Asian film, see this one.'[12] Faced with the like, it is easy to see why a post-colonial critic such as Ackbar Abbas might be rightly suspicious and declare his allegiance to avant-garde Hong Kong film-makers such as Wong Kar-wai. The latter, according to Abbas, depicts an atmospheric violence that 'exists as a ubiquitous and unavoidable dimension of the urban space itself, which offers the individual no choice'.[13] On the other hand, Abbas eschews violence that is 'celebrated as the voluntaristic act of an individual subject, as in John Woo's films'.[14] What Abbas finds in

Woo is a type of humanism that has traditionally been associated with capitalist economics and liberal politics: the subject as a self-contained and self-determining monad in the social order. This subject has been for the last few decades an object of various critiques – critiques that have not only suggested that no such subject exists, but have further declared that the ideologies that have produced this notion of the subject are themselves pernicious. Most importantly in this context, post-colonialist theorists have suggested that the supposed universality of the subject could only have been posited by constructing colonised peoples as particular exceptions to the rule and by suppressing the effects of differences in power.[15] To counter these tendencies, Abbas is interested in the way that violence in Wong Kar-wai undoes the construction of the individual by presenting the viewer with a 'neonoir of a colonial subject caught in the confusions of colonial space'.[16]

While I share many of Abbas's concerns about humanism, it seems fair to ask whether or not Bullet in the Head fits neatly into the dichotomy that the critic has set up. If we look at the narrative structure of the film, the individual as wilful agent does appear to rise out of the ashes of wartime chaos and personal betrayal. Thus Ben, after himself being shot by Paul and succoured by Buddhist monks, eventually confronts his childhood companion and kills him. The narrative of retribution seems to depict the return of the challenged agent – a sort of colonial castration anxiety covered over. This line of criticism, compelling in respects, nonetheless oversimplifies. For example, what should we make of the fact that agency in the form of Ben does not collude with capitalism (represented by Paul and the Triads) but is rather antagonistic? Moreover, what are we to make of the director's oft-cited interest in traditional Chinese notions of allegiance, honour, reciprocity, sacrifice – not to mention Christian agape?[17] Can we look away from the problem of community and solidarity that haunts Bullet in the Head throughout? Complications of the sort are in fact naggingly present in the case of Bullet in the Head, a film that even fans' guides, usually lavish in their praise of Woo, consider to stand somewhat apart from the exercises in controlled mayhem found in his other films (as well as similar fare by Tsui Hark, Ringo Lam and others). The authors of the appropriately titled Sex and Zen & A Bullet in the Head remark that the shootout at

the Bolero night club is the film's 'most exhilarating gunfight (a classic Woo-choreographed slugfest)'.[18] Yet because of the turn that the film takes, they consider it 'John Woo's most intense' and 'brutally intense'.[19] The guide Hong Kong Babylon calls Bullet in the Head 'John Woo's most uncomfortably violent film'.[20] Similarly, Hong Kong Action Cinema declares it 'a film that examines the outer limits of human experience in an often painful manner'.[21] Clearly, something about the violence of Bullet in the Head does not – at least not always – fit with models of the subject as individual and agent, post-colonial atmospherics or balletic formalism.

THEORISING AMBIVALENCE

What, then, is different or at least unusual about the type of entertainment that Bullet in the Head provides? The strongest moments of the film could hardly be described as exhilarating. They are rather disconcerting – some would say horrifying and sickening – and require an approach appropriate to this horror and its ambiguous attractions. Such an approach should exclude neither considerations of temporal and geographical specificity nor the ways that the film refers us to other mediations of violence. It should also allow us to retain the insights of Bordwell and Abbas while maintaining complications and critical distance. With respect to the theorisation of film experience, psychoanalytic inquiries have been the most widespread, and these by and large have focused on identification. Above all, reworkings of Lacanian Jacques-Alain Miller's notion of 'suture' by theorists in the 1970s have dominated the scene.[22] 'Suture' in these accounts names the processes by which the viewer's gaze is stitched to that of a specific character (notable is the technique of establishing point of view via shot-reverse-shot editing).[23] Identification of the sort is certainly at work in Bullet in the Head, especially in relation to Ben and Luke. Such a trajectory no doubt confirms some of Abbas's suspicions about the reinforcement of agency in the work of Woo. An interesting case of repression, however, in Laura Mulvey's seminal essay 'Visual Pleasure and Narrative Cinema', may point out a plausible complementary route.[24] When Mulvey characterises 'the pleasurable structures of looking in the cinematic situation', she limits herself to two types: one involving the sexual instincts (so-called 'active scopophilia' or sadistic pleasure in looking)

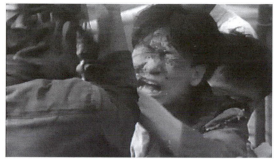

Shot-reverse-shot in *Bullet in the Head*

and another related to the ego and narcissistic identi-fication.[25] The problem for Mulvey is how these two contradictory pleasures – one involving separation from the objects on the screen and the other identi-fication with them – are brought together in the patriarchal fantasy world of classic cinema. Her view of how this problem is solved aside, what Mulvey leaves out in her characterisation of cinematic pleas-ure is another form of attraction that she had pre-viously and briefly posited: 'temporary loss of ego' and the 'sense of forgetting the world as the ego has subsequently come to perceive it'.[26] In classic narra-tive cinema, the destabilising return to such an undif-ferentiated state, which Mulvey tellingly labels a type of nostalgia, is compensated by simultaneous rein-forcement of the ego through identification with ego ideals (both characters and stars).

Mulvey's positing and subsequent repression of the loss of ego as a type of enjoyment clearly recalls Freud's death drive. With this concept, most thor-oughly addressed in the speculative text *Beyond the Pleasure Principle*, Freud attempts to come to terms with the suspicion that in addition to the types of pleasure we can easily accept – erotic pleasure and confirmation of identity – there lies another enjoy-ment, one linked to the release from community, identity, and ultimately from life itself.[27] In *Beyond the Pleasure Principle*, Freud first localises the death drive through an analysis of repetition based on observations of an infant who over and again throws away from himself a piece of string, accompanying this gesture with the word '*fort*' (German for 'away'). The infant then jubilantly reels in the string and pronounces '*da!*' ('there!'). Freud reads the *fort–da* scene in part as an attempt to master a situation. The child moves from passive victim of the mother's apparent whims to active controller of reality. The

game thus shows the hallmarks of an incipient sadism and might be linked to an examination of identification and enjoyment that we would expect to find in relation to violent action films. But what Freud ultimately finds disturbing about the *fort–da* game – and what is lost in the well-known Lacanian account of it – is neither the loss that entry into lan-guage entails nor this glimpse of sadistic mastery. Rather, what the compulsion to repeat a traumatic occurrence suggests to Freud is that somewhere in the psyche this pain is felt as akin to enjoyment. Why else would it be repeated?

We need not entirely acquiesce in Freud's specu-lations to affirm that his third type of 'pleasure' – the word is not particularly apt – operates at an almost unbearable pitch in *Bullet in the Head*.[28] In this regard, it is worth noting that the visual horror of *Bullet in the Head* reaches its apex in the selfsame sequence that recalls the killings of Tiananmen and quotes from *The Deer Hunter*. That is, both reference to extra-cinematic events and reference to cinematic history are here brought together under the rubric of *repetition*. But we still must ask in what ways this confluence affects the spectator. What *Bullet in the Head* does – and this is something it holds in common with *The Deer Hunter* and *The Wild Bunch* – is that it simultaneously 'sutures' viewers to charac-ters and then violently undoes the stitching by turn-ing the guns on us. In particular, the shot-reverse-shot editing in the scene where Frank is forced to kill American captives situates the spectator's gaze both as unwilling executioner and as pleading, bloodied victim. This would help explain why so many viewers find the film so deeply disturbing. Along with sadis-tic scopophilia and the satisfaction of ego reinforce-ment, there is a masochistic exposure to scenes of violence that shake any identity to its core. This is something it holds in common with *The Deer Hunter* and *The Wild Bunch*, as well as a significant number of ultraviolent Category III films that were increasingly produced in Hong Kong in the 1990s (director Herman Yau's gruelling festival of gore *The Untold Story* of 1993 is a perfect example of the type).[29] Indeed, while *Bullet in the Head* is in respects *sui generis*, we might also expect the types of mediated violence that it employs to crop up in the wake of traumatic events and at times of social uncertainty. I must point out at this juncture, however, that *Bullet in the Head* was a box-office failure on release in its so-called native territory. Apparently, trauma was still far too proximate for the kinds of spectacle the film had to offer. In fact, we know from psychologists that trauma victims actively avoid anything that might recall the occasion of the mental assault, even if re-enactments are common and may have a therapeutic value.[30] If there is a beyond of the pleasure principle that makes of horror an object of fascination and attraction, it must be contained, tempered, mediated or otherwise attenuated.

There is something deeply troubling, of course, about the notion of the beyond of pleasure, and we should certainly not unambiguously celebrate the violent breaking down of identities. There is also something more than ridiculous – we might say absurd or even obscene – about using an action film to probe the psychic wounds left in the wake of massacre. In a related vein, theorists of the Holocaust have often inveighed against attempts to represent the unrepresentable. Perhaps this is why Woo chose allegory as the mode of narrative, since it represents only indirectly. Yet at least since the Vietnam War, it has become clear that it is scarcely possible to avoid the spectacular mediation of terror. Here the issue of ambivalence in psychoanalysis rejoins post-colonial concerns and the anxiety of identity with which I began. Although some were obviously closer and more affected than others, Tiananmen was, after all, a trauma that, thanks to media of mass communication, was widespread in its impact. In this respect, Georgio Agamben places Tiananmen at the end of a process by which mass media and the state become oppressively linked (even where the intention of the former is to work against the latter). For Agamben, Tiananmen was a horrific instance of the 'state of the integrated spectacle': 'the ruinous stage toward which monarchies and republics, tyrannies and democra-cies, racist regimes and progressive regimes are all rushing.'[31] Against this state stood 'humanity' as a gathering of what Agamben calls 'whatever singularities'. That is, a community not bound by the traditional ties of identity but by the lack thereof – a lack engendered by the very hegemony of the spectacular. As emotionally compelling as Agamben's analysis may be, by painting the state of the spectacle as so radically inhuman, he thereby unwittingly reverts to a humanist individualism. It would appear, moreover, simply false that those present at Tiananmen and those in Hong Kong watching the massacre unfold on television did not share a variety of ties of identity irreducible to 'humanity' alone.

To conclude, I would simply suggest that we can retain what is valuable in Agamben's thesis if we reformulate his exclusive oppositions as inclusive. After all, it is surely not as simple as inhuman spectacle on one side and humanity on the other. Neither is it a matter today – in Hong Kong or elsewhere – of either traditional identities or 'whatever singularities'. As Glissant's call to chaos theory reminds us, binary schemes and models that remain progressive in their very apocalypticism cannot help us grasp the complexity of affairs to which a film such as *Bullet in the Head* bears witness.[32] Approached from this angle, we might see in *Bullet in the Head* a contingent function: to mediate for the viewer the traumas of Tiananmen and anxieties about the possibility of community under the coupled regimes of global capitalism and authoritarianism. In addition, while we can certainly be suspicious of the spectacular and treat it to analysis and critique, we might consider a film such as *Bullet in the Head* an occasion to learn about our own ambiguous pleasures and their relation to globalisation and media. Freud's supposition was that the inhuman or death drive is a part of us – and that masochism, in which the boundaries of the ego and its identifications are challenged, is an aspect of community. On the other hand, Eros and the bonds created by it are not necessarily positive – they do not always distinguish between society and sadism. Freud's ethical stance was that neither one side nor the other could save us, only a precarious tension between the two. Woo's *Bullet in the Head*, while not maintaining this tension, certainly presents us with the contrast in the most graphic terms.

NOTES

1. *Poetics of Relation*, trans. Betsy Wing (Ann Arbor: University of Michigan Press, 1997), 138.

2. Stefan Hammond and Mike Wilkins, *Sex and Zen & A Bullet in the Head* (New York: Simon and Schuster, 1996), 41.

3. See Bérénice Reynaud, 'Woo in Interview', *Sight and Sound*, 3, no. 5 (May 1993): 25

4. We might compare the nostalgia of *Bullet in the Head*, which idealises an imaginary past and communal unity while treating them ironically, to Rey Chow's reading of nostalgia in Wong Kar-wai as a simultaneously deconstructed and reconstructed longing for erotic union: 'Nostalgia of the New Wave: Structure in Wong Kar-wai's *Happy Together*', *Camera Obscura*, no. 42 (1999): 31–49.

5. Quoting Marx for support, Lisa Odham Stokes and Michael Hoover argue that the violent conflicts in Woo's films represent early capitalism: *City on Fire* (London: Verso, 1999), 38, 41–42, 49, 52. I would simply suggest that they are often a *figure* for late capitalism that renders *literal* the coercive and contradictory aspects of the system.

6. That Vietnam stands in for the People's Republic is also noted by David Bordwell in *Planet Hong Kong: Popular Cinema and the Art of Entertainment* (Cambridge, MA and London: Harvard University Press, 2000), 110.

7. On the 'apocalyptic' cinema of Woo in relation to space, hybridity and identity, see Tony Williams, 'Space, Place, and Spectacle: The Crisis Cinema of John Woo', *Cinema Journal*, 36, no. 2 (Winter, 1997): 67–84.

8. Various facets of *Bullet in the Head* as allegory and its relation to Cimino and Peckinpah's 'Mexico' are laid out in Kenneth E. Hall, *John Woo: The Films* (Jeffereson, NC: McFarland and Company, 1999), 135–147.

9. Tracking the multiple stylistic influences and plot citations in Woo is common in amateur and scholarly accounts of his films (and mention of Peckinpah is *de rigueur*). Stokes and Hoover, for example, note the presence of both *The Deer Hunter* and *West Side Story* in discussing *Bullet in the Head* and make earlier mention of Peckinpah in relation to other Woo films (*City on Fire*, 40, 49 and 184). See also Bordwell, *Planet Hong Kong*, 100–102. On Woo's influences, see Hall, *John Woo*, 33–64.

10. A point also driven home in a scene in which Woo recreates Eddie Adam's famous photograph of a Vietcong being executed by a pistol at point blank range. What we see is a real execution, first captured with a still camera and globally circulated, before being translated into narrative cinema and treated to slow motion and other effects.

11. See, in particular, the chapter 'Motion Emotion: The Art of the Action Movie' in Bordwell, *Planet Hong Kong*, 199–247.

12. *Asian Trash Cinema: The Book* (Kingwood, TX: ATC/ETC Publications, 1994), 58.

13. *Hong Kong: Culture and Politics of Disappearance* (Minneapolis and London: University of Minnesota Press, 1997), 34–35.

14. Ibid., 34.

15. For a recent and cogent overview of the critique of the subject, see N. Katherine Hayles, *How We Became Posthuman: Virtual Bodies in Cybernetics, Literature, and Informatics* (Chicago and London: University of Chicago Press, 1999), 4.

16. Abbas, *Hong Kong*, 34.

17. On the ways in which Woo's films combine Christian and traditional Chinese beliefs, see Stokes and Hoover, *City on Fire*, 39–40, passim. On both Christianity and the fundamental importance of *yi* (righteousness) in Woo's films, including *Bullet in the Head*, see Stephen Teo's *Hong Kong Cinema: The Added Dimensions* (London: British Film Institute, 1997), 174–183. Woo himself comments on the importance of Christianity to his films in Reynaud, 'Woo in Interview', 25. See also Bordwell, *Planet Hong Kong*, 98. The scene re-enacting Adam's photograph reminds us of the Christian facet of Woo's own peculiar hybridity: as the corpse falls out of the frame, it reveals a bronze Pietà.

18. Hammond and Wilkins, *Sex and Zen*, 42.

19. Ibid., 41 and 43.

20. Fredric Dannen and Barry Long, *Hong Kong Babylon: An Insider's Guide to the Hollywood of the East* (New York: Hyperion/Miramax Books, 1997), 199.

21. Bey Logan, *Hong Kong Action Cinema* (Woodstock, New York: The Overlook Press, 1995), 124.

22. Compare, however, Christian Metz's assertions that the spectator first and foremost identifies with the camera, before any relation to characters is established: *The Imaginary Signifier: Psychoanalysis and the Cinema*, trans. Celia Britton, Annwyl Williams, Ben Brewster and Alfred Guzzetti (Bloomington: Indiana University Press, 1977), 42–57.

23. See in particular: Stephen Heath, 'Notes on Suture', *Screen*, 18, no. 2 (1977–1978): 48–76; Daniel Dayan, 'The Tutor Code of Classical Cinema', in *Movies and Methods*, ed. Bill Nichols (Berkeley: University of California Press, 1976), 438–451.

24. Returning to Mulvey's essay to understand Woo better is also suggested by Anthony Enns in 'The Spectacle of Disabled Masculinity in John Woo's "Heroic Bloodshed" Films', *Quarterly Review of Film and Video* 17, no. 2 (2000): 137–145. Enns reads Woo's obsession with male disability as a reinvention of masculinity in the face of socio-political anxiety (see, in particular, pp. 138 and 142–143). See also Julian Stringer's oft-cited examination of male melodrama and the historical specificity of Hong Kong action cinema in 'Your Tender Smiles Give Me Strength', *Screen*, 38, no. 1 (1997): 25–41.

25. Laura Mulvey, 'Visual Pleasure and Narrative Cinema', in *Film Theory and Criticism: Introductory Readings*, third edition, ed. Gerald Mast and Marshall Cohen (New York: Oxford University Press, 1985), 808.

26. Ibid., 807.

27. Freud's analyses will be found in Chapter 2 of *Beyond the Pleasure Principle*, in Volume XVIII of *The Standard Edition of the Complete Psychological Works of Sigmund Freud*, ed. and trans. James Strachey (London: The Hogarth Press, 1955), 12–17.

28. Perhaps a better term would be Julia Kristeva's 'abject': 'L'Abjet d'amour', *Tel Quel*, no. 91 (1982): 17–32. Compare, too, Lacan's attempts to deal with what is left out of his account of the Symbolic, namely the Real, and particularly Lacanian Slavoj Žižek's theorisation of obscene enjoyment: see Žižek's *For They Know Not What They Do: Enjoyment as a Political Factor* (London: Verso, 1991), 239–241.

29. On the Category III rating and the rise of violent spectacle, see Darrell W. Davis and Yeh Yueh-yu, 'Warning Category III: The Other Hong Kong Cinema', *Film Quarterly*, 54, no. 4 (Summer 2001): 12–26.

30. See Judith Herman, *Trauma and Recovery* (New York: Basic Books, 1997), 41–42.

31. *Means Without Ends: Notes on Politics*, trans. Vincenzo Binetti and Cesare Casarino (Minneapolis: University of Minnesota Press, 2000), 86. Agamben situates his views in the context of a commentary on Guy Debord's *Society of the Spectacle*. Initial and largely identical observations on Tiananmen will be found in Agamben's *The Coming Community*, where his position on community is developed at greater length: trans. Michael Hardt (Minneapolis: University of Minnesota Press, 1993), 85–87 in particular.

32. We might compare here Rey Chow's argument that one of the functions of the mainland films by directors such as Chen Kaige and Zhang Yimou is not so much to address local audiences, whose often lukewarm reception belies concerns about oversimplification and exposing too much to 'outsiders', but rather visually to translate for others the violent construction of Chinese identity: *Primitive Passions* (New York: Columbia University Press, 1995): 176–202. See also Julian Stringer's mention of the problem of 'white spectators' and 'representations of violence against and between [other] ethnic groups' (40). On pedagogical approaches to trauma, see Shoshana Felman's 'Education in Crisis, or the Vicissitudes of Teaching', in *Trauma: Explorations of Memory*, ed. Cathy Caruth (Baltimore: Johns Hopkins University Press, 1995), 13–60.

4   *Centre Stage*: A Shadow in Reverse

Bérénice Reynaud

Maggie Cheung, star of Stanley Kwan's *Centre Stage*, won a Silver Bear at the 1991 Berlin Film Festival, the first Chinese actress to receive such an award. A few months later, the director's 146-minute cut was reduced to less than two hours for commercial release in Hong Kong.[1] This partial invisibility is poignant, for *Centre Stage* revolves around the search for the missing image of legendary star, Ruan Lingyu, most of whose films have disappeared.[2] It is also a metaphor for another form of hindered vision: the image is *there*, but *not seen*. The second unseen image is that of the Chinese queer subject.[3]

Stanley Kwan 'came out' through his documentary, *Yang + Yin: Gender in Chinese Cinema* (1996). Since then, he has directed performances, another documentary (*A Personal Memoir of Hong Kong*, 1997) and feature films (*Hold You Tight*, 1998; *Island Tales*, 1999; *Lan Yu*, 2001) with gay themes and/or characters. In the context of the frequent denial of *real* homosexual practices in Chinese culture, Kwan's courageous assertion of his sexuality was of paramount importance. It has allowed a number of queer analyses of the work he has completed since 1996, but so far this has not extended to his earlier films.[4]

Until the late 1990s, there were virtually no sympathetic or realistic representations of homosexuals in Hong Kong cinema. Like the left-wing Shanghai film-makers who got round Japanese censorship by inserting coded allusions, gay directors like Kwan resorted to metaphors and *double entendre* to suggest an alternative reading. The most effective strategy in *Centre Stage* is inspired by Foucault's 'reverse discourse' that duplicates and subverts 'the same vocabulary, the same categories by which [homosexuality is] disqualified' and rendered invisible.[5] The denials that structure the film are therefore also *double entendre* asserting *simultaneously* one thing and its opposite – 'I know very well, but . . .' Three such denials can be identified:

- Ruan Lingyu is not alive (*but* Maggie Cheung is).
- Ruan Lingyu did not live in Hong Kong (*but* she spoke Cantonese).
- Ruan Lingyu is not a man (*but* she is an object of desire and/or identification for male homosexuals).

Such identification maps out a space allowing for queer analysis. As a female spectator with a vested interest in the representation of women, I conduct this analysis *within* the framework of contemporary gender and feminist film theory. First, I examine how the figure of Ruan/Cheung is constructed through the cinematic equivalent of Freud's *fort–da* mechanism. Then I follow how, in the Republican era, 'the immoral woman' and 'the homosexual' were subjected to similar rebukes, ejecting them from what was socially acceptable in Chinese culture. Finally, I decipher the interplay of identification and objectification that connects male subjectivity to the figure of the 'suffering woman' through the double process of denial and displacement described by Tania Modleski: 'the male finds it necessary to repress certain "feminine" aspects of himself, and to project these ... onto the woman, who does the suffering for both of them.'[6]

RUAN LINGYU IS NOT ALIVE

An 'experimental biopic', *Centre Stage* recounts aspects of the life and legend of Ruan Lingyu. One of the most famous Shanghai silent cinema stars, she made her first film at the age of sixteen, and committed suicide at twenty-five on 8 March 1935 – International Women's Day – after being attacked by the media about her relationships with the bankrupt family scion, Zhang Damin, and the wealthy tea merchant, Tang Jishan.

Centre Stage's fragmented texture intertwines fictional reconstructions of Ruan's life with black-and-white video interviews with survivors from the Golden Age of the Shanghai studios and Ruan's biographer, as well as the cast and crew of the contemporary film; excerpts of footage from still-extant films; reconstructions of scenes from lost films; production stills; and photographs. This *mise en abyme* allows several Ruan Lingyus to co-exist, diffracting her image to the point of vertigo. Here she appears as Maggie Cheung, there in her role as *The Goddess* (Wu Yonggang, 1934), here again in Cheung's re-creation of the same sequence of *The Goddess*, and finally in black-and-white pictures taken on her deathbed. To 'capture' the elusive 'essence' of the star, Kwan stages several 'mirror scenes' such as the moment when Ruan stands alone at night, gazing at her diffracted reflection. She holds the bowl of *congee* that we have seen her pour two bottles of sleeping pills into. Under the shimmering seduction of appearances, Kwan weaves a dialectic between the visible and the *invisible*. He playfully uses cinema to indulge in a grown-up game of what Freud called '*fort–da*' ('gone–there'), after the exclamations of a little boy throwing and recovering a cotton reel to re-enact and master his mother's departure.[7] Now you see Ruan Lingyu, now you don't – or maybe a little bit of her, a reflection, a copy, or a trace: *mise en scène* creates a symbolic control over the appearance and disappearance of the object of desire.

'Cinema, like the *fort–da* game, constitutes itself as a continually renewed search for a lost plenitude', writes Mary Ann Doane, analysing *Gilda* (Charles Vidor, 1946)[8] – a film with barely disguised homosexual overtones.[9] The questions are: Whose loss? Whose plenitude? And at whose expense? Both *Gilda* and *Centre Stage* stage the punishment of their heroines by wounded and flawed males (Gilda's two husbands, Ruan's two lovers). In *Centre Stage* this also generates a friendly rivalry between the director and his star based on the tacit question, who will *benefit* most from identification with Ruan Lingyu?

Cheung first appears as herself, while offscreen Kwan asks if she hopes to be remembered in fifty years. She replies, 'If people do, it'll be different from Ruan, because she is remembered when she was at the pinnacle of her success. She's become a legend.' In his desire to use Cheung as a 'medium' to access the dead star, Kwan seeks overlaps between her and Ruan and to involve her in the (re)construction of her character. Yet Cheung refuses to be seen as an

icon. In turn, her resistance fuels the film's unspoken suggestion: isn't a *man* better equipped to incarnate Ruan Lingyu?

Centre Stage's first narrative sequence takes place in an all-male bathhouse. The camera glides sensuously over the bodies of half-naked men getting massaged, smoking and talking. In *Yang + Yin*, Kwan identifies this moment as a 'marker' of his homosexuality, adding: 'the person who first took me to a bathhouse was my father.' However, Kwan also acknowledges *two* patterns of queer identification. One is defined by the search for intimacy with an older man, the other by his love for gender-bending performances in Cantonese opera (starring women playing male roles), where his *mother* took him. The bathhouse sequence unfolds between allusions to these two 'founding moments'.

First, *before* she appears on the screen, the *fictional* Ruan is already constructed as a *figure of speech to be passed between a chorus of men*. The narrative part of the film is book-ended by two such choruses. To the brotherly banter of the beginning corresponds to the film-makers' bonding around Ruan's deathbed. The imaginary brotherhood of Shanghai film-makers is tightly knit first by passing Ruan on from film to film then through the death of 'their' common star.

Second, Kwan introduces a disruptive element: an unnamed young man sashays into the discussion of Ruan's acting abilities. Assuming the comical role of 'the sissy', he offers himself as the melodramatic lead for *Wayside Flowers* (Sun Yu, 1930), in case 'Ruan is not up to scratch'. Rebutted, he replies 'I'll go compare sizes with the others'. On the one hand, he suggests that he could be a *better female impersonator* than Ruan. On the other, he reasserts his manhood through both his desire to look at other men's penises and the existence of his own member. This brief exchange gives an edge to Kwan and Cheung's later conversation, when they good-naturedly compete to impersonate Ruan. An acknowledged director of melodrama (*wenyi pian*), Kwan mimics her saddest poses, while, as a modern young woman, Cheung reproduces her happy smile in *The Peach Girl* (Bu Wancang, 1931).

Some men, gay and straight, think the construction of femininity is too serious a business to be left to women. This attitude may be best exemplified by the tradition of female impersonators (*huadans*) in

Peking opera following a 1772 law barring women from the stage. The cognoscenti believed that the exquisite essence of femininity conveyed by the *huadans* was superior to anything a 'real woman' could do. *Centre Stage* poses the question of female impersonation (by men *and* women) in a way that denotes a queer sensibility in 'the awareness of the social constructedness of sex roles',[10] the suspicion that 'gender is a kind of persistent impersonation that passes as the real',[11] or the discovery, as Kwan aptly coins it in *Yang + Yin*, that 'gender need not be a boundary, but can also be a game'. Also queer is the implicit assumption that too-much-femininity may be a mask over masculinity, as in the case of Joan Riviere's patient.[12]

Examples of femininity-as-masquerade abound in the film. When future star Chen Yanyan tells Cheung/Ruan she has heard that in Peiping 'it takes you an hour to do one eyebrow', Cheung splendidly replies, 'in Harbin, it took me two hours'. The gesture of carefully painting an eyebrow over a face reduced to a blank canvas invokes the make-up sessions of the *huadan*. In their stylised femininity, did not the actresses of Shanghai's Golden Age try to compete with the *huadans* who had displaced their forebears? Filmic realism demanded 'an authentic object called "woman" – to be *seen*, and then "known" and "had"'.[13] But where did these bodies copy their version of the feminine from?

Ruan is also shown to face the double bind of fashion and male authority. As she and Tang Jishan are being sued for 'adultery' by her previous lover Zhang Damin, Tang ponders how he should dress to go to court. 'I'll wear a dark suit and a green tie to match that new dress of yours … . I want all Shanghai to know that we are high class adulterers', he says. Ruan replies, 'I live with you, knowing you're married. I admit being a loose woman. What we wear wouldn't make a difference.' Tang slaps her twice.

Later, when a friend invites her to a party that night, Ruan replies, 'Then I must look my best …' and extends her hand to Tang in a conciliatory gesture. However, the tension between them resurfaces at the party when Ruan, dazzling in a superb *cheongsam*, uses the very codes of feminine masquerade he's imposed upon her to upstage him. This is a strategy of 'self-parody' Doane identifies as 'double mimesis'.[14] A bit tipsy, Ruan kisses all the men, speaks too much and dances without restraint. As she

utters a mock feminist statement about Women's Day, Tang protests: 'You women have arisen, whereas we men have fallen.'

Later, Tang falls on the polished floor. Angrily refusing a helping hand, he screams, 'She's my mistress!', while Ruan continues to dance alone. Cheung's exuberant yet dreamlike dancing is spectacular, seeming to express Ruan's silent *jouissance* – a *jouissance* beyond the phallus, 'proper to her and of which herself may know nothing, except that she experiences it'.[15] However, what Cheung imitates is not the body language of the dead star, but that of Stanley Kwan, who had felt the need to demonstrate the appropriate movements,[16] yielding to the pleasure of 'dancing like Ruan Lingyu'. Kwan's performance, covered over by the glamour of his star, was nevertheless a way to experience 'the suicidal ecstasy of being a woman' which Leo Bersani identifies as a component of male gay *jouissance*.[17] By inter-cutting the party sequence with shots of the wake, Kwan further intimates that the whole 'act' gave its performer such intense pleasure that only death could follow, again closely linking it to male masochism.

While he stages the performance of femininity as a *contest* between women and gay men, Kwan also views it as an essential component of the *impasse sexuelle* between women and straight men. Whether contained and fabricated by the codes of acting or gender roles, or produced to excess as a covert form of retaliation and resistance, femininity is perceived by straight men as a challenge.

Against the grain of his noted sensual filmmaking, Kwan depicts Ruan's affairs as devoid of intimate sensuality; their physicality is reduced to male hysteria from Zhang Damin, abuse from Tang Jishan and emotional withdrawal from Cai Chusheng. Over-evaluated and fetishised, Ruan *can't* be 'possessed' by boorish men who don't 'deserve' her. That husbands and lovers tend to abuse, mistreat and demean 'woman' is a widespread queer belief – as seen in the cult of Judy Garland.[18] Femininity is too serious a business to be left to heterosexuals.

RUAN LINGYU DID NOT LIVE IN HONG KONG

By asking a famous Hong Kong star to embody Ruan Lingyu, Kwan 'reclaims' her by stressing her Cantonese origins. Like the modern Cheung in her conversations with Kwan, her fellow actors and the crew, Ruan speaks Cantonese at home. She uses Shanghainese for mundane exchanges and to talk with director Bu Wancang, while trying to master Mandarin when speaking to actresses Chen Yanyan and Li Lili. Kwan's oeuvre is thoroughly informed by a sense of fractured Chinese identity, leading to the intimate dialectic between Hong Kong and Shanghai in the 'nostalgic trilogy' formed by *Centre Stage*, *Rouge* (1988) and *Red Rose White Rose* (1994).

Rouge starts with a close-up of Anita Mui (as the courtesan Fleur) carefully making up her face, and segues into a scene in which she sings Cantonese opera in male drag, under the fascinated gaze of a young brothel patron. After committing suicide – on the same date, yet one year earlier, than Ruan[19] – Fleur returns as a ghost fifty-three years later in 1987 Hong Kong.

Red Rose White Rose is an adaptation by noted queer writer and artist Edward Lam, who later wrote *Yang + Yin*'s voice-over, of a novella by Eileen Chang – a cult figure among Chinese intellectuals, especially but not exclusively, in queer circles. Set in 1930s Shanghai, the story explores the relationships of a selfish Chinese businessman, Zhenbao, with two women, his mistress, the passionate adulteress Jiaorui and his wife, the masochist Yanli.

Nostalgia in these films has been thoroughly analysed,[20] but I will focus on its queer connotations, following Russo's interpretation of the longings expressed by cross-dressing *Queen Christina* (Rouben Mamoulian, 1933) as 'a nostalgia for something [gay people] had never seen on screen'.[21] Similarly, Kwan's investigation of Chinese cinema history in *Yang + Yin* articulated a longing for a symbolic *space* within pan-Chinese culture that would allow queer desire to unfold. However, this longing proves painfully contradictory, as homosexuality had been 'marked' as *un*-Chinese.

In spite of a classical Chinese homosexual tradition, colonial Hong Kong and Republican Shanghai perceived homosexuality as a 'recent importation from the decadent West …. going against traditional Chinese moral concepts'.[22] Moreover, 'prostitution and sodomy represented the two forms of non-procreative sex which needed to be eliminated for the sake of the family and the nation'.[23]

When Ruan Lingyu started acting in 1926, film actresses were equated with loose women and prostitutes. This changed in the 1930s, with increased professionalism in the industry and well-orchestrated publicity campaigns turning movie stars into media darlings. Escaping her working-class background, Ruan attained a glamorous lifestyle – once the privilege of imperial courtesans, who had been downgraded to prostitutes as movie stars now entertained the new urban elites.[24]

In a telling moment, Ruan is at home, rehearsing the role of the prostitute in *The Goddess*, smoking and striking semi-lascivious poses to inhabit her character. As Tang arrives, she blows smoke in his face and imitates the streetwalker's gait. Tang asks if this is her true self. Unruffled, she whispers, 'If Miss Liang upstairs and I were whores, tell me, who would you pick?' The situation might be fictional, yet the anxiety was not, for Tang is depicted as a womaniser.

It is in *New Women* (Cai Chusheng, 1934), where she is cast as Wei Ming, an intellectual who resorts to prostitution to buy medicine for her daughter, that the thin wall between 'acting' and 'being' collapses. The object of a slanderous media campaign much like Ruan herself, Wei Ming commits suicide, but on her hospital bed she has a last surge of energy and vows to live. The scene completed, Ruan/Cheung cries uncontrollably under the sheets. Cai Chusheng/Tony Leung stands uncomfortably by the bed. Kwan steps in: 'You forgot to lift the sheet to look at Maggie.' Who forgot? The fictional Cai? The Hong Kong actor? While a beautiful woman crying for the camera is an object of specular consumption, an excess of sobbing is potentially obscene, for it threatens the boundaries of the acting profession. So, an actress playing a prostitute may think she's become one. Maybe it is better not to look. Now you see her, when she's a star, now you don't, when she's a tart.

In the 1930s, 'movie actresses … were still placed … on this prostitute–courtesan continuum [that] gave them ambiguous status'[25] and put Ruan in the constant risk of 'falling'. Kwan shows her obsessed by the fear that people may not perceive her as a 'good woman'. His 'nostalgic trilogy' creates an association between sexual subjects traditionally thought of as 'bad': the courtesan in *Rouge*, the foreign-born adulteress in *Red Rose White Rose* and the actress in *Centre Stage*. Gliding along this chain, Kwan hides a fourth term, providing a hint with the bathhouse 'sissy'. As much the object of social reprobation as the prostitute, as 'influenced by foreign mores' as the

Centre Stage: Maggie Cheung as Ruan Lingyu

overseas woman, as vulnerable to gossip as the movie star, is the homosexual in Chinese society.

Public discourse in the Republican era equally condemned the prostitute, the socially mobile woman and the 'sodomite'. While often coupled with left-wing politics, the upsurge of nationalism caused by the war also gave way to xenophobic tendencies. It was believed that in treaty ports contacts with foreigners put prostitutes at greater risk of disease,[26] while young men were exposed to seduction by Western perverts.

Already *out of place* in 1930s Shanghai, the queer subject is neither here nor there, but has instead the tragic freedom to glide between worlds like a ghost. So Kwan can jump between 1934 and 1987, collapsing Hong Kong into Shanghai in *Rouge*[27] or creating a scintillating game of equivalences between 1930s Shanghai and 1990s Hong Kong in *Centre Stage*. For, if 'stories about Hong Kong always turned into

stories about somewhere else',[28] the 'negative hallucination (not seeing what is there)' facilitates the queer strategy of now you show it, now you don't. The moralising discourse of the 1930s 'was meant to exclude and delegitimise anyone who might become … influential through the medium of film – [a goal achieved] via the trope of "woman"'.[29] It attacked film actresses to take aim at an ineluctable modernity. By reversing the trope, a gay director may also reverse the exclusion. You thought you saw the victimisation of a woman – while I showed you the trials of a gay man.

RUAN LINGYU IS NOT A MAN

And yet Maggie Cheung triumphantly and effortlessly wins the contest with Kwan. As he fights as a director does with his star, he also gives her literally 'room to breathe', for example when the camera captures her breathing on the fictional Ruan's deathbed, and then sitting up laughing. However, this perpetual oscillation between different sides of the representation was hard on Cheung: 'To play Ruan Lingyu, Stanley and I agreed on one thing … she had to wear a mask at all time …. So I find my acting a little fake, hieratic …. Stanley wanted this alienation effect, he wanted representation to be visible as a process.'[30]

However, the effectiveness of Cheung's presence in the film goes beyond mere equivalence to Ruan. Like the *xiuyang* (mystique) of the Shanghai actresses of the 1930s, her charisma retains its opacity. So far, literature on the fascination of gay men for female movie stars has been limited to the West: Garbo, Dietrich or Garland. There is no such scholarship on the cult of Ruan. About one hundred thousand mourners attended her funeral,[31] and some *young men* committed suicide.[32] However, 'the majority of these mourners were women, especially female students'.[33] So, what does this say about the young men who 'adored Ruan'? At this stage, nothing. The queer subject was not only invisible, but he was also silent.

If the cult of certain movie stars has become a code of recognition for gay men in the West, has Ruan Lingyu's played a similar role in contemporary Hong Kong? *Yang + Yin* lists some of the denials encountered by Kwan when tracking down possible signs of queerness in Chinese cinema: 'I've never taken Brigitte Lin as anything but female' (film archivist Law Kar); 'You cannot project modern attitudes onto the friendship between two Peking opera actors' (Chen Kaige, director of *Farewell My Concubine*); 'We Chinese see this kind of relationship differently from Westerners' (veteran director Xie Jin); 'No Chinese reader thinks of homosexuals when he reads *Romance of the Three Kingdoms*' (martial-arts film director Chang Che). At the core of these denials is a suspicion of Western-induced modernity, which ejects the queer subject outside 'Chinese culture'. On the other hand, woman *is* marginalised as a subject, but as a figure of speech, she is *at the centre* of the discourse on the effects of modernity. So the female movie star, as the site of multiple contradictions, provides the Chinese queer subject with a possible anchor for identification.

Centre Stage explores many avenues through which this identification is possible. The issue of mask is central for gay men, who view 'performance [as] an everyday issue, whether in terms of passing as straight [or], signaling gayness in coming out …'.[34] Although Ruan's female masquerade is mostly performed for the benefit of men, Kwan throws clues that subvert this reading. When Ruan and Chen Yanyan discuss make-up, they achieve a subtle bonding, 'which demonstrates the masquerade's potential to draw women closer together and to function as non-verbal homoerotic expression'.[35] In several instances, Ruan is seen dancing with other young actresses, with whom she seems freer and more at ease than with men. At the final party, however, she theatrically overplays her heterosexuality by loudly announcing she 'won't kiss the girls'.

Another clue occurs when Ruan interviews another actress about the pain of childbirth – something she *knows* she will never experience herself – and explains her decision to adopt a little girl, Xiaoyu. Thus, the family composed of Ruan, her mother, Xiaoyu, and first lover Zhang Damin resembles a gay household. Zhang plays the role of a kept lover and Ruan, who keeps writing expenses in her ledger, is the responsible breadwinner. This role reversal continues throughout, with Ruan taking more 'masculine' responsibilities: she 'directs' her partner Li Lili in a crucial scene in *Little Toys* (Sun Yu, 1933), convinces Bu Wancang to let her play a more socially conscious role, and asks director Cai Chusheng to elope with her. While humouring Tang Jishan by pretending to be his kept mistress, she was actually financially independent.[36]

The mechanism of identification with a female actress/character by a male subject is complex, especially for films that foreground female suffering. The subjective position of the gay man complicates matters further, for his 'denial of the feminine' differs from that of the male heterosexual subject. His ambivalence toward femininity is best exemplified by the 'bifurcated position' of the bathhouse 'sissy' (identification, competition *and* phallocentrism). Moreover, queer subjects are often faced with a situation unknown to heterosexuals: the impossibility of identifying with a mirror image on the screen, where they are only constructed as *absent*. To draw a parallel with other misrepresented minorities, how is the Chinese queer subject 'sutured into a place that includes [him] only as a term of negation? *What* does [he] identify with when his own mirror image is structurally absent or present only as an Other?' This could be the explanation for James Baldwin's 'adolescent identification with Bette Davis',[37] since images of black gay men were unavailable onscreen.

Reading Lacan, Kaja Silverman stresses that it is through fantasy that the subject learns both how to desire and to build an identity. The two are 'complexly imbricated' through 'the insertion of the subject into a particular syntax or tableau', so the subject can only exist if under the gaze of the Other, as well while 'assuming a position within the *mise en scène* of desire'.[38] A subject whose desiring identity keeps being denied and/or rendered invisible has no other recourse than to project himself into a specular fantasy. While there are many avenues to queerness, including those far removed from feminine identification, recent scholarship has focused on the feminisation that overplayed male theatricality entails: 'masquerading as a man' feminises the 'macho' wearer's relation to the costume.[39] These analyses strengthen Silverman's thesis that 'woman seem[s] to function at times not only as the focus of gay identification, but as the pivot of gay desire'.[40]

What is more problematic – and interesting – is the *internalisation* by the queer subject of this feminine *mise en scène*. Of the variety of ways this phenomenon has been analysed, the one that concerns us here is narcissistic object-choice of 'what [the subject] once was' and/or 'someone who was once part of himself',[41] a process made more complex by the congruence between object of desire and object of identification. Identification and desire rest on the loss of both the little boy that the subject once was – and his mother loved – and the first object he ever lost – his mother.

Ruan Lingyu, the lost object *par excellence* of Chinese cinema, becomes a stand-in for all these losses. By mourning her, Kwan identifies with the mainstream Chinese culture that outlaws his queerness; with the community of film-makers, husbands, and lovers that used her 'glamour value' to strengthen their male bonds; and with all the Chinese gay men and women that secretly identify with her. By mourning her, he also mourns himself – what he never was, what he has lost without even ever possessing it.

The *pleasure* caused by *Centre Stage* stems from Kwan's ability to simultaneously play on several registers – while anchoring himself in the *wenyi pian* 'melodrama' tradition. *Centre Stage* may be the story of a female impersonator who thought s/he was Ruan Lingyu, who, in turn, thought she was Maggie Cheung. Or it may be the story of a modern Hong Kong actress who is asked to play a star of the past, as the latter discovers that she was only 'playing' at being Ruan Lingyu. 'Truth' lies in this interplay of surfaces and *trompe l'oeil*, this collage of eras, cities, genres and media, this hall of mirrors in which identity is many times diffracted and only exists as seduction.

NOTES

1. This essay is based on the director's cut.
2. Kwan mentions ten films, five of them 'lost'. Since 1991, four other films starring Ruan have been recovered.
3. Chinese lesbian representation is beyond the scope of this essay. Here, I refer to the 'Chinese queer subject' in the masculine only.
4. Existing texts on *Centre Stage* include: Natalia Chan Shui Hung, 'Memory, Gender, History: Female Sensitivity and Queer Spectatorship of Stanley Kwan's Films' (Jiyi, Xingbie, Lishi: Lun Guan Jin-peng Dianying di Nuxingchujue yu Kuyiguanzhao) in *City on the Edge of Time: Gender, Special Effect, and the 1997 Politics of Hong Kong Cinema* (*Shengshi di Bianyuan: Xianggang Dianying di Xingbie, Teji, yu Jiuqi Zhengzhi*) (Hong Kong: Oxford University Press, 2002), 43–72; Cui Shuqin, 'Stanley Kwan's *Center Stage*: The (Im)possible Engagement between Feminism and Postmodernism', *Cinema Journal*, 39, no. 4 (2000): 60–80; various essays in *Stanley Kwan: La Via Orientale al Melodrama*, ed. Giovanni Spagnoletti, Alessandro Bori and Olaf Möller (Pesaro: Fondazione Pesaro Nuovo Cinema/Il Castoro, 2000); and Julian Stringer, '*Centre Stage*: Reconstructing the Bio-Pic', *Cinemaction*, no. 42 (1997): 28–39. Queer analyses of Kwan's work include Helen Hok-Sze Leung, 'A Time to Dance: Stanley Kwan's Queer Fable of 1997 Past' (paper presented at the After the End – Hong Kong Culture After 1997 conference, UCLA, 26 May 2001; Yau Ching, 'Bisexuality and Duality in *Hold You Tight*', *Cinedossier: The 35th Golden Horse Award-Winning Films* (Taipei: National Film Archive, 1999), 116–122.
5. Michel Foucault, *The History of Sexuality*, vol. 1 (New York: Vintage Books, 1980), 101.
6. Tania Modleski, *The Women Who Knew Too Much* (London: Methuen, 1988), 13.
7. Sigmund Freud, *Beyond the Pleasure Principle* (New York: Norton, 1961), 8–9.

8. Mary Ann Doane, '*Gilda:* Epistemology as Strip-Tease', *Femmes Fatales* (London: Routledge, 1991), 102.

9. Vito Russo, *The Celluloid Closet* (New York: Harper & Row, 1987), 78–79.

10. Richard Dyer, *Heavenly Bodies* (New York: St Martin's Press, 1986), 178.

11. Judith Butler, *Gender Trouble* (London: Routledge, 1999), xxviii.

12. Joan Riviere, 'Womanliness as Masquerade', *The Inner World and Joan Riviere* (London: Karnac Books, 1991), 90–101.

13. Michael G. Chang, 'The Good, the Bad and the Beautiful: Movie Actresses and Public Discourse in Shanghai, 1920s–1930s', in *Cinema and Urban Culture in Shanghai 1922–1943*, ed. Yingjin Zhang, (Stanford: Stanford University Press, 1999), 129.

14. Mary Ann Doane, *The Desire to Desire* (Bloomington: Indiana University Press, 1987), 181.

15. Jacques Lacan, 'God and the Jouissance of The Woman', in *Feminine Sexuality*, ed. Juliet Mitchell and Jacqueline Rose (London: Norton, 1982), 145.

16. Interview with Kwan, April 1997.

17. Leo Bersani, 'Is the Rectum a Grave?', *October*, no. 43 (1987): 212.

18. Dyer, *Heavenly Bodies*, 141–194.

19. Ackbar Abbas, *Hong Kong, Culture and the Politics of Disappearance* (Minneapolis: University of Minnesota Press, 1997), 45.

20. Ibid., 39–47; Leo Ou-fan Lee, *Shanghai Modern* (Cambridge: Harvard University Press, 1999), 335–338; Kristine Harris 'The *New Woman* Incident', in *Transnational Chinese Cinemas*, ed. Sheldon Hsiao-peng Lu (Honolulu: University of Hawai'i Press, 1997), 198; Rey Chow, 'A Souvenir of Love', in *At Full Speed*, ed. Esther C. M. Yau (Minneapolis: University of Minnesota Press, 2001), 209–229.

21. Russo, *Celluloid Closet*, 66.

22. Bret Hinsch, *Passions of the Cut Sleeve* (Berkeley: University of California Press, 1990), 165.

23. Frank Dikötter: *Sex, Culture and Modernity in China* (Hong Kong: Hong Kong University Press, 1995), 137.

24. Chang, 'The Good, the Bad and the Beautiful', 150.

25. Ibid., 157.

26. Dikötter, *Sex, Culture and Modernity*, 127–130.

27. Lee, *Shanghai Modern*, 335.

28. Abbas, *Hong Kong*, 25.

29. Chang, 'The Good, the Bad and the Beautiful', 140.

30. *Libération*, 4 December 1999, interview with J. M. Lalanne.

31. Harris, 'The *New Woman* Incident', 291.

32. Shu Kei, '*La légende de Ruan Lingyu*', in *Le Cinéma Chinois*, ed. Marie Claire Quiquemelle and Jean-Loup Passek (Paris: Centre Georges Pompidou, 1984), 149–154.

33. Chang, 'The Good, the Bad and the Beautiful', 297, note 88.

34. Richard Dyer, 'Believing in Fairies: the Author and the Homosexual', in *Inside Out*, ed. Diana Fuss (London: Routledge, 1991), 188.

35. Chris Straayer, 'The Hypothetical Lesbian Heroine in Narrative Feature Film', in *Multiple Voices in Feminist Film Criticism*, ed. Diane Carson, Linda Dittmar and Janice R. Welsch (Minneapolis: University of Minnesota Press, 1994), 351.

36. Chang, 'The Good, the Bad and the Beautiful', 297, note 93.

37. Isaac Julien and Kobena Mercer, 'De Margin and De Center', *Screen* 29, no. 4 (1988): 9.

38. Kaja Silverman, *Male Subjectivity at the Margins* (New York: Routledge, 1992), 6–7.

39. See, in particular, Jamie Gough, 'Theories of Sexual Identities and the Masculinization of the Gay Man', in *Coming on Strong: Gay Politics and Culture*, ed. Simon Shepherd and Mick Wallis (London: Unwin, 1989), 121.

40. Silverman, *Male Subjectivity at the Margins*, 355.

41. Freud, 'On Narcissism: An Introduction', *General Psychological Theory* (New York: Collier, 1963), 71.

5 *A Chinese Ghost Story*: Ghostly Counsel and Innocent Man

John Zou

Whenever ghosts appear on a screen, we realise, intuitively and without hesitation, that they are going to do something. For all the illuminated or closed depths they suggest beyond this world of ours, ghosts cannot be described as contemplative beings. In that sense, ghost stories are always strangely human stories. Ghosts may act strangely, but we know what the strangeness is about. They are action figures of a special kind. However, the consequences of this reciprocity are not happy, for ghostly rationality tends to drive humans out of their wits. Ghosts may take different approaches but they all send one message: your life is in strange hands.

Maybe this is why we have flocked to the movies in modern times, savouring the maddening moments of our life embraced by the Other. We are not only scared stiff by ghostly liminality, but also immensely attracted to their predatory appetite that shocks us into living, into demanding our own being. It is not enough to reiterate Benjamin's idea that as messengers of death, ghosts impart counsels of great authority to the living.[1] In ghost stories, we, the frightened listeners, the barely breathing audience, are often more ghostly than human. Is it not we who have developed this insatiable appetite for human life that seems, alas, denied to us? Is it not true that it is ultimately 'we' who desperately want 'us'? The exceptional joy of scary movies is mischievously autoerotic. It registers the foreignness of our own touch on our half-numb bodies.

GHOSTS ARE US

This essay studies how the Hong Kong film *A Chinese Ghost Story* (1987) rhetorically positions and constitutes its audience in anticipation of the colonial city's traumatic repatriation in 1997. I employ the basic Lacanian notion of symbolic castration to discuss the anxious ghostly acquisition of 'live humanity', gendered male in the film and an element

perceived as fantastically complementary to the abject lack that energises an audience in need of masculine conquest. Beyond existing interpretations that emphasise the film's narrative and visual hybridity and innovation,[2] I highlight the configuration of masculine and feminine identities at the centre of the visual imaginary concerning 'post'-colonial Hong Kong.

In *Men, Women and Chain Saws*, Carol Clover argues that the cinematic constitution of the male gaze and subsequent male embodiment for the audience in the horror film may be facilitated by identification with a female victim-hero.[3] Moving beyond this thesis of cross-sexual identification, however, I argue that in *A Chinese Ghost Story* the cinematic subject's assumption of female embodiment and obsession with the acquisition of manhood manifest male homoerotic moments in the 'post'-colonial making of an allegedly 'straight' male gaze. Furthermore, the invitation of male conquest by the 'feminised' audience becomes a particularly compelling trope of political negotiation when it is reframed as an amorous process of seduction and castration. In the disorientating historical context of the Hong Kong Handover, I argue that seduction and castration register an ambiguous instrument of political engagement counterbalancing the tremendous weight of British and mainland Chinese powers of domination and conquest.

Since its 1987 release, *A Chinese Ghost Story* has become a cult classic of Hong Kong cinema. Its memorable music, outrageous randomness and fleeting eroticism precipitated two sequels and numerous imitations. Indeed, it is often said to represent the pinnacle of Hong Kong horror. Partly because of its impact, the retrospective section at the 13th Hong Kong International Film Festival in 1989 was dedicated to the ghost film. Although the film seems to haphazardly combine romance, martial arts and period drama, its programmatic imprudence, excessive self-mockery and dizziness resulting from hasty production all contribute to a uniquely potent configuration of sexuality, history and contemporary Hong Kong politics. A remake of an earlier picture, the film's prominent literary origin is a familiar episode in *Strange Stories from a Chinese Studio*, an eighteenth-century compilation of ghost stories and a favourite sourcebook for ghostly reverie in Hong Kong cinema. The story relates a young man's solitary encounter with a female ghost in a desolate place.[4] At the most accessible level, the film takes the form of a quest narrative. A young tax collector, Ning Caichen (Leslie Cheung), sojourns in a haunted temple and thus subjects himself to the mercy of a beautiful female ghost, Nie Xiaoqian (Joey Wang), and a cohort of zombies. These zombies are human victims wasted by her bloodsucking master, the hermaphroditic Tree Monster by the name of Lao Lao or, literally, 'Grandma'. Yet because of Caichen's innocent respect for her body and his feeble but sincere effort to keep her out of harm's way, Xiaoqian falls in love with him, and entrusts herself to him for delivery from Lao Lao and a prospective marriage to a more terrifying figure – the Black Monster. Also resident at the temple is a powerful Taoist hermit, Yan, who prefers the company of ghosts to human troubles. Finally, with the Taoist's help, Caichen succeeds in defeating Lao Lao and the Black Monster and sends Xiaoqian away for reincarnation and a new life.

According to Carol Clover:

> Students of folklore or early literature recognize in horror the hallmarks of oral narrative: the free exchange of themes and motifs, the archetypal characters and situations, the accumulation of sequels, remakes, imitations. This is a field in which there is in some sense no original, no real or right text, but only variants; a world in which, therefore, the meaning of the individual example lies outside itself.[5]

To greatly simplify the folklorist Vladimir Propp's basic terms, the narrative of the film may be said to consist of four classes of characters: the hero, Caichen, who sets out on a journey to acquire his desired prize; the prize, Xiaoqian, whose acquisition testifies to the hero's success and full self-realisation; the donor, Yan, with whose help the hero accomplishes his mission and fulfils his identity as hero; and the villainous guardian, Lao Lao/Black Monster, who initially blocks the hero's acquisition of the prize and then yields to the additional power he receives from the donor.[6] However, such a structural interpretation is only true to a limited extent. Those who are familiar with *A Chinese Ghost Story* may be aware that, in the end, it is revealed that the female ghost's interest in the travelling man far precedes and exceeds his interest in her. Caichen's initial attraction to Xiaoqian's music playing and personal charm is in fact a scenario she has orchestrated as a fatal scheme. In that first meeting between them, his love for her is not awakened by her 'spontaneous' presence but indeed conditioned by her premeditated and seductive design. His need for her is programmed to fulfil her objective of turning him into a sacrifice to Lao Lao. Therefore, we have also to acknowledge that the quest narrative works in both directions. It is not just a mundane and male-centred romance where 'boy sees girl, and boy gets girl'. At a less obvious, but certainly more primordial level, we may read an extraordinary ghostly quest in which 'girl sees boy, and girl gets boy'. Caichen's pursuit of Xiaoqian is always situated within a larger context in which he plays only a passive and compliant role. In Clover's terms, one may say that by identifying with the subject of both narratives, the audience is at once Caichen and Xiaoqian, male and female, conqueror and conquered.

The fact that Caichen, the boyish man, constitutes the ultimate object of desire is further demonstrated at the end of the movie, when his romance with Xiaoqian concludes with her departure. Whereas her loving gaze that has so far directed and framed the audience's attention on him is now formally withdrawn, Caichen nevertheless still occupies the centre of the screen. The last shot of the movie follows him and Yan riding off towards an open pasture under a rainbow. Besides the emotional catharsis and sublimation mediated through the disappearance of the female and ghostly figure, the importance of this seemingly impersonal and objective look of the camera moves the audience to take the position left open by Xiaoqian. Indeed, when Xiaoqian's desire for Caichen ceases to stage him as the object of desire, the film exposes the tenacious persistence of its audience's own fascination with such a male figure. Of course, like Xiaoqian's, this parting look by the audience at Caichen is filled with a sense of longing and discontent. But whereas Xiaoqian's unrequited love opens up a space of desire in which he is situated, the movie's structural longing for him seems to indicate the necessity for narrative continuation. Predictably, in the box-office driven Hong Kong cinema, both the cinematic character Caichen and its actor Leslie Cheung would soon be reincarnated for further commercial and narrative exploitation. In that partially sublimated but also somewhat ominous parting shot of Caichen, one could almost be sure that he was to be accosted by other ghosts down the road. *A Chinese Ghost Story* was followed by two successful sequels, and Leslie Cheung was soon cast in another equally, if not more famous, Hong Kong ghost movie, *Rouge* (1988), in which he is remembered and pursued by the spectre of his youthful lover fifty years after her death.[7]

What becomes clear in this reiteration of the desiring characters of Xiaoqian, the impersonal camera and the female lead in *Rouge* is that the immediately evident quest narrative of male agency is situated within a framing narrative, in which the male protagonist serves as a rather passive object of

desire with predetermined functions. Behind the masks of Xiaoqian and the figure of Caichen are pre-designated functions operative in a larger context that Clover compares to the folkloric in her discussion of slashers or low-genre horror movies in the West. Citing Andrew Britten's remark that '[The] highly ritualistic and formulaic character is the most striking feature of contemporary entertainment film', she argues that the modern Western horror genre consists of a 'set of fixed tale types that generate an endless shadow of what are in effect variants: sequels, remakes, rip-offs'.[8] The limitation of her reading, from the perspective of *A Chinese Ghost Story*, is twofold. First, when interpreting the female identification by the male audience as an essentially masochistic process that contributes to the constitution of male subjectivity, she largely lays aside the issue that whereas the male audience may cross the boundary of sex to assume cinematic womanhood, the same 'straight' male cohort may also cross the boundary of sexuality to assume a homosexual position in their quest for masculine self-realisation. Citing Kaja Silverman, Clover agrees that 'it is always the victim – the figure who occupies the pas-

A Chinese Ghost Story: Caichen and Xiaoqian

sive position – who is really the focus of attention, and whose subjugation the subject (whether male or female) experiences as a pleasurable repetition of his/her own story', and that 'the fascination of the sadistic point of view is merely that it provides the best vantage point from which to watch the masochistic story unfold'.[9] What is important in the present context is that when the cinematic gaze is focused upon Leslie Cheung, a gay man playing the heterosexual lead, the masochist identification with his threatened body by a 'straight' audience is inevitably correlated with a male homosexual projection of desire, for which the Final Boy constitutes the object of passion rather the designation of the self.

Second, the folkloric reading, though mindful of larger structures of social discourse and process, is somewhat underdeveloped to account for catalytic and revolutionary moments of historical trauma. The Hong Kong horror genre in the last two decades of the twentieth century, for all its borrowings from Western vampire themes and classical Chinese ghost stories, specifically addresses subject formation under the shadow of agonising and riveting anticipation of radical socio-political change – Hong Kong's 'post'-colonial repatriation. Here, the source of anxiety is not so much the reconfiguration of pre-existing structures as the advent of the absolutely new. In the following pages, I provide an analysis that may lead to some tangible means to critically engage this political and psychological subject and assess its formative impact upon colonial Hong Kong's imagination of its own terminal moment. Clover's Final Girl, the sole survivor among numerous dead female and male bodies, serves as a pivotal link that allows the cinematic gaze to assume male subjectivity through exhilarating pains gendered as female. In contrast, I argue that in the Final Boy – rather than the Final Girl – embodied in the charismatic Leslie Cheung, Hong Kong sets up a lucky, innocent but helplessly gullible, imperialist figure, to be eternally staged, tantalised and seduced by a feminised Hong Kong undergoing repeated colonising ravishment. The presumed straight male gaze of the cinematic subject undergoes a similar process of masochistic self-articulation, not through identification with a female final survivor, but by projecting a feminised passion by which the want for men is satisfied through a seemingly passive but indeed predatory entrapment.

MALE DIFFERENCE: THE EDIBLE AND THE LOVABLE

The modernist message of ghostly narratives may ultimately concern the Lacanian law concerning being versus having.[10] According to Lacan, the acquisition of language – fundamental to the achievement of human subjectivity – presupposes a fundamental loss of unmediated connection to material reality, which the linguistic subject tries forever to recuperate. He names the acquisition of language the symbolic stage of the subject's development and likens that fundamental loss to castration. Because of this loss, the subject may only 'have', but not 'be', what it is distanced from: the dimension of materiality to which the pre-linguistic infant had spontaneous access. In her adaptation of this Lacanian insight in the seminal *Powers of Horror*, Kristeva states that

> [t]he abject of the self would be the culminating form of that experience of the subject to which it is real that all its objects are based merely on the inaugural *loss* that laid the foundations of its own being. There is nothing like the abjection of self to show that all abjection is in fact recognition of the *want* on which any being, meaning, language, or desire is founded.[11]

For Kristeva, horror or its vehicle, the abject, is fundamentally an experience that brings the subject back into proximity with what the subject has to expel from itself in order to establish itself. Abjection is designated as an ambiguous process precisely because the desirable is here intrinsically related to the repellent.

In modern horror cinema, maybe since *Nosferatu* (Murnau, 1922), ghostly figures mark ambiguity for cinemagoers precisely because they are both attractive and disgusting, and because they are attracted to and disgusted by their own objects of desire. Like linguistic subjects, they are forever in pursuit of live human bodies as the latter may provide some form of material complement. The haunted Lanruo temple, the allegorical Hong Kong, is a breeding ground for just such forlorn ghosts neurotically waiting for male blood and lively being. There is an unambiguous preference amongst the ghostly population in the film for male blood and, together with it, male essence. Female victims do exist, but they are not sucked dry, as if their blood does not yield the same relished taste. Furthermore, in comparison to the wasted men, who are consistently turned into zombies and left in desolate places such as the temple, the female ghosts – the undead women – are at least selectively treated with favour by Lao Lao. They become members of his/her murderous retinue and reside in illusory but swanky houses, such as the one where Caichen's erotic rendezvous with Xiaoqian takes place. In the business of blood sucking, therefore, gender difference conforms unconventionally to the difference between object and subject. Whereas the coveted object is male essence, without which man becomes a zombie and loses his sexual identity, the desiring agency is perversely highlighted as female: Lao Lao is half-female, as indicated by the almost equal distribution of his/her voice between male and female registers; and his/her entourage seems to consist only of female ghosts. Since the victimization of men is prominently gendered as a female enterprise, the zombies' attempt on Caichen's life, by following the 'female' routine of blood sucking, serves only a female agenda.

This ghostly economy of consumption in human fodder, gruesome as it is, has counsel for the audience. An ideologically conformist project, the movie trains us to desire and mystify a certain version of manhood, and warns against its unhappy loss. Even in the ghostly world, the unethical loss of manhood is punished more severely than its mere absence. A good ghost, such as Xiaoqian, is redeemable. A bad ghost, such as Xiaoqian's 'sister', exercises supernatural powers, such as flying. But zombies, once men, either languish in that eternal want for manhood, or are haplessly crushed without compensation, as indicated in Caichen's (non)encounter with them at the temple. Furthermore, within the category of desirable men, there is a crucial distinction between Caichen and earlier visitors to the temple. Those visitors were turned into zombies for one main reason: their inability to resist Xiaoqian's ethereal charms. Caichen, however, is represented as exceptional when he manifests a certain unresponsiveness to her sexual form. Xiaoqian only withdraws her attempt on Caichen's life, allowing herself to note his other admirable qualities, when she recognises this strangeness in Caichen, which the movie – and then she – apparently interprets as 'heterosexual innocence'. In an interpretive leap, Caichen's deficiency in heterosexual responsiveness is understood as his surplus in heterosexual charm. When he fails to express interest

in her heterosexual advances – indeed for that reason – the Chinese Final Boy does not look too different from the Western Final Girl in her sexual inactivity. Unsurprisingly, Leslie Cheung's gay escapades were already common knowledge by this time, thanks to the tireless Hong Kong paparazzi.

'Heterosexual innocence' is not only a factor in Caichen's disinterested moral self-possession, but also an important self-defence protecting him from being devoured by his ghostly neighbours. Translatable into his male physical integrity, this moment of heterosexual default also lays the ground for the transformation of Caichen's vulnerable male body into an entirely different figure of desirability. His innocence converts her evil obsession with his physical body into a romantic and therefore positive fascination with his emotional, intellectual and spiritual being. Xiaoqian stops seeing him as a food item and begins desiring his attention, company and ultimately his help in delivering her from indenture to Lao Lao and the prospect of marriage to Black Monster. Caichen's heterosexual innocence thus miraculously turns him from wretched victim into a benefactor with considerable leverage over Xiaoqian.

If manhood is made the focus of attention and the ultimate figure of desire in *A Chinese Ghost Story*, innocent manhood is even more so, because it inspires a higher denomination of desire. A man is but meat, and thus a matter of mere digestive and nutritional consideration for a ghost. An innocent man, however, can be a ghost's lover, benefactor and superior. Caichen goes from being an object of palatal attachment to one of sentimental attachment. As an innocent man, he renders the ghost an exceptional service. A ghost remains a ghost while consuming licentious and ordinarily heterosexual men, but she acquires a chance to be reincarnated as a human when she is consumed by the love for an innocent and exceptionally 'heterosexual' man. A man's lack of heterosexual response is therefore the definitive apparatus that distinguishes a lovable man from an edible man. As a movie, *A Chinese Ghost Story* celebrates Caichen's triumphant metamorphosis from food to conqueror of evil, though at the behest and always to the benefit of his ghostly lover. The ghostly counsel to the innocent male conqueror therefore reads: 'Desire not my body, but my soul.'

There is one further point to be made about the figure of male heterosexual innocence. Given its false materiality, attraction to the ghost's form is by definition vain. In not fixating upon this form and in seeing through that medium into the depth of the ghost's 'body', Caichen, the innocent and therefore dubiously heterosexual man, not only discovers Xiaoqian's 'heart', the locus of her real worth as a caring and vulnerable woman. He also discovers us, the audience for whom Xiaoqian's ghostly appearance functions as our mask, our concealment. The astonishing fantasy of *A Chinese Ghost Story* is not one in which man redeems ghost, or ghost seizes man, but one about Caichen in love with us. Functioning as some external and separate form of power and figured as the Lacanian pound of mortgaged flesh, he miraculously comes into lively connection with us and willingly attaches himself to us, to our invisible and therefore ghostly bodies in dire need of a physical complement.

However, the desiring agency of the ghostly women also takes on a distinctly masculine gender within the Lacanian scenario, where the having of phallus – as inscribed in the pursuit of Caichen – is conventionally represented as male, whereas the being of such phallus – Caichen himself – is female. To the extent that Caichen is a figure to be had by Xiaoqian and the audience, he is fundamentally correlated with that inaugural loss (or rejection) that makes possible the cinematic subject. In this sense, Caichen incarnates a typically vulnerable woman embodied as man. The ghostly women, on the other hand, reveal a forbidding male countenance. Particularly in the figure of Lao Lao, we witness a phallic mother capable of penetrating or castrating men.[12]

HEART OF GHOSTLINESS

Critics and fans of Hong Kong cinema agree that *A Chinese Ghost Story* is one heck of a ghost story. However, to describe it as a statement about colonialism may raise some eyebrows. Where is the international relevance? Who are the colonised? What constitutes the economic incentive? To answer such queries, one has only to turn to the film's conspicuous conquest themes. An audience familiar with Conrad's Africa may appreciate the irresistible attraction of the dark, oppressive world of the spectral beings, its intrinsic madness, and the necessity for a drastic final departure on the part of the sane 'humans'.[13] There is also romance: the film is about a languid female member of the ghostly tribes falling in love with a vibrant male intruder and betraying her own kind. Behind her lie unspeakable intrigues, savageness and cruelty. With him stands triumphant 'human' technology: Sanskrit sutras, martial arts and a weapon called 'love' that is capable of melting Turandot's heart. Stepping into the heart of darkness, the intruder brings with him not just satisfaction but also therapy. He gives her happiness, but he also gives her a cure. On the other hand, there is the constant possibility of the intruder's own victimisation. He who enters the dark world by accident is under the constant threat of being consumed by darkness. Caichen could be food for Lao Lao at any point before he/she is finally defeated. To redeem Xiaoqian, Caichen makes a heroic exertion for which he can never be adequately rewarded. In the end, the narrative of colonial self-making is also central to the film. Whereas Xiaoqian's world remains in general ghostly and Caichen's frivolous, there is a magic mutual recognition that elevates them both. Caichen comes out of the ordeal not just a seasoned warrior against the forces of darkness, but also more of a man: sublimated, wiser and better prepared to meet with troubles in his future. Conquest here is represented as a formative experience, a *bildungsroman*.

But what does it mean for such a story of (con)quest to be placed within a reversed framing narrative? Whereas the ghostly audience of Hong Kong cinema implied in *A Chinese Ghost Story* comes forth as a coveted object of desire in Caichen's eyes, Caichen's quest for Xiaoqian obviously becomes meaningful only within Xiaoqian's primordial quest for him. Why does the positioning of Xiaoqian, our surrogate cinematic subject or audience, have to assume the narrative forms of a (con)quest of herself?

To answer these questions, we have to revisit the fundamental ambiguity and transgression of the ghostly beings, most sensationally articulated in the monstrous person of Lao Lao. Between Xiaoqian and Lao Lao there is a ghostly community torn between agendas to save and destroy men. Like the colonising figure, Caichen, who is also both masculine and feminine, the ghostly world is never one and the same, but always divided between rejection and invitation, and between murderous hatred of and sentimental longing for the intruder. If we take Xiaoqian and Lao Lao as two aspects of the self-same colonial subject, they complement each other in such a way that the conventional colonial object of desire becomes immediately recognisable.

As Homi Bhabha states, the designation of objects or values of English origin in the dark colonial world becomes necessary in colonial travels and conquests, because there they produce signs of difference within that world that help consolidate the discriminatory relationship between Europe and its colonies.[14] In *A Chinese Ghost Story* Caichen's discovery of some form of humanity in the heart of Xiaoqian fulfils that purpose. In Xiaoqian, Caichen locates a responsive human image among the dark cohorts. This image reminds him not only that his own 'humanity' is linked to the dark world around him, inspiring his anger and energy for conquest and cleansing, but also of the fundamental inconsistency of the ghostly world, giving him leverage and making his intervention practical.

Conversely, what stands out within the framing narrative of Xiaoqian's interest in Caichen is that unique desire for, and the attendant techniques to manipulate and victimise, the intruding conqueror. To Xiaoqian, love for Caichen always involves betrayal, violation and condemnation of the self. Even though her self-hatred may precede the intruder's advent, the latter certainly supplies a means for its sustenance and materialisation. Caichen's presence gives Xiaoqian opportunity to repeat confessions of past wrongdoings and to express yearning for future improvement. Xiaoqian, like Lao Lao, is a dualist figure. Whereas Lao Lao is both man and woman, Xiaoqian is both human and ghost, or a human value among the ghosts. Therefore, her *raison d'être* in the film is self-incrimination. She is totally subjected to the overwhelming power of Caichen's human interpellation. As explained in Judith Butler's recent discussion, the Althusserian allegory of the policeman's 'hey, you there' postulates that subjects achieve their identity by forming a conscience which systematically incriminates and demands compliance with the law.[15] Between Xiaoqian and Caichen, the scenario of interpellation may be a form of conquest that forever demands Xiaoqian's reform on account of her past crimes against masculinity, humanity and colonial consistency.

Yet, *A Chinese Ghost Story* is ultimately interesting because it does not stop at such a mode of colonial self-incrimination. The female, ghostly conscience that presupposes a debt to the masculine human runs side by side with mockery of masculinity. If nothing else, masculinity is the butt of the joke throughout the film. The romantic hero Caichen is almost pissed upon by Swordsman Yan. The archetypal warrior Yan is prone to emotional breakdowns, when he bewails his confusion about worldly affairs. He is even pierced in the buttock by a clumsy Caichen, his dignity compromised in his duel with Lao Lao. Lao Lao's swimming tongue, shaped like a oversized penis, is maybe visually the most striking and ridiculous metaphor of masculinity. Though its horrifying function is to force open the lustful heterosexual man's mouth, in the end Yan chops it off: the film's passion for masculinity is checked by a fundamental disbelief in its inherent powers.

More importantly, although Xiaoqian's agency as subject is delineated as female, wanting and often self-punishing, to a certain extent this is a camouflage, because the masculinity idealistically embodied in the intruder is not only undermined but also ultimately her victim, her toy, and a source of her pleasure and karmic gain. In the movie, at the same time as we the audience are engaged in conquering ourselves by imagining ourselves receptive of a robust and innocent masculinity, we realise that such a masculinity is as artificial as that simulated foreign touch. Leslie Chueng, the Final Boy, is not a triumphant figure in the end, but constantly subjected to the cinema's voluptuous, threatening and disabling gaze. Benjamin's great dictum about death that ghosts impart counsels of great authority to the living may therefore also require a different reading. Through the masks of death, the colonised subject does come forth, but only to tantalise and castrate the living presence of the colonising forces. Maybe such ghostly counsel for the innocent man is the ultimate and ambiguous message of the film, as Hong Kong cinema of the late 1980s foresaw another strange conqueror at the gate.

NOTES

1. Walter Benjamin, 'The Story Teller', in *Illuminations: Essays and Reflections*, ed. and intro. Hannah Arendt, trans. Harry Zohn (New York: Schocken Books, 1968), 93–94.
2. Stephen Teo, *Hong Kong Cinema: The Extra Dimensions* (London: British Film Institute, 1997), Chapter 14, 219–229; Lisa Odham Stokes and Michael Hoover, *City on Fire: Hong Kong Cinema*, (London and New York: Verso, 1999), 101–103; and David Bordwell, *Planet Hong Kong: Popular Cinema and the Art of Entertainment* (Cambridge: Harvard University Press, 2000), 165–168.

3. Carol Clover, *Men, Women, and Chain Saws: Gender in the Modern Horror Film* (Princeton: Princeton University Press, 1992), 16–17.

4. Pu Songling, *Strange Stories from a Chinese Studio* (*Liaozhai Zhiyi*), trans. Herbert A. Giles (London: T. W. Laurie, 1913). On this Chinese classic, see Judith Zeitlin, *Historian of the Strange: Pu Songling and the Classic Chinese Tale* (Stanford: Stanford University Press, 1993). The film is roughly based on a story entitled 'Nie Xiaoqian'. Another movie with the same Chinese title and known in English as *The Enchanting Shadow* was made in 1960 by the famed Hong Kong director Li Hanxiang.

5. Clover, *Men, Women, and Chain Saws*, 10–11.

6. Vladimir Propp, *Morphology of the Folk Tale*, trans. L. Scott (Austin: University of Texas Press, 1968). For a relatively recent discussion, see Frederic Jameson, *The Political Unconscious* (Ithaca: Cornell University Press, 1981), esp. Chapter 2, 151–84.

7. For a discussion of the ghostly business of memory, see Rey Chow 'A Souvenir of Love', in *At Full Speed: Hong Kong Cinema in a Borderless World*, ed. Esther C. M. Yau, (Minnesota: Minnesota University Press, 2001), 209–229.

8. Clover, *Men, Women, and Chain Saws*, 9–10.

9. Ibid., 62.

10. For a discussion of Lacan's binary divide between meaning and life, see Kaja Silverman, *Male Subjectivity at the Margins* (New York: Routledge, 1992), 35–48.

11. Julia Kristeva, *Powers of Horror: An Essay on Abjection*, trans. Leon R. Roudiez (New York: Columbia University Press, 1982), 5.

12. For a discussion of the castrating mother as a regulating factor in horror movies, see Barbara Creed, *The Monstrous Feminine: Film, Feminism, Psychoanalysis* (London and New York: Routledge, 1993), 88–104.

13. Joseph Conrad, *Heart of Darkness* (Harmondsworth: Penguin, 1983).

14. Homi Bhabha, 'Signs Taken for Wonders: Questions of Ambivalence and Authority under a Tree outside Delhi, May 1817', in *Location of Culture* (London: Routledge, 1994), 102–121.

15. Judith Butler, ' "Conscience Doth Make Subjects of Us All": Althusser's Theory of Subjection', in *The Psychic Power of Life* (Stanford: Stanford University Press, 1996), 106–131.

6 *Chungking Express*: Time and its Displacements

Janice Tong

The world as we see it is passing.

Paul of Tarsus

Four shots of an indeterminate steel-blue pre-dawn or twilight sky follow each other. Framed by the jutting contours of dirty housing commission flats and factory-like buildings, they offer a view of the 'world' between the gaps of an urban concrete jungle. White clouds pass, their motion is sped up. A voice-over begins in Mandarin: 'We rub shoulders every day … although we may not know one another now, it may be possible to be friends some day. My name is He Qiwu. I'm a cop, my number is PC 223.' Jostled and incoherent images of an overcrowded street provide glimpses of this plain-clothes detective in a *mise en scène* that is indistinguishable. A series of quick cuts interrupt this already over-loaded vision – handcuffs, a mannequin with a blonde wig, an Indian with a paper bag over his head who suddenly and doggedly runs off. The cop makes chase – around him the streetscape flashes by in a multitude of colours and frozen movement, recalling the multi-perspectival blur of Futurist paintings. The action freezes into stop-motion as He Qiwu bumps into a woman in dark glasses, beige raincoat and a blonde wig. An abrupt cut to a close-up of an old-fashioned electronic 'flip-card' clock interrupts the frame. It reads 'Friday, 28 April, 8:59pm', which, at that moment, changes over to '9:00pm'. Then the frame cuts back to a succession of mid to long shots of the blonde woman turning to look at the figure disappearing towards camera and out of frame. Over this image, we hear He Qiwu's voice-over: 'At our closest point, we were just 0.1 centimetres apart … 55 hours later, I fall in love with this woman.' This is the second part of the opening sequence to *Chungking Express* (Wong Kar-wai, 1994).[1]

The experience of time in cinema, particularly in post-World War II cinema, opens up a fundamental and irreversible change in our basic perception and conception of time and temporal relations. The technology of cinema directly calls for a manipulation of time and in doing so the visual fabric of time is altered definitively. The multitudinous presentation of time – time can be accelerated, compressed, stretched, spliced and even evacuated – means that time itself can be (re)produced in cinema. Directors such as Jean-Luc Godard, Alain Resnais and more recently Krzystof Kieslowski, David Lynch, Raoul Ruiz, Tsai Ming-Liang and Wong Kar-wai belong to a handful of directors whose films contribute to a new cinematic rendering of time by complicating the materiality, or the visuality, of time. What I mean by this is that these directors do not necessarily follow the convention of a narrative-driven structure. Instead, their films unfold in a kind of temporal exegesis. Their films toy with and challenge our experience of time as a linear succession of moments, as well as the rudimentary notion that time's trajectory is that of a past, present and future. Take Quentin Tarantino, for example. His *Pulp Fiction* (1994) throws this linear notion of time into disarray. At the end of the film, we are returned to the opening sequence to give this episode (and the film) closure. (Hitherto, the opening sequence has only functioned as a kind of adjunct to the story.) Not only is Tarantino able to neatly and inventively tie up loose ends, but he is also able to resurrect the heroes of the story, Jules and Vincent, from their respective exits – Jules's untimely retirement and Vincent's memorable but somewhat unheroic death. However, although the temporal structure of this film does indeed loop in on itself and is for the most part fragmented, with the story interlocking in a multi-perspectival and splintered way, I would argue that Tarantino's films are still unable to alter or challenge our perception of time. This is both because Tarantino's fragmentation and looping of time still obey a coherent narrative structure that is episodic, and, more importantly, because his films generally do not attempt to complicate or extend the boundaries of the *visuality* of time. It is this second idea, to do with stretching our perception of cinematic time that I believe Wong's films give access to and that fuels this essay.

This is not to say that Wong, Resnais or Ruiz are attempting to make non-diegetic films. In fact, what makes *Chungking Express* so compelling and delightful to watch is precisely its two unrequited love stories. What I am suggesting, however, is that in these films there is a lot more at stake than the storyline. Films like *Ashes of Time* (Wong Kar-wai, 1994), *Last Year at Marienbad* (Alain Resnais, 1961), *Mulholland Drive* (David Lynch, 2001) and *Time Regained* (Raoul Ruiz, 1999) bring to the fore certain kinds of images which are difficult to grasp through an analysis of narrative alone. In fact, this specific concern with images and their representational power are what constitute the film's aesthetic being, an ontology that is specifically of the temporal kind.

Chungking Express presents its viewers with such images. They are what I would like to call images of time. It is Wong's rendering of time in his cinematographic images that unhinges our perception of time when viewing *Chungking Express*. But how so? This essay sets out to describe what I mean by the visual fabric of time which constitutes Wong's images of time. It asks how Wong's film defies conventional readings of time by displacing temporal relations so as to open up possibilities for non-linear, disseminative, and discontinuous reading.

Tony Rayns rightly calls Wong Kar-wai the 'poet of time',[2] in whose films we see a vital engagement of time in its many guises – speed, recollection, memory, waiting. The cinematographic images in *Chungking Express* bear witness to this not only through the overlapping narrative's focus on deadlines and expiry dates, which are shown in close-ups of recurring images of clocks and dates stamped on tins of food. Also, his image repertoire and its incongruities suggest that Wong's manipulation of time is experienced more obliquely. For me, his films raise the question of what it means for time to be cinematic, whilst at the same time remaining open to how cinema, in turn, affects this temporal event. In other words, what sort of time is cinematic? And, furthermore, how can the 'substance' of cinematic

time be experienced, especially the substance of Wong's cinematic time?

In order to engage with these questions we need first to approach Wong's films from a historico-cultural viewpoint so as to contextualise and give a fuller understanding to their *image* of Hong Kong and its citizens.

HONG KONG: CULTURAL DIASPORA AND THE HORIZON OF LOSS

Hong Kong in the mid-1990s was experiencing the state of its own disappearance. A shroud of uncertainty has bathed the city-state since the 1984 Sino-British Joint Declaration returning Hong Kong to China. But even before this, the history of Hong Kong has always reflected a city in flux: from its origin as a territory of the Qing Dynasty, Hong Kong was then annexed to the British for a period of 99 years after the Opium War, during which time it also experienced a period of Japanese occupation. In its status as a British colonial-state it thrived as an entrepôt, an unparalleled 'nexus' through which the cultural and economic traffic of the East and West passed and still passes.

It is therefore not surprising to find Hong Kong as a city with an identity that is for the most part culturally fragmented. With its return to mainland China in 1997, instability and indeterminacy advances on its citizens. It is as though Hong Kong itself, along with its identity, is vanishing before the very eyes of its people. There is a rapid sense of time passing and, in this process, a calling forth towards an indeterminate future.

This experience of flux is reflected in Wong's destabilising cinematographic self-image of Hong Kong. The city epitomises Paul Virilio's description of geography as no longer the measuring of space alone, but now as determined by a 'chrono-space'; what he calls geography 'by speed'. Virilio sees this 'space of speed' as an image of the 'city of the beyond', which he calls 'the City of Dead Time'.[3] This is exemplified in the experience of having 'dawn and dusk in a single window' of an airplane: appearance and disappearance. This is how Wong presents the image of Hong Kong and its citizens to us. The images of Faye at the Midnight Express food-stall are typically 'slit-framed', giving us only a partial view of her actions (or inaction). Christopher Doyle's hand-held camera and William Chang's fast-paced editing combine to disorient the viewer. Take the opening sequence described at the beginning of this essay as an example. Only glimpses of the sky are visible and, even so, they are 'denatured' with the clouds moving at an abnormal speed. The following action sequence through the streets is a jumbled incoherent mess of colours, which makes the surrounding architecture and its location indistinguishable. The camera then freeze-frames on a woman we do not and cannot recognise, because she is in disguise. All this is combined with a haunting fairground-like music, its repetitive bass riff oscillating not more than three to four semi-tones apart, adding to our growing sense of displacement. These are not familiar images of Hong Kong. They are not even familiar cinematic images of Hong Kong. How, then, are we able to read these images of Hong Kong and to make sense of what escapes us visually?

These 'visual slippages' reveal that Wong's camera is not given over to a direct representation of the anachronistic spaces of Hong Kong. In fact, his images extend Ackbar Abbas's view of the new Hong Kong cinema as one that is sensitive to 'spatial issues', eloquently summed up in his phrase 'image[s] of history as palimpsest'.[4] Instead of trying to capture spaces, geography, architecture or location, Wong is 'trying to capture time'.[5] Wong's rendering of cinematic time can be experienced in the ambiguous nature of his images, and not only does time displace the characters and locations, but also it is *time itself* that is ultimately displaced in *Chungking Express*.

In Ewa Mazierska and Laura Rascaroli's essay 'Trapped in the Present: Time in the Films of Wong Kar-wai',[6] and in a recent interview with Hou Hsiao Hsien, both the critics and director have commented on Wong's ability to 'capture contemporary life'[7] or 'catch the spirit of the time'.[8] *Chungking Express* bears this out, as it has often been described as a post-modern slice of contemporary Hong Kong exemplified by 'a new wave editing style, on-location realism and narrative dissonance'.[9] But these readings have only located this experience of contemporary life as that of living in the *present*. Mazierska and Rascaroli refer to Hong Kong as a 'throw-away society': its citizens consume fast foods, rent 'small apartments furnished with simple, mass produced furniture', doing so through 'choice rather than necessity', because for them 'the past and memory matter very little'.[10] For Mazierska and Rascaroli,

Wong has no 'appetite for dead styles and fashions' and the 'contemporary culture he depicts … does not appear to be founded on past achievements, but on the strength of the present'.[11] This view echoes Abbas's description of Hong Kong people as having 'little memory and no sentiment for the past', their 'general attitude to everything sometimes indistinguishable from the spirit of enterprise', that is, to 'cancel out and pass on'.[12]

A focus on the narrative level alone indicates that the four main characters in *Chungking Express* do seem to belong to this kind of disposable and transient society: the two cops, He Qiwu and Cop 663, both live alone, renting small and inexpensively furnished apartments, and frequent the Midnight Express take-away food stall where a third character, Faye, works. But the images reveal a different story; in fact, their experience of Hong Kong is *not* of the present.

The first story in the film involves Cop 223 (He Qiwu) and a drug-trafficker (an unrecognisable Brigitte Lin in a blonde wig, dark glasses and trench-coat). Time is of paramount importance to both these characters. We can literally see the minutes ticking away for them. 223's presence was first 'documented' by a flip-card clock in the opening sequence, propelling him ceaselessly into the future. The significance of time for him is that of time running out. As Wong says, he has to make 'every minute of his life count for something'.[13] So, from the deadline of 1 May he sets for his ex-girlfriend, May, to return (represented by the expiry date stamped on tins of pineapples, her favourite fruit), to his pager password ('to love you for 10,000 years'), to counting the hours until he or someone else falls in love, he is trying to capture a bit of time. But these attempts are failures, and time slips from his grasp. Despite all the technology that enables immediacy, his phone calls never reach their destinations and become but a series of further detours and delays. Presence inevitably escapes him. Tellingly, his character appears in 'smudge-motion' more than any other character in the film, as if to suggest that change is always effacing his sense of himself.[14]

For the other two principal characters, 663 and Faye, the present is not a rapid succession of ceaseless moments, as suggested by the name of the take-away stall they frequent, Midnight Express. Instead, they are out-of-sync with the present: Faye listens compulsively to 'California Dreamin' and 663 to his lover's favourite tune, Dinah Washington's 'What a

Difference a Day Makes'. Both songs are from a different era and a different culture. In 663's case, we are doubly trapped in the past. The song belongs in his flashback of his time with his air-hostess former girlfriend. This flashback, in turn, plunges us into Wong's own memory of Hong Kong when he was a boy, his nostalgia for the toy planes he played with as a boy (no longer fashionable and difficult to find when Wong decided to have them in the film), and his fondness for this song (used in an PanAm advertisement several years ago).[15] The only song in the film current at the time of its filming is 'Dreams' by The Cranberries. But even as you hear the opening strain your familiarity is immediately displaced, because it is a Cantopop version remade and sung by Faye Wong.

Chungking Express offers us an experience of Hong Kong in Abbas's sense of '*déjà disparu*', the feeling that 'what is new and unique about the situation is always already gone, and we are left holding a handful of clichés, or a cluster of memories of what has never been'.[16] It is as though even this desire to preserve is problematic, Abbas writes that in the very 'act of looking … the more you try to make the world hold still in a reflective gaze, the more it moves under you'.[17] Let us return to the opening sequence where Takeshi's character is running through a background that is totally blurred. His movements seem to be staggered or disjointed, yet he is visible and in focus. In contrast, his surroundings are a mere blur of colours and movement. This sequence is shot in Wong's signature 'smudge-motion' or 'step-printing' technique,[18] for Wong feels that Hong Kong is too fast-paced, but that with this technique he can 'con-centrate on [things which] don't move while everything around them moves fast'. For him, this process is a way of 'trapping time', to 'change' and 'play with time', to do to time what you can't do to it in real life.[19] What happens to the visuality of time in these images? And what is our experience of Wong's cinematic rendering of time?

The scene is shot at double-speed, forty-eight frames per second, and played back at twenty-four frames per second through the projector. At the lab, frames one to twelve are allowed to run consecutively, then frame twelve gets repeated for the next twelve frames to achieve a 'pause' in the motion; frames thirteen to twenty-four are discarded, and frames twenty-five to thirty-six get to run consecutively, and so forth. By letting the same frame run through the projector this process distinguishes itself from the device of the 'jump-cut' − another editing process used to show temporal discontinuity.[20] Something gets lost in this process − we lose sight of our surroundings. Space becomes ambiguous, things and objects around the foreground and background merge and blend with each other. Hong Kong has been stripped of its appearance, the signs that are so easily recognisable have been replaced by an under-belly of non-signs. I would like to recall Virilio's metaphor here: appearance, disappearance. Sylvere Lotringer describes this as the tension between '[t]he urbanist … whose art made the city appear' and 'the acceleration of speed … now making it disappear'.[21] The urbanist is now the *cineaste* whose camera is able to not only speed things up, but also able to slow things down to make visible what is previously invisible to the human eye.

Takeshi's character caught in Wong Kar-wai's signature smudge-motion style. This technique offers up a new visuality to our experience of cinematic time.

TIME, MULTIPLE FRAGMENTATION, DISPLACEMENT

Wong's manipulation of time enables us to see incongruous and divergent states of time in the same image. Simultaneously represented, these states of time appear to be in the process of dissemination; the images dilate and stretch, and seem to slip and pull away from each other. It is this displaced sense of time that is experienced in the opening sequence and throughout *Chungking Express*. Perhaps the most significant scene supporting this view in the second story is when 663's past and future collide at Midnight Express: Faye (future air-hostess and 663's future love interest) and his ex-girlfriend (dressed in an air-hostess uniform) stand side by side, sizing each other up. It is an image that conjures up a visual representation of a present that is split, both past and future appearing in the one image. This image prefigures my reading of Wong's cinematic images, and specifically their visual activity in the displacement of time. Gilles Deleuze describes these images as time-images, when '[w]hat is specific to the image … is to make perceptible, to make visible, relationships of time which cannot be seen in the represented object and do not allow themselves to be reduced to the present'.[22] What is significant in Deleuze's concept of the time-image to Wong's project is that when 'a little time in the pure state … rises up to the surface of the screen' it privileges the 'seer'. In other words, Wong's cinema is a 'cinema of the seer'[23] which privileges seeing rather than acting, making images rather than following plot-lines, making visible time and temporal relations rather than spaces or movements.

A few image sequences can illustrate this. 663's ex-girlfriend leaves behind a letter for him at Midnight Express (having gone there on the wrong night), only to have 663 delay their 'end' by leaving it behind the counter indefinitely. Wong makes visible these temporal dislocations in a beautiful image sequence. A two-shot of 663 and Faye shows 663 frame left, leaning against the side of the counter and staring into the distance. Faye is frame right; motionless, she watches him drink his coffee. The two are almost entirely still in this whole sequence, and deep in their own thoughts. She is watching him and he is looking but doesn't see, for 663 has plunged into the past, into his memory. The foreground is a blur of shadows, indistinct figures whose movements are speeded up, an effect that punctuates the stark neon-lit backdrop of 'inaction'. This scene faithfully renders what Deleuze would call a 'pure optical situation',[24] where time can be seen as being freed from movement. In this scene, we can see how Wong makes visible this other temporality that exists for his characters. He renders visually the interiority of Faye and 663 – contemplative, waiting, weighed down by memory. The different components of the image come together to make time and temporal relations visible: the lack of a soundtrack; Faye's stillness; her quiet gaze at 663; and his banal everyday gestures, steeped in the past here. People speed past around them, in sync with each other and the world they live in. But Faye and 663 are isolated, absorbed in their own time frame, and for them time *drags*. The materiality of time is fractured visually, opening itself up to different temporal intensities in the one shot.

Jean-Marc Lalanne's analysis of Wong's images closely describes this rendering of cinematic time:

> The images break loose from any context of enunciation to drift through the narrative; space splits into pieces; the film's direction is no longer governed by a spatial scenography based on continuity, but becomes an abstract device of pure optic and sonic sensations; as in the sublime verse from *Hamlet*, 'the time is out of joint', it breaks up into atoms of disparate and overlapping lengths of time.[25]

This fracturing of time is not only present in special effects shots, but is found throughout Wong's film: in everyday gestures infinitely mutated with every repetition. This is especially the case with 663, who is not only out-of-sync with the present, but whose identity is also displaced. When his ex-girlfriend asks for him at Midnight Express, the owner of the stall

Cop 663 and Faye: caught in their own time-frame.

mistakenly refers to him as 633 (as he does through-out the film), but she does not seem to register this error. Later on in the film, one of the kitchenhands corrects his mistake, only to have him shrug his error off. To compound this displacement further, writing on the film perpetuates this slippage of identity. Neither Ackbar Abbas in his essay 'The Erotics of Disappointment' nor David Bordwell in his chapter on *Chunking Express* in *Planet Hong Kong* picks up on the cop's displaced identity. In *Hong Kong: Culture and the Politics of Disappearance*, Abbas slips from one badge number to the other. Perhaps these 'slippages' only testify to the inevitability of change and, in the end, it doesn't really matter whether his real number is 663 or 633. Even as he purposefully and inces-santly resists change by sticking to the same foods (we see huge stacks of Del Monte tomato sardines in his cupboard) or the same places to eat, or by even failing to notice the alterations Faye makes to his apartment (we see him reprimanding his dishcloth for changing when it should be steadfastly holding onto its sense of self). He seems to be unaware that his everyday gestures and habits are already made up of 'a daunting number of minutely varied repetitions of locales and routines'.[26]

Chungking Express shows Hong Kong to be a compressed space that forces its people to make physical contact with one another without making any connections, even effecting disconnections from their selves. Just as the city and its citizens embrace time in the express speed of communication via mobile phones, emails and faxes, so too these tech-nologies elicit distance and displacement between people. Therefore, it is not surprising to find the swift and efficient drug-trafficker contracting a group of drug-smugglers and concealing the heroin in the opening fast-paced sequence only to lose her charges at the airport, a place of transit with multiple destinations and time zones. When her own 'expiry date' is stamped on a tin of sardines she should be forced into action. Yet, paradoxically, she spends her last night in apparent inaction. The series of images of her and 223 sitting together at the bar show a motionless couple. Time passes. They are still motionless, except for their different poses and the collection of empty glasses in front of them. It is hard to say how much time has actually passed. More images of 223 and the blonde woman follow, this time in a hotel bedroom where she is sprawled out

asleep on the bed, still in her disguise. He is con-suming plates of chef's salads and chips while watch-ing Chinese opera on TV. Television is the only allusion to the present moment, encapsulated by the notion of televisual presence as the most immediate form of time, a perpetual presence, direct, continuous and uninterrupted, leaving one with no time to think or to dwell on the past. Why these images of listless-ness, of stillness, instead of the images of action usually associated with these characters?

Martin Scorsese's editor, Tom Rolf, talks about investing a little bit of time into the image when editing *Taxi Driver* (Martin Scorsese, 1976). In a particular shot, Robert de Niro's character, Travis Bickle, puts an effervescent tablet into his glass of water. We see his hands putting the tablet in the glass in a zoom-in, which cuts to a zoom-in of a motion-less de Niro staring fixedly at the fizzing water and then a final cut back to the glass – the camera zooms in slowly, until the bubbles fill the entire frame. The whole sequence took about twenty seconds, which is very long in terms of screen time for the little action that is taking place. Rolf explained Scorsese's insist-ence in 'hanging on to the shot' when he was about to edit it out: 'By hanging onto an image for an inor-dinately long time, the audience questions why they are looking at this image for such a long time … and they reinvest their interest into the image, and begin to look at it with a new perspective.'[27]

This investment of time is what leads to the sev-ering of the action/reaction response that many mainstream films offer their audiences. Traditional narrative cinema has conditioned audiences to respond in a certain manner to its conventions: for example, matching eye-lines, shot/reverse shots; or a close-up of a face used to induce an emotional response; or a special-effects sequence slowed down to heighten its effects which may not otherwise be visible to the naked eye. For Deleuze, the 'break in the sensory-motor link'[28] frees time from its subor-dination to movement. In traditional narrative cinema, time is subordinated to movement that allows the story to unfold in a logical, linear manner. Deleuze's 'time-images' are established by breaking with this convention. In Wong's films, especially in *Ashes of Time*, we are often shown a series of images that no longer follow a cohesive narrative structure. In turn, the narrative is further displaced by these images, which are aberrant and ambiguous. In fact,

Time stands still for Cop 663 at the California bar.

'we no longer know what is imaginary or real, physical or mental in the situation, not because they are confused, but because we do not have to know and there is no longer even a place from which to ask'.[29] In *Chungking Express*, Wong's rendering of a time freed from movement can be found everywhere, such as in the slow-motion images of Faye daydreaming, as if her daydreaming has altered even the camera's perception of time. Or it can also be found in the image of 663 and Faye sitting together at his apartment (their image is further displaced because it is their mirror reflection that we see), as if they are only able to be together when they are absent from each other, absent even in their presence. And again, it appears in the smudge-motion images of 663 whilst he was waiting for Faye at the California bar. His voice-over tells us that he is wondering whether she will remember their date in her California that evening. The fragmentation of time in this scene is experienced in 663's stillness by a juke-box contrasting the rush of bar-goers, and the slippage of place as well as time zones, between an imaginary California (from the song, which nonetheless conjures up images of Faye) and the real California, a destination where she will physically arrive. The temporal relations in these image sequences come together to testify to a new experience of cinematic time.

For the most part, *Chungking Express*'s images of mutability depict conditions of lostness in the characters – loss of identity, failure of communication, impossibility of reconciliation and the inability to hold on to time. These are conditions that, in turn, infuse Wong's images of Hong Kong with a sense of nostalgia, a kind of sentimental yearning for a history that has disappeared too quickly. In Wong's world it is not memory or the past that do not matter to his characters. In fact,

the very opposite seems to be true. Rather, it is as though for Wong, the people of Hong Kong do not know how to *think* the history of Hong Kong; the relationship between the people of Hong Kong and the place is displaced temporally. BBC Hong Kong correspondent Damian Grammaticas recently described Hong Kong as a 'rootless refugee city' that even six years after its return to the mainland is still 'struggling to find its own identity'.[30]

The last section offers a close reading of the opening sequence to *Chungking Express* as described at the beginning of the essay. In my analysis, I hope to further and more concretely describe how Wong's rendering of his cinematographic images illustrate a split or displacement in time itself, and how, as a viewer, the substance of his cinematic time can be experienced.

THIS IS NOT OF THE PRESENT

Time is out of joint.

Gilles Deleuze[31]

Chungking Express opens *in media res*, as if to suggest that time is always already split and could only open up to its 'variable present'[32] in every instance. The 'present' for Deleuze is a disjunction – it joins the present that is 'still to be' with a present 'that has already passed'. In other words, the present is 'variable', it is a paradox that speaks of a fold in time. Whilst the present calls forth a ceaseless opening towards an indeterminate future, it simultaneously disappears into a concrete but infinitely variable pastness. Made possible only through a loosening of the sensory-motor schema, the challenge now lies in the '*interstice* between images',[33] where temporal relations open up to all possibilities not based on determinate logic.

Wong's film begins with Cop 223's voice-over: 'We rub shoulders every day … we may not know each other, but we could be friends some day.' As the voice-over is the first thing we hear, the viewer is immediately compromised temporally. The device of the voice-over suggests a displacement in time, a casting back in time from a narrative point of view that normally places the viewer in a privileged position of knowing in advance the outcome of the narrative. But instead of shedding insight for the viewer, this voice-over conveys its message in Mandarin where the local dialect is Cantonese. Immediately, the audience is disadvantaged and a distance between audience and narrative effectively opens up. This displacement is further compounded by the subsequent voice-over – when 223 bumps into a woman in a blonde wig – that tells us: 'At our closest point, we were just 0.1cm apart … 55 hours later, I fall in love with this woman.' The use of the present tense here – 'I fall in love' – confuses the flashback convention of a voice-over, which would normally employ the past tense: '… 55 hours later, I fell in love …' This temporal incongruity found in the voice-over returns us to the present unfolding of events and to the temporally parallel stories that follow this space of encounter. It is only as the first story draws to a close that we will find a further and more destabilising fracture within his voice-over: that there was no possibility of 223's voice-over being a flashback, since he could not have known that this woman was the one he would fall in love with at the time they were 'closest' to one another. Thus, the fold doubles in on itself, the voice-over becomes a non-diegetic insert of time, and radically puts into question what the audience is seeing or experiencing.

Wong's image-narrative in *Chungking Express* presents Hong Kong as a city with an absent centre. In its place, we find a mobile state of rupture where images, space, time, characters and narratives fold in upon each other, weaving a skein of images that threaten to slip from our gaze. These are images of a little 'pure time' which rises to the surface of the screen: time that has taken flight from spatial relations, abstracted from the real world. Wong's visual fabric of time has more to do with affect, memory, displacement. It is about seeing, as well as not seeing: appearance, disappearance.

NOTES

1. All translations and descriptions of scenes from *Chungking Express* used in this essay are my own.
2. Tony Rayns, 'Poet of Time', *Sight and Sound*, 5, no. 9 (1995): 12–14.
3. Paul Virilio and Sylvere Lotringer, *Pure War*, trans. Mark Polizotti (New York: Semiotext(e), 1983), 6.
4. Abbas's new cinema is one that captures these kinds of spaces. Ackbar Abbas, *Hong Kong: Culture and the Politics of Disappearance* (Minneapolis: University of Minnesota Press, 1997), 27.
5. Wong says that he became aware of this when filming around the Wanchai area for *Fallen Angels* (1995). Jimmy Ngai, 'A Dialogue with Wong Kar-wai: Cutting between Time and Two Cities', in *Wong Kar-wai*, ed. Danièle Rivière (Paris: Dis Voir, 1998), 85.
6. Ewa Mazierska and Laura Rascaroli, 'Trapped in the Present: Time in the Films of Wong Kar-wai', *Film Criticism*, 25, no. 2 (2000–1), 2–18.
7. Lee Ellickson 'Preparing to Live in the Present: An Interview with Hou Hsiao-hsien', *Cineaste*, 27, no. 4 (2002), 13–19.
8. Mazierska and Rascaroli, 'Trapped in the Present', 3.
9. Stephen Teo, *Hong Kong Cinema: The Extra Dimensions* (London: BFI, 1997), 196.
10. The notion of the 'throw-away society' is Alvin Toffler's. See Mazierska and Rascaroli, 'Trapped in the Present', 4–5.
11. Here the writers use Jameson's ideas on post-modern societies. Mazierska and Rascaroli, 'Trapped in the Present', 16.
12. Abbas, *Hong Kong*, 26.
13. Rayns, 'Poet of Time', 14.
14. The same goes for Brigitte Lin's character, who is permanently in disguise. She says, 'Whenever I put on a raincoat, I put on sunglasses as well. You never know when it will rain and when it will be sunny.' She is in disguise so as to avoid the effects of change, be it a change in the weather or a change in her emotions. Is it possible that the only disguise she has on is, in fact, a disguise that hides her from herself?
15. These references are Wong's comments on the making of *Chungking Express*. Rayns, 'Poet of Time', 14.
16. Abbas, *Hong Kong*, 25.
17. Ibid., 26.
18. The two terminologies refer to the same device: 'step-printing' describes the actual lab process, whereas 'smudge-motion' describes what you can see.
19. John Ashbrook, 'Available Light', in *The Crime Time Filmbook*, ed. John Ashbrook (Harpendon: No Exit Press, 1997), 165.
20. All technical terminology here is the result of conversations with documentary film-maker, Rick Farquharson, whose documentary on Christopher Doyle, *Orientations: Chris Doyle – Stirred Not Shaken*, was part of the Sydney Film Festival programme in 2000.
21. Virilio and Lotringer, *Pure War*, 6.
22. Gilles Deleuze, *Cinema 2: The Time-Image*, trans. Hugh Tomlinson and Robert Galeta (Minneapolis: University of Minnesota Press, 1997), xii.

23. Ibid., 2.
24. For further reading, see Chapter 1 'Beyond the movement-image' and the last section in Chapter 2 'Recapitulation of images and signs', ibid., 2–24 and 34–43.
25. Jean-Marc Lalanne, 'Images from the Inside', trans. Stephen Wright, in Danièle Rivière, *Wong Kar-wei*, 25.
26. From David Bordwell's description of *Chungking Express*'s plot-line in *Planet Hong Kong: Popular Cinema and the Art of Entertainment* (Cambridge: Harvard University Press, 2000), 283.
27. Taken from a documentary on the shooting methods in *Taxi Driver*. *Taxi Driver* DVD special feature, Collector's Edition, Columbia TriStar Home Video Australia (1999).
28. Deleuze, *Cinema 2*, 173.
29. Deleuze, *Cinema 2*, 7.
30. Damian Grammaticas, 'Hong Kong Searches for New Identity', *BBC News: Asia-Pacific*, 4 February 2003: <http://news.bbc.co.uk/2/hi/asia-pacific/2721029.stm> (7 February 2003).
31. Deleuze, *Cinema 2*, xi.
32. For a Deleuzean description of the present as open-ended, see 'Peaks of Present and Sheets of Past: Fourth Commentary on Bergson', in ibid., 98–125.
33. Ibid., 179.

7 *Crouching Tiger, Hidden Dragon*: Cultural Migrancy and Translatability

Felicia Chan

Migration and cultural translation are symbiotic concepts. In the course of a migration, two or more cultures are inevitably brought up against each other requiring a process of translation of one culture to another. When a film like *Crouching Tiger, Hidden Dragon* (Ang Lee, 2000) makes the headlines around the world as a *unique* triumph for Chinese film, many issues are raised. What happens when a cultural text travels from one place to another? The wide disparity in responses to the film provokes larger questions of how we read what we see. How are cultural images and narratives translated by, or into, a different culture? What conditions our reading? Do Chinese audiences necessarily have a greater insight into the film compared with a Western one?

CULTURE MIGRATING

'Migration' usually refers to the movement of people from one locality to another, and physical migration usually involves the resettlement of an individual or community into a different geographical location. Whether the movement is of migrants in search of economic opportunities or the movement of imperial armies and missionaries across continents, each migrating community brings its own cultures to interact with those of the new location giving rise to a diasporic community. In the current technological environment, physical movement is no longer necessary to effect cultural change as ideas, cultures and ideologies are now brought in closer contact on a wider scale than ever before. The rate and reach of its impact on individuals and cultures is of an extent that one needs to speak of it as a state of cultural *migrancy* rather than an act of cultural migration.

In the face of *Crouching Tiger*'s success, Sony Pictures Classics executive Michael Barker was prompted to declare that the film had ushered in a 'new globalism in motion pictures'[1] and a majority of the Western press appears to echo this view. Lauren Hunter of *CNN.com* outlines in her article the international flavour of the 2001 Academy Awards and lists a whole string of 'foreign' contenders for the golden statue: for example, Judi Dench (Britain), Juliette Binoche (France), Russell Crowe (New Zealand and Australia) and Javier Bardem (Spain).[2] And yet, the entry of such 'foreign' talent into Hollywood's biggest industry award ceremony is not unique to 2001. Many Anglo-Europeans have made Oscar headlines over the years, including Laurence Olivier (Britain), Sophia Loren (Italy) and Peter Weir (Australia), though not specifically for their *foreignness*. Ang Lee and *Crouching Tiger* are the first East Asian entrants to attract such media attention since Akira Kurosawa was nominated for *Ran* in 1986. *Crouching Tiger* was nominated for an unprecedented ten awards and won four, including Best Cinematography and Best Foreign Language Film, encouraging the perception that East Asian cinema has finally 'arrived'. In other words, the Chinese language film is seen to have completed the global circuit for the Oscars, in the sense that *Crouching Tiger* now makes the Oscars even more 'global' than they had already been. Ironically, the film's success at this *American* sponsored event is what would open doors for it to the rest of the world, including East Asia itself.

When attempting to account for the film's phenomenal success, most credit its action sequences. Paul Dergarabedian, president of a box-office tracking service, Exhibitor Relations, says: 'The reason *Crouching Tiger* may transcend its foreign-language status is that it's an action film. There's a lot of visual information. That translates well in foreign markets.'[3] Similarly, Paul Tatara, also for *CNN.com*, gushes, 'The first fight, which springs to sudden, exquisite life ... surely will elicit rounds of applause from audiences the world over – action, after all, has become cinema's universal language.'[4] And yet many mainstream Hong Kong films, such as those by Jackie Chan, John Woo or Tsui Hark for example, boast a far higher and more spectacular action quotient, as well as a considerably higher body count. In fact one Hong Kong viewer even complained that, 'there's simply not enough action … *Crouching Tiger* is so slow, it's a bit like listening to grandma telling stories'.[5]

Perhaps the cultural phenomenon may be better explained as an economic phenomenon. Rather than any profound textual mystery, record earnings at the US box office are what actually catapulted the film into an international acclaim. The film earned about US$128 million at the US box office – in comparison, the threshold for 'foreign hit status' is a mere US$1 million[6] – and this in turn fuelled its international success (about US$208 million). However, the appeal of the film to mainstream US audiences was not a historical accident, but the result of a particularly shrewd marketing campaign, rendered even more exceptional given that American audiences are notorious for shunning subtitled films. If Tom Bernard, Co-President of Sony Pictures Classics, could suggest that 'Ang Lee has hit the button for every demographic',[7] it is only because his marketing team had cleverly tailored its publicity campaign at specific segments of the mass market.[8] Basically, the producers divided the US audience into five target groups – 'the arthouse crowd, the young, the females, action lovers, and the popcorn mainstream'[9] – and tailored the publicity of the film to each group by anticipating their respective needs. For example, one group was composed of the fans of *The Matrix* (1997). *Crouching Tiger* was sold on the strength that action choreographer Yuen Wo-ping was also responsible for the action in *The Matrix*. Ironically, the quasi-martial arts display in *The Matrix* is itself a modified cultural import from the Hong Kong martial arts and action genres. Such blurring of boundaries between primary and secondary texts is not new. Kurosawa's adaptations of the Western for his samurai films were later remade as Westerns by Hollywood, the most famous of which is *The Magnificent Seven* (1960) from *Seven Samurai* (1954). What is different and interesting about *Crouching Tiger* is that it was not *only* marketed as a Matrix-type film, but also as an art film, a woman's film, as well as a combination of all these, which complicates its positioning. According to David Saunders, 'Just 700 of

37,000 U.S. screens are available for foreign films',[10] but *Crouching Tiger* opened not only in arthouse venues but in mainstream multiplexes as well. This too was planned. In seeking to subvert the arbitrary association of foreign-language films with the arthouse, the producers deliberately withheld the film from competition at the Cannes Film Festival, in an effort to break from what they called 'the art-house ghetto'.[11] The fact that the move did not fail made distributors sit up and take notice. Daniel Battsek, Managing Director for Buena Vista International, says that the film 'acts as a vanguard for all foreign language films'.[12] Thus it would seem that the migratory success of this ostensibly Chinese text is made possible only when the *conditions* allowing for its (apparently) successful translation and favourable reception are adequately attended to.

However, the cultural migrancy of *Crouching Tiger* lies not only in the capture of Western markets but also in the re-capture of Asian ones. The lukewarm reception of the film in China and other parts of East Asia has been well publicised.[13] And once again numerous theories abounded, the most common of which is that Lee has simply pandered to Western tastes. Chinese film-maker Xie Fei bluntly suggests that 'Lee is clever. He knows what they like.'[14] Li Xun, director of the Graduate Programme of China Film Arts Research Centre, likewise surmises that 'What is appealing to American audiences is the exoticism: the totally fresh aesthetic of Chinese martial arts and the imaginary artistic conception. But that turned out to be mundane to Chinese viewers.'[15] While Hong Kong viewers appear to expect a greater dose of action, mainland Chinese viewers appear to expect a degree of realism. Zhong Gang, a bank employee, is quoted as saying: 'The action scenes weren't as good as the old kung fu movies …. People flew around way too much. If you put me on wires, I could fly around too …. There was no real martial-arts skill.'[16] Xie Fei expresses a similar view: 'Some in China say that the movie's *gongfu* [*kung fu*] is not very exciting because it's quite artificial. They can feel the wires and cables used.'[17] And yet, are aesthetic considerations the only reason for the film's lacklustre performance in China and Hong Kong?

While the West may be looking to reformulate its distribution strategies, China continues to be plagued by more mundane problems of excessive bureaucracy and video piracy. Attempting to distribute a film in the mainland is an arduous process. Films are not allowed to be independently distributed in China without official sanction. A private distribution company must form a joint venture with a state-run firm in order to have any access to the China market. In the case of *Crouching Tiger*, the rights to its distribution were shared by a private production firm, Asian Union Film and Entertainment, and China Film Co-Production, a state-run company. Of the US$1 million it cost to distribute the film in China, Asian Union invested 80 per cent and China Film 20 per cent. Problems arose when China Film, on realising that the film was about to be a hit, tried to oust Asian Union from the partnership. In the tussle, the film was withheld from exhibition for 'three crucial months'.[18] By the time permission was given to release the film, there was 'no time to remarket the movie'.[19] Furthermore, during that time, the streets became 'flooded with pirated DVD and video compact disc copies of the movie, selling for about [US]$2.50 each, or less'.[20] Ironically, it was precisely in the bid to combat piracy that the film was 'scheduled for almost simultaneous openings across the region'.[21]

In addition, the film's Oscar triumph saw a revived interest in many parts of East Asia, which basked in a collective cultural pride. This is evident in cinematographer Peter Pau's Oscar acceptance speech: 'It's a great honour to me, to the people of Hong Kong and to Chinese people all over the world.' Donna Tung, a spectator, called Lee a 'credit to all Chinese people'.[22] In Hong Kong, the film did not even make the top five box-office earners of that year, and yet 'as Oscar night neared, video discs of the movie were selling for nearly double the price of other local movies at around HK$95 (US$12)'.[23] In Taiwan, Lee was honoured with a personal visit from the Taiwanese President, Chen Shui-bian, who congratulated him on being the first Taiwanese national to win an Academy Award.[24] The Taiwanese premier Chang Chung-hsiung also offered public congratulations: 'We recognize the hard work and contribution that Ang Lee has made to our movie industry and his achievements on the international stage also honour us.'[25] Interestingly, the film's Taiwanese financier had backed out in the early stages of pre-production,[26] and the film's only links to Taiwan are the director's own ethnic origin as well as those of his Taiwanese actors, Chang Chen and

Cheng Pei Pei. Nevertheless, Scarlet Cheng, writing for the *Far Eastern Economic Review*, calls it a 'cultural homecoming'[27] for Ang Lee, while a Taiwanese office worker is reported to have exclaimed: 'I am so proud of Ang Lee …. He never forgot his roots in Taiwan, and he also traced his roots back to China.'[28] Never mind that Lee himself has said that the China he envisioned was a fantasy China of his boyhood dreams.[29]

Although in no way a Chinese culture specialist, my own personal observation from living in Chinese-dominated Singapore is that the attitudes towards the film's Western success seem to reveal a characteristic, though paradoxical, mix of cultural chauvinism and deference towards Western culture. Despite a great resistance to being dictated to by the West, a foreign success is at the same time almost always seen as something to be emulated, praised and welcomed. This cultural schizophrenia, at least with regard to *Crouching Tiger*, stems in part from a history of being inundated by high production value Hollywood films, which set a commercial standard, and a sense of self-effacement characterising Chinese culture. Chinese film scholars like Zhang Nuanxin and Li Tuo, for example, seem inordinately concerned with 'why the development of our film *lags behind* the rest of the world'.[30] Their essay calls for Chinese film-makers to learn from foreign films in order to 'hasten the development of our own cinematic language',[31] laying the blame for its aesthetic 'backwardness' on China's contemporary history and political struggles, specifically the 'stagnation and retrogression created by the Gang of Four'.[32] Even in Singapore, film-makers, artists and theatre practitioners often aim to make a name for themselves in international festivals before they are confident that the local public will accept them. So, while Chinese audiences may initially express reservations about *Crouching Tiger*, a Western success may not only convince them to the contrary, but also assure them that it was a winning product to begin with.

I should emphasise that for the sake of argument and convenience, I am making some unqualified assumptions about the unity of Chinese culture, which as history has shown is far from unified. However, the general situation is interesting and worthy of pursuit insofar as this process of what I can only call a 'double migration' – from East to West and back to East again – has an impact on local industries and films. The Hong Kong film industry for instance is already looking to emulate *Crouching Tiger*'s success. Joe Cheung of the Hong Kong Film Directors' Guild says, 'This movie is a benchmark and it shows that we must all be professional, that we must put together the best to create something of such high standards.'[33] Hong Kong cinema, which used to outsell Hollywood blockbusters in domestic markets, saw a reverse trend in the 1990s, caused in part by changing audience demographics, rampant piracy and the political uncertainty leading up to the British handover of the colony to Chinese rule in 1997. Thomas Chung, an influential Hong Kong producer, is described by *Asiaweek* as being on a 'mission – to revitalize Hong Kong's ailing film industry'.[34] Most of his efforts are directed at changing the signature slap-dash style of production in Hong Kong films in favour of stronger scripts and high value productions designed to appeal to foreign audiences as well as local audiences weaned on foreign imports. This includes writing most of the dialogue in English, as with *Gen-Y Cops* (2000) and the forthcoming *The Touch*, produced by and starring Michelle Yeoh. The kinetic energy of a regular Hong Kong film resulting from the spontaneity of churning out a film in forty days or less, and the rapid-fire witticisms tossed out in Cantonese, look set to be sacrificed in favour of Hollywood-style big-budget action flair.

In addition, the ersatz copies have surfaced. One example, *Flying Dragon, Leaping Tiger* (2001), starring Sammo Hung, is unabashed in its resemblance, complete with a brooding middle-aged hero, lengthy desert scenes, a feisty young heroine and the theme of lost love. Interestingly, Miramax is said to have acquired the film for distribution in the US,[35] and it was reported that the ending of the film was changed after a US screen test audience was found to have disliked the original ending. However, given the complex conditions for *Crouching Tiger*'s success, does it necessarily mean that *any* Chinese-language film could replicate its appeal? Have the traditional barriers to entry really been eradicated? It remains to be seen if Miramax's other acquisitions such as Stephen Chow's slapstick *Shaolin Soccer* (2001), released as *Kung Fu Soccer* in the US), a top-earner in Hong Kong, will translate well and take in any substantial box-office revenue in Western markets.

CULTURE TRANSLATING

To translate something generally means to express it in another language, and yet embedded in the act of translation is the notion of the untranslatable. Those on the receiving end of the foreign language or product need to translate it into a language they can understand; those on the producing end need to translate it into a language they think the other can understand. The fissure between the two is where the untranslatable lies – an *aporia*, if you will. *Crouching Tiger*'s migration to the West, and back to the East, necessitates a translation, not simply of language, but of *cultures* as well. By 'cultures' I mean more than the ethnological sense of culture; I mean also the culture of the medium itself – the culture of film developed over its history, and the culture of reading that has developed out of that history.

The main difficulty of translation in *Crouching Tiger* is the Chinese notion of *jianghu*. The closest equivalent in English to the term is 'world of knightly chivalry', which is mostly unsatisfactory since it conjures up images of Sir Galahad and maidens in need of rescue, which confines us still within the English context. *Jianghu* encompasses an abstract community within the Chinese literary tradition that is ruled not by state legislation but by moral principle and decorum. It exists simultaneously outside as well as within society. Its members are not above state laws, but are accorded the moral authority to reject the implementation of those laws should they serve corrupt ends. *Crouching Tiger* is sustained by the tension between the various characters and their varying abilities to adhere to *jianghu* principles. The inability of Li and Shu Lien to act upon their love for example stems from their *jianghu* code of honour. They are bound by a respect for Li's sworn brother and Shu Lien's betrothed, Meng Sizhao. That Meng was killed in battle does not free them from this obligation and in fact binds them further into honouring his memory. Li's responsibility to avenge the death of his master is another barrier between them. A viewer unfamiliar with the cultural resonances of this decision may ask why Li is unable to court Shu Lien and avenge his master at the same time. The answer is that that would mean privileging his personal desires over his social and filial responsibilities. Indeed, Li's initial attempt to retire from his *jianghu* obligations and give up on the search for Jade Fox only resulted in a situation that forced him to stay on and accomplish his mission.

The intrusion of Jade Fox and her disciple Jen into Li's life provides a different perspective on the notion of *jianghu*. Jade Fox sees the *jianghu* world as a world of freedom in which she can roam freely. At the end of the film, she tries to persuade Jen to remain with her: 'But why go home now? We've gone this far, we won't stop now …. At last we'll be our own masters. We'll be happy.' For Jade Fox, the life of a wandering pugilist represents an entirely different world from the life within the governor's household. She sees the *jianghu* world as an escape from society, though her excessive concern with the martial combat ('Kill or be killed. Exciting, isn't it?') over the moral aptitude necessary to operate within that world forces her to remain in hiding behind the walls of the governor's mansion.

Her protégé, Jen, is the most complex character in the film. The narrative momentum of the film is sustained mainly by her failure to comprehend *jianghu* etiquette and values. When chided for stealing the Green Destiny sword, she says it was just 'for fun'. Note that the brawl she causes in the tavern stems from her insolence and arrogance, causing her opponents to later complain about her lack of manners. It is Jen's waywardness that also leads Jade Fox to attempt to poison her, for Jen has committed the ultimate offence in *jianghu* terms: she has betrayed her own master. Li's desire to train her is in part an attempt to impart the moral discipline required to wield her talent responsibly.

No knowledge of the *jianghu* context is necessary to access or enjoy the narrative of the film. On a basic level, the film supplies sufficiently recognisable signs for the story to be understood. However, some of the gaps in the narrative can only be filled by a knowledge of the cultural context within which the film operates. When that knowledge is absent, and the narrative gaps are filled by signs from a different cultural system, the context for the narrative could be altered to the extent that meaning in the narrative is also altered.

One example is to read the film as a feminist film, as Matthew Levie has done:

> It is a sign of tremendous skill on Lee's part that he manages to insert into his epic such a profound

Crouching Tiger, Hidden Dragon: Jen

commentary on the situation of the modern woman. Imagine Jade Fox as the strong professional woman who is perceived as too 'aggressive' and even 'bitchy', while her equally aggressive male colleagues are spared this criticism; Shu Lien as the woman who works twice as hard as her male colleagues to reach the same stature, sacrificing her personal happiness for professional success; and Jen as a beautiful, capable teenager trying to set her priorities: career or family?[36]

Although the similarities may exist on the level of a Lévi-Straussian 'deep structure', the three categories of women Levie depicts represent problems women face within *Western* cultural discourse. This is not to say that Chinese women don't necessarily face the same problems of patriarchal domination, but that the discourse employed by Chinese films tends to approach gender roles differently. I refer to Esther Yau's article about the difference in representation of gender politics in Chinese and Western texts. Although the text she analyses is Chen Kaige's *Yellow Earth* (1984), the point she makes is relevant to my argument: 'Inasmuch as the sense of social identity defines the person within Chinese society, individuals in Chinese films are often cast as non-autonomous entities within determining familial, social and national frameworks.'[37] The familial and social, perhaps not so much the national, framework of *Crouching Tiger* is the framework of the *jianghu* world. Each character has a social role to play within this world, and the gender relations depicted in the film are but part of this larger framework. There is no direct evidence of male oppression in the film other than the one we are primed to expect from the period setting of ancient China. Li Mubai and Lo (Jen's lover) struggle as much with the restrictions of *jianghu* society as the women. Gender relations are not presented in dialectical opposition in the film, and if we assume that they are, then we run the risk of turning it into a different film.

A different kind of misreading involves the imposition of other cultural texts onto the film. One extreme case is Elvis Mitchell's review in the *New York Times*, which describes *Crouching Tiger* as a 'picture [with] a knockabout, screwball comedy bounce' and that it is 'just the film for an audience transfixed by the weekly girl-power cool and soap-opera bloodshed of "Buffy, the Vampire Slayer"'.[38] How far has the fissure widened between producer and receiver

that a film deemed too slow and tedious by a Hong Kong viewer can be perceived as one having a 'screwball comedy bounce'? The comparison with *Buffy*, though incongruous, is more understandable, although their similarity is acknowledged as based on the lowest common denominator between the two texts – the martial arts. This leads to questions of genre and how awareness of generic conventions may influence a reading of a film. Are genres dependent upon a particular culture? Can a genre sufficiently translate from one culture to another? In addition, do genres themselves create a culture of reading?

According to Stephen Neale:

> Genres … help render films, and the elements within them, intelligible and therefore explicable. They offer a way of working out the significance of what is happening on the screen: why particular events and actions are taking place, why the characters are dressed the way they are, why they look, speak and behave they way they do, and so on.[39]

In other words, genres depend on a spectator's familiarity with its conventions, built upon from knowledge gained from other films of the same genre. This inherently circular process can sometimes complicate rather than clarify readings of a film. For instance, while we can say Kurosawa's samurai films resemble Westerns, we cannot say that *The Magnificent Seven* resembles a samurai film. Different genres depend on different sign systems: a Western, it seems, can be recognised without the cowboy costumes and frontier setting, but a samurai film cannot be identified as such without the actual representation of a samurai figure or Japanese period setting. Like the samurai film, the Chinese martial arts film is identified mainly though its *mise en scène*, a criterion which *Crouching Tiger* fulfils, and which in turn influences audience expectations.

So Mitchell's identification of *Crouching Tiger* as possessing 'a knockabout, screwball comedy bounce' appears to be influenced by his expectations of a martial arts film. Before *Crouching Tiger*, American audiences used to experience these films as low-budget, low-quality 'chopsocky flicks', usually with poor to laughable English subtitles. While martial arts films are mainstream fare for Eastern audiences, for US audiences Hong Kong martial arts films tend to be available mainly from cult video stores and

Chinatown theatres. For this reason, *Crouching Tiger*'s mainstream release is seen to have crossed a major hurdle. Does the cultural context under which one had experienced a genre then affect one's response to a new film seemingly of that genre?

So far, I have been arguing that the lack of cultural knowledge and familiarity can impede the understanding of a cultural text. Ironically, that same knowledge and familiarity may conversely alienate viewers from the film as well. For instance, one of the reasons for which the film is said to be unpopular amongst Chinese viewers is that the characters are not portrayed according to type. Larry Teo reports that critics in the mainland 'assailed [the film] as a shallow story about anti-heroes – a debasement to the traditional martial arts genre'.[40] And indeed, Li Mubai fails as a traditional *wuxia* (knight errant) hero. Although he succeeds in killing his master's mortal enemy, he is killed by her *by accident*, and dies with regret on his last breath. Jen, whom he had set out to save, is not given a chance to redeem herself, arrives too late with the antidote and leaps to an uncertain death. There is no showdown in *Crouching Tiger*, no dialectical clash of good and evil, and thus no catharsis its resolution is expected to provide.

Instead what Lee has chosen to emphasise is the film's emotional quality, underscoring the personal price each character has to pay as members of the *jianghu* world. The heroism in *Crouching Tiger* is thus not the heroism of action but of *effort*. Early in the film, when Jen expresses a longing for the *wuxia* lifestyle, her fantasies are countered very quickly by the level-headed Shu Lien:

> Jen: I've read all about people like you. Roaming wild, beating up anyone who gets in your way!
> Shu Lien: Writers wouldn't sell many books if they told how it really is.
> Jen: But you're just like the characters in the stories.
> Shu Lien: Sure. No place to bathe for days, sleeping in flea-infested beds …. They tell you all about that in those books?

Central to the aesthetic of *Crouching Tiger* then is a degree of self-reflexivity about the conventions of the genre that does not yet resort to parody. This is achieved in part by merging two different cinematic sensibilities – the older Taiwanese melodrama and swordplay films and the more recent Hong Kong martial arts films.

Martial arts films are generally divided into two categories: the *wuxia* (or sword-fighting) films and the *kung fu* (or fist-fighting) films. According to Stephen Teo, swordplay narratives were traditionally set 'in medieval dynasties and other mythical fantasies which, in turn, became stylistic conventions of the genre', such as 'the effortless facility of swordfighting heroes and heroines to leap, somersault and generally levitate in defiance of gravity'.[41] *Kung fu* films on the other hand 'emphasised the body and training rather than fantasy or the supernatural'[42] as in the films of Bruce Lee and Jackie Chan. *Wuxia* films, mostly made in Taiwan, gave way to Hong Kong *kung fu* films by the early 1970s[43] and have currently adapted to television in the form of lengthy serials. The other difference between Taiwanese and Hong Kong films is that the former favoured domestic and rural themes (melodrama was popular) while the latter favoured a more kinetic cinema leaning towards action, comedy and mass entertainment.[44] In some ways, Ang Lee brings a Taiwanese sensibility into what is now commonly perceived as a Hong Kong genre. Indeed, there are several homages to earlier *wuxia* films, such as the tavern scene and the bamboo grove scene. Interestingly, the casting of Cheng Pei Pei as Jade Fox seems to be a nod towards a film genre long past. As the 'queen' of the *wuxia* films in the 1960s, Cheng symbolically makes way for a new generation of actor the way Jade Fox must make way for her disciple.

The translation of *Crouching Tiger* at the level of its cultural milieu thus requires knowledge not only of the conventions of genre but also of the history of the genre. This cultural milieu however extends equally to the circumstances under which it is received. Singapore audiences, for example, were extremely conscious of the fact that the four lead actors spoke with four different accents: Zhang Ziyi with a Beijing accent, Chang Chen with a Taiwanese accent, Chow Yun-fat a Cantonese one, and Michelle Yeoh with a Malaysian-English lilt to her Mandarin which she had memorised phonetically. Though Yeoh's acting was sufficiently nuanced, her awkward Mandarin drew laughter during the three occasions I watched the film at theatres in Singapore, mainly because Malaysia is the closest neighbour and the accent was so familiar to us, yet oddly unfamiliar in the context that it came across on screen.

Thus what I have tried to explore in this essay are the various conditions under which a cultural text may operate, which hopefully reveal that the processes of cultural migration and translation are never simply bilateral in nature. In fact, Rey Chow argues that, 'cultural translation needs to be rethought as the co-temporal exchange and contention between different social groups deploying different sign systems that may not be synthesizable to one particular model of language or representation'.[45] She calls for a reassessment of the 'transactional reading' when discussing the process of cultural translation, suggesting that the emphasis might fall less on the 'reading' than on the 'transactional' aspect of the process. She says:

> the translation between cultures is never West translating East or East translating West in terms of verbal languages alone but rather a process that encompasses an entire range of activities, including the change from tradition to modernity, from literature to visuality, from elite scholastic culture to mass culture, from the native to the foreign and back, and so forth.[46]

This transactional aspect is what I have tried to explore with my analysis of *Crouching Tiger*, in order to illustrate that while culture may be infinitely translatable, it is not easily translated. And when particular readings of culture can also be shaped by particular cultures of reading, its problems can be exponentially compounded.

NOTES

1. Richard Natale, 'The Film Business's New Globalism Makes Its Mark', *LA Times,* 26 March 2001, *calendarlive on latimes.com*: <www.calendarlive.com/top/1,1419,L-LATimes-Search-X!ArticleDetail-26825,00.html> (12 May 2002).

2. Lauren Hunter, 'More than Ever, Oscars Go Global', *CNN.com*, 22 March 2001: <www.cnn.com/2001/SHOWBIZ/Movies/03/22/international.oscar/index.html> (11 April 2002).

3. Quoted in Dan Biers, 'Chasing the Tiger's Tail', *Far Eastern Economic Review* (25 January 2001), 164, no. 3: 67.

4. Paul Tatara, ' "Crouching Tiger, Hidden Dragon": A Gripping Poetic Tale', *CNN.com*, 11 December 2000: www.cnn.com/2000/SHOWBIZ/Movies/12/11/review.crouching.tiger/index.html> (7 July 2001).

5. Quoted in Steve Rose, 'The Film Is So Slow – It's Like Grandma Telling Stories', *The Guardian*, 13 February 2001, *Guardian Unlimited*: <www.film/guardian.cu.uk/features/featurepages/0,4120,437326,00.html> (29 July 2001).

6. Robert Koehler, 'How auds Learned to Love Subtitles', *Variety* (14 January 2002), <www.findarticles.com/cf_∅/m1312/8_385/82262324/print.html> (23 May 2003).

7. Quoted in Biers, 'Chasing the Tiger's Tail', 66.

8. See John Lippman, 'Buzz Gets "Crouching Tiger" a Leg Up"', *Asian Wall Street Journal* (12–14 January 2001), 1 and M1; and Charles Pappas, 'Improbable Eastern Hit Proves It Can Fly in the U.S.', *Advertising Age* (Chicago) (26 March 2001), S2.

9. Pappas, 'Improbable Eastern Hit', S2.

10. David Saunders, ' "Crouching Tiger", hidden profits', *Chicago Sun-Times*, 8 April 2001, Sunday Late Sports Final Edition, F41.

11. Lippman, 'Buzz Gets', M1.

12. Quoted in Vanessa Thorpe, 'A Tiger Burning Bright', *Observer* (14 January 2001), 6.

13. See, for example, David Rennie, 'Chinese Unimpressed by "Crouching Tiger" ', *Chicago Sun-Times* (13 January 2001), Sunday Late Sports Final Edition, 30.

14. Quoted in Jessica Tan, 'Gongfu Not Good Enough?', *The Straits Times* (Singapore) (12 February 2001), L10.

15. Quoted in Dai Limin, ' "Crouching Tiger" Scoops 10 Academy Award nominations', *China Daily* (15 February 2001), 1.

16. Quoted in Henry Chu, ' "Crouching Tiger" Can't Hide from Bad Reviews in China', *Los Angeles Times* (29 January 2001), A1: 1.

17. Quoted in Tan, 'Gongfu Not Good Enough?', L10.

18. Chu, ' "Crouching Tiger" ', A1: 1.

19. Ibid.

20. Ibid.

21. Scarlet Cheng, 'Ready to Pounce', *Far Eastern Economic Review* (6 July 2000), 163, no. 27: 85.

22. Quoted in 'Asia Roars as "Crouching Tiger" Pounces on 4 Oscars', *Mercury News*, 26 March 2001: <www0.mercurycenter.com/justgo/special/tiger/feature-oscarroar.htm> (23 October 2001).

23. 'Asia roars.'

24. 'President Chen Meets with Ang Lee and Lee's Father', 24 April 2001, *The Office of the President of the*

Republic of China website, news release: <www.president.gov.tw/php-bin/docset/ showenews.php4?_section=5&_rid=586> (7 July 2001).

25. Quoted in Larry Teo, 'A Triumphant Roar for Taiwan Filmmaker Lee', *The Straits Times* (26 January 2001), A1.

26. See 'Interview with Ang Lee and James Schamus', *Guardian Unlimited*, 7 November 2000: <www.film.guardian.co.uk/interview/ interviewpages/0,6737,394676,00. html> (29 July 2001).

27. Cheng, 'Ready to Pounce', 84.

28. Quoted in 'Many Asians see "Crouching Tiger" as an example of China's power' (2001), *Mercury News*: <www.mercurycenter.com/justgo/special/tiger/ feature-power.htm> (23 October 2001).

29. Ang Lee, 'Foreword', *Crouching Tiger, Hidden Dragon: A Portrait of the Ang Lee Film* (New York: Newmarket Press, 2000), 7.

30. Zhang Nuanxin and Li Tuo, 'The Modernization of Film Language', trans. Hou Jianping, in *Chinese Film Theory: A Guide to the New Era*, eds George S. Semsel, Xia Hong and Hou Jianping (New York: Praeger, 1990), 10, my emphasis.

31. Zhang and Li, 'The Modernization of Film Language', 18.

32. Ibid., 19.

33. Quoted in ' "Crouching Tiger" Oscars Bring Hope to HK Filmmakers', *Mercury News*, 26 March 2001: <www.mercurycenter.com/justgo/special/tiger/ feature-hkfilm.htm> (23 October 2001).

34. Jeremy Hansen and Alexandra A. Seno, 'A Touch of Realism', *Asiaweek*, 20 July 2001: 1.

35. 'Copying Tiger, Ripping Off Dragon', *The Straits Times* (Singapore), 5 July 2001: L3.

36. Matthew Levie, *'Crouching Tiger, Hidden Dragon*: The Art Film Inside the Chop-Socky Flick', *Bright Lights Film Journal*, 33, July 2001: <www.brightlightsfilm.com/ 33/crouchingtiger.html> (23 October 2001).

37. Esther C. M. Yau, *'Yellow Earth*: Western Analysis and a Non-Western Text', *Perspectives on Chinese Cinema*, ed. Chris Berry (London: BFI, 1991), 69.

38. Elvis Mitchell, ' "Crouching Tiger, Hidden Dragon": Fans, Be Prepared for Heart and Feminism', *New York Times* on the web, 9 October 2000: <www.nytimes.com/2000/10/09/ arts/09TIGE.html> (27 July 2001).

39. Steven Neale, 'Questions of Genre', *Film Genre Reader II*, ed. Barry Keith Grant (Austin: University of Texas Press, 1995), 160.

40. L. Teo, 'A Triumphant Roar', A1.

41. Stephen Teo, *Hong Kong Cinema: The Extra Dimensions* (London: BFI, 1997), 98.

42. Ibid.

43. Ibid., 102.

44. See Chiao Hsiung-Ping, 'The Distinct Taiwanese and Hong Kong Cinemas', *Perspectives on Chinese Cinema*, ed. Chris Berry (London: BFI, 1991), 155–165.

45. Rey Chow, *Primitive Passions: Visuality, Sexuality, Ethnography, and Contemporary Chinese Cinema* (New York: Columbia University Press, 1995), 197.

46. Ibid., 192.

8   *Crows and Sparrows*: Allegory on a Historical Threshold

Yiman Wang

Crows and Sparrows (Zheng Junli, 1949) was produced by the Shanghai-based and left-leaning Kunlun (Peak) Film Company. Production started in April 1949 but did not finish until after the Chinese Communist Party (CCP) overcame the Nationalist Party (Kuomintang: KMT) government in October. The film has been canonised in mainland China's official film history as a masterpiece that realistically reflects the disintegration of the KMT government in the storm of the Communist revolution.

> Armed with exuberant revolutionary zeal, sharp social observation, and masterful skills, the filmmakers created biting political satire. By depicting the gradual transformation of a group of ordinary cityfolk … from pessimism and fantasy to heightened consciousness in their struggle against the oppressive and reactionary KMT government represented by Mr. Hou, the film delivers a realistic and vivid reflection of the social landscape in the KMT-controlled area on the brink of Liberation, a landscape vacillating between chaotic darkness on one hand and brightness on the other.[1]

The screenwriter, Chen Baichen, agrees with this judgment, recalling that all the film-makers were motivated by the desire to act 'as witness to the disintegration of the Chiang Kai-shek dynasty, and an urge to record the last page of its wicked history so as to welcome Liberation'.[2] This agreement has two important implications: first, the film-makers were convinced of the possibility and necessity of a *realistic* cinematic representation of social circumstances; and second, realism was established as a primary criterion for judging good films.

Contrary to the official evaluation that emphasises the film's sympathy with the CCP, Leo Ou-fan Lee seeks to wrest the film from the CCP co-optation by re-evaluating it as a paragon of what he calls 'social realism'. According to Lee, where social-ist realism compels ideological conformity to the CCP's radical political agenda and the subjugation of art to politics, social or critical realism represents 'a social stance of discontent' and leads to 'a committed art burdened with ethical and emotional weight but not necessarily with doctrinaire propaganda'.[3] *Crows and Sparrows* demonstrates precisely that:

> … in China artistic creativity prospered on the eve of the revolution … [Committed art] is 'revolutionary' only in the sense that through its exposé ethos it lays bare the darkness before the revolution, rather than glorifies propagandistically the revolutionary victory itself … [Leftist film-makers'] independence of spirit and their critical conscience were given full release precisely because in the last years of the Kuomintang (Guomindang) rule they had to confront the chaos and darkness of a disintegrating society.[4]

Lee's analysis achieves two things for my purpose. First, he demystifies the canonised 'socialist realism' by proposing 'social realism' as a positive counter-term. Second, he usefully emphasises the on-the-eve mentality inscribed in the film diegesis as well as the *ambiguous* political conditions of its production. Nevertheless, his thought-provoking rethinking of realism is limited to a concern with the indexical tie between the film and its *immediate* context.

This begs an important question: if the value of the film exists solely in its indexical tie with its time, whether in a straightforward or an ambiguous manner, why does it remain significant now? To address this question, I re-focus on the other side of realism, that is elements that exceed indexicality, thus making it possible to relocate the work in a different context. These elements remain in the textual substratum as moments of 'excess', defined as 'the random and inexplicable, that which remains ungovernable within a textual regime presided over by narrative'.[5] Excess in fiction films is built into the very attempt to represent an external world. Such extra-textuality, according to Nichols, can be generalised as 'history', which 'always stands outside the text'; 'Always referred to but never captured, history, as excess, rebukes those laws set to contain it; it contests, qualifies, resists, and refuses them.'[6] My refocus on excess sheds a new light on realism and enables us to read *Crows and Sparrows* with a different frame of reference.

In this essay, I question the orthodox realist discourse by showing how realism is inevitably imbricated with excess. On this basis, I propose an alternative approach to *Crows and Sparrows* as an *allegory*. This allegorical quality, as analysed below, is inscribed in the film's temporal and spatial configurations. However, I will conclude counter to the usual understanding of allegory as utopian by arguing that in this case excess reverses into a dystopic ideology.

My reading of the film as an allegory is premised on Jameson's re-conception of this device as 'an unstable and provisory solution to an aesthetic dilemma which is itself the manifestation of a social and historical contradiction'.[7] The aesthetic dilemma in question is precisely the dilemma of representation. That is, whereas available strategies of representation are necessarily circumscribed by certain conditions, they are nonetheless indispensable for one's speculation on the realm beyond representation. If Nichols considers history as the origin of excess, Jameson similarly sees history as an ultimate term that exceeds representation, but nevertheless is accessible *only through* representation: 'History is *not* a text, not a narrative, master or otherwise, but ... as an absent cause, it is inaccessible to us except in textual form, and ... our approach to it and to the Real itself necessarily passes through its prior textualization, its narrativization in the political unconscious.'[8] When history exceeds the extant conceptual categories, it results in a crisis of representation, which in turn demands new representational parameters. This is precisely how Jameson's 'allegory' becomes necessary. Jameson's conceptualisation of history and allegory casts a new light on the signifying system of *Crows and Sparrows*.

Produced at the crucial historical moment of 1949, when KMT control was giving way to the would-be CCP government, *Crows and Sparrows* straddles a historical threshold moment, the complexity and instability of which constituted a representational problem. This problem, following Nichols and Jameson, leads to moments of excess, which can be located in director Zheng Junli's 1979 reflections on the film.

Entitled 'Recording an Outline of the Transitional Moment between the Old Times and the New Era', Zheng's essay displays pronounced reservation, even scepticism, despite surface agreement with the orthodox position on the film. His claim that the film succeeds in recording (*jilu*) its time is bracketed by qualifications such as 'to a certain degree' and 'one aspect' or 'a sidelight'. As a result, realism in the film becomes conditional and partial at the best.[9] Written in 1979 shortly after the end of the Cultural Revolution, Zheng's self-deprecating recount echoes schoolteacher Mr Hua's self-criticism at the end of the film, when he urges all the characters – himself included – *and* the film audience to transform themselves into new people in the new society.

The major 'defects' of the film, according to Zheng, lie in the framework of the film, which was not modified according to the changed situation after the CCP conquered Shanghai. The concentration on the struggle for a two-storey lane house forecloses the possibility of a more penetrating exposé of the KMT in a wider social context. Also, due to KMT censorship and the screenwriter's limitations, the film focuses on the 'sparrows', or narrow-minded urban residents who lease rooms from a domineering KMT official, Mr Hou the 'crow'. Thus, it overlooks the more organised workers and peasants who were named as the masters of the new China. Consequently, the film fails to represent the awakening of the real people – the creators of the new era and the gravediggers of the old dictatorship.[10] Zheng further pinpoints three faulty characterisations. First, the transformation of Mr Hua and the old newspaper editor Mr Kong from weak conciliators to unyielding resistors seems too abrupt and unconvincing. Second, the film fails to highlight Mr Kong's enthusiasm for the People's Liberation Army (PLA), which should be a spontaneous response given his son's CCP affiliation. Third, the film fails to portray Ah Mei, maid of Mr Hou's mistress, as a pivotal figure. As a sheer oppressee, Zheng reasons, Ah Mei should have the strongest sense of justice and the deepest class sympathy, and her good personality should be instrumental for the other characters' transformation.[11]

Zheng's self-criticism is circumscribed by the

CCP ideology that dictates who should be the hero, how a hero should behave and why. Ironically, however, his recount carries the CCP terminology overboard, thus undermining the orthodox discourse by converting what the People's Republic official critics have praised as realistic details into subversive moments of excess. These moments undermine the real-to-reel correspondence assumed by the ideology of realism and joins Jameson's 'allegorical spirit'.

To view the film as an allegory entails an emphasis on the temporal-spatial 'edge', which is arguably connected with utopian futures. Allegory thrives at the threshold moment insofar as it provides a provisory solution to the problem of representation by way of a visual projection, that is proffering a figure as proxy for the pre-formed and not-yet-representable realm. The film stemmed precisely from a historical threshold moment, registering a series of images that presumably point toward a desirable future. The film's investment in the future is manifested in three interweaving timelines, all spanning the transition from KMT to CCP control. They are diegetic time, production time and historical time. Diegetic time covers the last two weeks before lunar New Year's Day on 18 January 1949. Production time started in April 1949, was soon suspended by KMT censorship, resumed in May, nearly finished by the end of 1949 and released in early 1950. Historical time includes the CCP conquering north-east China, beating the KMT along the Huai River in the winter of 1948, taking over Shanghai in May 1949 and finally establishing the People's Republic on 1 October 1949. Although diegetic time slightly precedes production time, radical future change is already clearly prefigured in the film. Largely couched in the present tense, indicating contemporariness, diegetic time nevertheless takes on a pronounced forward-looking, or allegorical, dimension. Within the framework of this progressive timeline, diegetic time is strictly chronological. Flashbacks are laboriously eliminated and current happenings consciously extended toward the future – the future delivered by the CCP. The intersection of the film's progress with the pace of CCP victories not only sutured the film into the socio-historical fabric, but was also calculated to visually prefigure the future from this side of the threshold moment.

The investment in the present and the future

determines that events that took place fours years ago right after China's victory in the anti-Japanese war (1937–1945) are consigned to mere verbal references, instead of being fleshed out in flashbacks. These events are referred to by Boss Xiao, the American merchandise peddler nicknamed 'Little Broadcast' for his rumour-spreading habit,[12] and Mr Kong, the original house owner. They cover how Hou, the former collaborator with Japan during the anti-Japanese war, was suddenly transformed into an undercover agent, obtaining a high KMT position, subsequently framing Kong's son as a Communist soldier, having him jailed, and usurping Kong's lane house. In the absence of visual flashbacks, these brief verbal allusions in the past tense fill in the background without distracting the audience, so that the present events, fully visualised in the film, can be emphasised and endowed with forward momentum. To modify Winston's comments on pre-war Griersonian documentaries, "the 'problem moment" structure [the problem of housing and class struggle in my context] has an implicit narrative trajectory … there was a [problematic past]; there is a current problem; there will be a [hopeful] future'.[13] Such a linear and irreversible plot-line implies inevitability, or the 'weight of the temporal axis. The parallel between plot development and temporal progress allows the latter to be perceived and experienced as concrete materiality.'[14] In this light, the chronological narrative in *Crows and Sparrows* implies a specific future-oriented perspective.

In accordance with the weight of the temporal axis, the confrontation between the 'crows' and the 'sparrows' can be viewed as a struggle to control *time* for their individual interests. The film starts with a newspaper advertisement about an urgent house sale. The hasty sale advertised by the 'crow' Hou causes an instant housing problem for the 'sparrow' tenants. The ensuing story describes their unsuccessful struggle to find other housing before the last day of the year, the deadline set down by Hou. Failure forces them to rebel against Hou's timeframe, replacing it with their own simple one: 'We will unite together. None of us will budge. Let's see what he can do.' The ability to determine their own timeframe (which really means frustrating that of Hou) marks the emergence of a certain subaltern agency. Passive as it seems to be, it outlasts Hou, whose timeframe turns out to be determined not by himself but by the larger historical force of the CCP tug-of-war with the KMT. This larger force is conveyed through the headlines Little Broadcast disseminates, which serve as a timepiece tolling the knell for Hou and the KMT government.

The tenants' tactic of procrastination implies their vague, sometimes blind, optimism about what the future can bring. For Little Broadcast, the headline news reporting CCP's victory means that peace is coming, that Mr Hua the schoolteacher and Mr Kong's son will be released from prison, and that his business in American goods will prosper. Similarly, Mr Hua tries to ameliorate Mr Kong's pessimism by proclaiming that 'Your account will be settled one day. The forces of evil will be eradicated one day, but the time is not ripe yet …' Hua's inaction and ostrich-like reliance on the future are largely ineffectual. Nevertheless, he provides a verbal harbinger for future fulfilment. When the calendar in the last sequence turns to the last day of the old lunar year in close-up, the original deadline set up by Hou has become the sparrows' day of celebration. The threshold date finds a perfect visual illustration in the 'happy ending' sequence.

After the fall of Nanking, the base of the KMT government, Hou the crow hurries to leave Shanghai, then a financial centre approximately 400 kilometres to the south of Nanking, reluctantly leaving the house to the sparrow tenants, who represent a wide range of urban classes oppressed by KMT to different degrees. The unexpected resolution of the housing problem, resulting from Hou's hasty escape leads to the final sequence, with all tenants gathering for a joyful lunar New Year. A medium shot toward the end includes all the major characters, significantly positioned on the threshold of the front gate and arranged as in a theatrical tableau, with Mr Kong and Mr Hua – the two intellectuals among the sparrows – delivering clinching remarks for the entire film. After Kong, the original owner, rejoices about regaining his house and looks forward to a promising New Year, Hua, whose consciousness was raised by recent imprisonment, voices his self-criticism and determination to renew himself: 'A new society is coming! We should get rid of our old weaknesses. We must live a new life as new people!'[15] This anticipation of a utopian society merges with the traditional New Year couplet (duilian) that Kong pastes on the gate: 'The firecracker sends off the past; a

peach wood mascot brings in the new (baozhu yisheng chujiu, taofu wanhu gengxin).' This couplet is framed in a close-up at the end, when the tenants-turned-masters go back 'home', closing the gate behind them. A few neighbours run past the gate, setting off firecrackers amidst loud festival music. The music track continues long after the image track has turned black. If the gate suggests these characters' on-the-eve and anticipatory mentality,[16] the prolonged music suggests continuation into a utopian future that literally exceeds and lies beyond visual representation. During actual screenings in early 1950, the music track would have accompanied audiences of the New Chinese exiting the theatre after the show, probably around lunar New Year, inspiring them with great expectations for a new year and a new society. By telling an ultimately triumphant story set in the recent past, the film strives toward an undefined yet apparently utopian future.

The encounter between the crows and the sparrows operates not only along the temporal axis, but also on the spatial level. The allegorical dimension of the film accordingly shifts from utopian projection to the spatial reconfiguration of the lane house. Director Zheng recalls that the five-person scriptwriting group (including Zhao Dan who plays Little Broadcast) had to resort to allegory or metaphor (yingyu) in order to dodge KMT censorship. As a result, they deployed

> Hou as a figure for the reactionary KMT, and centred the main story on the house. The house is like the nation (jiangshan), which had belonged to the people, but was usurped by collaborators and KMT lackeys …. their doomsday is approaching … and the house is returned to its original owner. [17]

Interestingly, Zheng dismisses this allegory as too obscure to be understood by the audience.

Nevertheless, I argue that spatial allegory structures the central conflict by allowing it to develop in a site orchestrated by elaborate camerawork.

First, the two-storey house epitomises and literalises the social hierarchy of the crows and the sparrows. Hou and his mistress lord it over the tenants and live upstairs, where Kong used to live as the original owner. The tenants divide up the rooms below according to their social positions and professions. As part of 'garret literati' (tingzijian wenren) in 1930s and 1940s Shanghai, the schoolteacher Mr Hua and his family live in the garret room to the right of the stairway landing, an intermediate position between upstairs and downstairs.[18] The peddler Little Broadcast and his relatively better-off family live in the front living room, next to the kitchen. In contrast, the original owner Kong, an old and poor newspaper editor, is crammed into the windowless back room. Besides these 'family rooms', there are two 'communal spaces' – the kitchen downstairs and the clothes-drying terrace on the roof. The sparrows gather here to discuss their tactics against the crow. Also, Little Broadcast and Hua's children play games in these places and sing a satirical song that compares Hou to an ugly and oppressive 'monkey'.[19]

This spatial configuration not only epitomises the social hierarchy, but also inscribes its self-deconstruction. The opening sequence, for example, powerfully illustrates porosity between contrasting worlds. The camera first shows Hou's mistress lighting a cigarette in her room upstairs, then tilts down past the floor to reveal the noisy and messy room of Little Broadcast downstairs. This cross-section shot underlines the co-implicating relationship between the oppressor class and the oppressed class by visualising their simultaneous distance *and* proximity. Such proximity produces porosity that allows the sparrows to monitor the crows, thus facilitating their subversion of social hierarchy. The resultant leaking of information is shown often when the sparrows, especially Little Broadcast and his wife, eavesdrop on

The camera tilts down vertically from the warlord's mistress (her legs seen in upper part of the frame), across the floor (the black plank running horizontally through the frame), to 'Little Broadcast's' wife (lower part of the frame) taking off her hoarded American goods.

the stairs. The porous boundaries in the house both intensify the conflict and render it susceptible to subaltern corrosion.

As a major site of adjacency and porosity, the stairs constitute an important stage for conflict and struggle as well as connection. Director Zheng emphasises shots at the stairs and the door area in that they help to alleviate the theatrical look resulting from the large quantity of shooting within rooms.[20] The stairs not only diversify the shots, but also imply vertical mobility, thus converting encounters between crows and sparrows into a metaphor for class conflict and re-negotiation of social hierarchy, threatening to collapse boundaries and reverse the hierarchy. This is born out in changes in Hou's physical relationship with other characters and the audience.

Hou, referred to as the 'master' from the very beginning, remains mysteriously invisible to the audience for the first third of the film. The audience hears his voice and coughing sound as '*acousmatre*', a disembodied voice that commands ubiquity, panopticism, omniscience and omnipresence.[21] The authoritative voice is located in a body after a set of deferring shots that whet the audience's desire to see Hou. His final materialisation is couched in satiric terms. The camera first tracks up to a close-up of Little Broadcast announcing with a heavy Zhejiang accent: 'Now we've found a solution [to my housing problem].' A graphic match cuts to a picture of the uniformed Chiang Kai-shek (a Zhejiang native) in Little Broadcast's posture, accompanied by a stern offscreen voice. The camera tracks right, stopping briefly at another picture of an ugly uniformed man, then resumes tracking right until it falls upon the back of a man, subsequently revealed to be Hou – the ugly man in the picture. This scene begins with Little Broadcast parodying the dictator Chiang and ends by satirising Hou as a self-important monkey who ludicrously mimics Chiang, his master. The move to locate the domineering voice in Hou's body, or de-acousmatisation, serves to undermine his power, as Chion argues.[22]

Further demystification takes place in an important stairs sequence, where Hou is forced to literally lower himself to face the united tenants at the bottom of the stairs. Zheng recalls that this scene was shot with a wide-angle camera to elongate the stairs and increase the distance between the two par-

A wide angle over-shoulder shot of Mr. Hou (the warlord and crow) from the prespective of 'Little Broadcast', his wife, and other tenants (sparrows) behind them outside the frame.

ties, thereby to enhance the tension.[23] Two other types of camerawork contribute to building the tension. First, the clash is deferred by focusing on the tenants listening attentively to offscreen steps walking down the stairs, approaching them. Second, the encounter is registered visually by alternating high-angle and low-angle shots that take the positions of Hou and the tenants in turn. This confrontation on the stairs is a transitional point when the crows and the sparrows switch positions. Their confrontation on the stairs begins with Hou's aggressive threat. Then, with Mr Kong visibly animated by Little Broadcast's words, the children starting to chant their satirical song, and the other tenants forcing their way up the stairs, Hou is compelled to retreat and the old social hierarchy is visually subverted.

This trajectory illustrates Zheng's allegorical conception of the house as a nation usurped by dictators but eventually returned to its original owners, who promise to construct a new future. Insofar as the house is poised on the threshold between the old and the new, bearing marks of both, it evokes Benjamin's 'dialectical image'. Benjamin describes the dialectical image as 'that in which the Then and the Now come into a constellation like a flash of lightening .... the image is dialectics at a standstill.'[24] The collapsing of the past and the present serves to liberate the utopian potential buried in the 'prehistory' (*Urgeschichte*) of the object into an 'afterlife' (*Nachleben*).[25] Such liberation depends precisely on an 'allegorical gaze', because allegory is a form of premonition that 'sees the object as it will appear in its "afterlife"'.[26]

In these terms, the house is wrested from its previous context and reconstructed as a home by, of and for the former sparrows. The moment when the maid Ah Mei replaces Hou's picture with one of Mr Kong and his son suggests momentary superimposition of the past, the present and the future in a montage that quickly turns out to be a dissolve, one image giving way to the other. The whole house *and* the wall thus become a palimpsest, inscribed with multiple temporalities and competing meanings, from Kong's home to Hou's loot, and then to the home of Kong *and* the other sparrows.

Having established the forward-looking and promising side of allegory, I now proceed to discuss how this vision is fractured by excessive moments when viewed with historical hindsight. In other words, I show how history is both figured in the film and exceeds its parameters, turning the utopia of the film upside down, thereby complicating the notion of allegory. To recall Zheng's 1979 reflection on the film, the film fails to focus on the broader social landscape and the more politically conscious classes, and instead limits itself to the self-interested petty bourgeoisie. By reconsidering these apparent faults in terms of excess, we can see how allegory entails constant transformation and inversion when placed in a new context.

In order to show how inversion takes place in the film, I refer to Benjamin's comments on the Soviet experiment with socialism in the late 1920s. Regarding the elimination of private space in late 1920s

A close-up shot of a photography of Mr. Kong (the original owner of the lane house) and his son being hung on the wall, replacing the usurper warlord's picture, illustrating Walter Benjamin's notion of the 'dialectical image'.

Moscow, Benjamin observes, 'apartments that earlier accommodated single families in their five to eight rooms now often lodge eight'.[27] While he sees the socialist vision as a potential redemption of what he contemptuously calls 'the petty-bourgeois interior' and its de-politicisation, he implicitly voices a concern, even anxiety, about over-emphasis on the 'correct political tendency' to the exclusion of 'free intellect'.[28] This concern was to become prevalent amongst Chinese intellectuals as socialism unrolled in the post-1949 China. The film's release was to be followed by similar sweep of collectivisation, which was to provoke ambivalence and even alienation among Chinese people, especially intellectuals, as it did in Benjamin.

Ironically, the film itself contains instances that begin with utopic potential only to turn into their own opposites. With the completion of collectivisation by 1952, a private house-owner like Mr Kong would have had his house appropriated – again – for public use this time. Peddlers, especially those trading in foreign merchandise like Little Broadcast, would have been phased out due to economic and political reorientations and re-channelled into socialist collective units, instead of being allowed to expand their private business. Mr Hua's voluntary self-criticism in the happy ending would become the staple in the state-sponsored ideological interpellation that constantly prodded the entire intellectual sector toward self-reflection and realignment with the masses. The encouraging vision of becoming masters of a nation offered at the end of the film was soon to flip into something unexpected, even dystopic, to the sparrows. If hope and utopia lie in the provisory and dream-like quality of the vision, they become disillusioning when realised in the form of an ossifying and imposing ideology. The utopia postulated in the film can be described as Raymond Williams's 'structure of feeling'. Contrary to an ideology more concerned with maintaining the status quo, 'structure of feeling' is 'at the very edge of semantic availability', and therefore characterised by 'pre-formation' or 'intensity of experience'.[29] The choice to focus the film on the so-called self-interested petty bourgeoisie instead of more politically conscious classes tends towards the production of excess that subverts the original vision. The petty bourgeois conviction in private ownership will ultimately clash with the socialist ideology, although it may be tem-porarily harnessed as a rebellious voice against the KMT government and a demand for social change.[30] Reconsidered with the benefit of historical hindsight, the film becomes a complex allegory, its figures being reversible, and its apparently straightforward narrative closure giving rise to indeterminable excess. In this sense, 'realistic' details take on multiple shifting significations as allegorical nexuses.

NOTES

1. Cheng Jihua, Li Shaobai and Xing Zuwen, eds, *The History of Chinese Film* (*Zhongguo dianying fazhanshi*) (Beijing: Zhongguo Dianying Chubanshe, 1963), vol. 2, 248.

2. Chen Baichen, 'Thoughts on the Re-release of *Crows and Sparrows*' ('Cong "Wuya yu Maque" chongying shuoqi'), *People's Daily* (*Renmin ribao*), 11 January 1958. Quoted in Cheng *et al.*, *The History of Chinese Film*, 244.

3. Leo Ou-fan Lee, 'The Tradition of Modern Chinese Cinema: Some Preliminary Explorations and Hypotheses', in *Perspectives on Chinese Cinema*, ed. Chris Berry (London: BFI, 1993), 7–8.

4. Ibid., 11.

5. Bill Nichols, *Representing Reality: Issues and Concepts in Documentary* (Bloomington: Indiana University Press, 1991), 141.

6. Ibid., 142.

7. Fredric Jameson, *Fables of Aggression: Wydham Lewis, the Modernist Fascist* (Berkeley: University of California Press, 1979), 94.

8. Fredric Jameson, *The Political Unconscious: Narrative as a Socially Symbolic Act* (Ithaca: Cornell University Press, 1981), 35.

9. Zheng Junli, 'Recording an Outline of the Transitional Moment between the Old Times and the New Era' ('Jiluxia xinjiu jiaoti shidai de yige ceying') in *Voiceover* (*Huawai yin*) (Beijing: China Film Press, 1979), 19–38.

10. Ibid., 21.

11. Ibid., 27–28.

12. 'Xiao' functions as a pun referring to 'Xiao', his last name, and 'xiao', meaning small or little.

13. Brian Winston, *Claiming the Real: The Documentary Film Revisited* (London: BFI, 1995), 107.

14. Li Suyuan, 'Narrative Modes in Early Chinese Cinema' ('Zhongguo zaoqi dianying de xushu moshi'), in *Melting National Characteristics into Film – Chinese Film-Television and National Culture* (*Minfeng*

hua jing – Zhongguo yingshi yu minzu wenhua), ed.
Zhou Xuan (Beijing: Beijing Normal University
Press, 1999), 238.

15. Interestingly and unfortunately, the reformation of
intellectuals through the practice of repeated self-
criticism and confession was to become a means of
persecution during the Cultural Revolution
(1966–1976). Ironically, among the persecuted
intellectuals were well-known film workers, including
Zhao Dan who plays Little Broadcast.

16. It is significant that the front gate appears in the film
only in this sequence. Throughout the film, characters
enter and exit through the run-down back door. The
implication is that only the legitimate master of the
house can use the front door, which is associated with
the future and progress.

17. Zheng, 'Recording an Outline', 20.

18. Intellectuals in 1930s and 1940s Shanghai were
conventionally known as 'garret literati' because their
meager income could only afford the rent of a garret
room in a lane house, a cheap accommodation due to
its narrow space and noisy environment.

19. Hou's name and the Chinese character for 'monkey'
are homophones.

20. Zheng, 'Recording an Outline', 35.

21. Michael Chion, *The Voice in Cinema*, trans. Claudia
Gorbman (New York: Columbia University Press,
1999), 24.

22. Ibid.

23. Zheng, 'Recording an Outline', 38.

24. Quoted in Gary Smith, ed., *Benjamin: Philosophy,
Aesthetics, History* (Chicago: University of Chicago
Press, 1989), 49.

25. Graeme Gilloch, *Myth and Metropolis: Walter
Benjamin and the City* (Cambridge: Polity Press,
1996), 111.

26. Ibid., 137.

27. Walter Benjamin, *One-Way Street and Other Writings*,
trans. Edmund Jephcott and Kingsley Shorter
(London: Verso, 1985), 187. Quoted in Gilloch, *Myth
and Metropolis*, 50.

28. Quoted in Gilloch, *Myth and Metropolis*, 53.

29. Raymond Williams, *Marxism and Literature* (Oxford:
Oxford University Press, 1985), 134.

30. A similar reversal is mapped out in Jameson's
comparative study of *The Godfather I* and *The
Godfather II*:

> It is as though the unconscious ideological and
> Utopian impulses at work in *Godfather I* could in the
> sequel be observed to work themselves towards the
> light and towards thematic or reflexive
> foregrounding in their own right. The first film held
> the two dimensions of ideology and Utopia together
> within a single generic structure, whose conventions
> remained intact. With the second film, however, this
> structure falls as it were into history itself, which
> submits it to a patient deconstruction that will in the
> end leave its ideological content undisguised and its
> displacements visible to the naked eye. ('Reification
> and Utopia in Mass Culture', in *Signature of the
> Visible* [New York: Routledge, 1990], 33.)

9 *Ermo*: (Tele)Visualising Urban/Rural Transformation

Ping Fu

Focusing on Zhou Xiaowen's 1994 film *Ermo*, this essay asks how contemporary Chinese film-makers use visual motifs to delineate the new urban space that has been socially reconfigured by transnational capital and globalised cultural practices. The corresponding urban–rural dichotomy reflects new political assertions, ideological underpinnings, historical conditions, social transformations, and cultural practices and negotiation. In the late 1980s and early 1990s, a striking number of films about rural migration, and the plight of rural women migrants in particular, appeared on the screenscape, counter-intuitively focused more on economic reform than gender issues *per se*. For example, one of the earliest films about rural women seeking business opportunities in the city, Peng Xiaolian's 1987 *Women's Story*, attracted the attention of international film critics for its portrayal of women's changing role in the labour force. And Zhang Liang's 1990 film, *Girls from the Special Economic Zone*, tells the story of a group of rural women becoming employees of a joint-venture electronic factory in Shenzhen, the Special Economic Zone near Hong Kong.

Film-makers started to question economic reform, re-embracing humanitarian themes concentrating on women's identities and their social repositioning in the course of unanticipated side effects from this socio-economic revolution. Based on the novel by Xu Baoqi, *Ermo* keenly depicts the dislocation of gender, society and culture faced with the lure of new work roles and economic prosperity. Rural women like the leading figure, Ermo, embody all the contradictory effects of this 'dislocation' in relation to transnational capital and heterogeneous cultural practices.

Most of existing writing on *Ermo* examines how the film's content demonstrates issues concerning the power of capital, economic development, technological phantasmagoria, consumer culture and the role of women's bodies in the formation of power.[1] My project is to treat the 'technologised visuality'[2] of both the film itself and its televisual theme as a discourse in which the filmic spectacle demands further critique by pointing to its own ideological connotations and social implications. By elaborating on how these elements interact with the story, I analyse the urban–rural dichotomy as it is condensed into the vivid depiction of a rural woman in pursuit of the biggest TV in town.

My close reading aims to supplement exiting critiques by unpacking visual clues to scrutinise the representational value of the commodity-on-display and its cinematic iconography. I discuss how experiencing the power of a spectacle is transmitted by the film, and how post-socialist consumerism and the new urban phantasmagoria are turning the commodity form into an ideology in its own right. If, as Michel Foucault puts its, 'urban space has its own dangers',[3] how does 'danger' intersect with emergent hybrid political and economic cultures and change human behaviour? How do people in post-socialist China, including the film-maker, comprehend and respond to modernity in this period of political and economic transition?

Cultural representations of rural and urban identities are taking on increasing significance in China today under conditions of state retreat and marketisation. These conditions are creating a space shared by the desirable and profitable grandeur of transnational capital, and the unexpected and debatable splendour of the global culture – the two most prominent inputs from Western culture. Transnational capital provides Chinese people with mobility and autonomy while global culture moves society toward post-industrial ideological practice. In this filmic instance, the parallel economic and cultural inputs reflect the political economics and cultural politics at play in contemporary Chinese modernisation. And in this mirrored hybridity, we see an emerging dichotomy of China and the world, the rural and the urban, the individual and the collective, the traditional and the modern, and woman and man.

THE SOCIAL BACKGROUND AND SYNOPSIS

Launched in the late 1970s, reform of the old socialist state-owned economy has penetrated every fibre of people's lives with irresistible force. The leading-edge sectors of this economic transformation are foreign investment and domestic private enterprise. The influx of imported goods and foreign culture, and the experiences and expectations that travel with them, have followed three decades of relative isolation.[4] The combination of these two sectors with the continued existence of the old state-run sector signals the emergence of a hybrid state and society. Less politically and ideologically harsh policies have provided farmers, in particular, with more chances to take advantage of the market economy, leading many to seek out business opportunities and new roles in the urban landscape. In major cities, the presence of multinational corporations signifies speedy modernisation of the economy while also posing a challenge to domestic enterprises. Hence the contest and compromise of the domestic and the foreign, the traditional and the modern, and the rural and the urban, forming a landscape of hybridity. These heterogeneous cultures, politics and regional practices and traditions have found common ground to invent the Chinese urban scenario of the 1990s. But the global reach of capitalism, which has transformed China's old integrated economic system and hybridised its culture, has come at the price of human and cultural dislocation.

'Ermo' in the Chinese north-western dialect literally means 'the second daughter' of the family. 'Mo' in classic Chinese refers to a plain woman. Nevertheless, the female protagonist Ermo is a good-looking and hard-working peasant woman, whose journey to modernity is one of spatial transition and mental transformation. As a mother and the wife of a physically, sexually and politically impotent man, Ermo is the breadwinner and decision-maker in her family. Her aspirations include buying a huge colour television set for her son, whose spare time is spent watching the television of a sharp-tongued neighbour with a daughter his age. The neighbour's husband Xiazi (literally meaning 'blind') is the *nouveau riche* owner–driver of the only truck in the village. He encourages Ermo to take her roadside business selling twisted noodles and hand-woven baskets to the city. There she sets her sights on a 29-inch colour television that attracts daily crowds and that not even the mayor can afford. Her new obsession with the large television fuels her ambition to enter the city marketplace and increase her earning power. She commutes with Xiazi, and, through his connections, becomes a noodle-making expert in a city restaurant. Her new job requires her to relocate to an urban women's hostel. When a co-worker suffers an accident demanding a transfusion, she discovers that cash is paid for blood. Selling her blood regularly, her health declines.

Sharing rides with Xiazi promotes their relationship. He praises her ability to support her family and produce a son. Denigrating his own wife as a narrow-minded couch potato, he suggests they each divorce their spouses to be together. This intensifies their clandestine love, until she discovers that Xiazi secretly boosted her wages through an arrangement with the restaurant manager. Outraged at being treated like a whore, she quits her job and returns home to resume making and selling twisted noodles in the local market.

Finally, Ermo makes enough money to buy the highly sought-after 29-inch television set and bring it home. It has to be manoeuvred in through the window and placed on the bed – the only place large enough to hold the monstrosity. As soon as the television set is settled in, Ermo collapses from exhaustion. As the coloured light display of the television and the promise of viewing the outside world attracts the villagers to squeeze into the room, Ermo leans on the set, helplessly turning herself into part of the show.

SEARCHING FOR MODERN CIVILIZATION

Ermo does not have the typical Chinese glamour that Zhang Yimou and Chen Kaige intentionally and effectively created to attract the gaze of the international film market. It is not a tale of 'a helpless victim or self-sacrificing saint who has suffered the usual varieties of sexist exploitation'.[5] Nor does the story reveal feudal Chinese oppressiveness in the

Ermo: to market with twisted noodles.

form of an unreasonable and domineering male figure, which was Zhang Yimou's trademark 'secret weapon' in international film festivals. Rather, *Ermo*, anchored in contemporary rural China, depicts a strong-willed peasant woman on a mission to buy a 29-inch television. According to director Zhou Xiaowen, the film is about 'a peasant's pursuit of a new lifestyle and her wish for upward mobility'.[6] In other words it is, as most Chinese critics say, about 'modern civilization'.

Evidently, 'modern civilization' here is largely and loosely associated with material abundance, foreign commodities and modern technology. As a symbol of Western influence, the city and the television set embody the new urban phantasmagoria equated with 'modern civilization'. The term indirectly but forcefully manifests a challenge to the past, a denial of tradition, and a belief in social advancement and historical progress. It is the lure of modern civilization that initiates Ermo's desperate pursuit of the symbolic television, which is a perfect cipher for the meaning and effect of change in rural China. Never-

theless, the meanings of her mission are multiple. They include a fight for dignity, an emotional competition with her neighbour, an overwhelming desire to possess the best, the capacity to consume within the new national economic environment, a woman's effort in a domestic power struggle and an unconscious departure from patriarchal tradition.

However, the misfortune that Ermo experiences in pursuit of her dream undermines all the above positives. Modern civilization and all it signifies becomes a new hegemony that monitors, justifies and shapes the thoughts and deeds of each individual. What most represses rural women like Ermo is no longer traditional ethics but modern civilization itself in the form of the commodity. Showing how Ermo is captured by the power of the commodity and in the end turns herself into a commodity to realise her dream further illustrates the dialectic and contradiction of the promise of modern civilization.

Ermo begins with her hawker's cry as she sells her twisted noodles by the roadside. The tightly framed shot of Ermo squatting behind her noodle basket becomes the film's visual leitmotif and associates her with the arena of commerce, suggesting a woman farmer's separation from the land and changing identity. Her stubborn bargaining demonstrates that she is an inflexible but profit-minded rural business-woman. This new image of a rural woman suggests this will not be a tale about the countryside but about the city where a woman farmer's social status and identity are dislocated, as indicated by the basket-selling episode in the film.

After Xiazi has found a shop where Ermo can sell the hundreds of surplus baskets she wove all summer, she is shown sitting on top of the load of baskets in his truck and heading to the busy urban marketplace. A freeze-framed close-up of her fearful face cuts to a moving long shot, which captures the fully loaded truck rumbling through the village gate and into the distance, where it becomes a dot hovering across the mountains. Ermo can hardly be made out anymore as a human being on top of the pile of baskets. This cinematic effect dislocates Ermo to associate her with the baskets, registering the subjugation of human consciousness to the form of the commodity, in which human alienation and its reification find their expression.

The filmic presentation of Ermo's fetishistic desire for a 29-inch colour television set further illustrates how human desire for material civilisation has been alienated by irresistible global commercialisation. No sooner does Ermo wander into a city department store than she finds a horde of people mesmerised by the television set and watching a Chinese-dubbed tape of a Western soft-core sex film. The scene baffles her; she cannot understand why the foreign actors are speaking Chinese. Her first encounter with the 'Other' – the foreign commodity as well as the foreigners on television – in such a hybridised condition 'infuses the fetish's initial role as the material sign of a cross-cultural agreement' and an in-between experience.[7]

As a spectacle, the object – the TV set – becomes image and belief, secured by an erotic aura manifested through the Western soft-core sex film. Such a display emphatically registers both the television show and the set itself as commodities to the consuming world by directing consumers' libidinal drives towards the whole package. Susan Buck-Morss's interpretation of Walter Benjamin's *Arcades Project* gives an even more precise account of the quietly persistent process of commodity fetishism:

> For Benjamin ... the key to the new urban phantasmagoria was not so much the commodity-in-the-market as the commodity-on-display, where exchange value no less than use value lost practical meaning, and purely representational value came to the fore. Everything desirable, from sex to social status, could be transformed into commodities as fetishes-on-display that held the crowd enthralled even when possession was beyond their reach. Indeed, an unattainably high price tag only enhanced a commodity's symbolic value. Moreover, when newness became a fetish, history itself became a manifestation of the commodity form.[8]

Indeed, what attracts Ermo's gaze are the representational value of the television set, its giant size, its unaffordable prize and the incomprehensible conversation on it. Its status 'beyond reach' transforms the television into a spectacle, in the sense elaborated by Debord. Debord's core thesis is that the spectacle constitutes a social relationship mediated by images:

> The spectacle is both the outcome and the goal of the dominant mode of production .... It is the very heart of society's real unreality .... [It] epitomizes the prevailing model of social life. It is the omnipresent celebration of a choice already made in the sphere of production, and the consummate result of that choice. In form as in content the spectacle serves as total justification for the conditions and aims of the existing system [transmitted visually].[9]

In Ermo's case, the affect of visuality that upholds the power of the spectacle is not just individual; rather, it is group-based. Collective viewing in the department store leads to collective enthusiasm for the TV show and comments about the unaffordability of the set, reflecting a shared vision of the modern, the foreign and the Other, as well as shared and visualised imagination of the near future. The Chinese dubbing of the US soap opera *Dynasty* minimises verbal signification and further emphasises the visual. In the end, it is the visual – both the show and the set – that counts and hunts.

The spectacle is what drags Ermo into the imaginary space where she can fantasise the power of possession, and also propel herself towards empowerment.

'The real consumer, in this case, thus becomes a consumer of illusion.'[10] This illusion enriches and enlarges her original goal, which was simply to buy a television for her son so he would not have to run next door to endure the neighbour's insults while he watched their television.

The iconography develops further by emphasising her compulsive viewing of the television, demonstrating the perfect logic of capitalist commercialism whereby 'watching' leads to 'wanting'. Ermo is captured by this cunning logic in the name of pursuing modern civilization. Through the other visual leitmotif of counting money, which draws attention to her role as bread-winner, decision-maker and bookkeeper, Ermo anticipates being able to count body hair in the clearness of the television image: 'the TV set is so big, its colour is so beautiful, and its picture is so clear that you can see every strand of the foreigners' blond body hairs.' This demonstrates her naive perception of the foreign/Other through the window of the 'global village',[11] which also perfectly echoes Anne Friedberg's analysis of a 'mobilised virtual gaze':

> Cinema and television – mechanical and electronic extensions of photography's capacity to transform our access to history and memory – have produced increasingly detemporalised subjectivities …. The cinema developed as an apparatus that combined the 'mobile' with the 'virtual'. Hence, cinematic spectatorship changed, in unprecedented ways, concepts of the *present* and the *real*.[12]

The department store television set and the television show have profound effects on Ermo. They open up her 'optical unconscious',[13] letting her experience what they present and represent as *real*. The set attracts her 'virtual gaze' and the show mobilises her desire to possess the set, which holds the promise of foreign eroticism. This opening of her 'optical unconscious' makes her more desperate than ever to pursue the set as icon of modern civilization. She takes more aggressive steps to reach her goal, such as leaving home for a city job and selling her blood. The latter underlines the fact that she is turning her body into a commodity valued only for its exchange value – its worth as another commodity. Her reaction to 'the external culture'[14] turns civilization into fetishism.

Broadly speaking, fetishism involves the attribu-

tion of autonomous power to a manmade artefact. It is therefore dependent on the ability to disavow knowledge and suspend disbelief. However, the fetish is always haunted by the fragility of the mechanisms that sustain it. Both Freud and Marx use fetishism to explain a refusal or phobic inability to understand a symbolic system of value, one within the psychoanalytic and the other within the social sphere.[15] For Freud, the body that is the source of fetishism is the mother's body, uncanny and archaic. For Marx, the source of fetishism is in the erasure of value of the worker's labour. Both are repressed as the unspeakable and the unrepresentable in commodity culture.

However, the unspeakable and unrepresentable are openly, cheerfully and sarcastically exhibited by the film-makers through the image of Ermo selling blood and repeating, 'I have plenty of blood. Women lose their blood anyway.' To mistakenly and innocently identify medically drawn blood with menstrual blood signifies Ermo's need to become 'civilized', or educated, about human physiology. Instead of showing a block or phobic inability of the psyche, her innocence about her own body manifests itself as a natural impulse driving her search for modern civilization. However, at the end of the film, she appears to be a fragile, totally worn-out and lifeless object compared to the gigantic television set with all its vibrant and colourful movement, implying the internal and external dislocation that is the price of achieving modern civilization.

(RE)ENVISIONING THE GLOBAL–LOCAL AND THE URBAN–RURAL

The market economy has speeded up urbanisation as urban migration has become an avenue to make money. Throughout the 1980s, rural migrants including women like Ermo overturned the social immobility imposed on them by the old collective system.[16] The proliferation of markets made commerce a significant alternative for rural women. Saskia Sassen remarks that migration is a representation of globality in terms of economics, politics and culture. It transcends locality, Otherness and marginality, transforming all three into the core of power.[17]

The filmic imagery of Ermo's country-to-city trips not only showcases her geographical travelling but also the way in which her identity and power travels, elevating her gender and social status, and releasing her from rural exclusion from the urban, the modern and the global. Ermo's power is never visualised on the screen through her role as a farmer but only in her role as an agricultural migrant entering the urban sphere. On the one hand, her naiveté, diligence and endurance in her efforts to make a better life for herself and her family challenge patriarchal dominance and empower her. On the other hand, the same imagery diminishes the significance of farming in contemporary China and signifies its constant movement towards further modernisation and globalisation.

The visual juxtaposition of her husband's physical and political impotence simultaneously signifies the diminution of his male power and his once respected rural leadership. He is almost always confined to the edge of the frame, consuming medication as a dietary staple, reminding everyone that he is no longer the village chief. He pushes for a larger house instead of the television, insisting that 'A TV set is an egg but a house is a hen'. Ermo's powerful status, as someone mobile and autonomous, is symbolised by her frequent business trips to the city, her taking over the role of male labour in her household and her new buying power. Her geographical border crossing and gender crossing in terms of labour seem to help her win female subjectivity and agency. Sassen contributes a keen insight into such power formations:

> We learn something about power through its absence and by moving through or negotiating the borders and terrains that connect powerlessness to power: Power is not a silence at the bottom; its absence is present and has consequences.[18]

Superficially, Ermo is empowered. When she fills the vacancy at the 'International Grand Restaurant' as an expert noodle maker, she designates a new element in a new urban regime, facilitating its operations. Her noodle making expertise changes her urban status from temporary to permanent, and also empowers her as master of her own family. The film-makers communicate this to the audience in a distinctive way during one of Ermo's rare home visits.

Following a close-up of two naked male backs, the audience sees Ermo sitting in front of the two half-naked males – her son and her husband – giving them new shirts purchased from a city store. This symbolic act not only signifies that she is a caring wife and mother, but also that she is in financial control. The visible nakedness and their passive seated position suggest their vulnerability compared to her fully clad mobility, as she stands over them and even dresses her husband. From this position, Ermo's husband looks remarkably similar to his son in height and stature, further marking out his loss of power.

Ermo returns to powerlessness when she breaks up with Xiazi, quits her restaurant job and resumes her position selling twisted noodles in the local market. Her husband's renewed bossiness signifies the power shift associated with these changes. Power is suddenly lost because of her withdrawal from the city. Furthermore, this loss is exacerbated by her husband's suspicion of her infidelity. Her infidelity compensates for the diminution of his patriarchal power because of his physical mutilation and loss of political power when he ceased to be the village chief, because it propels him to reaffirm his role as husband and father.

Ermo's body is inscribed by sexual politics demonstrated in the circulation and transformation of power, which director Zhou Xiaowen communicates through recurring boundary crossings.[19] These male–female and urban–rural transpositions can be regarded as a modern allegory of location where power, morality and economics construct and deconstruct the power of individuality, subjectivity and autonomy.

In conclusion, by almost any measure, China's opening to the world economy has been a spectacular success. Film-makers participate in this transformation when they focus on the geographical and cultural spheres that make up the rural–urban context. In John Revne Short's analysis:

> Cities are embedded in a world economy; they are nodes in a global network of production, consumption and exchange of commodities, goods, and services. The cities of the world make solid in time and space the nature of changing economic transactions. They are the physical embodiment of social and economic change.[20]

His remark echoes Raymond Williams's canonical thesis on the relation of *The Country and the City*,[21] denoting the city as an achieved centre of learning, communication and light (an embodiment of modernisation). However, because the city is situated in globalised politics, economics and cultural conditions, the moment is only 'solid' as a snapshot in time, forever moving forward and then backward in our memory-banks. Furthermore, travelling between the city and the country does not necessarily entail a struggle between advancement and backwardness. As Aihwa Ong suggests, understanding it requires the new concept of 'flexible citizenship'.[22] She suggests there is an internal logic in capitalist consumption and that the movement between different spheres is such that, in order to improve one's political and economic situation, some fluidity is necessary.

The city as a 'physical embodiment of social and economic change' in the Chinese context sustains a complex hybridisation, which enhances the contact between the global and the local, the foreign and the indigenous, and the centre and the marginal. This loosens the ties between the rural and the urban, and produces a new 'cultural logic', in which transportability and transformation become possible. In the final frame, the world-weather forecast is ending the China Central Television (CCTV) broadcast on the large 29-inch screen. This underscores the reality and existence of a larger world and climate. This modernisation that has invented the Chinese contemporary urban scenario – viewed by Foucault as a 'danger', by Jameson as 'commodity production', by Benjamin as an 'aura-killer' and by Debord as a 'spectacle' or as fetishism – does in fact bring Chinese people, and especially farmers, substantial wealth alongside the ineluctable confusion that accompanies the rupture and dislocation of their culture and traditions.

Ermo's overwhelming pursuit of the symbolic icon of the 29-inch television set forces her to take on all the baggage associated with the above-mentioned discursive practices, irreversibly intertwining the beautiful and the ugly. In the end, any judgments about either the intent or outcome of China's ongoing modernisation and modernism must be suspended, for they cannot be read as more than an unfinished script.

Furthermore, the visuality of Ermo's rural-city-rural journey enacts ceaseless but clueless debates on the dichotomy between mobility and stability, the domestic and the foreign, and the national and the global throughout the century-long process of Chinese modernisation. This specific cinematic visual cipher, to echo Rey Chow's thesis on visuality,[23] 'enables us to notice [our] position of spectator and

observer', reminding us of the reciprocity of viewing and receiving, and warning us to ponder what projects our gaze upon the spectacle and what shapes our vision of the social panorama, particularly in the age of globalisation.

NOTES

1. David Leiwei Li, 'What Will Become of Us If We Don't Stop?: Ermo's China and the End of Globalization', *Comparative Literature*, 53, no. 4 (2001): 442–461; Beth Notar, 'Blood Money: Woman's Desire and Consumption in *Ermo*', *Asian Cinema*, 12, no. 2 (2001): 132–153; Stephen J. Gould and Nancy Y. C. Wong, 'The Intertextual Construction of Emerging Consumer Culture in China as Observed in the Movie *Ermo*: A Postmodern, Sinicization Reading', *Journal of Global Marketing*, 14, nos. 1 and 2 (2000): 151–167; Judith Farquhar, 'Technology of Everyday Life: The Economy of Impotence in Reform China', *Cultural Anthropology*, 14, no. 2 (1999): 155–179; Anne T. Ciecko and Sheldon H. Lu, 'Televisuality, Capital and the Global Village', *Jump Cut*, 42 (December 1998): 77-83; Tani E. Barlow, 'Green Blade in the Act of Being Grazed: Late Capital, Flexible Bodies, Critical Intelligibility', *Difference: A Journal of Feminist Cultural Studies*, 10, no. 3 (1998): 119–158; Tony Rayns, 'The Ups and Downs of Zhou Xiaowen', *Sight and Sound*, 5, no. 7 (1995): 22–24.

2. Rey Chow, *Primitive Passions: Visuality, Sexuality, Ethnography, and Contemporary Chinese Cinema* (New York: Columbia University Press, 1995), 16.

3. Michel Foucault, 'Space, Knowledge, and Power' in *The Foucault Reader*, ed. Paul Rabinow (New York: Pantheon Books, 1984), 243.

4. Margaret Peterson, *China's New Business Elite: The Political Consequences of Economic Reform* (Berkeley: University of California Press, 1997).

5. Tony Rayns, 'The Position of Women in New Chinese Cinema,' *East–West Film Journal*, 1, no. 2 (1987): 32–44.

6. Chai Xiaofeng, *Zhou Xiaowen is Also Crazy* (*Zhou Xiaowen ye fengkuang*) (Changsha: Hunan Wenyi Chubanshe, 1996), 313. For more detailed discussion, see Dai Jinhua, '*Ermo*: Modern Allegorical Space' ('*Ermo* Xiandai Yuyan Kongjian'); Wang Dehou, '*Ermo*: a Crystallization of Sturdiness and Blindness' ('*Ermo*: Zhuozhuang yu Mangmu de Jiejing'); and Wang Yichuan, 'A Realistic Representation of Power

Exchange and Repetition' ('Rushi Biaoyan Quanli
Jiaohuan yu Chongfu'), in *Film Art* (*Dianying Yishu*),
no. 5 (1994): 39–43, 36–38 and 44–47.

7. See Patricia Spyer, ed., *Border Fetishism: Material Objects in Unstable Spaces* (New York: Routledge, 1998) for details.

8. Susan Buck-Morss, *The Dialectics of Seeing: Walter Benjamin and the Arcades Project* (Cambridge: MIT Press, 1991), 81–82.

9. Guy Debord, *The Society of the Spectacle*, trans. Donald Nicholson-Smith (New York: Zone Books, 1994), 13.

10. Ibid., 32.

11. In Marshall McLuhan and Bruce Power's book, *The Global Village* (New York: Oxford University Press, 1989), McLuhan invents this term to refer to globalised telecommunication. According to McLuhan, all Western scientific models of communication are linear, sequential and logical as a reflection of efficient causality. McLuhan thinks speed-of-light technologies could be used to postulate possible futures (globalisation). The 'global village' (or 'international arena') is controlled by those with the most advanced technology. To a great extent, an advanced telecommunication determines the legitimacy of speech, information flow, and in short, global control in this 'global village'.

12. Anne Friedberg, *Window Shopping: Cinema and the Postmodern* (Berkeley: University of California Press, 1993), 2–3.

13. The term originates from Walter Benjamin's thesis of mimesis with reference to the camera, which he suggests is capable of generating 'the aura' of works of art in the age of mechanical reproduction. For a detailed analysis of the notion, see Michael Taussig's *Mimesis and Alterity* (New York and London: Routledge, 1993), 44–69.

14. Georg Simmel states that 'the deepest problems of modern life derive from the claim of the individual to preserve the autonomy and individuality of his existence in the face of overwhelming social forces, of historical heritage, of external culture, and of the technique of life'. See his 'The Metropolis and Mental Life', in *Classic Essay on the Culture of Cities*, ed. Richard Sennett (New Jersey: Prentice Hall, 1969), 47.

15. See Sigmund Freud, 'Fetishism', *Standard Edition of the Complete Psychological Works*, vol. 21 (London: Hogarth Press, 1961) and Karl Marx. *Capital*, vol. 1 (Moscow: Foreign Languages Publishing House, 1961) for details.

16. Ashwani Saith, ed., *The Re-emergence of the Chinese Peasantry* (London: Croom Helm, 1987), and Kate Zhou, *How the Farmers Changed China* (Boulder: West View Press, 1996).

17. Saskia Sassen, *Globalization and Its Discontents* (New York: The New Press, 1998), 81–111.

18. Ibid., 86.

19. Rong Weijing, 'Zhou Xiaowen, a Director Knocked Dead by Films' ('Zhou Xiawen bei Dianying Kesi de Daoyan'), *Film Art* (*Dianying Yishu*), no. 3 (1994): 45–49.

20. John Short, *New Worlds New Geographies* (New York: Syracuse, 1998).

21. Raymond Williams, *The Country and the City* (New York: Oxford University Press, 1973).

22. Aihwa Ong, *Flexible Citizenship: the Cultural Logics of Transnationality* (Durham and London: Duke University Press, 1999).

23. Rey Chow, *Primitive Passions: Visuality, Sexuality, Ethnography, and Contemporary Chinese Cinema* (New York: Columbia University Press, 1995), 6.

10   *Evening Bell*: Wu Ziniu's Visions of History, War and Humanity

Yingjin Zhang

PROLOGUE: FOR WHOM THE BELL TOLLS?

One evening in 1987, double security was posted outside a screening room at the August First Film Studio in Beijing, which was under the direct supervision of the Culture Department of the People's Liberation Army, a stronghold of conservatism in contemporary China. When the lights came up after the censorship screening of *Evening Bell* (1986), uniformed officials and studio leaders were completely silent, temporarily stunned by the powerful, radically unsettling images of war they had just seen. A few veteran film directors spoke in sympathy with what Wu Ziniu had attempted in the film, but most mounted trenchant criticism in frustration or fury. Needless to say, the film did not pass censorship. During the subsequent two nerve-racking years, *Evening Bell* went through four major revisions, and Wu was frequently assailed by the question: 'When are we going to hear your funeral bell (*sangzhong*)?'[1]

Although *Evening Bell* was eventually released to critical acclaim in 1988, the question persists as to for whom (or for what) Wu's film tolls. For those conservative old-timers who believe in the Communist cause and the justice of revolutionary wars? For Wu who insists on the *auteurist* right to cinematic art and a tragic vision of humanity? Or for the kind of avant-gardism Fifth Generation directors such as Chen Kaige and Tian Zhuangzhuang were pursuing in the mid-1980s? Several critics have opted for the third possibility. Thus comments Bei Cun, an avant-garde fiction writer:

> *Evening Bell* contains the humanist content of *One and Eight*, the ascetic vision of *King of the Children* and the visual impact of *Red Sorghum*. But most of all it represents Wu Ziniu's personal style: his enigma, his unpredictable insights, his heart-wrenching suspense

and his unique take on war and humanity. The appearance of *Evening Bell* signals the end of Fifth Generation films; *Evening Bell* is therefore a glorious act.[2]

Dai Jinhua, a leading Chinese film critic, agrees:

> the Fifth Generation directors look forward to salvation: not only their own salvation, but also the salvation of memory, history, nation, and subsistence. The basic narrative thrust of *Evening Bell* is precisely to bury wars – to bury the corpses left after the war is over. Perhaps the film also signifies the burial and termination of a tragic but heroic era.[3]

Like Bei Cun and Dai Jinhua, I treat *Evening Bell* as an outstanding text in the Fifth Generation's early development; but unlike them, I am not interested in pinpointing a 'terminal' point for Fifth Generation films in the late 1980s.[4] Instead, I am interested in retrieving war-related *images of dissent* as an *alternative* route of cinematic exploration that has been largely abandoned by the avant-garde directors in their subsequent pursuit of 'ethnographic cinema' or historical epics.[5] From *One and Eight* (Zhang Junzhao, 1984) through *Red Sorghum* (Zhang Yimou, 1987) to *Farewell My Concubine* (Chen Kaige, 1993), the Fifth Generation directors have achieved a series of spectacular international successes while constantly readjusting their cinematic priorities. Amidst all the media fanfare from the mid-1980s to the mid-1990s, Wu Ziniu maintained a posture of dissent, presenting himself as a loner in Chinese avant-garde cinema and repeatedly testing the limits of Chinese censorship – significantly from *within* the studio system rather than from underground film operations.[6]

This chapter approaches *Evening Bell* as an exceptional case in the cultural politics of contemporary Chinese cinema. First, I scrutinise images of dissent in Wu's film against the backdrop of the Fifth Generation's avant-gardism in the mid-1980s. Second, I discuss Wu's efforts to reconstruct the genre of war films by upholding humanism and downplaying nationalism, which crystallises in his rebellious visions of transcendent humanity and barbaric civilization. Third, I analyse the controversy surrounding the censorship, distribution and reception of this film and map out the terrain of film criticism and political intervention. Finally, I refer to Wu's projects at the turn of the millennium and re-evaluate his career trajectory from dissent to consent in the era of post-socialism and transnationalism.

IMAGES OF DISSENT IN
EVENING BELL

Evening Bell offers little narrative plot. A team of five Communist-led Eighth Route Army soldiers is dispatched to bury corpses on a battlefield. They witness the cruelty of war but control their rage when they discover thirty-three Japanese soldiers hidden in a cave full of ammunitions, unaware of Japan's surrender and almost starved to death. After giving food to these hungry souls, the Chinese soldiers convince the Japanese to surrender the next morning, and they leave as the cave explodes behind them.

Produced two years after *Yellow Earth* (Chen Kaige, 1984), *Evening Bell* continued the Fifth Generation's initial avant-garde practice of minimal plot and scanty dialogue. Yet, more radical than *Yellow Earth*, *Evening Bell* does not rely even on musical scores or song lyrics to convey its meanings. Instead, images *alone* speak to the viewer and build an ambience of deadly silence and suspense that carries an extra emotional weight. Significantly, the images in *Evening Bell* are not those found in *Yellow Earth* suggestive of the 'profundity' of Chinese culture and history, such as the Yellow River and the loess plateau.[7] Rather, they are visually disturbing images that assault the viewer and keep them on an emotional edge, very much in the fashion of *One and Eight*. 'We do not narrate, but we hope to experience together with the audience', declares Wu in his director's notes.[8] In accordance, before the title *Evening Bell* appears, the viewer is confronted with a scene of utter desolation: the autumn wind blows over reeds, and a sea of white funeral banners flutters over a seemingly endless stretch of tombs in the wilderness. When the Communist soldiers arrive, the camera tracks past the injured bodies and the burned faces of Chinese and Japanese soldiers littered around broken walls and bombshell pits and piled up on the ravaged battlefield.

The preference for *images over narrative* in *Evening Bell* is in line with Wu Ziniu's pursuit of *poetry*: 'If you believe poetry can be uttered by a wild animal's roar, then this film is a poem.'[9] In *Evening Bell*, Wu's sense of poetry is conveyed by recurring symbolism and imagery. Apart from dead bodies and death motifs such as the starved Chinese woman and cannibalised Chinese labourer in the cave, Wu offers numerous other images apparently unrelated to the narrative but subtly suggestive of the pent-up anger of war. In one such instance, an old peasant is silhouetted against the rising sun, cutting at the base of a Japanese watchtower with a long axe. The chops echo across the empty horizon, as the image is repeated in a series of close-up, medium, long and extreme-long shots. The sequence is repeated in the middle of the film, this time at sunset, suggesting both the lingering effects of war and the steadfast effort to eradicate its remains. The sequence is repeated a third time at the end of the film: with a thundering sound, the tower crumbles down as the sun rises.

These three scenes of chopping down the watchtower illustrate what Bei Cun describes as Wu's four avant-garde techniques: suspense of narrative, isolation of images, re-enactment of rituals and enlargement effects (*fangda*). By repetition, the ritual of chopping at the watchtower adds a sense of cadence and coherence to *Evening Bell*. Moreover, it also foregrounds the film's pacifist theme, thus logically linking this otherwise isolated image to other symbols such as a stray Japanese army dog and intermittent bell sounds in the film. In each occurrence, the chopping ritual arrests the narrative flow and forces the viewer to reflect, at an abstract level, on the meaning of war. In other words, Wu has 'enlarged' the chopping ritual to symbolic proportions, making the peasant's re-enactment parallel to the Communist soldiers' rituals: both bury the war but at the same time remind the viewer of its cruelty.

Other rituals in *Evening Bell* include an initial sequence of the Japanese soldiers' group suicide and the hungry Japanese singing a song in the cave near the end. Both sequences are presented sympathetically, the latter in particular testifying to the eventual triumph of humanity over bestiality. However, as far as emotional impact is concerned, *Evening Bell* excels in exposing the atrocities of war. Again, isolated images of ritual performances keep intruding into the film and seem to take on *a life of their own*. A blind man gropes along a hillside and scatters pieces of paper money to the wind. Two young widows cry by tombs, their moans echoing into the distance. In flashbacks, a Chinese soldier's wife hangs herself from a tree after being raped by the Japanese, and another soldier's wife is gang-raped by the Japanese after trying to jump down a well. Indeed, hatred and rage run deep in *Evening Bell*, and distant moaning and deadly silence fill the screen with flammable tension, as if any single utterance would explode the entire screen. Such is the power of Wu Ziniu's *aesthetic of violence*. No wonder Wu has been depicted as 'a blood-thirsty king' or 'assassin' (*shashou*), who 'launches wars on screen' and creates 'suspense on the basis of anger'.[10]

It would be wrong to assume that Wu is angry at wars alone, for his cinematic images carry a disturbing message of *dissent* vis-à-vis the political and cinematic conventions of contemporary China. In *Evening Bell*, such dissent is articulated at multiple levels. In ideological terms, the film departs from standard Communist history and challenges the justification of violence in the name of nation and race. In genre terms, it departs from the paradigm of nationalism and heroism in the mainstream war film and offers an alternative of humanism and pacifism.[11] In narrative terms, it departs from melodrama in socialist realism and opts for minimal plot and characterisation. In aesthetic terms, it departs from revolutionary romanticism and deploys tragedy to expose the frailty and utter irrationality of human existence on the threshold of life and death. Arguably, it is precisely these instances of dissent – all strategically masked as ideological ambiguity and narrative obscurity – that provoked outrage after the censorship screening of *Evening Bell* detailed above.

TRANSCENDENT HUMANITY AND BARBARIC CIVILIZATION

But why did Wu want to provoke the authorities and challenge convention? For one thing, he was fed up with the mainstream war films that had dominated the Chinese screen from the 1950s to the 1980s. In a 1988 interview, he argues:

We cannot forever stay with the heroism of the past decades, promoting national spirit and endorsing the invincibility of the Communist Party and its armies … We have too many such films. Can't we do something different? Can't we represent war from a higher angle?'[12]

Evening Bell represents a positive answer to Wu's rhetorical questions. The 'something else' Wu had in mind is embodied in a number of notable shifts he has implemented in the Chinese war film: from propagandist messages to symbolism and imagery, from idealisation of heroism to cultivation of ambivalent moods and pathos, from pure patriotic spirit to prolonged psychosomatic suffering. Painful sufferings, indeed, are integral to Wu's tragic vision of humanity, and it is through suffering together with screen characters that Wu hopes his viewers will rethink the meaning of war.

A more direct cause of Wu's confrontation with the authorities is his artistically justifiable but politically naive dedication to 'representing wars from a higher angle' – the angle of transcendent humanity. What Wu says of *The Dove Tree* (1985), his earlier film about the 1979 Sino-Vietnamese border war that became the first Fifth Generation film banned by the government, applies to *Evening Bell* as well.[13] 'Wars are merciless, … but people do not forget they are human. This is a victory for morality, a sacred, most grandiose victory of all human wars!'[14] Based on such an abstract conception of humanity, Wu intended to explore human relationships in wartime from a sweeping perspective (*hongguan*). Hence, in *The Dove Tree*, he creates a situation where a Vietnamese army nurse treats two fatally wounded Chinese soldiers before another Chinese arrives and kills her. Similarly, in *Evening Bell*, the Chinese soldiers leave food for the starving Japanese. It is worth noting that Wu gives no names to either Chinese or Japanese soldiers, thereby suggesting a generic war situation and elevating *Evening Bell* to an abstract height of humanity that aspires to transcend otherwise unbridgeable national and racial divides.

Paradoxically, Wu has depended on an aesthetic of violence to convey his pacifist message and fortify his posture of dissent. The excessive graphic images of war atrocities from his *Joyous Heroes* (1988), *Between Life and Death* (1988), *The Big Mill* (1990) and *Nanjing Massacre* (1995) foreground Wu's tragic vision of history and humanity. To a considerable extent, Wu's vision approximates Walter Benjamin's famous verdict – 'There is no document of civilization which is not at the same time a document of barbarism.'[15] The rationale behind Benjamin's verdict poses a potential challenge to any political establishment: 'Whoever has emerged victorious participates to this day in the triumphal procession in which the present rulers step over those who are lying prostrate.'[16]

To convey his double vision of transcendent humanity and barbaric civilization, Wu is fond of blurring or even collapsing otherwise rigid boundaries or categories such as Chinese and Japanese, Chinese and Vietnamese, Communist and Nationalist, landlords and peasants, and friends and enemies. In *Between Life and Death*, local factions change their affiliations with either the Communists or the Nationalists and engage in a confusing battle at the end that kills all the principal characters. In *The Big Mill*, a former Red Army soldier serves as an irrational assassin who murders local militia members one by one in revenge and grinds their bodies to pieces in a giant mill. In *Nanjing Massacre*, Wu restages a holocaust that claimed 300,000 lives by following a mixed-race family with a Chinese husband and a Japanese wife from Shanghai to Nanjing. In cases like these, if Wu's vision of transcendent humanity remains abstract, his images of 'those who are lying prostrate' present a concrete threat to the Communist authorities. In the final analysis, what is at stake in Wu's war films is the sanctity of Communist rhetoric, which has always used nationalism and revolution as a perfect justification for violence of all kinds.

A ROLLER COASTER RIDE THROUGH CENSORSHIP AND CRITICISM

In retrospect, Wu's recruitment to the August First Film Studio appears extremely ironic. After *The Dove Tree* was banned, Wu felt his prospects with Xiaoxiang Film Studio in Hunan were murky at best, so he accepted an invitation from Lu Guozhu, a noted fiction writer and then deputy director of August First Film Studio. Lu had seen *The Dove Tree* and valued Wu's talent, and Wu was transferred to the PLA studio to develop projects on military topics. Nevertheless, Wu rejected a pile of mainstream screenplays and decided to write his own script for *Evening Bell*, a film he designed from the outset to be 'pacifist' (*fanzhan*) in nature.[17] The resulting adversity was inevitable. For a film that took less than two months to shoot, *Evening Bell* went through two years of screenings at various levels of censorship and four stages of requested revisions. In January 1988, Wu completed the third revision, but the film still did not pass. The censors ruled that, 'the Japanese watchtower must crumble down'. So Wu had another tower built and did the fourth revision. As time dragged on like this, Wu saw his classmate Zhang Yimou achieve international fame with *Red Sorghum*.

On 18 March 1988 the Film Bureau finally approved *Evening Bell* for release. But to Wu's great disappointment, the initial order in May 1988 was for zero prints. This was a record low for any domestic film, a record that indirectly confirmed the avantgarde nature of Wu's film and his dissent from the mainstream war film. Later in 1988, the order climbed to one print, and Wu's fortune seemed to take a positive turn as the authorities named *Evening Bell* one of the ten outstanding films for the first half of 1988. Wu's fortune peaked in February 1989, when *Evening Bell* won the prestigious Silver Bear at the Berlin International Film Festival. In addition, Wu was awarded the Best Director at China's 1989 Golden Rooster Awards (*Jinji jiang*) for *Evening Bell* as well as for his two sequel films, *Joyous Heroes* and *Between Life and Death*.[18] With Wu's belated recognition, the order for *Evening Bell* eventually went up to forty-seven prints.

Closer investigation of the behind-the-scenes discussions at the 1989 Golden Rooster Awards reveals that the jurors were sharply divided about *Evening Bell*. According to Yu Min, the conservative film critic and editor-in-chief of *Film Art* (*Dianying Yishu*), the official film journal based in Beijing, the awards deliberations started on 4 May 1989, during the crisis of the pro-democratic student demonstrations centred in Tiananmen Square. The majority of the twenty-five jurors were in favour of *Evening Bell*, praising its artistic impact, humanist profundity and significance for international peace. A minority of jurors supported the film with reservations, uncertain about the film's abstract representation of war and emotionally disturbed by Wu's sympathy for the Japanese. Only a few among the minority, Yu himself included, denounced the film's ideological content: its pacifism and its objection to all wars. For Yu,

Evening Bell.

the jurors' heated debate over *Evening Bell* concerned not so much differences in artistic vision as differences over principles related to war and peace, policy on enemies and humanitarianism. Yu asserts that *Evening Bell* is based on Wu's own subjective perception, and his symbolic portrayal of the Chinese feeding the armed Japanese soldiers is 'by no means humanitarian, merciful or transcendental'.[19] Due to strong opposition by critics in positions of authority like Yu, *Evening Bell* gathered eight votes in both the preliminary and final votes and did not qualify for Best Film. No other nominated films received more than half of the total votes, and 1989 became an unprecedented year in the history of the Golden Rooster Awards because no film won Best Film.

The debate over *Evening Bell* continued after the awards. Yu published an article in August 1989 exposing the hidden meanings in *Evening Bell*. His article was criticised in September 1992 in *Wenhui Film Times* (*Wenhui dianying shibao*), a Shanghai film magazine, which defended the Fifth Generation films and specifically praised *Evening Bell*. What I find interesting in the exchanges between Yu and his diplomatically unnamed critic in this case is that it took exactly six years before Yu decided in 1995 to vent his pent-up frustration publicly regarding the 1989 Golden Rooster Awards. Why? My guess is that in the early 1990s Yu represented a minority voice during China's transition to the market economy. Apart from his denunciation of *Evening Bell*, Yu also complained about the 'smart film leaders' who prescribed 'entertainment films' (*yule pian*) as a moneymaking strategy to save the film industry.[20]

It must be evident by now that one does not exaggerate when naming Wu Ziniu 'the most controversial Chinese film director of the past decade',[21] which is exactly what Chen Mo does. A prolific film scholar with the China Film Arts Research Centre in Beijing, Chen Mo describes Wu as 'a subjective, romantic poet' like Chen Kaige. For Chen Mo, as for Wu's wife Sima Xiaojia, Wu behaves like a big child who stubbornly refuses to see the world from the adult point of view.[22] His persistent naiveté determined that *Evening Bell* could never pass the rudimentary test of common sense – for example, why do the Japanese not return fire when a Chinese soldier fires his machine gun twice to vent his anger? – and could only be a humanitarian fantasy. Likewise, by following a mixed-race family and a half-Chinese, half-Japanese child named Nanjing, the history of the Nanjing massacre is re-presented as a conceptual game in *Nanjing Massacre*. What bothers Chen Mo is not exactly Wu's ideological ambivalence, which infuriates conservatives like Yu Min, but rather Wu's own brand of romanticism masquerading as naiveté. To paraphrase Chen's reserved criticism, Wu's propensity for abstraction has reduced human beings – heroic, tragic or otherwise – to mere symbols or signs for such loaded terms as humanity, nation and race.

EPILOGUE: FROM DISSENT TO CONSENT

As Chen Mo correctly observed in 2001, Wu Ziniu has changed his positions 'from internationalism to nationalism, from humanitarianism to patriotism, from an articulation of love to an education in hatred, ... from the frontline of avant-gardism to the centre of military headquarters'.[23] Although some critics want to see *Evening Bell* as the end of the avant-garde in Fifth Generation films, Wu proved himself as a lone explorer of the incomplete avant-garde project with *Sparkling Fox* (1993), a meditation on an urbanite's efforts to solve his existential crisis in snow-covered forests. However, beginning with *Nanjing Massacre*, Wu came closer to the mainstream by emphasising harmony and symmetry and returning to dramatic conflict and detailed characterisation. Wu's change since the mid-1990s, one suspects, might have more to do with China's transition to the market economy than his personal preferences. Wu's close collaborator, Zhang Xuan, notes: 'Just as society changes, so does an artist. Expectations and hopes arise because of changes, and changes stimulate human creativity, thereby supplying an artist with inexhaustible energy.'[24]

After an unprecedented hiatus of four years, Wu

returned to film-making with *The National Anthem* (1999), a self-acknowledged 'mainstream film' (*zhuliu dianying*) that cost the Xiaoxiang Film Studio twenty million *yuan*. Dedicated as 'a monument to the national spirit, to the Chinese nation, and to outstanding Chinese people like Tian Han',[25] the film depicts the birth of a patriotic film theme song in 1935 that would eventually be adopted as the national anthem of the People's Republic of China.[26] Wu has renounced his earlier position on transcendent humanity. Instead, he embraces the ideology of nationalism and believes – in complete *consent* with the authorities – that 'some education in humiliation and hatred is still necessary for a nation that has suffered so much' in modern history.[27] 'I think that the gene of patriotism must reside in the thick blood of the Chinese people', he states in an interview, and 'I want to tell the audience that they must love their nation, or otherwise they would have no way to sustain their individual existence'.[28] Wu's passionate endorsement of nationalism thus places in ironic light 'the film-making motto' he reportedly wrote as a student at the Beijing Film Academy between 1978 and 1982: 'Don't be captive to any "ism" (*zhuyi*) or school (*liupai*).'[29]

Wu's radical change *from dissent to consent* in recent years appears rather embarrassing, if not alarming, even to seasoned critics. Chen Mo admits that he did not know where to start when confronted with the 'mercurial' nature of Wu's films, but he certainly is not pleased with what *The National Anthem* does to its audience, who seem to be 'listening to an official speech' (*ting baogao*) while watching the film.[30] No traces of Wu's trademark images of dissent such as minimal plot and dialogue or ambivalent imageries and symbolism are to be found in *The National Anthem*, and even the slightest hint of sympathy for the Japanese would be outrageous in this state-sponsored 'leitmotif film' (*zhuxuanlü dianying*). Sure enough, *The National Anthem* was officially named one of the must-see films in the season celebrating the fiftieth anniversary of the People's Republic of China and went on to win several domestic awards.[31]

It should be pointed out that Wu's transition from dissent to consent was actually foreshadowed in his award speech at the 1989 Berlin Film Festival: 'If foreign enemies invade China, I would not hesitate to defend my nation. But if I had a chance to say something before death, I would say this: "I hate war!" '[32] This logic determines that Wu's obligation to the nation outweighs his pronounced hatred of wars. And since his hatred of wars was only conceived and represented at an abstract level, it is a small conceptual step for Wu to sublimate his hatred and consent to the mainstream ideology of nationalism, which thrives on a rigid definition of nation, race and ethnicity. In his next film, *National Hero Zheng Chenggong* (2000), Wu therefore conceives of two different kinds of war. First, the war between the Ming (the Han loyalists) and the Qing (under the Manchu rule) is one between compatriot 'brothers' and thus involves no bloodshed at all. Second, the war between the Chinese and the Dutch is the Chinese defence against foreign invasion, and it must be 'bloody and extremely violent'.[33]

The 'mainstream' (*zhuliu*), indeed, has become a magic word with which Chinese avant-garde filmmakers justify their transition from dissent to consent in the late 1990s. As Wu himself acknowledged in 2000, 'it was inevitable for the Fifth Generation directors to take the road many new directors in international film history had done before: to participate in and advance mainstream filmmaking'.[34] At the turn of the millennium, numerous younger directors, some labelled as 'the Sixth Generation', have also made the transitions to the mainstream.[35] Given this latest development in the cultural politics of contemporary Chinese cinema, when new alliances are forged between cinematic art, official ideology and transnational capitalism, it is of particular significance for us to ask the troubling question *Evening Bell* posed in the mid-1980s again: for whom does the bell toll?

NOTES

1. Zhang Xuan, the film's scriptwriter, compares this screening of *Evening Bell* to what André Bazin describes as the Columbia Pictures' preview of Orson Welles's *The Lady from Shanghai* in 1947 – an initially puzzling masterpiece. See Zhang Xuan, ed., *For Whom Does* Evening Bell *Toll?* (*Wanzhong wei Shui er Ming*) (Changsha: Hunan wenyi chubanshe, 1996), 73–76.

2. Quoted in ibid., 75–76.

3. Dai Jinhua, *Handbook on Film Theory and Criticism* (*Dianying lilun yu piping shouce*) (Beijing: Kexue jishu wenxian chubanshe, 1993), 44.

4. Dai Jinhua, for instance, argues that *King of the*

Children (Chen Kaige, 1987) marks a terminal point 'when the Fifth Generation dissolved': see Dai Jinhua, 'Invisible Women: Contemporary Chinese Cinema and Women's Film', *Positions*, 3, no. 1 (1995): 268.

5. Representative examples of such 'ethnographic films' include *Raise the Red Lantern* (Zhang Yimou, 1991) and *Red Firecracker, Green Firecracker* (He Ping, 1994). For more discussion, see Yingjin Zhang, *Screening China: Critical Interventions, Cinematic Reconfigurations, and the Transnational Imaginary in Contemporary Chinese Cinema* (Ann Arbor: Center for Chinese Studies Publications, University of Michigan, 2002), 220–239.

6. Wu thus distinguishes himself from many so-called 'Sixth Generation' directors such as He Yi, Wang Xiaoshuai and Zhang Yuan, who launched their careers with underground film-making.

7. For a discussion of the 'cultural' meaning of *Yellow Earth*, see Mary Ann Farquhar, 'The "Hidden" Gender in *Yellow Earth*', *Screen*, 33, no. 2 (1992): 154–164.

8. Zhang Xuan, *For Whom Does* Evening Bell *Toll?*, 74.

9. Ibid.

10. The term 'blood-thirsty king' comes from Jiang Hao; quoted in Chen Mo, 'An Honest Person's Quest – Reading Wu Ziniu's Films' ('Chizi de yixu – du Wu Ziniu dianying zhaji'), *Contemporary Cinema* (*Dangdai dianying*), no. 3 (2001): 54. The term 'assassin' comes from Bei Cun, who compares Zhang Yimou to an 'onlooker' and Chen Kaige to a 'lone meditator' in relation to Chinese psychological mechanisms and historical conceptions.

11. The paradigm of nationalism and heroism is still operational in *Garlands at the Foot of the Mountain* (Xie Jin, 1984). For more discussion of Chinese war films, see Yingjin Zhang, *Screening China*, 173–205.

12. Liu Weihong, 'An interview with Wu Ziniu' ('Yu Wu Ziniu tan Wu Ziniu'), *Contemporary Cinema* (*Dangdai Dianying*), no. 4 (1988): 112.

13. In the wake of the official ban on *The Dove Tree*, Wu was forced to publicly acknowledge his errors at a national meeting on film production in Beijing in April 1986 after a number of top film authorities had 'criticised and encouraged' him in person. See Zhang Xuan, *For Whom Does* Evening Bell *Toll?*, 290.

14. Ibid., 63.

15. Walter Benjamin, *Illuminations: Essays and Reflections*, ed. Hannah Arendt, trans. Harry Zohn (New York: Schocken, 1969), 256.

16. Ibid.

17. Zhang Xuan, *For Whom Does* Evening Bell *Toll?*, 74.

18. Additionally at the 1989 Golden Rooster Awards, *Evening Bell* won Best Cinematography, Best Actor and Best Supporting Actor, while *Joyous Heroes* won Best Actress. *Between Life and Death* also won the 'Government Award for Chinese Films' and Best Supporting Actor at the Hundred Flowers Awards (*Baihua jiang*) in 1989.

19. Yu Min, 'Judging Right or Wrong First, then Evaluating Beauty and Ugliness' ('Bian shifei er houlun meichou'), *Film Art* (*Dianying yishu*), no. 5 (1999): 72.

20. Ibid., 68-71.

21. Chen Mo, 'An Honest Person's Quest', 54.

22. Ibid.

23. Ibid.

24. Zhang Xuan, *For Whom Does* Evening Bell *Toll?*, 109.

25. Wu Ziniu, 'My Original Intentions of Shooting *The National Anthem*' ('Pai Guoge de chuzhong'), *Contemporary Cinema* (*Dangdai dianying*), no. 5 (1999): 5.

26. The theme song, 'March of the Volunteers' ('Yiyongjun jinxin qu'), was written by Tian Han and composed by Nie Er for *Children of Troubled Time* (Xu Xingzhi, 1935). Tian Han was then an underground Communist and a leading leftist writer in Shanghai.

27. Wu Ziniu, 'My Original Intentions', 5.

28. Wu Ziniu, 'A Passionate Eulogy of the National Anthem' ('Jiqing benyong song guoge'), *Film Art* (*Dianying yishu*), no. 5 (1999): 6.

29. Jia Leilei, 'Wu Ziniu's Film World' ('Wu Ziniu de dianying shijie'), *Contemporary Cinema* (*Dangdai dianying*), no. 3 (2001): 66.

30. Chen Mo, 'An Honest Person's Quest', 54, 61.

31. *The National Anthem* won Outstanding Film and Outstanding Director at the state-sponsored *Huabiao* Awards, Best Film at the Hundred Flowers Awards and second place for outstanding screenplays at the Xia Yan Prizes for Film Literature.

32. Zhang Xuan, *For Whom Does* Evening Bell *Toll?*, 80.

33. See Jia Leilei, 'The Heart of Film – an Interview with Wu Ziniu' ('Dianying de xin – Wu Ziniu fangtan lu'), *Contemporary Cinema* (*Dangdai dianying*), no. 3 (2001): 51.

34. Ibid., 50.

35. For a critique of the recent vogue of the mainstream film, see Yingjin Zhang, *Screening China*, 324–331.

11   *Farewell My Concubine*: National Myth and City Memories

Yomi Braester

The dazzling images and sweeping narrative of Chen Kaige's *Farewell My Concubine* (1993) might blind the viewer to the more intimate associations of the film's locations and themes. The director insists, however, that the film is 'not an epic … It's a personal story about a few individuals.'[1] By paying homage to Chen's native Beijing and to Beijing opera, *Farewell* engages in personal memories, contrapuntal and even conflicting with collective memory. I argue here that the film shows how memories are fetishised and re-articulated through intimate objects, bodily scars and perhaps most importantly urban spaces, all of which resist the myths of the Chinese nation-state.

My essay challenges the existing critical response, which has mostly accused the film of presenting a patronising national allegory. Together with Zhang Yimou's *Raise the Red Lantern* (1991), *Farewell* marked a turning point in so-called 'Fifth Generation' movies. Critics had hailed earlier films by the new directors, which presented alternative models of nationhood. A shift away from the focus on rural themes – notably in Chen's own *Yellow Earth* (1984) and *King of the Children* (1987) – to epic plots coincided with a novel reliance on foreign investment. In this context, *Farewell* was deplored as backsliding to an emphasis on national narratives and to the dominant culture represented by Beijing opera, and as catering to an Orientalising overseas audience's taste for the exotic.[2] Hong Kong critic Yar See, punning on the film's title – literally 'hegemon king bids farewell to his concubine' – alluded to the domineering position of PRC culture and called the movie 'hegemonic cinema' (*bawang dianying*).[3]

Yet such criticism does not fully take into account the politics of memory in Chinese cinema. Since the establishment of the People's Republic, the government has used specific public spaces to forge a collective national identity. Even these places, however, have often been re-appropriated for contending meanings, and urban locations have largely resisted national myths. *Farewell* uses political changes as a backdrop for the story of a locale whose inhabitants strive to retain an identity free from the state's ideological manipulations. As such, Chen's film foreshadows the 'Sixth Generation' film-makers' use of urban settings as spaces of personal memory.

The tension between these different uses of memory is exemplified by the two sequences that open *Farewell*. In the first, presented before the credits, two Beijing opera actors walk onto the floor of a dark sports hall. The attendant recognises them: 'Oh, it's you two! … It's been over twenty years since you performed together, hasn't it?' One actor answers, 'twenty-one', and the other rebukes him, 'twenty-two!' The scene introduces some of the film's major themes – the failure of recognition, the fickleness of memory, the use of recollection as a stake in personal grievances and the staging of these issues in theatrical spectacles. The scene also links personal memories to larger historical narratives, foreshadowing the film's epic span of fifty-three years, marked by key political events. The next sequence, immediately following the credits, transports the viewer to another place and time. A transition to black-and-white photography cues spectators that the scene takes place in the more distant past, and an intertitle identifies the place and time as 'Beijing, 1924: The Warlord Era'. A woman makes her way through food and porcelain stalls, itinerant vendors of toys and musical instruments, and advertisers of foreign tobacco. The crowded alleys can be recognised as Tianqiao district, which lies to the west of the Temple of Heaven in Beijing's southern, lower-class quarters. This carnivalesque space presents the underbelly of respectable performance.

The two opening sequences – the last and first, respectively, in the story of the two opera actors –

frame the epic and foreground the film's main symbols. The two scenes are, however, also very different in tone and may stand for two diverging ways of reading the film. The first sequence places the operatic spectacle and the gender roles played by the two actors in the context of larger political changes. The second shows the street savvy of the child apprentices and the power struggles among local groups in the dusty alleys of old Beijing. Critical discussion of *Farewell* has largely targeted the more heavily ideological issues, and in particular the construction of national history and the performance of queer desire, at times mentioned in the same breath.[4] Yet the actors' hesitant and contradictory answers in the pre-credits sequence cast doubt on the validity of translating personal experience to the national level. In response to the attendant's statement that their troubles are all due to the Gang of Four, leaders of the Cultural Revolution, the actors concede in a hollow voice and without conviction. One should notice the director's choice to frame the film as a story about personal memories of old Beijing. The detailed representation of the Tianqiao stalls, vendors and performers indicates the importance of the

film's location in Chen Kaige's native city. Through references to urban landmarks and earlier cinematic representations of Beijing, *Farewell* offsets the national narrative with a focus on the intimate spaces of the city and their past. The references to Beijing locales present a parallel plot-line that mitigates the melodrama and the national historical narrative.

Farewell's myth-making has overshadowed Chen's use of cinema as a facilitator of personal memory. *Farewell* commemorates old Beijing, makes urban spaces into places of post-traumatic recall, and works through the director's unresolved memories of growing up in the capital during the Cultural Revolution. *Farewell* offers not only a grand national epic but also intimate urban vignettes, amounting to a statement about the interaction between personal and collective memory and on the importance of film for reclaiming otherwise lost experience.

BEIJING'S ARCHITECTURAL SYMBOLISM

Farewell does not offer grand vistas of Beijing, nor does it show many recognisable landmarks. Indeed,

Farewell My Concubine: Leslie Cheung as Cheng Dieyi

the film is shot mostly on sets or in enclosed court-yards and opera houses, and is sprinkled with occasional glimpses of an old alley or an ancient wall. Yet it is precisely by turning inward, to the more inti-mate architectural spaces typical of Beijing, that *Farewell* captures the experience of the lived-in city. Rather than reproduce camera-ready images of touristy sites, Chen's film re-creates the practices that have defined local identity. At the heart of the film, visually and thematically, is the *siheyuan*, a rectangu-lar courtyard surrounded by one-storey tile-roofed houses, typical of Beijing's residential architecture since the thirteenth century. The opera school where the two opera actors meet is made of three court-yards strung together; when the actors move out, they settle in private courtyards. Images of the court-yards are complemented by typical Beijing sounds, from the tell-tale accent to street peddlers' cries and pigeon whistles.[5]

Even though the film presents also extravagant operatic and political spectacles, Chen gives as much attention to aspects of everyday life in Beijing's alleys. *Farewell* follows earlier filmic depictions of Beijing's southern quarters, notably *My Memories of Old Bei-jing* (1982), which shows unabashed nostalgia for the city's layout and customs before its transformation since 1949. Like the cameraman for *My Memories*, the cinematographer for *Farewell*, Gu Changwei, has been careful to block out views of the rapidly mod-ernising metropolis. The resulting eye-level photog-raphy of the enclosed alleys and courtyards adds to an intimate and sometimes claustrophobic atmos-phere.

The visual and auditory clues not only help locate the plot but also motivate the story-line. A case in point is the architectural symbolism that stresses the theme of the overlap between operatic spectacle and political struggles. The film tells the story of two Beijing opera apprentices, Douzi and Shitou, who grow up to become famous actors under the names Cheng Dieyi (played by Leslie Cheung) and Duan Xiaolou (Zhang Fengyi). The friendship between the two is marred by Dieyi's undeclared attraction to Xiaolou and jealousy of his wife, Juxian (Gong Li). The two protagonists' schooling extends to using their acting skills off stage, whether to confront gangsters in a brothel or procure the favours of pol-itically connected patrons. The intimate theatrical spaces protect the two protagonists, even as the opera

hall hosts political rallies and riots. On one occasion, a rehearsal in the school courtyard turns into a cruel display, when Shitou forces a pipe into Douzi's mouth as ostensive punishment. Despite the brutal-ity, the episode further strengthens the bond between the two actors. Later the two grown-up actors return to the same courtyard to enact another punishment upon each other, in a scene that stresses the ties between the actors and their teacher, to the point of excluding Juxian, an outsider to the courtyard.

The symbolism of the courtyards as private spaces, seemingly impenetrable to outside regulation, is made clear when the plot turns to the Cultural Revolution. After the establishment of the PRC in 1949, Dieyi's adopted son, Xiaosi'r, refuses to take part in the operatic tradition. He gives up his train-ing, resists his adoptive father's discipline and denounces him before leaving for good. A pivotal scene takes place in Dieyi's residential courtyard, where the established opera singer uses against Xiaosi'r the same punishments that had been inflicted upon him. The younger man, however, rebels; instead of letting Dieyi flog him, Xiaosi'r leaves for the 'new society' and joins the revolution-ary masses. Xiaosi'r's betrayal of his adoptive father is coded also in spatial terms by his departure from the courtyard, in a shot-reverse shot sequence that places Dieyi in the middle of the *siheyuan* and Xiaosi'r behind the screen that blocks the line of vision from the street. The courtyard and the street stand for two separate viewpoints.

When the conflicts are no longer contained within the private courtyards and erupt in public spaces, the protagonists face their undoing. The spec-tacles of the Cultural Revolution spill into the streets. Dieyi and Xiaolou are dragged into a 'struggle session'. Unlike previous personal and political con-flicts, the scene takes place in an open space, large enough to contain a big crowd. The actors are made to wear opera costumes and make-up that mocks their profession. The protagonists' stage skills do not help them this time. In fact, they are drawn into making mutually incriminating accusations. Without the protective traditional architecture around them, they are reduced to complicity in the cruel spectacle staged by the state. The difference between the small Beijing courtyards and the large, barren public square foregrounds the distinction between personal and collective narratives.

FACING PERSONAL MEMORY

By Chen Kaige's own testimony, the film allows the director to return to Beijing's intimate spaces and come to terms with his experience of growing up in the city. In particular, the director associates the city's spaces with his parents' home and with his betrayal of his father. In a recent autobiographical account, Chen expresses his desire to return to live in a *siheyuan* like the one in which he grew up and laments the recent gentrification of old courtyards, which have become status symbols for new entrepreneurs. Chen also tells about his interest from childhood in the capital's history. He associates Beijing opera with his memories and wonders 'whether Beijing opera has impacted Beijing people or Beijing people influenced Beijing opera'. Chen also identifies specific Beijing locations used in the film, in particular a fortress in Xiangshan, in the capital's north-west suburbs. 'When shooting *Farewell* I felt an unknown force taking hold of me,' he recalls. 'I believe that I put into the film all my understanding of Beijing and all that old Beijing left in me. After the shoot, I dreamed that Leslie Cheung as Cheng Dieyi was bidding me farewell; I wept in my dream.'[6]

Farewell may thus be seen as Chen's farewell to the city of his childhood. I do not suggest reading the film as an autobiography in disguise. Yet Chen admits that he used film-making to reflect upon his relation with his father, Chen Huaikai, who was a celebrated film-maker in his own right. The son grew up among the Beijing film establishment until he was sent down to the countryside together with many youths of his generation during the Cultural Revolution. Upon his return to Beijing and graduation from the Film Academy in 1982, Chen Kaige directed four films reflecting his experience as a sent-down youth and as a People's Liberation Army soldier, and then turned to *Farewell*, in which he pays tribute to his birthplace.

Chen's experience in the period from 1966 to 1978 is of major importance to his subsequent career and stands at the centre of his autobiography.[7] Chen tells how as a Red Guard he denounced his father, who had been associated with the KMT Nationalist pre-1949 regime, and how he has lived with the ensuing guilt ever since. *Farewell*, which starts with a reference to the Gang of Four and depicts a son's betrayal of his adoptive parents only to be exposed as their successor, is Chen's closest brush with his guilt-ridden past. It is apt that the movie should pay homage to film-makers of his father's generation, both in showing the torture to which stage professionals were subjected during the Cultural Revolution and in alluding to the locales they had frequented and portrayed in their films.

Many have commented on the formative importance of the Cultural Revolution for Chen and his peers. Critic Dai Jinhua notes that the Cultural Revolution may be viewed as a collective patricide – the fathers, formerly regarded as 'valiant hero[es] of revolutionary historical myth', were denounced and victimised by their children.[8] Sheldon Lu draws attention to the obsessive interest in child–parent relations in Fifth Generation films. This concern informs *Farewell*'s focus on the rapport between the two opera actors and their master on the one hand and their adopted disciple, Xiaosi'r, on the other.[9] The director would continue to try to come to terms with his past in *The Emperor and the Assassin* (1998).[10] Chen is explicit about the relation between film-making and his family history in his comments on the later film. Chen plays the court historian Lü Buwei, who according to the fictional script is the Emperor's unacknowledged father. Explains the director:

> One reason I wanted to play this part is that I wanted to pay respect to my father …. [During the Cultural Revolution] I was asked by the revolutionaries to denounce my father. I did that, and it did huge harm to my father and my family. He was deeply hurt by what I did to him …. What I learned from my father was the word 'forgiveness' …. I was sent to the countryside, and my father came to the train station to see me off …. Then I realised how much he loved me, despite the terrible things that I had done to him. This is [similar to] the situation between the prime minister and the emperor.[11]

The mature Chen Kaige takes over the role of the forgiving and self-sacrificing parent to re-enact his father's actions during the Cultural Revolution. Acting the role becomes Chen's belated atonement, repaying his father by forcing himself into a position of identifying with the father's pain.

Chen draws attention to the scene in *Emperor* in which the son is confronted with the choice to either implicitly acknowledge his illegitimate provenance and imperil his legitimacy as Emperor or kill his father. Comments Chen: 'That's when I understood my father better and better … I had tears in my eyes … I can't forgive myself … I did it because I was selfish.' The younger Chen's conflicting emotions are transferred to the Emperor, who cannot bring himself to kill his father but is nevertheless relieved by the latter's subsequent suicide and then denounces him as a traitor.

While the director has not made similar remarks to explicitly link *Farewell* to his personal memories, the plot alludes to the problem of facing the past. Both *Emperor* and *Farewell* contrast two men who deal with their memories in diverging ways. In the later film, the Emperor is motivated by his pledge never to forget his plan to unify the empire; he faces an assassin brought to inaction by the memories of his own past conduct. The final showdown between the two protagonists takes place on a bridge that literally floats up from the king's memory. In *Farewell*, Dieyi struggles to keep memories alive, while Xiaolou pays little attention to them. Their memories finally resurface during the Cultural Revolution, where their past is held against them and claims the life of Xiaolou's wife. In light of the director's comments on *Emperor*, one may better understand his interest not so much in Xiaosi'r (roughly his own age) as in that of Dieyi and Xiaolou (of his parents' generation). Inasmuch as the two protagonists' fate reflects Chen's view of the Cultural Revolution, it shows that the dynamics of mob persecution not only caused the victims to betray one another and themselves,[12] but also that the period's most devastating effect was the betrayal of memory itself, by remoulding recall of the past into a tool of torture.

BEIJING AS THE SPACE OF TRAUMA

In *Farewell*, Chen sets out to rescue memory from state ideology, such as the one that taints the recollections of the Mao-like emperor in *Emperor*. Many ways in which the film addresses memory lie outside the scope of this essay, yet one should notice that the plot foregrounds the existence of unresolved mental traumas by constant reference to unhealed scars. Douzi's road to success starts when his mother chops off a sixth finger on his right hand, and Shitou dresses the wound. Later, Shitou's forehead is bruised; Dieyi tenderly applies make-up to the scar before each performance. Their relationship is sealed in the film's last scene with another wound, as Dieyi slits his throat. The scene takes up the episode at the sports hall, presented in the film's beginning. Surprisingly, it is Xiaolou, usually resistant to nostalgia, who brings up the past and starts to recite an aria that re-establishes the bond between the two actors. Next, they play a routine from *Farewell My Concubine*, an opera piece that has earned them fame. At this moment, when the two return to the experiences that defined their relationship, Dieyi avails himself of Xiaolou's sword – also an object that evokes multiple memories – and commits suicide. Dieyi has consistently tried to remind Xiaolou of their common past, at times addressing Xiaolou by his childhood name. The film's last shot, in which Xiaolou relinquishes his dramatic persona as Hegemon King and calls Dieyi by his childhood name, denotes the return of memory, in the form of a freshly opened wound.

The reunion scene brackets the film and is key to understanding not only the role of reminiscence but also the specific kind of memory at stake and the importance of place. The significance of the scene can be glimpsed from comparing the filmed version to the description in the 1985 novel of the same name by Li Bihua (aka Lillian Lee). Chen and Li collaborated on the script, and following the film's success Li published a revised edition of the novel in 1993. Yet Li's novel retains scenes excised or modified in Chen's film. Two specific changes in the concluding scene stand out: the novel locates the actors' reunion in Hong Kong and Dieyi only feigns suicide. Dieyi derives satisfaction from Xiaolou's renewed recognition, then gets up, parts with his former stage partner and leaves for his home in the People's Republic.[13]

By placing the scene in Hong Kong, Li touches on questions never mentioned in the film. Hong Kong residents often regarded the British colony as a sanctuary of a Chinese culture, such as Beijing opera, vandalised in Maoist China. Xiaolou, now a resident of Hong Kong, worries about its freedom after the impending 1997 handover. The film, on the other hand, is set in Beijing from beginning to end. Anchoring the narrative in the capital of the People's Republic pre-empts a contending narrative based on Hong Kong identity. Moreover, the novel fashions the concluding scene as a relocation if not dislocation of memory, whereas the film emphasises the return to the original point of departure – Dieyi becomes Douzi again, in the city where the two actors grew up.

The semblance of return is of course illusory.

Reopening the wounds of memory on the floor of the empty hall stresses the failure of constructing a collective memory outside the landscape of old Beijing. The modern, barren sports hall draws attention to the urban restructuring projects that destroyed much of the old capital and left Beijing short of good opera stages at the end of the Cultural Revolution. The failure to reconstitute the spaces of memory is echoed also in Dieyi's self-immolation. His suicide, whether real or feigned, is the last of many dislocations of the operatic spectacle. Dieyi, who has consistently fetishised scars, reopens his old wounds, literally and irrevocably. Posthumously triggering Xiaolou's recognition, in an empty Beijing arena, is Dieyi's paradoxical and misplaced attempt to bring his memories back to life.

THE CINEMATIC MEMORY OF BEIJING

The thematic reference to belated recognition, reified memories and displaced recall goes hand in hand with the use of cinematic allusions that pay tribute to the old capital, its vanishing spaces and earlier films that have captured Beijing's image.

In the context of post-Cultural Revolution cinema, the casting alludes to Beijing's place in earlier fiction and films. Side by side with Gong Li and Leslie Cheung, most likely chosen for their international star power and appeal to Hong Kong investors, the cast includes some of the capital's better-known actors. Ge You, as Master Yuan, had often been typecast as a young Beijing hooligan, from *The Troubleshooters* (1988) to *Conned Once* (1992) and *After Separation* (1992). Of special note is Zhang Fengyi as Xiaolou. Although Zhang had attained some fame in Hong Kong by the time of shooting *Farewell*, he had risen to fame in films about the capital, from his debut in *My Memories of Old Beijing* and his successful lead role in *Camel Xiangzi* (1982) to *No Regrets About Youth* (1992). In his performances in *My Memories* and *Camel Xiangzi*, Zhang Fengyi took an active role in rehabilitating an image of Beijing that had been erased during the Cultural Revolution. *Camel Xiangzi* invokes also the memory of Lao She, the author whose novel provides the film's plot and whose works document 1930s Beijing. *No Regrets* (and *The Troubleshooters*) were among the earliest scripts inspired by Wang Shuo's vision of a new consumerist society in post-Mao Beijing. *Farewell* joins these pieces and can be considered among the earlier Chinese urban films after the Cultural Revolution. *Farewell* lacks the rough edge of Wang Shuo's plots and the documentary-like realism of later 'Sixth Generation' urban cinema. Yet in important ways, *Farewell* demonstrates an important link between the grand productions of Fifth Generation film-makers and the understated pieces usually associated with urban cinema.

Farewell not only pays homage to recent Beijing cinema but also alludes to earlier, largely forgotten films. Many have noted the precedent set by Xie Jin's *Stage Sisters* (1965). Set in the Republican period, the film depicts the life of two opera singers who are separated by their political views. Even though *Farewell* is indebted to *Stage Sisters*, Chen disregards the local opera variation in Xie Jin's film, which draws much of its vitality from representing the southern-style Shaoxing opera, with its unique costume, singing and staging. Yet *Stage Sisters* is itself homage to an earlier film, namely Zheng Xiaoqiu's *Opera Heroes* (1949). Despite its historical importance, *Opera Heroes* has largely been neglected by critics. The assistant director was Xie Jin, in his debut, and his *Stage Sisters* reworks themes present already in *Opera Heroes*. The earlier film describes the careers of two actors dedicated to the Communist cause. Yuan Wenguang drops out of high school to become an opera singer, under the stage name Yuan Shaolou, and teams up with female singer Liu Yanyun. Yuan is imprisoned by the Japanese, and Liu saves him at the price of her chastity. Liu drifts in and out of Yuan's life, but the latter becomes involved in political protest. Many of the political and social messages are conveyed by modifying existing opera plots. *Opera Heroes* paves the way for *Stage Sisters* and *Farewell* in foregrounding the political use of the stage.

Reading Chen's film may be informed not only by the similarities with Xie Jin's films but also by the dissimilarities. While the earlier pieces stress the positive propagandistic value of theatre, *Farewell* foregrounds the abuse of the stage for political means. As such, *Farewell* is clearly a product of post-Maoist ideology. Chen's film also differs in that it challenges Xie Jin's national epics by placing the plot in Beijing and depicting Beijing opera. The focus on Beijing opera, rather than invoking 'national essence', can also be seen as the director's tribute to his city and to his father – Chen junior mentions that his advisor on the history of Beijing opera was Chen Huaikai.[14] Counter to the logic that made some critics identify Beijing opera with the nation-state, it was the opera of the area around Shanghai that had become a symbol for revolutionary nationalism in earlier films. In fact, in the 1930s and 1940s – the period in which *Opera Heroes*, *Stage Sisters* and much of *Farewell* take place – the capital was moved away from Beijing, which was renamed Beiping. It was not until 1949 that Beijing became identified with the modern Chinese nation-state, and Chen's emphasis on Beijing should not be confused with reference to political hegemony.

Farewell acknowledges portrayals of Beiping also by re-using earlier cinematic form. *Opera Heroes* features teahouse shows typical of the capital and a sequence of Beijing opera training remarkably similar to the ones in *Farewell*. Like Zhang Shichuan's *Fate in Tears and Laughter* (1932), *Farewell* starts with establishing shots of Beijing at Qianmen and Tianqiao District. However, Chen's consistent focus on Beijing diverges from the earlier films – unlike *Farewell*, *Fate in Tears and Laughter* and *Opera Heroes* shuttle between Beiping and the south. In terms of the cultural rivalry between the Beijing and Shanghai styles, *Farewell* is a rare proponent of Beijing, and as such it promotes a local and decentralised identity no less than its southern equivalents. In the context of earlier cinematic treatments of Chinese opera, the film's relocation of the ending from Hong Kong to Beijing should not be mistaken for siding with nationalist hegemonic discourse.

In retrospect, *Farewell* signals the beginning of a shift of emphasis in non-government sponsored Chinese cinema away from a national grand narrative to the history of specific cities. It is easy to understand why the film's attempt to use Beijing symbolism to counter nationalist myth has been misread. Chen himself admits to the difficulty of parting with the myths of the People's Republic, which was established only three years before his birth: 'You have no way to disbelieve a rhetoric as old as you, of which you have become part, until you muster the bravery to deny yourself first.'[15] *Farewell My Concubine* turns to Beijing's local history to displace national myth. To reshape personal and collective memory in post-Maoist China, Chen Kaige reframes the political theatre within a filmic screen of personal memories.

NOTES

1. Jianying Zha, *China Pop: How Soap Operas, Tabloids, and Bestsellers Are Transforming a Culture* (New York: The New Press, 1995), 98.

2. See, for example, Jenny Kwok Wah Lau, ' "Farewell My Concubine": History, Melodrama, and Ideology in Contemporary Pan-Chinese Cinema', *Film Quarterly*, 49, no. 1 (1995): 16–27; Liao Binghui, 'Time and Space and Gender Disorder: On *Farewell My Concubine*' (*Shikong yu xingbie de cuoluan: Lun Bawang bieji*), *Zhongwai Wenxue*, 22, no. 1 (1993): 6–18; Lin Wenji, 'Drama, History, Life: National Identity in *Farewell My Concubine* and *The Puppetmaster*' (*Xi, lishi, rensheng:* Bawang bieji *yu* Ximeng rensheng *zhong de guozu rentong*), *Zhongwai wenxue*, 23, no. 1 (1994): 1139–1156.

3. Yar See, 'The Hegemon's Film' (*Bawang dianying*), *Sing Tao Evening News*, 11 December 1993, quoted in Lau.

4. See for example Benzi Zhang, 'Figures of Violence and Tropes of Homophobia: Reading *Farewell My Concubine* Between East and West', *Journal of Popular Culture*, 33, no. 2 (1999): 101–109.

5. For a description of Chen's childhood in Beijing's old quarters, see Ni Zhen, *Memoirs from the Beijing Film Academy: The Genesis of China's Fifth Generation Filmmakers*, trans. Chris Berry (Durham: Duke University Press, 2002), 13.

6. Chen Kaige, 'Sometimes Growing Up Takes Only an Instant' ('Zhangda youshi zhishi yishunjian de shi'), in *'The Fifth Generation' in the '90s* (*90 niandai de 'diwudai'*) (Beijing: Beijing Guangbo Xueyuan Chubanshe, 2000), 251–260.

7. All references are to the Hong Kong edition, entitled *The Dragon-Blood Tree* (*Longxieshu*) (Hong Kong: Cosmos, 1992). The book has also appeared under the title *Young Kaige* (*Shaonian Kaige*).

8. Dai Jinhua, 'Severed Bridge: The Art of the Sons' Generation', trans. Lisa Rofel and Hu Ying, in *Cinema and Desire: Feminist Marxism and Cultural Politics in the Work of Dai Jinhua*, ed. Jing Wang and Tani E. Barlow (London: Verso, 2002), 16.

9. Sheldon Hsiao-peng Lu, 'National Cinema, Cultural Critique, Transnational Capital: The Films of Zhang Yimou', in *Transnational Chinese Cinemas: Identity, Nationhood, Gender*, ed. Sheldon Hsiao-peng Lu (Honolulu: University of Hawaii Press, 1997), 105–136.

10. 'Director's Commentary', included in the DVD

edition of *The Emperor and the Assassin* (Culver City: Sony Pictures Classics, 2000).

11. Minor changes made to comport with standard English grammar and style.

12. In his autobiography as well as in the Director's Commentary to *The Emperor and the Assassin*, Chen describes in detail the dynamics of betrayal and self-betrayal, and attributes them to the fear of becoming an outcast and the need to remain part of the collective. See for example Chen Kaige, *The Dragon-Blood Tree*, 69.

13. Li Bihua, *Farewell My Concubine – New Edition* (*Bawang bieji – xin banben*) (Hong Kong: Tiandi tushu, 1993), 352.

14. Chen Kaige, *The Dragon-Blood Tree*, caption for photo on unnumbered page.

15. Ibid., 3.

12 *Floating Life*: Nostalgia for the Confucian Way in Suburban Sydney

Kam Louie

In an article discussing the 1998 Asian-American International Film Festival in New York, Somini Sengupta remarks that films such as Clara Law's *Floating Life* show the emergence of a new generation of Asian-Americans who have been raised on a diet of multiculturalism and who no longer accept stereotypes of Asians in American movies.[1] The films they produce 'are no longer just tales about the trauma of immigration to the United States, nor are they set in such archetypal Asian immigrant enclaves as San Francisco's Chinatown'.[2] By 'San Francisco's Chinatown', Sengupta is no doubt referring to the 'yellow peril' images so prevalent in Hollywood (and by extension Western) depictions of Asians throughout the twentieth century. These images are masterfully analysed in Gina Marchetti's seminal *Romance and the 'Yellow Peril'*, In her conclusion, Marchetti observes that even in the present time, 'Chinatown functions as pure style with neon dragons, pop songs, lion dances, and displays of martial artistry, forming a part of postmodern popular iconography'.[3]

Marchetti's observation can be substantiated by recent popular films about the Chinese in America. Even movies such as *First Strike* and *The Corruptor*,[4] though conveying a more favourable image of the Chinese, still contain the predictable Chinatown 'style' she mentions as a backdrop. This Chinatown motif may not to lead to a 'realistic' portrayal of Australian or American Chinese life, but it does generate rapport with audiences by harking back to the unmistakable stereotype of the sinister Chinaman so powerfully and consistently invoked in the fiction and cinema of Europe and America from the 1920s to the 1950s.[5] This representation of the Chinese was so ingrained in the culture of the West that Fredric Jameson cites Roman Polanski's 1974 film *Chinatown* as an example of a 'nostalgia film'.[6] It doesn't matter that despite the title Chinese people do not feature in this film: what matters is that it imitates a style, and it

is a style to which audiences could readily respond. Jameson believes that such films are not meant to present the past (or even the future) in its totality, but rather to reawaken the feel of an older period, whether or not that period is 'real'.

But if Sengupta is accurate in suggesting that the younger generation of film-makers who have grown up with multiculturalism no longer accept the Chinatown icon as an artefact to emulate, it is imperative that we ask questions about the ownership of memories. For example, if Polanski's *Chinatown* is a 'nostalgia film', one must ask 'whose nostalgia'? Certainly not that of the recent Chinese immigrants whose immersion in Hollywood Chinatown paraphernalia may not be sufficient for them to immediately recognise *Chinatown* as pastiche. Nonetheless, the new 'multicultural' films did not materialise out of thin air. They too imitate older materials, but these materials do not come just from Hollywood culture, but emanate from a range of disparate places and time zones. Thus, the younger generation of diaspora Chinese film-makers, including Chen Kaige and Ang Lee, appeal to a different set of iconographies and memories.[7] In *Floating Life*, the setting has moved away from 'Chinatown' into the suburbs, but the nostalgia it invokes draws from times and places that go back to a distant Chinese tradition.

Using *Floating Life* as a case study, I will demonstrate that while it does not pretend to imitate earlier classical Hollywood styles in regard to the 'Chinese' and the iconography thus seems unfamiliar in that context, the movie is nevertheless a type of 'nostalgia film'. The nostalgia that is invoked, however, goes beyond classic Hollywood or even kung fu movies. It harks back to a patriarchal Chinese tradition, as manifested in filial piety and familial propriety, as a means of salvation. Rather than the sinister old Chinese (man), we now have the wise old Chinese (man). Thus, while Sengupta's observations about multiculturalism are accurate, they represent only a partial truth. Behind the assertiveness of the new breed of film-makers who are attempting to debunk the 'yellow peril' myth, another myth (in the sense of an enabling fiction) is emerging: that of the wise Confucian who will fix the chaos brought about by migration and materialist pursuits. Such a myth may be aimed at a different audience with different memories, but it is a myth nevertheless.

In her response to the question 'what will survive' in Chinese culture, Clara Law, the director and co-writer of *Floating Life*, provides the key to understanding the reason for the creation of the new mythology. She believes that what will survive are 'All those traditional beliefs – new Confucianism. The family thing – father and son and brothers and sisters.'[8] Clara Law is a keen observer of different cultural practices. She was born in Macau and moved to Hong Kong, where she attended university and worked in television before spending a few years in London for further study. After returning to Hong Kong, she made several award-winning features including *Temptation of a Monk* (1993), *Autumn Moon* (1992) and *Farewell China* (1990) before migrating to Australia, where she directed *Floating Life* in 1996. Law's family is also a transnational one. Originating from China via Macau and Hong Kong, members of her family have moved to different corners of the globe: a sister in Germany, and brothers, another sister and parents in Australia.[9] Her family's experiences mirror those of the Chan family in *Floating Life* and heighten the film's verisimilitude. The *Floating Life* family is as 'real' a contemporary family as that depicted in *American Beauty*.

The plot of the film is relatively simple. Ma and Pa Chan, with their two youngest sons, emigrate from Hong Kong to Australia, joining their second daughter Bing in her outer-Sydney suburban house. Meanwhile, the eldest daughter Yen, who lives in Germany with her husband, worries about her parents and goes to Australia to visit them. The family argue incessantly. The eldest son Gar Ming remains in Hong Kong and makes his Chinese-Canadian girlfriend pregnant. They opt for abortion and Gar Ming buries the foetus before joining his family in Australia. The parents move out with the boys and Bing has a nervous breakdown. The film finishes with Bing pregnant and reconciled with the family, and successful settlement in Australia seems assured.

The final scene has Yen's daughter in Germany narrating an idyllic future in which all of the family live under the one roof. From this brief summary, it is easy to see that the film consciously undertakes to raise and discuss issues of immigration and multiculturalism. As Tom O'Regan has pointed out, even the making of *Floating Life* is a direct result of the Australian government's adoption of multiculturalism as a national cultural policy in 1989.[10]

The focus of *Floating Life* is on life in Australia, and members of the Chan family apparently do not suffer from what Stephen Teo calls 'Hong Kong's China Syndrome'.[11] Teo coined this term to describe the anxieties and fears Hong Kong film-makers showed towards a China that they felt they had to identify with. This syndrome is manifested in films such as *Farewell China*, which was made a year after the Tiananmen Square incident and a few years before Hong Kong was due to be 'returned' to China. *Farewell China* is packed with all of the clichés associated with both the Chinatown Syndrome and Hong Kong's China Syndrome. The protagonist Nansheng and his wife Hong do everything possible to migrate to America. She even gets pregnant because she thinks her beauty prevents her from getting a visa. As Sheldon Lu observes, 'The film is an overt criticism of the Chinese Mainland itself, which has deprived its citizens of a home.'[12] Furthermore, the film is a standard 'traumatised migrant' movie in its unrelenting accounts of the horrors of life in America. Both Nansheng and Hong encounter nothing but betrayal, exploitation, violence and prostitution – all of the elements that one finds in old movies of the 'yellow peril' genre. In this film, Law clearly reverts to the 'Chinatown' formula, a formula totally absent in *Floating Life*.

Yet, the ideological underpinnings of both movies are prompted by a sense of longing for the familiar and, more importantly, the familial. Both movies are about problems associated with migration, but in *Floating Life*, instead of having members of the family separated by oceans, the majority (most importantly the parents) stay together. The message here is that peace and happiness can only be achieved when the parents are respected and there is harmony in the family. As Kathleen Murphy puts it, 'Law quietly cherishes, with Ozu clearly in her mind's eye, the kind of salvation – of body and spirit – generated by familial circuits, plugged securely into the past and the future.'[13] In the same way, as much as *Farewell China* is about the horrors of immigrant life in the West, it is also about the afflictions facing a splintered family. At his most despondent, Nansheng rings his parents in China and asks to go 'home', only to be told that he should stay in America for the sake of his own son. Without parental and familial support, both Nansheng and Hong disintegrate, with Hong becoming schizophrenic and ultimately suicidal. Bing can be seen as Hong's counterpart in *Floating Life*. Bing (meaning 'ice' in Chinese) is the second oldest sister who migrated alone to Australia, three years before her husband joins her (and seven years before her parents do). The isolation and lack of family support causes her to become depressed, melancholic and paranoid, and she imagines that all sorts of deadly dangers, such as savage dogs and biting insects, are lurking in the Australian suburbs. When the family joins her, she inflicts her phobias and draconian lifestyle on her younger brothers. More significantly, she reverses the traditional power hierarchy by attempting to dominate and tyrannise her parents as well, advising them that 'you are here as migrants, not to enjoy yourselves'.

Bing's atrabilious behaviour is, however, the only thing that is reminiscent of the stereotypical traumatised Chinese migrant – standard in other diaspora films such as *Farewell China*. Bing's suffering is not caused by evildoers in Chinatown. In fact, the only other Chinese she meets, the owner of the Chinese take-away food bar where she regularly eats, is portrayed as sympathetic to her obvious anxiety and loneliness. Her suffering is produced by self-induced paranoia about the dangers presented by the new environment of Australia, ranging from natural phenomena such as the ozone layer to exaggerated imagined disasters such as cancers from passive inhalation of cigarette smoke. These fears are based on a systematic 'misreading of signs' produced by the crisis she is plunged into by years of enforced separation from her husband and parents.[14] Bing cannot survive alone. Her phobias may be based on misreadings, but her terror of living in the apparently empty and soulless suburbs is genuine enough. Without the family, she is incapable of forming any meaningful human relationships, rejecting both the friendly overtures of her colleagues and the Chinese take-away food bar owner. Without familial support, she reads all normal social signs and human signals as threats.

The tragedy of the Bing character is not explicable simply by reference to the migrant experience. The film offers intimations of another, more fundamental, explanation. Her forced self-reliance in the first few years in Australia causes her to become more and more unforgiving, both towards others and towards herself, and she adopts an increasingly masculine and 'tough' identity. Thus, in the episode where she tells her story, the first shot of her shows a terrified young woman, in a flimsy nightdress and cowering on a table, yelling into the phone to her husband that she cannot cope with having a rodent in the house. Progressively, however, her manner and attire become more masculine, and she wears a man's suit and has a short haircut. Her whole demeanour becomes more precise and hard. This masculine exterior and her subsequent illness resonate strongly with female figures in Chinese tradition who transgress gender roles. Empress Wu in *Flowers in the Mirror* (*Jing hua yuan*) and Wang Xifeng in *Dream of Red Mansions* (*Honglou meng*) are classic examples. These women either do not have husbands or have weak husbands who let them dominate family matters. Their tyrannical rule is seen as reversing the 'natural order' of things. As a consequence, the family declines and/or the nation disintegrates. Often, the women are punished with death or by gynaecological or mental illnesses presumed to be peculiar to females. In *Floating Life*, Bing suffers from melancholia and hysteria. Her salvation only comes when she reverts to a feminine role. Thus, by the end of the film, she becomes a proper wife and, contrary to her adamant insistence earlier that she would never have a child, becomes pregnant, thus ensuring a more 'natural' family.

This transformation results directly from prayer to the ancestors. The practice of ancestor worship is mentioned several times in the film. Pa and Ma Chan are prevented from burning incense to the ancestral spirits when they live with Bing for fear that it could spark a house fire. When Bing has a nervous breakdown, Ma sets up the ancestors' altar in Bing's house and proceeds to implore the ancestral spirits to come to Australia and bring Bing back to health. This is perhaps the most touching and poignant scene in the film. Many in the audience would no doubt empathise when Ma asks tearfully why, with the whole family now united in Australia,

Floating Life: Gar Ming and his
girlfriend contemplate her pregnancy.

a paradise on earth, they cannot find any joy, and why the family cannot plant roots in this new soil. Unbeknown to Ma, Bing is sitting on the stairs listening to all this, and despite her hitherto adamant opposition to all things Chinese, she is moved to tears. The 'ice' finally melts. As the camera zooms in on the tears of Ma and then Bing, it would indeed be hard to imagine a viewer who is not also rendered moist-eyed by the scene. Thus, the matriarch's heartfelt invocation to the ancestors invites not only Bing, but also the audience to be complicit in adopting traditional family values as part of personal salvation. In his discussion of Wong Kar-wai's *Fallen Angels* (1995) and *Floating Life*, Dominic Pettman concludes that even though neither movie is a horror film as such, they do illustrate the gothic in times of displacement, where, using Homi Bhabha's words, 'the borders between home and world become confused' but where 're-establishing contact with dead kin serves to confirm the new portability of the past'.[15] By exhorting the dead kin, Ma thus re-enacts a vital function played by matriarchs in traditional China: to worship and honour the (patriarchal) family line and to ensure that it is continued.

The continuity of the family line also means that having a nuclear family is not sufficient for contentment. Thus, Bing's sister Yen is married to a decent German and has a lovely daughter, but is plagued by psychological problems (though not as severe as Bing's). She tries to explain her psychosomatic itches and pains through traditional Chinese philosophy and folk practices such as geomancy. She appears to be the direct opposite to Bing, who disavows Chinese traditions altogether. For example, whereas Bing forces the younger sibling to speak English, Yen

makes her daughter speak Cantonese, on the grounds that she should know Chinese. However, even though the house in Germany is very comfortable and Yen seems happily married, painting and redecorating with her German husband and nurturing a child who is bilingual, something is amiss. The house falls short of being a home. By talking constantly about *feng shui*, she is unable to make her white husband understand what is bothering her. In the end, Yen astutely verbalises the fact that she misses her parents and feels guilty about not being with them. She and her half-German daughter visit them in Australia, where she also clashes with Bing.

Meanwhile, left on his own in Hong Kong, the oldest brother Gar Ming is also depressed and unsettled. After aborting the foetus of his Canadian-Chinese girlfriend who is holidaying in Hong Kong, he is wracked by guilt and remorse. By neglecting his duty as a father, he has disrupted the continuity of the family line, if only temporarily. The feeling of unfulfilled obligation is highlighted in the foetus burial scene where he speaks a Hamlet-like soliloquy about life and death. This philosophising on the transience of life is repeated when he has to relocate his ancestors' bones because of lack of space in Hong Kong. The gravedigger's comment that in China there is so little space that people have to be cremated again reflects the 'Hong Kong China Syndrome' so forcefully revealed in *Farewell China*. Gar Ming is at a difficult age, and his moodiness can be attributed to the distress resulting from aborting his 'child' and being away from his parents rather than to the traumas of migration. Certainly, immigration seems to affect him less than his sisters.

The two younger brothers, who are left to explore their sexuality and new environment in Sydney with fewer restrictions than the older members of the family, are the least traumatised. Although they rarely speak in their 'mother tongue', they have not been separated from their parents. Thus, even though their memories will contain elements common to all new arrivals, they yearn for assimilation in Australia, and not for things found in China or Chinatown. All indications are that they will be acclimatised quickly. While the lives of the boys are 'floating', they are less prone to be frightened of the imagined paranormal found outside China. They certainly do not seem to need to appeal to the 'spiritual' as much as the women – a point highlighted in their beach conversation about women and sex, in which they consciously mock 'the spiritual'.

In keeping with the traditional notion that men are rational while women are emotional, the patriarch, Pa, acts as the voice of reason and wisdom. As Clara Law herself remarks, when the family disintegrates, 'the central moral force of the father pulls them together again'.[16] While he does not speak often, silently moving in the background and comforting Ma when necessary, what he says is mostly sensible and moderate. Pa's strong sense of his own being is not shared by anyone else in the film. He and Ma are presumably the only members of the family who have not grown up in Hong Kong or abroad. And they can still recall the 'real China'. This self-identity is very different from all of the young people in Law's other films such as *Autumn Moon* and *Farewell China*, who seem to be perpetually alienated. Pa is the only one in the film who appreciates and treasures Chinese tradition. This is illustrated by two recurrent motifs in the film: tea and houses. Right at the beginning of the movie when he is still in Hong Kong, Pa shows his profound knowledge of Dragon Well tea. The nostalgia for fine tea (and by extension Chinese tradition)[17] is shared here with an old friend, who is waiting to go to Canada. Tea is the symbol of the best from the Chinese past for these old friends cut adrift by a China that no longer appreciates tradition. In Australia, Pa is presented with a packet of Pu Erh tea by another old friend who has come to visit. This takes place in the episode titled 'A House in China', and these old friends reminisce about the days before they and their peers moved to Hong Kong in 1949 and then dispersed overseas. This is the only scene in which Pa talks at length, expounding his views on life. Unlike other members of his family, his nostalgia for the past takes on a concrete form.

In the discussion with his friend, Pa gets nostalgic over the houses in China, commenting that they are old but radiate 'harmony and strength'. He remembers his house with a lotus pond at the back. The peace and tranquillity of that existence were only disrupted by the advent of the Communists. The nostalgia for the past in China is even more poignant at the end of the movie when Pa fantasises about a house in the Australian suburbs where they will grow tea in the backyard. In his mind, he pictures a 'big house' where he offers his three sons space to build their own houses so that all the (male) members of the family can live in one place (a notion politely scoffed at by his sons). He muses that it is important to have water as Australia is too dry, a statement confirmed in the film by the harsh lighting of the Sydney scenes. This makes a lotus pond in the backyard necessary. It is by such careful planning and cultivation that tea can grow. Thus, Pa actively plans to re-create the ancestral home in the foreign land. His blueprint for a pond and growing tea stands as a potent metaphor for the continuation of Chinese tradition in Australia.

Pa's emotional stability and wisdom are not accidental, but are based on a faith in the goodness and durability of the Confucian tradition. His visions of a Chinese pond and tea growing in his Australian backyard display a willingness to sever ties with the geographical China and establish a new China in the West. He is an excellent example of the new breed of Chinese migrants whose wish is '*luodi shenggen*', or 'the planting of permanent roots in the soils of different countries', a phrase uttered by Ma in a lament before the ancestral tablet. This sentiment is quite new. In the old days, Chinese who went abroad saw themselves as sojourners who would one day return to China, or powerless minorities who would need to eliminate their cultural heritage and assimilate. Both views, as Wang Ling-chi argues, 'can now be characterised as chauvinistic, regressive and approaching the anachronistic. The *luodi-shenggen* approach rejects the extreme position of both and views the Chinese minority to be an integral part of each country's citizenry.'[18]

The Chan family's tribulations and eventual success in establishing a Chinese home in Australia thus reflect a general tendency in interpretations of the fate of Chinese overseas. Bing's attempt to completely assimilate is shown to be woefully misguided. On the other hand, there is never any doubt that the family wants to settle in Australia, and even the ancestral spirits are invited to join them. No doubt, the 'Hong Kong China Syndrome' has helped in this recent phenomenon. What is most fascinating about this trend is that at a time when China is becoming less rigidly Communist, the number of Chinese who have chosen to sink their roots in foreign lands have dramatically increased. More ironic is the fact that many of the Chinese who now live outside the China mainland believe that the centre of Chinese culture no longer resides in China but among the Chinese diaspora. Such a thesis is put most succinctly and influentially by Tu Wei-ming in 'Cultural China: The Periphery as the Center'.[19] This essay reflects a world-wide trend to revive traditional Chinese culture, with Confucianism as its core.[20] While the New Neo-Confucianists are understandably eager to cash in on the economic prosperity in East Asia and to argue that Confucianism should be treasured, there is something incongruous about the claim that the practitioners of 'real' Chinese culture live not inside China, but abroad.

In *Floating Life*, the incongruity of this claim is illustrated in the title itself. The term 'floating life' was used by Zhuangzi some two thousand years ago in his statement that 'his life seems to float'[21] (*qi sheng ruo fu*). This idea is repeated throughout Chinese history, and one of the best-known expressions of it is in the 1809 autobiographical *Six Records of a Floating Life* (*Fusheng liuji*).[22] Despite the feelings of transience invoked in these works, there is no question that authors like Zhuangzi and Shen Fu were very sure of their positions in life, one being a Daoist and one a Confucian. Both assert that life 'floats', but both were firmly entrenched in Chinese culture. However, the case of Pa and Ma Chan, and all those who attempt to rebuild Chinese traditions in other lands, is completely different. As new migrants in a strange land, their sense of 'floating' is more a result of culture shock than existential angst. Being out of context, they must choose the right elements from their cultural heritage – ones that will suit their new lands. These migrants look with nostalgia to a past 'floating life', but the rit-

uals and sentiments associated with that nostalgia are as disjointed and fuzzy as the 'yellow peril' or 'Chinatown' symbols in Hollywood cinema.

Clara Law has avoided the favourite Hollywood (and Hong Kong's China Syndrome) images and metaphors in *Floating Life*. In the process, however, another form of nostalgia is called upon. The result is a schizophrenic film that tries to be didactic and entertaining at the same time, two aims that do not always gel. The moving deeds of the Chan family often turn into farcical antics, and scenes that are meant to be tragic or heroic often degenerate into melodrama. The line between these contrasts is not always clear, and the audience is required to exercise tremendous good will so that serious drama is not interpreted as parody. For example, Bing's dire warnings of the dangers present in daily Australian life have the family cowed. In their first outing, they are dressed ridiculously in order to prevent skin cancer and eye damage. A small dog barks at them and the family scatters. This is a humorous scene, and those who are frightened are Ma and the boys, the weaker sex and the children. Pa remains, and he alone comes across a kangaroo. Pa adopts a kung fu posture, ready to combat this wild animal. The kangaroo hops away and Pa 'wins' the battle over the supposedly deadly Australian fauna.

The audience can simply treat this scene as an attempt at humour and have a laugh. However, its comical nature highlights the difficulties of the 'cultural China in the periphery' thesis. We can read this episode as an amusing expression of the migrant experience, or we can see it as an old man's triumph over nature by using traditional martial arts. But in either case, we are left with an uneasy chuckle at seeing an inappropriately attired 'foreigner' in a sunny Sydney suburb acting out a misplaced nostalgia. Pa's kung fu posturing is simply incongruous here. While incongruity may generate humour, it also reveals the ludicrousness of the proposition that Confucianism may be superfluous in contemporary China, but should be lionised in the West. The Chinese people, even those living abroad, may need to 'inherit' aspects of Chinese tradition,[23] but if Confucianism is prescribed as an antidote for the 'yellow peril' and 'Chinatown' nostalgia that still plague the silver screen, what emerges is unlikely to provide anything that could anchor the 'floating lives'.

NOTES

1. Interestingly, *Floating Life* was made in Australia and not America – Law has lived for extended periods of time in Europe and Australia, but not in America. Her honorary status as a member of this new young generation illustrates the assumption that anything Western must be American.

2. Somini Sengupta, 'Asian-American Films Speak a New Language of Multicultural Variety', *Migration World Magazine*, 26, nos 1–2 (1998): 40.

3. Gina Marchetti, *Romance and the 'Yellow Peril': Race, Sex, and Discursive Strategies in Hollywood Fiction* (Berkeley: University of California Press, 1993), 203.

4. This is despite the fact that actors Jackie Chan and Chow Yun Fat have tried very hard to reverse the sinister villainous image traditionally accorded the Chinese. See my discussion in Kam Louie, *Theorising Chinese Masculinity: Society and Gender in China* (Cambridge: Cambridge University Press, 2002), 141–159.

5. The Chinese are not the only ones to suffer from this othering process. The Arabs probably fared worse. See Jack G. Shaheen, *Reel Bad Arabs: How Hollywood Vilifies a People* (New York: Olive Branch Press, 2001).

6. Fredric Jameson, 'Postmodernism and Consumer Society', in *The Anti-Aesthetic: Essays on Postmodern Culture*, ed. Hal Foster (Seattle: Bay Press, 1983), 116.

7. See my discussion of this phenomenon in Bob Hodge and Kam Louie, *The Politics of Chinese Language and Culture* (London: Routledge, 1998), 143–172.

8. Diana Giese, *Astronauts, Lost Souls and Dragons* (St Lucia: University of Queensland Press, 1997), 164.

9. See ibid., 110–112 and 204–207.

10. Tom O'Regan, *Australian National Cinema* (London: Routledge, 1996), 23.

11. Stephen Teo, *Hong Kong Cinema: The Extra Dimensions* (London: British Film Institute, 1997), 207.

12. Sheldon H. Lu, 'Filming Diaspora and Identity: Hong Kong and 1997', in *The Cinema of Hong Kong: History, Arts, Identity*, ed. Poshek Fu and David Desser (Cambridge: Cambridge University Press, 2000), 284.

13. Kathleen Murphy, 'Toronto (The 1996 Toronto Film Festival, Ontario)', *Film Comment*, 32, no. 6 (1996): 55.

14. Audrey Yue, 'Asian-Australian Cinema, Asian-Australian Modernity', in *Diaspora: Negotiating Asian-Australia*, ed. Helen Gilbert, Tseen Khoo and Jacqueline Lo (St Lucia: University of Queensland Press, 2000), 196.

15. Dominic Pettman, 'The Floating Life of Fallen Angels: Unsettled Communities in Hong Kong Cinema', *Postcolonial Studies*, 3, no. 1 (2000): 77–78.

16. Giese, *Astronauts*, 205.

17. See discussion in Lili Ma, 'Reconciliation between Generations and Cultures: Clara Law's Film *Floating Life*', in *Bastard Moon: Essays on Chinese-Australian Writing*, ed. Wenche Ommundsen, a Special Issue of *Otherland*, 7 (2001): 159–160.

18. Wang Ling-chi, 'On *Luodi-shenggen*', in *The Chinese Diaspora: Selected Essays*, vol. 1, ed. Wang Ling-chi and Wang Gungwu (Singapore: Times Academic Press, 1998), xi.

19. Tu Wei-ming, 'Cultural China: The Periphery as the Center', *Daedalus: Journal of the American Academy of Arts and Sciences*, 120, no. 2 (1991): 1–32.

20. See my discussion in Kam Louie, 'Sage, Teacher, Businessman: Confucius as a Model Male', in *Chinese Political Culture 1989–2000*, ed. Shiping Hua (Armonk: M. E. Sharpe, 2000), 21–41.

21. Liu Wendian, *Zhuangzi buzheng* (*Zhuangzi Explained*), vol. 1 (Kunming: Yunnan renmin chubanshe, 1980), 494.

22. Shen Fu, *Six Records of a Floating Life*, trans. Leonard Pratt and Chiang Su-hui (Harmondsworth: Penguin, 1983).

23. For the case of China, see my discussion in Kam Louie, *Inheriting Tradition: Interpretations of the Classical Philosophers in Communist China 1949–1966* (Oxford: Oxford University Press, 1986).

13 *Flowers of Shanghai*: Visualising Ellipses and (Colonial) Absence

Gang Gary Xu

Flowers of Shanghai (1998) is Hou Hsiao-hsien's fourteenth film. Based on the eponymous 1892 novel by Han Bangqing (1856–1894), it presents sensuous visual details of the inner space of the most elegant brothels in Shanghai's foreign concessions during the late nineteenth century. While fascinated again by Hou Hsiao-hsien's stylistic innovations, including the daring use of low-key lighting, low-contrast colour, the long take, and the fade-in and the fade-out, audiences and critics also raised questions about the drastic differences between *Flowers of Shanghai* and Hou's previous films, which were exclusively about Taiwan's culture and history: Why not Taiwan? Why colonial Shanghai one century ago? Why the adoption of Shanghai-dialect for most of the dialogue? To some, it seemed Hou Hsiao-hsien had gone too far in pursuit of individual style and artistic idiosyncrasy,[1] so much so that he had departed completely from his concern for his native land at conspicuous historical junctures.

Hou Hsiao-hsien answered some of these questions during an interview in Cannes. When asked why he chose to make a film on 'China' instead of 'Taiwan', he explained:

> On the one hand, the choice was random. I happened to come to like the novel *Flowers of Shanghai*, which I stumbled upon when preparing materials for another film. On the other hand, I felt that I was artistically mature enough to jump out of Taiwan and make something new.[2]

The pursuit of innovation in both theme and style seems to be the motivation behind Hou's daring attempt. However, on closer examination of the film and its production process, I find that he has neither 'jumped out of Taiwan' nor departed completely from his previous stylistic and thematic patterns. Stylisti-cally, Hou's camera is still slow moving, and his trademark long takes still dominate the entire film. Although fades are rare in Hou's previous films, in *Flowers of Shanghai* they are used in such a way as to enhance long-take continuity; the scene does not change after the fade-out and fade-in, which seems to function as if the camera were pausing to take a deep breath. Thematically, although 'Taiwan' is no longer relevant to the story of the film, its absence becomes present in *Flowers of Shanghai* because of Hou's increasing awareness of MIT – Made in Taiwan.

In fact, the entire film was shot in Taiwan for logistical and political reasons. Hou originally planned to shoot street scenes in Shanghai after finishing the interiors in a Taiwanese studio. His request to shoot was rejected by the mainland Chinese authorities, because the film's subject of 'prostitutes' indicated 'decadence'.[3] Therefore, Hou had to sacrifice all the outdoor scenes and build the indoor set from scratch. From the perspective of the local Taiwanese film industry, this forced choice nevertheless has had trailblazing significance. For the first time, as this film's screenwriter Zhu Tianwen exclaims, Taiwan was able to build and maintain a set for late imperial-period Chinese scenes. Antique furniture was carefully designed and hand-crafted by Vietnamese carpenters; clothes were hand-sewn in Beijing; jewellery, decoration, make-up and other props were purchased in Nanjing, Suzhou and Shanghai. All these were shipped back to and assembled in Hou's studio in Yangmei, thus establishing a new way of producing Chinese history films. 'Building files, maintaining reserves, and building up productivity'[4] are major contributions this film has made to Taiwan's independent film industry, which simultaneously resists and co-oper-ates with the increasing trend towards globalisation and syndication in film production.

The complete indoor enclosure of *Flowers of Shanghai* seems a drastic departure from Hou's famous panoramic representations of Taiwan's natural scenery and calm observations of characters from a distance, and it was forced upon him. However, the enclosure also better conveys Han Bangqing's original understanding of space under the colonial situation. On one hand, Han emphasises the importance of enclosure for the interactions between patrons and high-level prostitutes, who are exclusively Chinese. On the other hand, this stands in contrast to a complete absence of colonial authority in a colonial territory, so much so that the absence itself becomes questionable. The more enclosed the space of the brothels, the more fearfully unknown and vast the colonial territory. Without displaying colonial presence, Han's enclosed pleasure quarters thus paradoxically reveal the colonial presence in a more emphatic way, which may be termed a 'non-present presence'. Similarly, without referring to 'Taiwan', Hou's representation of Shanghai's brothels points to Taiwan's 'non-present presence' by touching upon the peculiar invisibility of Taiwan in a post-colonial setting. The 'MIT' assembly of sets from materials made outside Taiwan, for example, symbolises the difficulty and irony of establishing a 'Taiwanese' identity, which also had to be built from scratch using the 'imported materials' of the histories and identities of various ethnic groups including mainland immigrants after 1945 and 'local' Taiwanese, who were also immigrants in earlier times. For the different ethnic groups to co-exist peacefully under political and military pressure from mainland China, 'Taiwan' as a geographical and political entity must be upheld but also downplayed to the extent that it seemingly fades into the shadows of superpowers. In what follows, I will detail how Hou Hsiao-hsien masterfully visualises the 'non-present presence' originally rendered by Han Bangqing's narrative manoeuvres, and how Taiwan's invisibility becomes part of Hou's reflections upon film-making and his previous films.

The film begins with a drinking scene in a brothel. Facing the audience are Pearl (Carina Lau) and her primary patron Hong Shanqing (Luo Zaier), a merchant. To their left are Jasmine (Vicky Wei) and her patron Wang Liansheng (Tony Leung), a foreign-affairs official from Guangdong. To their right are some other patrons. During the carousal, Wang Liansheng remains silent. No sooner than he takes leave does the crowd turn to gossip about him:

Wang is said to be trapped in a triangular relationship with Crimson (Hada Michiko) and Jasmine. Since it is hard to catch all the names and events in this first glimpse of brothel life, the gossip may interest the audience less than its presentation – the entire scene is shot in an eight-minute long take. The slow action and the unusually long duration allow the audience to observe not only the mannerisms of the characters, but also the way the camera moves and *observes* the characters. Although the camera cannot appear in the scenes it shoots, in this long take it becomes like a character. It is alert – when hearing someone speak, it immediately turns in the direction of the sound; it remains at the same level as the characters' eyes, evidenced in the picture's lack of depth. The camera, in other words, forcibly asserts its 'non-present presence' through cinematographic manoeuvres from the very outset.

This prefatory scene is representative of the entire film, which is shot exclusively in long takes. The total number of forty shots is the lowest of all Hou Hsiao-hsien's films. But this does not necessarily signify a drastic change. As Shen Xiaoyin points out, lengthening each take and decreasing the total number of shots has been a consistent tendency of Hou's films. In *The Boys from Fengkuei* (1983), for example, there are three hundred and eight shots, averaging twenty seconds per shot; while in *The Puppetmaster* (1993), there are only one hundred shots, averaging eighty-five seconds each.[5] Limiting the number of shots also guides Hou Hsiao-hsien's focus, which is on three groups of characters picked from amongst hundreds of characters in the original novel. The go-between Hong Shanqing, Pearl and her understudy courtesan Jade belong to the first group based in the brothel in Gongyang Enclave. There is almost no intimacy between Hong and Pearl, who only talk about happenings in the pleasure quarters. This demonstrates that Hong uses the brothel not for pleasure but for business, skilfully squeezing ten thousand *taels* of silver from Jade's inexperienced lover Zhu Shuren as compensation for her fabricated marriage with someone else when Zhu himself is forced by his family into an arranged marriage.

The second group, associated with the brothel in Shangren Enclave, consists of Emerald, her patron Luo Zifu and her madam Dame Huang. Sold into the brothel at the age of seven, Emerald understands the value of her body better than anybody. She gains

Flowers of Shanghai.

control of Dame Huang by swallowing raw opium in a suicidal gesture. However, her renowned intractability attracts patrons such as Luo Zifu, who believes that Emerald is an exemplar of virtue in a place where virtue is not supposed to exist. Relying on Luo, Emerald buys herself out from the brothel and exits from the film in a spectacular scene where she carefully counts every piece of jewellery and returns them one by one to Dame Huang.

The third group, consisting of Wang Liansheng, Crimson and Jasmine, is at the centre of the film's plot. Crimson, who lives in Huifang Enclave, is bitter about Wang's courtship with Jasmine. As Wang is her only customer, this points to financial disaster for her. Hong Shanqing arranges for Wang to offer compensation to Crimson, only to have his proposal flatly turned down. Crimson claims that she wants Wang's exclusive affection, not money. After they resume their relationship, however, Wang catches Crimson in bed with an opera singer. Infuriated by her transgression of the implicit 'ethical' rule of the pleasure quarters that a courtesan should be loyal to her exclusive customer much as a wife is faithful to her husband, Wang trashes Crimson's

room and immediately marries Jasmine. However, during the farewell banquet marking Wang's return to Guangdong, it is revealed that Wang has kicked Jasmine out because she has had an affair with his nephew. The final scene witnesses Wang's return to Crimson; they face each other silently, letting the surroundings fade into complete darkness.

These three groups often mingle, and the storyline is difficult to follow, especially for general audiences unfamiliar with the original novel. But for Hou Hsiao-hsien, clarity of story seems to be of less concern than the *aura* of the brothels. His focus is not on character interaction but on the unique surroundings enabling interaction. To emphasise the 'elegance' of the most expensive brothels, the prostitutes' rooms are filled with furniture, decorations and other details unrelated to plot. An antique oil lamp, sitting on a round Ming-style redwood dining table, often occupies the centre of the frame, and the lighting is deliberately subdued, as if the lamp is the only source of light. The yellowish light enhances the soft and elegant profiles of the prostitutes, adding a feeling of cosy intimacy. Other details include engraved beds, doors, windows, screens, exotic clocks, silver tobacco pipes, opium utensils, and so forth, which combine to create a beguiling atmosphere. The details, however, are by no means extravagant. In fact, they exhibit both the usefulness and the uselessness of the everyday furnishing, so much so that they create an aura that is thoroughly familial and indicates the brothel's mimicry of family relationships.

The familial aura made possible by the laboriously created *mise en scène* is Hou Hsiao-hsien's true focus. As a special costume consultant, Hou Hsiao-hsien hired the mainland novelist Ah Cheng, known for the tranquil, concise and 'natural' writing in his famous 'three king' novellas: *King of the Children*, *King of Trees* and *King of Chess*.[6] Ah Cheng told the costume designers: 'What you have so far found are all useful things; let's start to look for useless ones.'[7] These 'useless' items could be anachronistic, since they would not have any particular use. A Chanel lipstick, for example, was placed on a plate full of opium-smoking utensils. Bombarded by the excess of visual detail, the audience would not notice the anachronistic lipstick. According to Zhu Tianwen, 'useful things are stage props, while useless things are traces of real life', but the anachronism and unsuitability of the added items raise questions regarding not only the claimed naturalness of the *mise en scène* but also the very notion of naturalness in representation.[8] Ah Cheng's own fiction often juxtaposes highly polished language with closeness to life, so it seems Hou may have been striving to extend his own trademark style of pushing naturalism to the point where it becomes artificial and vice versa.

The familial aura in the film is both natural and artificial. It is natural, because of the family-like settings and because brothels from the era of polygamy and arranged marriage provided rare chances for one-to-one bonding between romantically attracted men and women. Naturalness in acting is also consistent with Hou's performance ideals. For example, Tony Leung was repeatedly reminded by Hou to act 'as little as possible' and to 'give up all your weapons as a great actor'.[9] Therefore, Leung had to remain silent and emotionless, especially in his dinner scene with Hada Michiko in her room. Both say nothing, yet the silence suggests the quiet intimacy of a married couple.

It is ironic, of course, that domestic bliss between husband and wife can only be found in a brothel, which threatens family structures. This irony also indicates the artificiality of the seemingly natural family atmosphere and performances. The more carefully the prostitutes and their patrons create and maintain the mock family, the more incompatible the aura and setting – as incompatible as the verisimilar *mise en scène* and the Chanel lipstick. Likewise, the more restrained the actors' performances, the more artificial they actually are.

The technique of creating a familial aura in the most improbable place that Hou visualises is borrowed from Han Bangqing. Unlike most authors of traditional Chinese fiction, Han was clearly conscious of technique. In particular, he proudly points out in his preface that he makes two narrative inventions: 'knitting' (*chuancha*) and 'hiding and eluding' (*cangshan*). By 'knitting', he refers to overlapping plot threads by ellipsis and recollection: 'Before one wave subsides another comes chasing its tail … When reading the novel, you feel there are many more words hidden underneath the text – even if they are not explicitly written into the narrative, you can sense them hermeneutically.' 'Hiding and eluding' refers to similar techniques:

> Something suddenly flies out of nowhere, giving no hint to readers and making them more curious about what will come next. However, the passage that follows turns away to other events. The first event is not picked up again until after some unrelated events, and the whole story does not become clear until the very end. Only then can readers grasp the relevance of every little detail.[10]

Han Bangqing deploys these principles, best termed 'strategies of ellipsis', to create numerous discrepancies between what has been announced by chapter titles and pretexts and what is actually hidden or omitted. Han's consistent use of these strategies calls attention to an intriguing dialogical imagination between the silent and the obvious. One of the most conspicuous discrepancies in the novel, for example, is the exclusively Chinese presence in the foreign concession. Hidden clues, however, often point up this obvious discrepancy between historical reality and fictional representation. In one case, the guests are startled by a dark shadow on the roof of the house across the street:

> It turned out to be a foreign policeman, standing straight up on the top of the building opposite. He was all

wrapped up in a black uniform, with a big steel knife in his hand. Illuminated by the electric light, the knife flashed brilliantly.[11]

The stunned guests are quickly distracted by an ensuing incident in which policemen arrest several gamblers. (Gambling was illegal in the concessions, while whoring in a brothel registered with the concession authorities was legal.) Flirting with the courtesans, they appear undisturbed by the incident. But the towering image of a foreign policeman in dark uniform lingers on as an unknown and heterogeneous force, threatening to end the banquets at any time. This episode also highlights the 'extraterritoriality' enjoyed by foreigners in Chinese treaty ports – although physically on Chinese land, Western citizens possessed the privilege of immunity from Chinese laws. In other words, they were untouchable – 'invisible' or 'non-present' – while Chinese citizens were subjected to the laws of the concessions.

In Hou's film, the towering image of the colonial presence does not appear. Hou has kept the scene, but all we see is a stir of excitement among the crowd in a courtesan's room. People whisper about gamblers next door being caught and one having plunged to his death. They rush to the window, but the focus of the camera stays with Wang Liansheng, who seems preoccupied and ignores the disturbance. Although the foreign policeman is not shown, this is the only reference in the film to the existence of a world beyond the brothel, further intensifying the sense of a self-sufficient enclosure threatened by non-present presence. This subtle example of offscreen space is reminiscent of Hou's use of offscreen radio sound and other similar devices to hint at the existence of a larger world in such films as *City of Sadness*.[12]

Han Bangqing's strategies of ellipsis also harbour an essential visuality. The visual image, as correctly understood by Rey Chow

is characterized by two seemingly opposite features: obviousness and silence. While the obviousness of the image expresses an unambiguous presence, the silence of the image suggests, instead, nonpresence – that is, all those areas of 'otherness' that are an inherent part of any single 'presence'.[13]

Han Bangqing's novel is fraught with moments of 'nonpresence', such as the absence of romantic passion and erotic desire in a place where they are supposed to be present, the deliberate disruptions and ellipses in the plot, and the lack of colonial presence in colonial territories. These 'nonpresences' nevertheless point up their surprising 'nonpresentality' in places where presences are expected, thus emphasising the contrast between silence and obviousness. Such a contrast is precisely what makes things 'visible'. Furthermore, in order to 'make sense' of the novel, readers must engage in incessant backtracking to locate and fill in the ellipses whenever a seemingly displaced clue pops up. New for Han Bangqing's time, this reading technique uncannily anticipated the arrival of the motion picture and its accompanying viewing habit of suturing, which relies on the viewer's incessant retroaction to fill in previously created ellipses whenever new hints are given. As Jean-Pierre Oudart notes in his seminal essay on suture, after their initial jubilant response to filmic images, the audience tends to be reminded that any single filmic image is but one link in the chain of signification that is not 'being there' but 'being there for' – for indicating the necessary filling up the 'absent field' in the viewer's imaginary. Suturing, at once 'retroactive at the level of the signified' and 'anticipatory at the level of the signifier', is precisely the way of coping with the dialectics between the present and the absent in the cinema.[14]

It is the contrast between silence and obviousness, or absence and presence, which Hou Hsiao-hsien visualises through filmic technique. Hou's *Flowers of Shanghai* is in this sense a 'meta-film', a film about how visuality is visualised and how film is apprehended. The long take is one visual means of conducting the dialogue between silence and obviousness, for it draws the audience to observe the observation of the camera. Other means include the use of the fade. Conventionally used to transition from one scene to the next, in *Flowers of Shanghai* fades do not mark changes of scene. While the characters and the settings remain the same, the angle of the camera changes slightly, as if the animated camera has just taken a closed-eye yawn and shifted its attention. In the scene immediately following the prologue, for example, there is a fade after Hong Shanqing and another friend take leave of Wang Liansheng and Crimson. The audience would assume this marks a cut to another scene in another place. However, after the fade-in, this assumption is proven wrong, for the only change is that Wang Liansheng has moved from the left to the right of the screen. Crimson suddenly begins to cry, and Wang goes over to comfort her. This fade in mid-scene raises many questions: What has happened between the fades? What triggered Crimson's crying? How long is the real interval? Could it have been one minute, one night, or even several nights, during which Wang Liansheng first left and now has returned? In other words, the gap between the fade-out and the fade-in, albeit very brief, implies infinite elliptical possibilities in its very mode of silence, and points to the gap between filmic representation and reality exemplified in temporal differences.

During an interview, Hou discusses his new understanding of camera movement:

> From *The Boys from Fengkuei* to *Flowers of Shanghai*, my understanding of space has changed. I used to think that the camera had to be set at a distance to show emotion-less and objective observation. But in *Flowers of Shanghai*, I realized that objective observation had to depend on subjective manoeuvres in presenting characters. I could be cool or emotional toward the characters when shoot-ing. My feelings are not important in terms of objectivity, because there is another pair of eyes simultaneously watching the characters. No matter how close the camera is, there is same effect of a double gaze. The camera is like a person standing beside me watching the group of characters.[15]

Hou's words imply that the camera becomes a char-acter in the film by participating in the banquet. The role of the camera thus helps us to achieve a doubled viewing experience. On one hand, our eyes follow the camera, so that what we see is exactly what is shot by the camera. On the other hand, the animated camera reminds us of its limitations in the field of vision, pushing us to reflect on how filmic scenes are pre-sented by an optical device.

The subtlety of Hou's reflections on film-making makes them easy to overlook. Without taking this self-reflexivity into consideration, one might suspect Hou of eroticising the image of Asian women. The lack of movement seemingly makes the camera the equivalent of the male gaze, which caresses the pas-sive, hyper-feminised and exotic female characters, performed not only by Chinese but also by Japanese beauties. Nicholas Kaldis, for example, easily equates this male gaze with a tendency towards Orientalism in *Flowers of Shanghai*. He does try to defend Hou Hsiao-hsien, emphasising that the excessive sensuous detail tends to 'overstuff' the audience, so much so that surface Orientalism is subverted.[16] Maybe this is another 'meta-filmic' feature, in the sense that Hou deliberately creates Orientalist imagery to reflect on the film's own Orientalism. However, without recog-nising the silent beyond the obvious or the absent hidden beneath the present, Kaldis's explanation seems at best far-fetched and at worst reduplicative of the Orientalist logic that emphasises the glossy results of the Orientalist imaginary instead of the process and the agent of cultural production behind it.

By reflecting upon visuality itself, Hou's visual dialogue between the silent and the obvious conveys well Han Bangqing's understanding of space in a colonial situation. In the context of the late nine-teenth century, how to redefine space became a major concern for Chinese intellectuals after West-ern colonisers forcibly demystified the notion of the 'Central Kingdom'. The most representative and widespread redefinition of space was Liang Qichao's polemics that imagined a new Chinese citizen inte-grated into the world system of modernisation against the old China as an isolated, closed and dilapidated house.[17] As a well-informed Shanghai intellectual, Han Bangqing must have been aware of Liang's rhetoric, but he chose to retreat back into the old house full of opium smoke and etiolated desires. However, his retreat reveals a much more acute sen-sibility about the colonial implications behind the drive to redefine space than Liang's utopian vision. His depiction of the lethargy and gluttony of the banqueting crowd in a completely closed and self-sufficient space would have been a mere celebration of decadence without the reference to the 'absent-presence', symbolised by the towering image of the coloniser whose gaze from *outside* keeps the colonis-ed under constant surveillance. Space, therefore, is understood by Han as a closed and homogenous entity, but its closedness and homogeneity are enabled by colonialism, an outside and heteroge-neous force made invisible by its disguise as a call for modernisation and global participation.

Closedness in this understanding of space is manifested in Hou's exclusive focus on the sealed and isolated inner space of the brothel. Defining cine-matographic space has always been at the centre of

Hou's experiments. In his previous films, Hou has often juxtaposed a space that is wide open and infinitely extending with an inner space of enclosure and self-sufficiency. In *A Time to Live and a Time to Die* (1985), for instance, the isolated life of a family of three generations does not prevent Grandma from going out in search of the bridge leading to Meixian, the home town she and her family left behind in the retreat from the mainland. Combined with the infinite possibilities posed by identical bridges and rivers is the frequent intrusion of outside space into the family's enclosure. The dialectics between these two spaces, as Li Zhenya points out, reflect Hou's conscientious construction of history through redefining a space in which the relics of historical events are preserved and constantly excavated.[18] However, as in many other Hou Hsiao-hsien films, the apparent message in *A Time to Live and a Time to Die* is too direct and obvious to disclose the truth of history. Grandma's search for home clearly signifies the tragic nature of the migrants' forced choice of Taiwan as their home; caterpillar tracks from tanks on the ground speak volumes about the Nationalist military occupation of Taiwan. In other words, the interaction between the outside space and the inner space is clearly associated with historical traces, to the extent that personal histories are subordinated to the grand history of the nation-state, which is retrievable based on traces of the former.

Much as the construction of grand history has been questioned by the likes of Foucault, the visual representation of history and space in Hou's previous films is reflected upon, if not completely overturned, by Hou himself. The absence of an outside space in *Flowers of Shanghai* enables Hou to distance himself from overtly immediate concerns about Taiwan's local history. This deliberate distancing is discernable in the dialogue Hou's stylistic innovation performs with his previous films, a dialogue that helps make the ellipses and absences in *Flowers of Shanghai* full of implications.

NOTES

1. For example, 'With *Flowers of Shanghai*, Hou seems to have reached an aesthetic dead end, a breakthrough, or both.' Peter Keough, 'Cinema of Sadness: Recapturing Lost Illusions in the Films of Hou Hsiao-hsien', *The Boston Phoenix*, 2–9 March 2000.

2. Zhu Tianwen, ed., *The Ultimate Dream: The Complete Record of* Flowers of Shanghai (*Jishang zhi meng: Haishanghua dianying quan jilu*) (Taipei: Yuanliu, 1998), 16.

3. Ibid., 9.

4. Ibid.

5. Shen Xiaoyin, 'Meant to be Watched Several Times: Film Aesthetics and Hou Hsiao-hsien' ('Benlai jiu yingai duo kan liangbian: Dianying meixue yu Hou Xiaoxian'), in *Performance that Loves Life: Researching the Cinema of Hou Hsiao-hsien* (*Xilian Rensheng: Hou Hsiao-hsien Dianying Yanjiu*), ed. Lin Wenqi, Shen Xiaoyin and Li Zhenya (Taipei: Maitian, 2000), 76.

6. For an analysis of the film version of *King of the Children*, see Rey Chow, *Primitive Passions: Visuality, Sexuality, Ethnography, and Contemporary Chinese Cinema* (New York: Columbia University Press, 1995), 108–141.

7. Zhu Tianwen, *The Ultimate Dream*, 126.

8. Ibid.

9. Ibid., 99.

10. Han Bangqing, *Flowers of Shanghai* (*Haishanghua liezhuan*) (Taipei: Sanmin, 1998), 1.

11. Ibid., 274.

12. I am indebted to Chris Berry for this observation.

13. Rey Chow, *Primitive Passions*, 117.

14. Jean-Pierre Oudart, 'Cinema and Suture', *Screen*, 18, no. 4 (1977/78): 35–57. In the same issue, see also Stephen Heath's article 'Notes on Suture' (48–76), which clarifies some of the confusions in Oudart's as well as Dayan's conceptualisation of suture based on Lacanian psychoanalysis.

15. Rey Chow, *Primitive Passions*, 344.

16. Nicholas Kaldis, 'Desire-denying Oriental Exoticism: On Hou Hsiao-hsien's *Flowers of Shanghai*', *Jintian* (*Today*), no. 52 (2001): 266–272.

17. See Xiaobing Tang, *Global Space and the Nationalist Discourse of Modernity: The Historical Thinking of Liang Qichao* (Stanford: Stanford University Press, 1996).

18. Li Zhenya, 'Historical Space and Spatial History' ('Lishi Kongjian/Kongjian Lishi'), in Lin Wenqi et al., *Performance that Loves Life*, 113–139.

14 *The Goddess*: Fallen Woman of Shanghai

Kristine Harris

The goddess … struggles in the whirlpool of life … In tonight's streets, she is a cheap goddess … When she takes her child into her arms, she is a pure, holy mother. In both these lives, she has shown great moral character.

Accompanying this elliptical epigraph, a cryptic emblem of a female figure huddled over an unclothed child foreshadows the precarious cycle of humiliation and devotion propelling *The Goddess*. The title itself conveys this sense of duplicity: literally it means 'divine woman', but colloquially 'goddess' was a mordant euphemism for streetwalking prostitutes. This haunting prelude portends the uneasy tensions embedded in this silent film. The background image, rendered in a Western-style relief sculpture of a nude woman and child, looms behind two Chinese characters conveying the mocking title. Juxtaposing imported aesthetics and local idiom, physical sacrifice and immortal divinity, vilified prostitution and glorified motherhood, *The Goddess* invokes the idolatrous, if ambivalent, obsession with female icons that so occupied the urban imagination of 1930s China.

This particular goddess is an unnamed young woman raising a child alone in the city, and surviving only by streetwalking. One night, she is cornered by the police, but saved from arrest by a small-time crook offering protection in exchange for submission. He blackmails her into a mock marriage, then siphons off her meagre earnings for his gambling habit. The goddess moves away and searches for other work, but continually fails to escape. She secretly saves up for her son's schooling, but wary parents discover her true occupation and have the child dismissed, despite the headmaster's impassioned speech condemning their intolerance. The hoodlum, meanwhile, wagers away all her remaining cash. The goddess confronts her adversary, inadvertently killing him. Sentenced to twelve years in prison, she receives a visit from the sympathetic educator, who assures her he will raise her son attentively. Hoping to free her child from ill repute, the woman beseeches the headmaster to tell the boy his mother has died.

When *The Goddess* premiered at Shanghai's Lyric Theatre on 7 December 1934, it played to full houses and instantly won attention from critics.[1] Newspapers and movie magazines lauded Wu Yonggang's directorial debut for his sophisticated use of expressive film language, hailing the 27-year-old film-maker as the new wonder boy of Chinese cinema.[2] They also showered praise on the mature, nuanced performance by actress Ruan Lingyu, then at the pinnacle of her career.[3] This popular release from Lianhua film studios was one of its last silent productions, and politically more reticent than its previous releases.

Depicting marginal outcasts of the urban underclass, *The Goddess* stimulated public debate over the capacity of individual action and cinematic representation to effect social change. Some journalists were concerned about the film's fatalistic ending, but even these critics considered *The Goddess* 'one of the three best films of 1934', and praised its courage in taking on such sensitive subjects as unemployment, intolerance and prostitution.[4]

Half a century later *The Goddess* came into global circulation, through retrospectives of Chinese cinema across Europe, Asia and North America.[5] International festivals foregrounded Ruan Lingyu alongside renowned stars like Marlene Dietrich and Barbara Stanwyck with the affectionate moniker 'Garbo of the Orient'.[6] Chinese and foreign critics alike reclaimed *The Goddess* as a masterpiece of 'the first golden age of Chinese cinema'.[7] These viewers considered Wu's use of the silent medium world-class, recognising resonances in genre and technique between *The Goddess* and European or American films. They also discerned a certain restraint and apparent Confucian conservatism.

This essay examines *The Goddess* closely in the context of writings by Wu Yonggang and his contemporaries. What we discover is that the director was indeed intimately engaged with global developments in cinema, including the 'fallen woman' film and maternal melodrama, but that he was also compelled to craft his film to conform with the changing outlines of China's cultural politics during 1934. Seen in this light, the strikingly restrained visual language in Wu's film dramatised not only the sacrifices of his nameless protagonist, but also, implicitly, the film-maker's own sense of limits demanding self-regulation.

FALLEN WOMAN OF SHANGHAI

Focusing on a prostitute, *The Goddess* resonates with narratives about the 'fallen woman' who violates conventional codes of sexual morality incurring tragic consequences. Early Chinese film-makers, enamoured with this genre, drew upon local and foreign precedents to produce titles like *New Camille* (Asia-Xinmin, 1913; Li Pingqian, 1927), based on the nineteenth-century novel *La Dame aux Camelias*, and *A Lady of Shanghai* (Zhang Shichuan, 1925). For the 1920s and 1930s New Youth culture emerging in Chinese cities, this complex 'fallen woman' figure embodied the predicament of individuals flouting restrictive boundaries of social convention.

Wu Yonggang's early education in cinema was filled with 'fallen woman' films from the United States and Europe. In a memoir written shortly before his death in 1982, the director recalled his teenage years watching third-run features at Shanghai's Carter Theatre during the mid-1920s.[8] American silents like *Way Down East* made an especially deep impression on Wu. Released in China as *Laihun*, or 'Mock Marriage', D. W. Griffith's classic featured Lillian Gish as a young woman duped into a false marriage and then maligned for bearing a child out of wedlock.[9] Shot through with the tensions of intolerance, such films provided powerful inspiration for the young Wu Yonggang.

Just steps away from the pathos of these tarnished screen heroines were the 'miserable sights', Wu remembers, of desperate women milling about the Shanghai streets at dusk. Unlicensed prostitutes, proliferating there during the late 1920s and early 1930s, were more vulnerable to danger and uncertainties than the city's legally registered courtesans in tax-

paying brothels, and were scorned as criminals polluting public health and morality.[10] Wu pitied these streetwalkers 'forced to sell their own flesh to live': 'Every time I watched this scene, my heart was filled with indignation. I sympathised with these misfortunate women and detested this dark society. I was dissatisfied; I was despondent; I wanted to cry out!'[11]

Wu Yonggang eventually realised he could channel this indignation into a film of his own. He abandoned a frustrating job in set design at the Shaw Brothers' Tianyi Film Company, and completed art-school training in Western painting. Inspired by new films of social conscience released by studios like Lianhua in 1933, Wu began to envision *The Goddess* as a film with universal, allegorical weight: 'I thought that speaking out about so many women's misfortune and oppression through the concrete images of cinema might serve as a repudiation and denunciation of this dark society in general.'[12]

MATERNAL VIRTUE

To develop the pathos of this 'fallen woman' figure, Wu lavished attention on her daytime life as a virtuous mother. Wu's camera respectfully observes her nursing the baby after staggering upstairs at dawn. He tracks her tireless missions to locate a new boarding house, a factory job, a school for her son. Even the final expository intertitle underscores her self-effacing devotion: 'The lonely, quiet prison cell is the only rest she has had in this life. In her hopes and dreams, she imagines with great yearning a bright and glorious future for her child.'

The woman who sacrifices everything for her child's future was, of course, a mainstay of Hollywood maternal melodramas like *Stella Dallas* (Henry King, 1925; King Vidor, 1937), *Madame X* (Lionel Barrymore, 1929), *The Sin of Madelon Claudet* (Edgar Selwyn, 1931) and *Blonde Venus* (Josef von Sternberg, 1932).[13] Yet the goddess's maternal virtue also conjured up local ideals, including the renowned mother of Mencius, who worked night and day to provide for her son's Confucian education, and the contemporary 'good wife, wise mother' model, which encouraged women to contribute to the nation by raising children.[14]

Seen in the same Confucian framework, the headmaster typifies paternal benevolence and righteousness as he extols the need for education: 'It's true the child's mother is a streetwalker, but this is due to broader social problems. … Education is our responsibility and we must rescue this child from adversity.' Embedded in a series of long, didactic intertitles (in a film where dialogue is otherwise minimal), the headmaster's indictment of intolerance is conspicuous; he even addresses the camera straight on, directing his speech at the trustees *and* the film audience. Indeed, Wu Yonggang subsequently explained that he had 'borrowed' the 'conscientious' voice of the educator to register his own cry for social justice.[15] If the headmaster offers a possible source of legitimate male authority, then the imprisoned goddess's final request that he tell her son 'his mother is dead' would appear to represent a parallel surrender of maternal influence.

When viewed alongside American melodramas and social conditions in Shanghai during the mid-1930s, *The Goddess* certainly seems to project a conservative morality. William Rothman points out, for instance, that this female character's only fulfilment comes vicariously, through her son and his education. Comparing *The Goddess* to *Blonde Venus*, Rothman sees in the Chinese film a virtual absence of the eroticism, romance, feminism or self-fulfilment so common in American 'fallen woman' films.[16] Along similar lines, Rey Chow searches for hints of sexuality in the film, concluding that 'even though she is a mother, the prostitute's access to her own feminine sexuality is continually obstructed, policed, and punished by society's patriarchal codes of female chastity'.[17]

Yingjin Zhang likewise interprets the film's emphasis on motherhood as an evasion and concealment of female sexuality, ultimately 'marking the film as conservative'. Supporting his conclusion that *The Goddess* is primarily a male fantasy, Zhang offers some compelling examples: the goddess's virtue does appear to depend on the fulfilment of an 'expected role in cultural reproduction'; the headmaster, as a potential surrogate father, seems to 'secure patrilineal continuity on a symbolic level'; and the camera's focus on locked gates and prison bars does indeed lock the goddess away.[18]

Some of Wu's contemporaries likewise took issue with the conservatism in *The Goddess*, though from a different angle. Critics influential in China's 1930s left-wing underground admitted *The Goddess* surpassed other releases that year, but questioned whether the film's ending was sufficiently revolutionary. Wang Chenwu contended that if prostitution is a 'broader social problem' rather than an isolated moral failing, as Wu's headmaster asserts, then *The Goddess* should offer a 'total indictment of social forces' and clear-cut resolution, emulating recent Soviet fiction.[19] A Ying concurred; he felt the plot focused excessively on the goddess's personal misfortune and her ill-fated conflict with the gambler, when in reality only a wholesale dismantling of the entire social system could resolve this woman's adversity.[20] Notably, neither critic took issue with patriarchal morality in *The Goddess*; instead, both worried that the film's protest against social injustice was politically inconclusive.

A NEW LIFE

Was *The Goddess* simply a maternal melodrama that accommodated and reinforced the social or political status quo, as these reactions might suggest? In response to his contemporary critics, Wu Yonggang promptly responded in print: 'When I first set out to write about the goddesses, I wished to show more of their real lives, but circumstances would not permit me to do so.'[21] The obliqueness of Wu's reference to 'circumstances' and 'permission' implies that the specific obstacles were sensitive, even unspeakable.

The Goddess would have been a likely target for censors. During the film's production in October and November 1934, China's KMT Nationalist Party was already intensifying its ideological efforts to regulate literature and cinema, concurrent with military campaigns targeting Chinese Communist Party bases in the hinterland. Under the government's broad censorship law, reinforced by increased police powers, any imported or domestic film that might 'harm good customs or public order' was ineligible for a licence.[22] This included any works advocating class conflict or socialism. By some counts, the script inspection committee rejected over eighty submissions from November 1934 to March 1935.[23] Surprisingly, however, extant public records provide no evidence of formal directives requiring alterations to *The Goddess*.[24]

More conceivably, Wu self-censored to navigate the diffuse and pervasive anxieties about ideology, politics and the market confronting China's filmmakers in 1934, when official censorship was reinforced by broader conservative restrictions and state surveillance. The government's New Life Movement, designed to bolster popular loyalty to the Nationalist cause, had been unveiled in February 1934, just months before *The Goddess* went into production.[25] Film-makers were encouraged to champion this cultural mobilisation effort, promoting Confucian revivalist morality along with sacrifice, discipline and endurance in everyday life. Just months later, Lianhua's weekly newsletter prominently reported that New Life organisational committee members, as well as high-ranking government ministers like Chen Gongbo, had paid several visits to the set half-way through the shooting of *The Goddess*; they were lavishly banqueted by studio head Luo Mingyou.[26]

The Goddess's idealisation of domesticity and virtuous motherhood dovetailed conveniently with the New Life Movement's prescribed roles for women. One line in *The Goddess* may even be interpreted as an allusion to the movement. After the goddess enrols her son in school, an expository title at this juncture declares emphatically, 'The start of a new life gives her new happiness.' Wu's self-conscious appropriation of New Life rhetoric would appear to fulfil national mandates and public expectations.

Additionally, Chinese studios like Lianhua were competing in a market dominated by imports. By 1934, the new talking pictures playing in Shanghai were generally light-hearted musicals, comedies, mysteries and adventures from the United States and Britain. American films, especially, seemed to be taking fewer risks, owing to new Production Code limitations and concomitant self-regulation.[27] Cumulatively these factors made the miserable 'social and economic conditions of fallen women' – Wu's stated concern – virtually unrepresentable on Shanghai screens.

Thus the street scenes of the 1920s and early 1930s that had first inspired Wu Yonggang's despondent indignation gradually evolved into a new, arguably more complex, narrative. Wu explains how he came up with the idea of a double life for the film: 'The story's emphasis shifted to maternal love, with the life of the streetwalkers as a background, until it became about the struggle of a streetwalker living two lives for her child.'[28]

A DOUBLE LIFE

Moving beyond the straightforward 'fallen woman' narrative, and also transcending a 'New Life' conservative maternal melodrama, Wu Yonggang silently dramatised the implications of the protagonist's double life through suggestive visual language. The film shifts between a few recurring spaces, and between the two 'regions' of public and private.[29] Nearly all – exteriors and interiors alike – are deliberately confined: the street corner set, her single-room dwelling, a pawn shop threshold, the tight alleyway, a montage of factory smokestacks. The artificiality and alternation of these spaces underscores the highly circumscribed patterns of daily life for this goddess, as she attempts to maintain a separation between her two roles as mother and streetwalker.

Wu's careful use of lighting also helps establish a 'double life' for the goddess. Offsetting daytime exterior shots are frequent night scenes, when the sun sinks below the horizon, gas lamps illuminate otherwise dark streets and incandescent bulbs cast shadows across interiors. Oscillating between natural and artificial lighting, the film conveys a sense of the passage of time, a sense of inexorable routine reinforced by frequent close-ups on the clocks that regulate this goddess's brutal schedule.

The 'double life' in *The Goddess* is as skilfully crafted as the best American silent melodrama or Weimar street tragedy. Wu Yonggang augments the film's oppressive claustrophobia through a rhythmic repetition of spaces and shots.[30] He also heightens its stark melodramatic contrasts by making the characters virtually anonymous, with almost mythological power. In fact, by transforming these figures into transcendent types, Wu arguably succeeds in extending the significance of *The Goddess* far beyond the individual to the universal.[31]

The film's restrained visual style effectively expressed the otherwise unnameable limits Wu had referred to as 'circumstances'. He conveyed his bleak vision less through intertitles than through spare sets, stark lighting, and jarring montages. Granted, this economy was partly borne from necessity – as a first-time director, Wu was given a spartan budget and a schedule that involved shooting at night. But the evocative *mise en scène* demonstrates Wu's decade of artistic training and experience designing sets for studios like White Lily and Tianyi, where he had managed with even fewer resources.

In fact, shortly after *The Goddess*'s nation-wide release, Wu Yonggang published an article about the 'power of suggestion' [*anshi*] that sets and lighting design could instil in a film.[32] Wu's advice would be useful to any film-maker trying to move beyond the narrow limitations of written scripts deemed acceptable. Seen in this light, the story of a marginalised woman striving for her ideals while maintaining a secret life might also be understood as an allegory of the 'double life' a film-maker might construct by necessity, to negotiate the constraints of 'circumstances'.

Silent actress Ruan Lingyu seemed to incarnate such duplicity. On the one hand, Ruan was a mother herself, and had attained public acclaim by playing tragic, suffering women in films such as *Peach Blossom Weeps Tears of Blood* (Bu Wancang, 1931), *Little Toys* (Sun Yu, 1933), *Life* (Fei Mu, 1934) and *Return* (Zhu Shilin, 1934). This element of Ruan's star persona translated into *The Goddess* well, generating sympathy for this solitary woman striving to maintain maternal virtue. On the other hand, the image of actresses was highly commodified, and at this peak period of her career, pictures of Ruan adorned advertisements for perfume, soap and other consumer products. These images played into the popular notion that female movie stars, like prostitutes, were merchandise for public display and consumption – making Ruan seem even more plausible in the role of the goddess.

Wu Yonggang attributed much of the film's success to Ruan's skill in character development, which often went far beyond what he could possibly have envisioned. Noting her talent for complex scenes, Wu commented on Ruan's masterful gestures and facial expressions, which could convey conflicting emotions simultaneously (hysteria, fear, sorrow, anger, resignation), enhancing key moments such as the incarceration scene. The director even intimated that the actress's self-effacing performances were inseparable from her own painful life and past experiences – a reference to Ruan's wretched childhood as a servant girl and her troubled relationships while making this film, which culminated in suicide only months later in March 1935 at age 24.[33]

SHATTERING THE GAZE

If the goddess at first manages to survive by maintaining a double life, any attempt to keep the two spheres separate is constantly frustrated. She becomes a target of surveillance, and the camera's voyeuristic gaze intimates her vulnerability to physical violation and abduction. The opening scene of the film, for instance, wends its way from the rooftops of Shanghai through a window to enter the goddess's home.

This pursuing, consuming gaze gets replicated in successive scenes. In the dark streets, potential clients casually survey the goddess's figure. Vigilant police and the gambling scoundrel stalk her in back alleys. Echoing the film's opening shots, the headmaster's initial housecall methodically scans her room for signs of vice; soon afterwards, the gambler similarly searches crevices in her room for cash.

One might interpret this visual surveillance as a 'male fantasy' of 'penetration' into a 'female world of prostitution', reaffirming male authority and 'control of the city', as Yingjin Zhang argues.[34] Or one might determine, as William Rothman does, that it demonstrates the camera's 'capacity for violence, for villainy', indicating that even the film-maker himself is 'implicated in the hypocrisy [he] attacks'.[35] Zhang and Rothman make absolutely crucial points. Yet in the light of our understanding about Wu's circumstances, it is possible to conclude that his camera does not simply participate in the controlling male gaze; rather, by foregrounding the camera's potential for visual domination and physical violation, Wu also presents coercion and force as part of the goddess's problem.

The gambler's imposing perspective and physical frame visibly dominate his scenes with the goddess. When this gambling thug takes her child hostage, the stunned goddess shrinks to a diminutive powerlessness in a disorienting shot framed by his legs. Then, lunging his hand directly at the camera – at

Held hostage.

the goddess, and the spectator – the grinning gambler slowly tightens it to a steely grip, warning, 'The monkey king struggles but he can't jump out of the palm of the Buddha's hand.' This line asserts the omnipotence of an enormous Buddha prevailing over misguided sinners, and it is full of bitter irony. For if the hoodlum once offered a moment of salvation for the fallen woman absconding from police raids, his underworld blackmail schemes soon approximate eternal damnation.

Wu's camera condemns this male domination in other ways too – replaying scenes structurally to magnify their impact, or positioning the camera as antagonist. By presenting analogously the police pursuit, the headmaster's investigation and the scoundrel's encroaching search, Wu's reiterations cumulatively insinuate a critique of such harassment.

When the goddess's anger finally erupts in the film's penultimate murder scene, Wu offers a brief moment of settlement for this fallen woman struggling to escape the grip of her oppressors. Bloody and beaten, the goddess musters up a bottle and smashes it on the unsuspecting gambler, instantly eliminating the antagonist. This murder scene fulfils an earlier moment of symbolic patricide in the film. When asked about the head of household's occupation, the goddess replies after some thought, 'His father is dead.' She cautiously conceals the truth for her son's sake; the film never reveals his phantom paternity.[36] Even the child's surrogate father (headmaster and film-maker stand-in) finds himself powerless to lead in the face of intolerance, and can only secede in righteous resignation.

Shattering the gaze

Yet if *The Goddess* is permeated with anxiety about the absence of legitimate authority, paternity is only one aspect of the crisis dramatised here; Wu Yonggang also implicates class relations as part of the problem. Gossiping parents and neighbours scorn the disreputable woman and her son; school trustees expel the child to satisfy the parents' 'call for accountability'. As these men and women track the goddess's behaviour, the film conveys their 'looks' as menacing surveillance shots through extreme high angles or apertures: a next-door woman spies on the goddess and gambler through a keyhole; other women look down on her child in the street from overhead. The class scrutiny becomes even more troubling when shots that appear to convey a point-of-view actually have no direct source – such as an isolated bird's-eye view of the goddess soliciting on the pavement below.

The goddess's violent blow of vindication against the scoundrel becomes a blow against the totality of this surveillance. As she smashes the bottle against the camera lens, Wu Yonggang's brief shot shatters the film spectator's gaze upon the action, single-handedly positioning its audience as complicit in the power structure. But if this 'symbolic attack', as Rothman rightly calls it, succeeds in stunning the viewer into a consciousness of the lethal consequences of intolerance, then what happens to that awareness during the anti-climax of the film? Wu's concluding sequence dramatises the court's judgment of this goddess; newspapers report her twelve-year prison sentence; she is incarcerated. These disciplining scenes could well have satisfied the public (and

Surveillance.

state censors) that the lethal threat of streetwalkers was properly contained and neutralised, as Yingjin Zhang suggests.

Yet again, Wu's film insinuates a compelling alternative interpretation. In the courthouse, the camera eye looks down upon the goddess through high-angle shots (from the judges' perspective), and up at the bench far above (low-angle shots from the goddess's position). The angles suggest an indictment not simply of this fallen woman, but also of a repressive justice system subordinating powerless individuals before the law. This double meaning was, of course, not fully speakable under the censorship code, but at least one contemporary reviewer noticed it, commenting obliquely that 'only through thoroughly skilled techniques [like these] can the fullest content be expressed'.[37]

ENDINGS

Wu Yonggang allows us to understand *The Goddess* in two ways. On the one hand, his narrative appears to fulfil Confucian convention and patriarchal moral codes: it affirms the maternal aspirations of this sympathetic female protagonist and enacts a final punishment for the fallen woman. But on the other hand, key visual cues in the film (especially sets, lighting and camera angles) imply that social convention is not always reliable or just.

Wu implicates the goddess, but he also incriminates the anxieties and hypocrisies of neighbours, parents, children, the justice system and even her last resort, the educational system. The fallen woman is left to negotiate the brutalities of the underworld alone, with all routes to reform closed off. Seen in this light, the school gates, walls and prison bars represent not simply protection and reassurance, but also bulwarks between the ruling powers and the defenceless. Wu deconstructs these barriers as artificial, even permeable, yet the confinement remains.

The child embodies her aspirations for the future, but by the end of this film, any hope for the goddess, even through her offspring, is bleak. Having implored the headmaster to tell her son that his mother has died, she now sits alone in a bare jail cell. The woman hallucinates a dim vision of the future – a vignette of her boy appearing against the blank prison wall – but then even this picture fades to 'the end'.[38] As his image vanishes, so does the goddess's joyful expression. The film's earlier faith in her

redemption through her son's education – as 'the start of a New Life' and 'a new happiness' – now seems to have paled, even disappeared.

If, as Wu Yonggang's technique and his writings imply, *The Goddess* dramatises the individual's struggle within 'circumstances' that limit free expression, might a resolution of that 'double life' be found in his subsequent cinematic retelling of the story? Only four years after he made *The Goddess*, Wu created a new version of the film, entitled *Rouge Tears* (1938). Rather than concluding his new scenario with a grim scene of imprisonment, Wu now showed the freed goddess twelve years hence, eager to see her grown child graduated from music conservatory and engaged to be married. The mother approaches the headmaster's home, and observes through a window her son performing 'Ode to a Devoted Mother'.[39]

The remake may have offered a somewhat more rousing glimpse of future freedom for the goddess – and a potential source of hope for a public now surrounded by the Anti-Japanese War – especially since it incorporated the new technology of sound, along with an established entertainer from drama and comedy, Butterfly Woo, in the lead role.[40] The revised conclusion, where the fallen woman gains reassurance of her child's survival and success, was certainly consonant with American maternal melodramas like *The Sin of Madelon Claudet*, and particularly *Stella Dallas*, remade by King Vidor just a year earlier, in 1937.[41]

Yet Wu's 1938 conclusion turned out to be no less disquieting than the original. Content to know the boy has been raised well, and adhering to her own erasure and anonymity, the woman ultimately resists the opportunity to meet her grown son. Instead, she slowly walks away from the headmaster's house in the falling snow.[42] Like *The Goddess*, Wu's remake offers neither a conventional 'happy ending', nor a fully reformist one: mother and child remain separated, and the social stigma of the goddess persists.

ACKNOWLEDGMENTS
I am grateful to Margherita Zanasi and the University of Texas, Austin, China Seminar, for valuable feedback on an earlier draft, presented 22 March 2002.

NOTES

1. *Lianhua Huabao*, 4, no. 23 (9 December 1934): 1; *Lianhua Huabao*, 4, no. 24 (16 December 1934): 1.

2. Mu Miao, '*The Goddess*: Review 2' ('*Shennü* ping er'), *Chenbao* (December 1934), reprinted in *The Chinese Left-Wing Film Movement* (Zhongguo Zuoyi Dianying Yundong), ed. Chen Bo (Beijing: Zhongguo Dianying Chubanshe, 1993), 553.

3. *Lianhua Huabao*, 4, no. 24 (16 December 1934): 2.

4. Chen Wu (pseud. Wang Chenwu), '*The Goddess*: Review 1' ('*Shennü* Ping Yi'), *Chenbao* (December 1934), reprinted in *Chinese Left-Wing Film*, 551–552; Wei Yu (pseud. A Ying), 'Painful Words Transcribed – On *The Goddess* and *Plunder of Peach and Plum*' ('Kuyan Chao – Guanyu *Shennü* yu *Taoli Jie*'), *Wenyi dianying*, 1 (1934), reprinted in *Chinese Left-Wing Film*, 554–555.

5. For instance, Turin, Italy (1982); China Film Archive, Beijing (1983); National Museum of Modern Art, Tokyo (1986); Hong Kong Arts Centre (1988); Pordenone, Italy (1995); Guggenheim Museum, New York (1998).

6. Programme notes, *Three Goddesses of the Silver Screen from the Thirties* (Hong Kong Arts Centre, 1988).

7. For example, Marie-Claire Quiquemelle and Jean-Loup Passek, ed., *Le Cinema Chinois* (Paris: Centre Georges Pompidou, 1985); Miriam Hansen, 'Fallen Women, Rising Stars, New Horizons: Shanghai Silent Film as Vernacular Modernism', *Film Quarterly*, 54, no. 1 (2000): 10–22.

8. Wu Yonggang, *My Explorations and Pursuits* (*Wode tansuo he zhuiqiu*) (Beijing: Zhongguo dianying chubanshe, 1986), 176–177.

9. Ibid., 176. *Way Down East* (1920) first appeared in China in 1921. On Griffith's film, see Robert Lang, *American Film Melodrama: Griffith, Vidor, Minnelli* (Princeton: Princeton University Press, 1989), 65–78; Lucy Fischer, *Cinematernity: Film, Motherhood, Genre* (Princeton: Princeton University Press, 1996), 56–72.

10. See Gail Hershatter, *Dangerous Pleasures: Prostitution and Modernity in Twentieth-Century Shanghai* (Berkeley: University of California Press, 1997), 286–287; Yingjin Zhang, 'Prostitution and Urban Imagination: Negotiating the Public and the Private in Chinese Films of the 1930s', in *Cinema and Urban Culture in Shanghai, 1922–1943*, ed. Yingjin Zhang (Stanford: Stanford University Press, 1999), 160–180.

11. Wu, *My Explorations*, 130.

12. Ibid., 131.

13. See Christian Viviani, 'Who is Without Sin?: The Maternal Melodrama in American Film, 1930–39', and E. Ann Kaplan, 'Mothering, Feminism and Representation: The Maternal in Melodrama and the Woman's Film 1910–40', in *Home Is Where the Heart Is: Studies in Melodrama and the Woman's Film*, ed. Christine Gledhill (London: British Film Institute, 1987), 83–99; 113–117.

14. See Sally Taylor Lieberman, *The Mother and Narrative Politics in Modern China* (Charlottesville: University Press of Virginia, 1998), 27–35.

15. Wu Yonggang, 'After Completing *The Goddess*' ('*Shennü* Wancheng zhihou'), *Lianhua Huabao*, 5, no. 1 (1 January 1935); reprinted in *My Explorations*, 134.

16. William Rothman, '*The Goddess*: Reflections on Melodrama East and West', in *Melodrama and Asian Cinema*, ed. Wimal Dissanayake (New York: Cambridge University Press, 1993), 59–72; see esp. 66.

17. Rey Chow, *Primitive Passions: Visuality, Sexuality, Ethnography, and Contemporary Chinese Cinema* (New York: Columbia University Press, 1995), 24.

18. Zhang, 'Prostitution and Urban Imagination', 169–171.

19. Chen, '*The Goddess*: Review 1', 552.

20. Wei, 'Painful Words Transcribed', 554–555.

21. Wu, 'After Completing *The Goddess*', in *My Explorations*, 134.

22. See 'Film Inspection Law' ('Dianying Jiancha Fa') (3 November 1930) in *Chinese Left-Wing Film*, 1089. Also see Zhiwei Xiao, 'Film Censorship in China, 1927–1937' (PhD dissertation, University of California: San Diego, 1994).

23. Cheng Jihua, Li Shaobai and Xing Zuwen, ed., *History of the Development of Chinese Cinema* (*Zhongguo Dianying Fazhanshi*), vol. 1 (Beijing: Zhongguo Dianying Chubanshe, 1963, 1980), 304.

24. I thank Zhiwei Xiao for confirming the censorship record.

25. See Lloyd E. Eastman, *The Abortive Revolution: China under Nationalist Rule, 1927–1937* (Cambridge: Harvard University Press, 1974).

26. *Lianhua Huabao*, 4, no. 15 (14 October 1934): 1; *Lianhua Huabao*, 4, no. 16 (21 October 1934): 1.

27. Accompanying self-regulation, institutional enforcement of the 1930 US Production Code intensified in spring 1934. Lea Jacobs, *The Wages of Sin: Censorship and the Fallen Woman Film, 1928–1942* (Madison: University of Wisconsin Press, 1991), 153.

28. Wu, *My Explorations*, 134.

29. On 'regions of the camera', see Rothman, '*The Goddess*: Reflections on Melodrama', 71.

30. On such techniques in Weimar melodrama, see Patrice Petro, *Joyless Streets: Women and Melodramatic Representation in Weimar Germany* (Princeton: Princeton University Press, 1989), 176.

31. For a stimulating reading of Wu's minimalist film language and the 'archetypal' effect of the nameless characters, see Chow, *Primitive Passions*, 24–25.

32. Wu, 'Speaking of Film Sets' ('Lun Dianying Bujing'), *Lianhua Huabao*, 5, no. 5 (1 March 1935): 3; reprinted in *My Explorations*, 171–174.

33. Wu, *My Explorations*, 132–133. Ruan made several dozen popular melodramas during her eight years on screen. On her suicide, see the film *The Actress/Centre Stage* (*Ruan Lingyu*) (Stanley Kwan, 1992); also, Kristine Harris, '*The New Woman* Incident: Cinema, Scandal, and Spectacle in 1935 Shanghai', in *Transnational Chinese Cinemas: Identity, Nationhood, Gender*, ed. Sheldon Hsiao-peng Lu (Honolulu: University of Hawaii Press, 1997), 277–302.

34. Zhang, 'Prostitution and Urban Imagination', 168.

35. Rothman, '*The Goddess*: Reflections on Melodrama', 71–72.

36. This marginalisation of the father echoes China's literary trends in the 1920s and 1930s, when male intellectuals rehearsed their own sense of 'general emasculation and powerlessness in the modern world', according to Lieberman, *The Mother*, 81.

37. Mu Miao, '*The Goddess*: Review 2', 553.

38. For a thoughtful analysis of this scene's analogies to the cinematic experience, see Rothman, '*The Goddess*: Reflections on Melodrama', 71–73.

39. Zhang Junxiang and Cheng Jihua, ed., *Dictionary of Chinese Cinema* (*Zhongguo Dianying Dacidian*) (Shanghai Cishu Chubanshe, 1995), 1162.

40. Several Chinese film historians have commented that the remake was a more commercial venture; Wang Yunman finds it inferior to Wu's original silent version. Neither Wu nor Woo (Hu Die) mention *Rouge Tears* in their memoirs. Zhu Jian, *Movie Queen Butterfly Woo* (*Dianying Huanghou Hu Die*) (Lanzhou Daxue Chubanshe, 1996), 252; Wang Yunman, '*The Goddess*: Simple yet Profound' ('Supu Yunhan de Shennü'), in *My Explorations*, 192; Hu Die and Liu Huiqin, *Memoirs of Butterfly Woo* (Hu Die Huiyilu) (Beijing: Wenhua Yishu Chubanshe, 1988).

41. In fact, the ending of *Rouge Tears* is nearly identical to *Stella Dallas*. On the debate over ambiguous closure in *Stella Dallas*, see E. Ann Kaplan, 'The Case of the Missing Mother: Maternal Issues in Vidor's *Stella Dallas*' (1983), and Linda Williams, 'Something Else Besides a Mother': *Stella Dallas* and the Maternal Melodrama' (1984), reprinted in *Feminism and Film*, ed. E. Ann Kaplan (Oxford: Oxford University Press, 2000), 466–478; 479–504.

42. Zhang and Cheng, *Dictionary of Chinese Cinema*, 1162.

15   *Hibiscus Town*: Revolution, Love and Bean Curd

Charles W. Hayford

Bean curd meets the simplest of human needs, revolution the most complicated, and love the most essential. Xie Jin's *Hibiscus Town* (1986) tells a story whose message was welcome to audiences in the 1980s: the Cultural Revolution is over, now 'to get rich is glorious'. Based on a popular novel by Gu Hua,[1] the plot is relatively straightforward. In a scenic provincial river town in the 1950s, a handsome young woman entrepreneur and her husband set up a street restaurant and get rich selling spicy bean-curd soup; they build a house; in the early 1960s, local cadres, carrying out leftist policies of class struggle, label them New Rich Peasants; her husband is hounded to death; she takes up with a poet/folk-song researcher who had been criticised as a rightist and set to sweep the town streets; she and the rightist conceive a child; after the Cultural Revolution, they are rehabilitated and set up her street restaurant again. Yet the film raises far more complex issues than this plot summary can imply. After the historical hurricane, what do we return to? On what moral ground do we build? How can society meet human needs?

Critics both inside China and abroad characterise the films of Xie Jin as cinematically elegant and politically orthodox.[2] One Shanghai critic attacked Xie for making 'Confucian films' (*ruxue dianying*) that served Party prerogatives. A tart Western commentator characterised Xie as China's 'leading film apparatchik'.[3] Still, Zhang Xudong's study of Fifth Generation film categorises Xie's earlier films as 'the Chinese equivalent of John Ford or *Casablanca*', with 'cultural and political importance in their own right', and comments that they 'reached the public in a way unmatched by the Fifth Generation (the only two new wave films that come close are *Yellow Earth* and *Red Sorghum*)'.[4] Critics also locate Xie's films in the genre of 'melodrama' – not in the disparaging colloquial sense of cheap clashes of pure good and evil, but the literary historical sense of a mode that

emerged in the aftermath of the Enlightenment. The French Revolution destroyed the spiritual authority of the Church and the moral sway of the aristocracy; secular dramas could no longer be 'tragedy' nor 'comedy', but fables of middle-class domestic moral and social conflict.[5] Paul Pickowicz thoughtfully observes that the melodramas of the New Culture (1916-1923) period, sometimes known as the Chinese Enlightenment, had political heft, attacking imperialism, capitalism and feudalism, with the assumption that an anti-capitalist, working people's socialist revolution would expel evil and save China. *Hibiscus Town*, he adds less persuasively, turned the New Culture 'on its head', presenting absolute good and absolute evil, with no middle ground, for now it is 'the demonic agents of the Communist Party and their poor peasant running dogs who represent evil, whereas hard-working entrepreneurs and "counter-revolutionary rightists" represent virtue and purity'.[6] However, Nick Browne persuasively concludes that Xie's 'critique of social deformation in the past neither excuses the Party nor supports calls for dismantling it.'[7]

These are all helpful observations, yet it seems to me that they do not do balanced justice to the experience of watching the film, which is cinematic, multivalent and suggestive, nor do they do full justice to the moral sophistication of the film in the political and historical context of the 1980s. I argue that the cinematic presentation of *Hibiscus Town* tempers the characterisation of the film as generic melodrama and that it is worth developing Nick Browne's suggestion that Xie Jin uses Confucian humanism as the moral reference to condemn the class struggle and political polarisation of the Cultural Revolution.[8] One recent appreciation of the Confucian persuasion sums up its basic principle as the 'secular as sacred', that is, a this-worldly centring on the 'human community as holy rite'.[9] This humanist strain was popularly understood to centre on how to '*zuo ren*' (literally to 'be a person', 'perform human-hood' or 'conduct oneself in society') in such a way as to bring the individual, the family and the state into moral alignment.

STORIES OF REVOLUTION: CHOICE, VOICE AND HISTORY

Xie Jin's film, of course, does not make a programmatic argument, but does make artistic, political and moral choices, some conscious or transparent, some not. Contrasting them with other ways of telling the Story of Revolution will clarify the nature of these choices. The heroic Maoist narrative long held centre stage. This Big Story, familiar from 1789 and 1917, depicted a triumphal state-building revolution which produced a New China strong enough to defy imperialism and destroy feudalism: Liberation. Mao encapsulated this nationalist story on 1 October 1949: 'China has stood up.'

For a nationalist story to succeed it must unify differences and cover over conflicts. Before 'Liberation', from 1921 to 1949, the Communist Party followed at least two political strategies, each with its own story. Beginning with the New Culture Movement (1916–1923) many intellectuals saw an antithesis between 'traditional' China and the 'modern' West; tradition had to be destroyed in order for China to modernise. New Culture leaders saw 'traditional' villages not as cultural ground for a new China, but as 'hell on earth', the opposite of everything modern: dark, weak, backward and shameful. This vision led to an innovative construction of China as 'feudal', populated by 'peasants' rather than 'farmers' (historians argue that actually late imperial China was hardly feudal, but this is a question better discussed elsewhere).[10] In 1927, Mao famously told the story of a feudal China awaiting liberation in his canonical Report from the Hunan Countryside: 'Several hundred million peasants will rise like a mighty storm, like a hurricane … They will sweep all the imperialists, warlords, corrupt officials, local tyrants, and evil gentry into their graves.' To destroy feudalism, he said, mobilise the poorest peasants to destroy the landlord class. But after the outbreak of the war with Japan in 1937, another strategy and story of revolution emerged – or re-emerged; it was, after all, the strategy of Sun Yat-sen. This United Front programme was based on confederating and leading all patriotic elements, whether landlord or merchant or village patriarch; this entailed accepting their traditions, including the entrepreneurial and patriarchal family. The Revolution came to power on this New Democracy platform. In many ways, the struggles of the 1950s and 1960s were between these two approaches to nationalist revolution, both subsumed into the story of New China.

After Mao's death in 1976, new stories implicitly or explicitly challenged the founding myths. One type, exile memoir literature, has become a recognised genre, or at least a publishing niche. Emerging in the early 1980s period of awakening Western interest, these books are first person coming-of-age or survival stories by Chinese who came out of China to live in the West; most were written first in English but limit their accounts to what happened in China (as opposed, for instance, to immigrant memoirs which focus on life in the new world or Chinese student-abroad stories of the 1990s). Examples include Liang Heng and Judith Shapiro, *Son of the Revolution* (New York: Random House, 1983), Gao Yuan, *Born Red: A Chronicle of the Cultural Revolution* (Stanford University Press, 1987) and Jung Chang, *Wild Swans: Three Daughters of China* (New York: Simon & Schuster, 1991).[11] Their eyewitness, bottom-up presentations of the Cultural Revolution radiate an authenticity that we are tempted to accept at face value as sincere, accurate and apolitical. In much the manner Pearl Buck's *The Good Earth* did before 1949,[12] they constructed a China for Western audiences.

The 'once upon a time' starting point in these memoirs typically is 1950s New China; the narrator is a 'son', 'daughter' or 'born red'. In this Golden Age, Liang Heng's second word as a baby was 'Mao', for he knew Mao 'presided over us like a benevolent god' and 'believed the apples, grapes, everything good had been given us because he loved us'.[13] Although we now know of the deaths of tens of millions of Chinese, mainly in the countryside during the Great Leap Forward, the memoirs do not generally dwell on this aspect. They do tell of awakening or epiphany in the Cultural Revolution, which they see as a fall into madness and disorder. Mao sabotaged New China and destroyed their families. As Peter Zarrow puts it, the refugee memoirs thus set the 'ideological dichotomies of the Cold War – Western freedom, rationalism, individualism, and order' against

'Chinese despotism, irrationality, group-think, and chaos'.[14] The memoir typically ends with a call from London or New York for human rights and education in China, in effect calling for Western cultural solutions to Chinese political problems.

A different tale was shaped in the Fifth Generation films. Lu Tonglin has well observed that for them, 'Chinese tradition has been negated by the Communist revolution; consequently the past must be re-created from ground zero in their films'.[15] To cite examples which thematically overlap with *Hibiscus Town*, some of these films are set in village China, such as *Yellow Earth* (1984), *Red Sorghum* (1987) and *The Story of Qiu Ju* (1991), while others follow families from the 1940s through the Cultural Revolution, including *Blue Kite* (1993), *To Live* (1994) and *Farewell My Concubine* (1993). Like the Maoist story, their baseline is Old China, sometimes merely an unspecified 'way back when', but they rarely depict the 1950s as a Golden Age; 1949 is an uneasy, foreshadowing, military reshuffling. Their view of Old China resonates with pessimistic New Culture polarities and intimates that the 1949 Revolution produced not Liberation but a perpetuation of isolation, cultural involution, patriarchy, totalitarian politics and economic stagnation. As also seen in the 1988 TV series, *Heshang*, the sedentary inland village allied with imperial despotism to abort the globalising, creative commercial revolution of the cities and coast.[16] Their films present a China that is culturally hobbled: not 'China has stood up', but 'China staggers on'.

THE STORY OF *HIBISCUS TOWN*

Hibiscus Town tells a story of the decline and fall of canonical Maoism in ways different from the refugee memoirs and Fifth Generation film, grounding its critique of the Cultural Revolution within China. The fictional town is based on places in Western Hunan, famous for craggy scenery and hot peppers, where the author of the novel grew up; the story of Hu Yuyin was inspired by actual people and events. In his preface to the novel, Gu Hua evokes a moneyless but rich childhood of swimming naked in clear streams, studying hard in the village school, going away for middle school and being 'sent down' to his home town during the Cultural Revolution. The remembered place is moral as well as physical. Fifth Generation films and refugee intellectuals tell stories

which either stay mired in earthbound China or blithely pass through it; their stories tend to end up in village death or New York. By locating his moral tale in a small town full of the ever present weight and beauty of history, Xie Jin sets up a space for historical judgment which does not disparage tradition, but builds on enduring, adaptable values as a basis for reform China.

The film opens in 1963, politically a period of return to the pragmatic policies of the early 1950s: shots of shadowy curved roofs and tiles just before dawn, then a match striking in the dark, then the comely Hu Yuyin and her husband Guigui turning the handle of a venerable quern to make 'rice bean curd' (*midoufu*). She is singing a haunting 'folk' song. Then we cut to a busy street with the stove, tables and stools of their street restaurant. The opening sequence thus juxtaposes a warm domestic space against a bright, bustling public stage where we meet the other major characters, set against a chorus of villagers: bearded Director Gu, supervisor of the granary, a grizzled war veteran from the north who sells Yuyin the rice sweepings to make her bean curd; burly young Party Secretary Li Mangeng, who once had wanted to marry Yuyin, an innkeeper's daughter, but gave in when the Party denied permission to marry a bourgeois element (he now agrees to help her adopt a child); Mangeng's dishevelled wife, Peppery, who distrustfully shoos her children away from Yuyin's bean-curd stand; poor peasant activist Wang Qiushe (a homophone for 'Autumn Snake' Wang), who received land in the land reform, drank himself into debt and sold it to Yuyin for her new house; and, almost in passing, Qin Shutian ('Crazy Qin'), first sent to the village in the 1950s to collect folk songs, but declared a rightist and set to sweep the cobbled streets.

The new Four Clean-ups Movement (*siqing yundong*), which was to lead to the Cultural Revolution, arrives in the form of the cadre Li Guoxiang, a politically righteous woman, worried about 'rural polarisation' and the relapse from revolutionary values. She soon goes to Yuyin's new house to demand an accounting of the grain she bought from the public granary. (Is it significant that Yuyin sees Li first in a mirror she is polishing? In traditional tales, a demon cannot be seen in a mirror.) The domestic space, which in many Fifth Generation films is the place for patriarchy, isolation and secret desire, is here

Hibiscus Town: Hu Yuyin.

the refuge for intimacy and family; Hu Yuyin's reward for hard work is to replace the dark old house with a bright new one. But the public space can be either the place for Hu Yuyin's useful commerce or used for political shaming. Li calls a mass-struggle meeting to expose Yuyin and the 'capitalist roaders'. As Jerome Silbergeld notes, this meeting is set up physically as a staged theatrical performance, after which local cadre Wang Qiushe orders the poet Qin to paint new slogans in white paint on the town walls: 'NEVER FORGET CLASS STRUGGLE.' Yuyin fearfully gives her bundles of cash (attentively photographed to fill the screen) to Mangeng for hiding, then flees to Guangxi to wait for the storm to die down. Mangeng, tearfully nagged by Peppery, fearing for his family, hands over the cash to the Revolutionary Committee.

'EAT, DRINK, MAN, WOMAN' OR 'A REVOLUTION IS NOT A DINNER PARTY'?

The emotional and moral heart of the film now plays out in three inter-cut domestic sequences; each centres around a dinner, wine, and involves forgiveness or forgetfulness of the past; in the first and third

sequences, the couple end up in bed. The moral valence of each couple is demonstrated in their food, drink and bedding, with a little dance thrown in for good measure.

Mao, as Jerome Silbergeld points out, shared the Confucian concern with 'rectification of names' which requires proper classification and public labels. His 1927 Hunan Report proclaimed that 'a revolution is not a dinner party' for revolution 'cannot be so refined, leisurely and gentle, so temperate, kind, courteous, restrained and magnanimous', specifying the virtues which, as noted in the official translation of his works, 'were the virtues of Confucius'. Revolution is 'an act of violence by which one class overthrows another'. Feudalism was a class system held together by the 'three bonds' of the state, the family and the spirits.[17] On the other hand, popular Confucianism saw the proper life as centring around the decorous handling of this-worldly 'eat, drink, man, woman,' and this 'decorum' (*li*) was the ritual which separates humans from animals.[18] Fifth Generation films, following Mao's condemnation of the 'three bonds', presented the village in terms of oppressive hierarchy, patriarchy and hegemonic culture, while *Hibiscus Town* shows family, reciprocity and community not as oppressing individuals but as constituting them morally.

The first sequence follows the step-by-step wooing of Crazy Qin and Yuyin, ending with them as a family (one which conforms to the One Child policy at that!). When Yuyin returns and hears that her husband Guigui has been hounded to death, she goes to the mountain cemetery. A figure emerges from the misty gravestones – 'are you a man or a ghost?' she asks. It turns out to be Crazy Qin – 'sometimes I'm a ghost, and sometimes a man', he replies. Yuyin hysterically shuns Qin, but is set to work sweeping the streets with him. When she falls ill, Qin goes into her house and makes a restorative soup; Yuyin accepts Qin's sustenance in spite of his rightist past, then reciprocates by making him a meal of her spicy bean curd, not for cash but for love. Now that they have prepared food for each other, the relationship progresses. Qin teaches her that when you do it right, sweeping is not shameful (literally, 'dehumanising' *diuren*); he turns street sweeping into a dance or ritual – '*one*, two, three … *two*, two, three … *three*, two, three'. The choreographed brooms and rainy streets bring to mind Gene Kelly's classic street dance scenes in *An American in Paris* (1951); the rain is not a hurricane, but a soft mist. Yuyin lets the poet and rightist into her kitchen, heart and bed. Lying with her in what one takes to be a post-coital glow, Qin brings out his family pictures and has her call his mother by the rightful name 'mother-in-law'.

The second sequence shows the manly reconciliation of two honest cadres both attacked by the leftists for their connection to Yuyin but caught in the middle by their loyalty to the party: Secretary Li Mangeng and old comrade Director Gu sit around a table in Li's kitchen, sharing dinner and a jug of homemade corn liquor (in the novel, they kill, flay and eat a dog which Peppery has raised). When Mangeng tearfully confesses that he had seen no choice but to refuse to marry Yuyin or to turn in her incriminating cash, Gu forgives him; his remorse shows that Li has 'retained some conscience' (*liangxin*). Eventually Yuyin and Qin organise a secret wedding dinner – a softly lit and cultured ritual, with a wine toast – and the two good-food sequences merge as Director Gu notices their preparations and invites himself to join the ceremony in Yuyin's house.

Meanwhile, the third sequence depicts the cou-

pling of the leftists, almost a parody of the other two sequences. Initially based on politics, the relationship between Li Guoxiang and Wang Qiushe goes sour as a Red Guard team sweeps into Hibiscus Town waving their charismatic Little Red Books (*Quotations from Chairman Mao Zedong*). 'Poor Peasant' Wang joins them as they taunt and parade power holder Li Guoxiang through the streets. They force her to line up in the drenching rain next to rightists Yuyin and Qin. Li is outraged, pitiful, reduced to hot, sincere tears: 'There must be some misunderstanding. I was never a rightist. I am a leftist.' The Red Guards tie a pair of worn shoes around her neck (in village vernacular, old shoes are like a loose woman – anyone can get into them). Qin quietly offers her his broom, saying in good Confucian fashion, 'After all, you're a human being too' (*ni ye shi ren*). Later Wang returns from a trip to Beijing, giddy with red fervour and new-found power. The awed locals are eager to hear the latest ways to work revolution. Dancing, announces Wang, is the new thing, and waggles around to demonstrate, keeping time with a chicken leg; the village crowd can hardly choke back their guffaws. In the background, an army jeep pulls up, and a figure emerges. As she turns we see it is a now rehabilitated Li Guoxiang. Wang, still munching on the chicken, slaps himself on the head, muttering 'Idiot! Idiot!'

How he will ever worm his way back into her good graces? First Wang visits the barber, getting slicked up, admiring himself in the mirror (the mirror again!), then climbs the worn wooden stairs to Li's spartan and shallowly lit room, where she is fixing a solitary dinner. He falls on his knees to beg forgiveness for having joined in her persecution, saying that he is uneducated: 'I'm not a human being' (*wo bushi ren*). Li dismissively forgives him – 'I don't dwell in the past'. As Wang, Iago-like, goads her with the rightist plots against her, she allows him a stewed chicken leg, which he gnaws as she distractedly pours a drink for them. She fondles him, but adds 'you didn't wash your neck'. In the morning, when the cocks crow, Qin is on duty sweeping the street, and spies Wang climbing down from Li Guoxiang's window; the following morning, he places a pile of manure under Li's window where Wang lands, slips and twists his leg.

This triangle of sequences contrasts the caring table and bed of Yuyin and Qin, the comradely country drinking of the two chastened but honest Party members, and the leftist cadres' nervous, dyspeptic feeding, careless drinking and illicit coupling. There follow separated scenes between Qin and each of the two leftist cadres. In the first, he petitions Wang for permission to marry, pleading that even chickens and pigs are allowed to be couples. When Wang finds that they are going to have a baby, he commands Qin to write a 'white couplet' to paste on their door (white being the colour of funerals and reactionaries) to publicly label them 'black couple: a bitch and a dog'. Qin is quick to comfort Yuyin: it doesn't matter if they are black or white, they are now labelled a 'couple'. But Qin is sent to labour camp.

Years pass. Off-camera Mao dies and reform commences. Yuyin's house and money are returned. We have seen Li Guoxiang enter the village from the river twice before, first on foot, then in an army jeep, and this final time on the ferry, misty river scenery in the background, in a *nomenklatura* rank car with a handsome young driver. When she emerges to stroll on deck, someone is standing at the rail, his back to us. Only when he turns do we see that it is Qin. Li smilingly slaps her head to jog her memory, and comes up with his name: 'Comrade Qin, I signed your rehabilitation.' 'Comrade?' he replies, as this a term reserved for the politically pure. 'That sounds strange.' In a phrase that echoes her conversation with Wang Qiushe, Li says, 'well, what's past is past'. Qin hesitates, nods, but adds, 'now you high Party people should be more kind to us commoners'.

The final scene: we are back where we started, at least physically, at Yuyin's again prosperous street restaurant. The bean curd is as sweet and the peppers as hot as ever. Yuyin has lost two men to politics (Mangeng and Guigui), but now has a family in Comrade Qin and their son, who is named 'Jun' (army). But Xie Jin does not allow us to think that all is happy bean curd. Abruptly all laughter stops at the sound of a clanging, and the screen fills with a battered and corroded cymbal carried through the streets, just as in the opening sequence of the film. What's 'past' is present. The camera pulls back to show a mad and hairy Wang Qiushe, hoarsely shouting 'Another movement! Another movement!' (*Yundongle! Yundongle!*), which reverberates on the soundtrack. Playing against the official message of the 1980s, the camera leaves us with a pensive, lingering sequence of motionless, maybe even apprehensive family portraits – Mangeng and Peppery, Yuyin and her new family, Old Gu, the bachelor … but no family for Li Guoxiang, and certainly none for Wang Qiushe.

END OF STORY?

By circling back to the opening of the film for an echoing closing tableau not found in Gu Hua's novel, Xie Jin ironically poses a dramatic challenge: 'what has changed?' The characters have not transformed or achieved self-knowledge or even gotten visibly older, but they have emerged for us to apprehend. 'Autumn Snake' Wang emulously betrayed humanity and trivialised the revolution, while Li Guoxiang is destructive, self-willed and makes an intimate connection only with Wang, the consummate toady. But she is sincere (the film leaves her in a more favourable light by omitting her racy sex life in the novel) and does not personally profit. These leftists are more acidly satiric than evil. They have their reasons, and if they appear in mirrors, can they be demons? The middle characters, also Party cadres, Li Mangeng and Director Gu, are restored – in the novel, they both are now concerned with fighting the pollution and uncontrolled growth produced by the local factories! Peppery, Mangeng's wife, counteracts the dangers of sentimentality; her children are snotty and squalling, shown in tight close-ups. But in the intimacy of their bed, she tells Mangeng not to swat mosquitoes (*wenzi*), since even they should be allowed to 'pass their days' (*guo rizi*).

Hu Yuyin has the insipidity problem common among virtuous heroines. Although she does choose her husbands and is profitably entrepreneurial, far more engaging women appear in Fifth Generation films – dare we call them 'Aunty Heroes'? Mao's 1927 Hunan Report defined the oppression of women as the 'feudal patriarchal system and ideology' and claimed that authority of the husband could only be destroyed with the abolition of the landlord system.[19] But, as a shrewd anthropologist notes, one of the central tropes in Fifth Generation film is the capacity of the market to change power and gender relations.[20] Like Qiu Ju, who markets red peppers, and Granny Nine in *Red Sorghum*, who sells liquor, Yuyin sells consumer goods to do what she wants and get the family she needs.[21] Unlike them, she does not take action, but only waits to be rehabilitated.

The pivotal character is Qin Shutian, whose label

changes from 'the poet', to 'Crazy Qin', to 'sometimes a ghost, sometimes a man', to 'Comrade Qin'. Cinematically, Qin emerges from an almost anonymous, passing figure in the opening tableau to a central one in the closing. Qin, like any number of Confucian heroes in history, suffers political frustration and displays moral fortitude; the 'gentleman' (*wenren*) serves, forbears, witnesses and endures. Qin the poet went to the village in search of folk songs, as does the poet soldier in *Yellow Earth*, but his village was not the New Culture 'hell on earth'; rather, the enduring humanism of the village and the recurring good sense of the villagers rebukes the agenda of class struggle. For Mao and for many New Culture intellectuals, Confucianism consisted of feudal ignorance and hierarchical oppression. *Hibiscus Town* evokes a street Confucianism free of late imperial authoritarianism and evokes a perhaps mythic tradition usable in the modern world, one centred on human reciprocity, the family ... and bean curd.[22]

ACKNOWLEDGMENT
During the writing of this essay, my father became very ill and died. I would like to dedicate it to his memory.

NOTES

1. Gu Hua's novel, *Furong Zhen* (Beijing: Renmin Chubanshe, 1981), was first serialised in the journal *Dangdai* 1981 and translated by Gladys Yang as *A Small Town Called Hibiscus* (Beijing: Chinese Literature Panda Books, 1983; reprinted San Francisco: China Books, 2001).

2. The major studies are: Jerome Silbergeld, 'The Force of Labels: Melodrama in the Postmodern Era', in his *China into Film: Frames of Reference in Contemporary Chinese Cinema* (London: Reaktion Books, 1999), 188–233; Ma Ning, 'Spaciality and Subjectivity in Xie Jin's Film Melodrama of the New Period', in *New Chinese Cinemas: Forms, Identities, Politics*, ed. Nick Browne, Paul G. Pickowicz, Vivian Sobchack and Esther Yau (Cambridge University Press, 1994), 15–39.

3. Zhu Dake, quoted in Geremie R. Barmé, *In the Red: On Contemporary Chinese Culture* (New York: Columbia University Press, 1999), 381 n. 14, and Barmé's comment in the same place.

4. Zhang Xudong, *Chinese Modernism in the Era of Reforms: Cultural Fever, Avant-Garde Fiction, and the New Chinese Cinema* (Durham: Duke University Press, 1997), 220–221.

5. The classic is Peter Brooks, *The Melodramatic Imagination: Balzac, Henry James, Melodrama, and the Mode of Excess* (New Haven: Yale University Press, 1976, with a new preface, 1995); also Wimal Dissananayake, ed., *Melodrama and Asian Cinema* (New York: Cambridge University Press, 1993).

6. Paul Pickowicz, 'Melodramatic Representation and the "May Fourth" Tradition of Chinese Cinema', in *From May Fourth to June Fourth: Fiction and Film in Twentieth Century China*, ed. Ellen Widmer, David Der-wei Wang (Cambridge, MA: Harvard University Press, 1993), 295–326, quote on 321.

7. Nick Browne, 'Society and Subjectivity: On the Political Economy of Chinese Melodrama', in Browne et al., *New Chinese Cinemas*, 51–52; Paul G. Pickowicz, 'Huang Jianxin and the Notion of Postsocialism,' in ibid., 58.

8. Browne, 'Society and Subjectivity', 53–54.

9. Herbert Fingarette, *Confucius: The Secular as Sacred* (New York: Harper, 1972).

10. Charles W. Hayford, *To the People: James Yen and Village China* (New York: Columbia University Press, 1990), esp. 60–65; Myron Cohen, 'Cultural and Political Inventions in Modern China: the Case of the Chinese "Peasant"', *Daedalus*, 122, no. 2 (1993): 151–170.

11. Peter Zarrow, 'Meanings of China's Cultural Revolution: Memoirs of Exile', *positions*, 7, no. 1 (1999): 165–191. I have also profited from King-far Tam, 'Private Memories and Public Memoirs: What Are They Telling the World about China?' (Association for Asian Studies Conference, Washington DC, 8 April 1995).

12. Charles W. Hayford, 'The Storm Over the Peasant: Orientalism, Rhetoric and Representation in Modern China', in *Contesting the Master Narrative: Essays in Social History*, ed. Shelton Stromquist and Jeffrey Cox (Iowa City: University of Iowa Press, 1998), 150–172; Charles W. Hayford, 'What's So Bad about *The Good Earth*?', *Education About Asia*, 3, no. 3 (1998): 4–7.

13. Liang Heng and Judith Shapiro, *Son of the Revolution* (New York: Random House, 1983), 7.

14. Zarrow, 'Meanings of China's Cultural Revolution', 172.

15. Tonglin Lu, *Confronting Modernity in the Cinemas of Taiwan and Mainland China* (Cambridge: Cambridge University Press, 2002), 17.

16. Su Xiaokang and Wang Luxiang, trans. R. W. Bodman and P. P. Wan, *Deathsong of the River: A Reader's Guide to the Chinese TV Series 'Heshang'* (Ithaca: Cornell East Asian Center, 1991).

17. *Quotations from Chairman Mao Tse-tung* (Peking: Foreign Languages Press, 1966), 11, from 'Report on an Investigation of the Peasant Movement in Hunan', *Selected Works of Mao Tse-tung*, vol. 1 (Peking: Foreign Languages Press 1967), 28, 56 n. 4, 44.

18. As well as being the title of the Ang Lee film, the phrase appears in *Book of Rites* (*Liji*).

19. Mao, 'Report on an Investigation', 44.

20. Ann Anagnost, 'Chili Pepper Politics', in *National Past-Times: Narrative, Representation, and Power in Modern China* (Durham: Duke University Press, 1997), 138–160.

21. In *Hibiscus Town* the Party Secretary is a woman, implying a choice to de-gender the power relation. See Andrew Kipnis, 'Anti-Maoist Gender: Hibiscus Town's Naturalization of a Dengist Sex/Gender/Kinship System', *Asian Cinema*, 8, no. 2 (1996–1997): 66–75.

22. Richard Madsen, 'Confucian Conceptions of Civil Society', in *Alternative Conceptions of Civil Society*, ed. Simone Chambers and Will Kymlicka (Princeton: Princeton University Press, 2001), 190–204.

16   *In The Mood for Love*: Intersections of Hong Kong Modernity

Audrey Yue

INTERSECTION AND MODES OF PRODUCTION

Hong Kong, 1962. Two neighbours meet and seek solace in each other as they discover their respective spouses are having an affair. They play-act what they will say to their spouses when they confront them with what they know. As they begin to spend more time together, they soon find that they too are falling in love and drifting into an affair. To allay neighbours' gossip, one moves to work as a reporter in Singapore. Four years later, in Cambodia covering General de Gaulle's visit, he finds himself unburdening the secret of this affair.

The above synopsis of Wong Kar-wai's *In the Mood for Love* (*IMFL*) reveals three sites of intersection. First, there is the theme – the mood of love is rendered through the intersection of the sanctity of marriage and the restraint of the affair. Second, there is the space – the narrative of the story is structured through Hong Kong's intersection with its region, including Cambodia, Singapore and Thailand (where the film was shot). Third, there is the time – history is replaced by a Jamesonian display of post-modern historicism, where the past surfaces as an intersection through the aesthetics of style.

The device of the intersection is a Wong Kar-wai hallmark. He has used two parallel stories since his directorial debut in 1988: triad big brother Ah Wah and his younger buddy-lackey, Fly, in *As Tears Go By*; teddy boy Yuddy and the cop-sailor in *Days of Being Wild*; cop 663 and 223's relationships with their respective lovers in *Chungking Express*; the hit man and his assistant in *Fallen Angels*; Evil East and Poison West in *Ashes of Time*; and Yiu-fai and Bao-wing in *Happy Together*. Ackbar Abbas formulates this as 'metonymic substitution', a device of doubling where characters are interchangeable in a narrative cycle of repetition.[1]

IMFL features a similar parallel-story structure, with reporter Chow Mo-wan (Tony Leung Chiu-wai) and housewife Su Li-zhen, usually referred to as 'Mrs Chan' (Maggie Cheung Man-yuk). Instead of Wong's usual protagonists' voice-over monologues interweaving the narrative, the film follows his period martial arts epic, *Ashes of Time*, by opening and ending with titles quoting from popular fiction:

It is a restless moment.
She has kept her head lowered,
To give him a chance to come closer.
But he could not, for lack of courage.
She turns and walks away.

That era has passed.
He remembers those vanished years.

Nothing that belonged to it exists any more.
As though looking through a dusty window pane,
The past is something he could see, but not touch.
And everything he sees is blurred and indistinct.

This adapted narration from Liu Yichang's novella *Duidao* reveals the three sites of intersection: a theme evoking a mood about two lovers and their failed encounter, a story that spatialises here and there, and a temporality that freezes memory in a perpetual present.[2] Wong explains the significance of intersection in a book accompanying *IMFL*:

The first work by Liu Yichang I read was *Duidao*. The title is a Chinese translation of *tête-bêche*, which describes stamps that are printed top to bottom facing each other. *Duidao* centres round the intersection of two parallel stories – of an old man and a young girl. One is about memories, the other anticipation. To me, *tête-bêche* is more than a term for stamps or intersection of stories. It can be the intersection of light and colour, silence and tears. *Tête-bêche* can also be the intersection of time: for instance, youthful eyes on an aging face, borrowed words on revisited dreams.[3]

This essay takes Wong's evocation of *tête-bêche* as a point of departure for an exploration of intersection in the film. Two practices of *tête-bêche* as intersection are evident in *IMFL*. First, *tête-bêche* is the intersection of *Duidao* and *IMFL*. The film intersects with the novella through the cinema, the space of Hong Kong and China, and popular media from Hong Kong, Taiwan, and South-east Asia.[4] Second, *tête-bêche* resonates with the temporality of Hong Kong before and after 1997, when the British colony returned to its socialist motherland, China. I have written elsewhere about how Hong Kong cinema expresses this temporality of pre-post-1997 as a culture that simultaneously forecasts and recollects.[5] I extend that idea here, to suggest that intersection functions as a point in Hong Kong's period of transition – both pre-1997 to Chinese rule and post-1997 in the following fifty years of the unique 'one

country, two systems' administration. This can be seen in *IMFL*'s conception and release. The film originated when Wong visited Beijing for a month in 1996, and he gave it the working title *Summer in Beijing*. He writes: 'Between *Summer in Beijing* and *In the Mood for Love*, eras changed, locales changed, and the music changed. We moved from contemporary jazz to nostalgic waltz.'[6] *IMFL* is Wong's first post-1997 film, shot on location in Thailand while filming *2046*, a science-fiction film set fifty years after Hong Kong's 1997 return, highlighting its status as a product of temporal (before and after 1997) and spatial (China, Hong Kong and South-east Asia) intersections. In *IMFL*, '2046' is the number of the hotel room occupied by Chow.

These two practices of *tête-bêche* produce intersection as a point in transition characterised by convergence and divergence. In the next section below, I use convergence to explore the cinema. I critically review the politics of recent theorisation of Hong Kong cinema to interrogate how the mood of the popular is produced in the global reception of *IMFL*. In the section after that, I use divergence to examine the space between Hong Kong and China by exposing how the film uses Asian popular media to construct Hong Kong's relationship to the region. I argue that convergence and divergence question the presumed intersections of Hong Kong modernity. *IMFL* captures this modernity as that which is accented by its specific history of emergence. My conclusion addresses the politics of its present by evaluating the film's temporality through its aesthetics of style.

A THEME OF CONVERGENCE: IN THE MOOD FOR THE HONG KONG POPULAR

Convergence is a practice synonymous with media globalisation. In the past five years or so, the globalisation of Hong Kong cinema has witnessed the popularity in the West of the industry's martial arts action genre, which has resulted in Hollywood produced blockbuster 'remakes', celebrity advertising and the emergence of a new breed of pan-Asian superstars in Hollywood. Against such a backdrop, the Wong Kar-wai film has also gained popularity, through the patronage of the likes of Quentin Tarantino and the art-house and independent festival circuits. Using convergence as the first moment of

In the Mood for Love: Tony Leung and Maggie Cheung.

intersection, I suggest here that the Wong Kar-wai genre functions as a site that crosses the high–low divide stereotyping Hong Kong action cinema in the West. I argue that as a site of convergence, the genre reveals the practices of current Hong Kong cinema theorisation and consumption to expose the politics surrounding Hong Kong cinema's transnational success. This success is the result of Hong Kong's transition that has witnessed the migration of people, cinema and industry throughout the world.

IMFL was released internationally in 2000 and 2001, around the same time as Ang Lee's award-winning *Crouching Tiger, Hidden Dragon*. Equally as critically acclaimed, the film's numerous awards included Best Actor (Leung) and Grand Prix technique (Christopher Doyle, Mark Li Ping-Bin and William Chang) at Cannes 2000 and Best Actor, Best Actress (Cheung), Best Costume Design (Chang), Best Art Direction (Chang) and Best Editing (Chang) at the 20th Hong Kong Film Association Awards. These accolades attest to Wong Kar-wai's popularity. After the licensing of *Fallen Angels* to thirty-four countries in 1994, his UCLA interview with Tarantino in 1995, and the US release of *Chungking Express* in 1996, Wong's meteoric rise was unprecedented, culminating with the Best Director award for *Happy Together* at Cannes 1997, on the eve of Hong Kong's return to Chinese rule. *IMFL* crossed the high–low divide in 2000 when it was listed in various global annual top-ten film polls.[7]

As art-house, Wong's films repeat the comfort of a familiar formula. But as 'Hong Kong art-house', they disrupt the larger generic economy. The prefix 'Hong Kong' is a signifier of difference, as a post-modern and post-colonial space that attenuates the gap between cult and mass, and hip and unhip. As a practice of convergence between action and art, the Wong Kar-wai genre exposes the politics of the Hong Kong popular. It modulates the cult of martial arts films and the mass appeal of the new Hollywood action by suggesting that there is a difference between what is 'hip' and 'unhip' in the global consumption of Hong Kong cinema. By problematising the Hollywood-produced action blockbusters of Jackie Chan and John Woo as mass and almost B-list unhip, the genre's hipness produces the Hong Kong popular as a mood that structures a mode, reflecting the intersections of the post-modern collapse of categories, the global celebration of difference and the neo-colonial new modern. The film's theme – its mood – governs this structure.

Most popular reviews of *IMFL* speak of it as 'a veritable mood piece'.[8] It communicates claustrophobic desire. Bound by the legal union that a marriage demands and the transgression of an illicit affection, Mr Chow and Mrs Chan try to curb their emotions. Claustrophobia is literalised through tight shot composition. Alleyways are angled from the turns of corners whilst interior shots of the apartments and the rooms are encased by windows, corridors, stairways and hallways, with characters framed through mid-shots, small tilts and slight pans. Yearning is structured through the finesse of Chang's editing and cinematography – a brush of fabrics, a turn of looks, a change in the film speed and tempo.

Theorisations of Wong's films have attributed the claustrophobic effect of his trademark fish-eye wide-angle lenscape to his unique understanding of the city.[9] These theorisations consign the city to a subject and a subjectivity by pointing to a prevailing Hong Kong structure of feeling concerning intensity, proximity and modernity. Some of these celebrate Wong's style often at the expense of undermining the specificity of Hong Kong, where the Hong Kong popular emerges only as a mood that is hip in current theorisations about the cinema and as a mode that structures a genre of film, maintaining the universality of film-as-art formula.[10] It is ironic that the modernity of Hong Kong that is used to characterise Wong's style is now the same site used to wipe out the specificity of the Hong Kong locality. For example, writing about the post-modern hipness of *IMFL*, Teo suggests that the privileging of 'abstraction rather than plot' allows the audience to engage in 'a ritual of transfigured time … and … each member of the audience, depending on their ages, could in theory go as far back in time as they wish to the moment that holds the most formative nostalgic significance for them'.[11] Abstractions such as this deny the politics demanded by the transfiguration of Hong Kong modernity's 'emergence of qualitatively new desires, social relations, and modes of association within the … community … *and* between that group and its … oppressors'.[12]

Such a politics consists of a desire to enact new modes of expression consequent on exposing the internal fissures of the transition. Elsewhere, I have argued that the politics of transition has produced a cinema post-1984 (the year of the Sino-British Joint Declaration that announced British Hong Kong's 1997 return to Chinese rule) that expresses Hong Kong's post-colonial identity as modern, mobile, transnational and hybrid. Both Hong Kong action and art-house films have emerged in such a milieu as instances of their own socio-cultural circumstances: the former, a high-octane genre that resonates with Hong Kong's panic culture and saw the emergence of the first modern, romantic-thriller, gangster hero (e.g. Chow Yun Fat in John Woo's 1984 *A Better Tomorrow*); the latter, the maturity of a style and an indigenous subject matter that achieved international acclaim and recognition.

I extend this here, to suggest that in *IMFL*, the mood of claustrophobia can be read as an effect of the inscription of phobic spaces by a transnational film-maker such as Wong, reflecting his experience of 'liminality and multifocality'.[13] This is evident in both the film-maker's intent and his filmic strategies. Of *IMFL*, Wong noted that he was influenced by his own experience as an immigrant child growing up in the 1960s in Hong Kong amongst the diasporic Shanghainese community where rumours, lies and gossip were rife and people tried to pretend that all was well. Gossip and pretence are anchored in the film through Mrs Suen's disapproval of Mrs Chan's late nights out alone, the protagonists' make-believe marriages and play-acting of their partners' infidelity. These events mediate social order (duty, propriety, monogamy) and disorder (love affairs, extra-marital relationships, adultery) and encode, in the process the subjectivity of claustrophobia. As noted earlier, the film's formal strategies attest to this desire.

More significantly, this desire is the desire for a forbidden love that has to remain a secret. Hence, the film is an ode to the acting of acting where everyday practices such as eating and walking are denaturalised to convey the oscillation between feeling secure and trapped. Not surprisingly, the use of Shigeru Umebayashi's 'Yumeji's Theme' as the main love theme for the encounters between Mr Chow and Mrs Chan captures the breathlessness of this desire. In these sequences, the camera pans are longer and wider, and the movement stylised and slowed. Rather than displacing intimacy to outside public spaces as Abbas and Siegel have suggested about Wong's earlier films, these sequences punctuate the film through the labour of its haunting rhythm, and function as a non-diegetic (interstitial) space for the consummation of love.[14] Clearly, this non-diegetic space returns to the liminality of Hong Kong-in-transition, as a third 'border' space caught between the East and the West. Here, the politics of transnationality exposed by the popularity of the Wong Kar-wai genre helps return the film to its cultural location. The following section further suggests, maybe ironically, that *IMFL* returns to Hong Kong via the mobility of transnational routes engendered by Asian popular media, only to produce a space of regionality.

A PROJECT OF DIVERGENCE: REGIONALITY AND MODERNITY

Jeffrey Ressner's *Time International* report on the 'controversy' created by *IMFL* – together with Ang Lee's *Crouching Tiger, Hidden Dragon*, Jiang Wen's *Devils on the Doorstep*, Shinji Aoyama's *Eureka* and Edward Yang's *Yi Yi* – at Cannes exposes regionality as a benchmark for measuring standards of acceptability.[15] Its headline, 'Asia Scores: The Region's Movies Come of Age at the Cannes Festival, with Four Big Awards', foregrounds the discourse of regionality as part of the politics of transnationality. The article once again marks 'Asia' as the other evaluated against the normative orthodoxy of international film acclaim. 'Coming of age' is an event that intersects the disjunctive projects of Western and Asian modernities as claims to both representation (of the films) and self-representation (from the films). This section shows how regionality is produced in *IMFL* through the emergence of Hong Kong modernity.

Regionality highlights divergence through the reterritorialisation of place as an effect of the cultural-economic contradictions of globalisation. The changing geopolitical configurations of Asia and Europe have witnessed culturalist, statist and economic projects of self-representation that construct new regional imaginations to patch the fissures of identity and difference.[16] Against such a backdrop, regionality produces the image as a practice of the transnational imagination, as a way of negotiating between different sites, individuals, and agencies.[17]

IMFL belongs to such an imagination where, as the previous section has shown, the 'hipness' of the Wong Kar-wai genre has produced an image of style. I argue that this image is characterised by a pan-Asian pastiche of Eastern and Western influences.

These influences question the authenticity of cultures and the different histories of the West in Asia. In *IMFL*, this pastiche is evident not only in the nostalgic 1960s *mise en scène* (e.g. modern apartments, modular furniture, pattern-design and floral wallpapers) but also in the use of Asian popular media. This use locates and problematises Hong Kong as an intersection for regional flows. As a strategy of divergence, intersection shows how the hegemony of Hong Kong cinema mobilises the process of reterritorialisation to produce its cultural location as a centre for Asian popular culture.

The eclectic references to Asian popular media in the film highlight Hong Kong as a modern space of regional cultural mix. For example, the use of Liu's *Duidao* archives an indigenous literary tradition in Hong Kong. A Shanghainese immigrant like Wong, Liu is one of Hong Kong's leading fiction writers. He is also the founder and chief editor of the journal, *Hong Kong Literary Monthly* (*xianggangwenxue*). The protagonists' penchant for reading martial arts pulp serials and Mr Chow's desire to write one himself show the popularity of the genre, one that Wong has also referred to in his use of Jin Yong's *Eagle Shooting Heroes* in *Ashes of Time*. Wong's quotations inscribe not only local literature and vernacular pulp fiction, but also Japanese film, art and music. 'Yumeji's Theme' is borrowed from Suzuki Seijun's 1991 film, *Yumeji*, a bio-fantasy about the turbulent life of Japanese artist Takehisa Yumeji (1884–1934), played by popular singer Kenji Sawada, who embodied the romanticism of Japan's Taisho era (1912–1926) with his hybrid woodblock and art nouveau style, and was renowned for his sketches of nude women. Other influences include the use of Cantonese, Beijing and Zhejiang operas. Notably, the recorded excerpts of *silangtanmu* and *sangyuan jizi* pay tribute to Tan Xin Pei, a legendary figure in the Beijing opera who was also involved in *Ding Jun Shan* (1905), China's first indigenous film.

Clearly, Wong's pastiche samples images and sound bytes from the present and the past, producing Hong Kong as a modern space constructed by its location as an intersection for regional Asian influences. In particular, I argue that the strategy of divergence reterritorialises the space between Hong Kong and China by engendering the image through the female voice and the female star as constitutive sites for the emergence of Hong Kong modernity.

First, the space between Hong Kong and China is rendered through Shanghai in the film. The story partially uses Shanghainese and is set in an immigrant Shanghainese community where everybody knows each other. The advent of Chinese communism in 1949 saw the fall of Shanghai with the emigration of its people and capital and the consequent emergence of modern Hong Kong. Since the 1997 return and China's vigorous economy, Shanghai has returned to its former status as the more 'senior' city in the Chinese cultural imaginary. Writing on heritage renewal projects in Shanghai and Hong Kong, Abbas suggests different histories of colonialism: Shanghai exhibits 'a cosmopolitanism of extraterritoriality' whilst Hong Kong displays 'a cosmopolitanism of dependency'.[18] Although both forms of cosmopolitanism show how colonial presence is used to 'construct a Chinese version of modern cosmopolitan culture',[19] I suggest here that the regionality of Shanghai rendered in the film complicates the chronology and shows the incommensurability of Chinese cultural history: the film functions as an axis of divergence revealing a Hong Kong modernity also shaped by the social imagination of Shanghai.

Hong Kong exists in the film as a space of displacement. Shot on location in Thailand because Wong could not find enough old buildings in Hong Kong, Hong Kong exists as an effect of two forces, migration and modernity. Both are evident in the narrative. Migration appears as Mrs Chan works for a shipping company selling tickets, Mr Chow leaves to work as a reporter in Singapore and Mrs Suen joins her family in America. Modernity appears, for example, in the use of radio broadcasts, Japanese electric rice-cookers, the telephone, and dining on steak and mustard sauce.

The setting of the film in 1962 is significant because the 1960s marked the beginning of Hong Kong's post-colonial modernity. Historian Frank Welsh dates Hong Kong's 'official' period of 'autodecolonisation' to 11 April 1963, when Hong Kong's House of Commons reviewed post-war Hong Kong. Welsh observes that it was in the 1960s that Hong Kong 'acquired what have become its typical modern attitudes: that single-minded dedication to money-making which powered the engine of expansion'.[20] The film inscribes this history through the narrative by using the displacement of Shanghainese and South-east Asian migration, and the politics of transition. Transition here is evident from the use of the archival footage of Charles de Gaulle's visit to Cambodia in 1966, on the eve of the Vietnam War and the start of China's Cultural Revolution, as a historical and metaphorical staging for Hong Kong, as a transit destination for Chinese migrants and Indo-Chinese and Vietnamese refugees, as well as for Hong Kong's 1997 return to Chinese rule.

The radio broadcast of popular 1930s and 1940s Shanghainese singer Zhou Xuan's '*Huayang de Nianhua*' consolidates the film's narrative as a transitional history between Hong Kong and China. Indeed, the film even pays homage to the singer through its Chinese title, *Huayang Nianhua*. The practices of radio listening (and listening to imported music) and making song requests in the film highlights radio in the 1960s as a form of popular domestic technology. It also locates the popular memory of Zhou as Shanghai's 'golden voice' of the 1930s and 1940s. Her repertoire included more than one hundred songs. More significantly, she sang in the national language of Mandarin Chinese (*putonghua*). Jonathan Stock suggests that her use of the national language, along with radio broadcasts, and gramophone replays in nightclubs, restaurants and bars, 'mark [her] music as "popular"' through 'its intimate relationship with the mass media'.[21] Andreas Steen states that she is placed at 'the heart of a cult of romantic nostalgia which has accompanied the growth of modern Shanghai since the early 1990s'.[22] The film's broadcast not only inscribes this history; its aurality functions as a technical device that disembodies Mr Chan's love through the cult of Zhou, relaying a romance with an image made present by technology as a female voice.

Another female voice in the film is that of Rebecca Pan, who plays the landlady, Mrs Suen. Like Zhou Xuan, Pan is also a Shanghainese who recorded songs in Mandarin and English in Hong Kong, but in the 1970s. *IMFL*'s official website acclaims her as a Chinese popular music legend throughout East Asia. This legendary status is anchored in the film through her rendition of 'Bengawan Solo', the national song of Indonesia. Margaret Kartomi notes the post-colonial significance of this song not only in Indonesia but also in East and South-east Asia through its reflections on anti-colonial resistance and political independence. Tracing multiple renditions in Tagalog in the Philippines and in Cantonese or Mandarin in Singapore,

Hong Kong, Taiwan and China, she notes that it has been performed 'in virtually every popular style, from *kroncong* to swing, jazz to bossanova, rock-and-roll, national song to march band, and brass band to symphony orchestra', becoming 'a regional symbol' that represents 'the hegemony and power struggles within Indonesia and the East/Southeast Asia as a whole, with its economic dynamism and self-assertiveness'.[23]

This song anchors the arrival of Mr Chow in Singapore. An interior shot of his office pans across the *Singapore Daily* sign, echoing an earlier pan in Hong Kong of Mr Chow at his *Sing Man Yit Pao Daily* newspaper office. The references to print media further add to the film's narrative of modernity through its role as a technology for the formation of the modern nation-state. More significantly, this narrative of modernity also reveals a self-reflexive return to the cinema of Wong Kar-wai and the politics of its emergence where *tête-bêche*, as the intersection of Mrs Suen (Pan) and Mr Chow (Leung), functions as a form of binding between *IMFL* and *Days of Being Wild*. Styled with the same vaselined hair, attired in the same mod suit and tie, the intersection of Leung and Pan re-places the song through the intertextuality of *Days of Being Wild*. Hence, the use of Nat King Cole's 'Aquellos Ojos Verdes', 'Quizas Quizas Quizas' and 'Te Quiero Dijiste' in *IMFL* makes sense when rendered through the surface of the Philippines as an image without memory, a cultural plastic of sound bites that makes familiar the foreignness of style. Like the band musicians in Hong Kong's nighclubs that croon familiar, romantic and exotic Latin ballads, here post-modern historicism produces a presence of the image as style.

CONCLUSION: AD(DRESS)ING ASIAN POP

The modishness of Cheung's *cheongsam* dresses in the film also foregrounds this post-modern historicist practice of making the image present as style. Her costumes epitomise the temporality of the film as a form of presentness marked by the new, where the progress of time is ritualised in the changing of her wardrobe. This temporality connotes a dailiness accentuated through the ephemerality of fashion. The style of the dress is not only newly fashionable again in the global consumption of Chinoiserie. The actualisation of style is also heightened through the aestheticisation produced by slow pans, low speeds and close-ups. This exteriority reflects the image of the Wong Kar-wai genre as a cinema of style, speaking to the politics of global fashion tourism. However, its literalness not only translates the logic of cross-cultural exchange; the style of dress also locates a politics about the history of modern Hong Kong cinema. This is also the style of dress adorning Cheung in *Centre Stage*, a film archiving the life of the legendary pan-Chinese movie star Ruan Lingyu and the attendant emergence of film in Hong Kong.[24] Cheung's performance won her the Best Actress Silver Bear award at the 1991 Berlin International Film Festival, considered as the first international acclaim for new Hong Kong cinema, but also marking the modernity of that cinema as one that questions the form of its relationship to the present and itself, signalling a self-consciousness about its presence in a world structured by the fissures of transition. Popularly described as the most recognisable female Asian face in the world, Cheung's image has not only appeared in films by Wong Kar-wai, Tsui Hark and Jackie Chan, but it also has currency as the face of the namesake style magazine, the hair of Lux shampoo advertisements and 'the latex fit' of French vampires[25] (*Irma Vep*) and martial arts cult aficionados (*Augustin, roi du Kung-fu*). Her iconicity converges to address the Oriental, neo-Oriental and self-Oriental commodification of contemporary pan-Asian popular culture. It problematises the Hong Kong cinema interface as a form of marginal imperialism in the Asian region,[26] a genre of fusion pan-Asian kitsch in the global imagination[27] and a structure of mood in the nostalgic present. This is a cosmopolitan image that tells the modern story of the intoxication of love, but also a passion that returns to the politics of cinema, its look and its tale.

NOTES

1. Ackbar Abbas, *Hong Kong: Culture and the Politics of Disappearance* (Minneapolis: University of Minnesota Press, 1997), 48–62.

2. Liu Yichang, 'Intersections (*Duidao*)', trans. Nancy Li, *Renditions*, nos. 29–30 (1988): 92.

3. Wong Kar-wai, *Tête-bêche: A Wong Kar Wai Project* (Hong Kong: Block 2 Pictures, 2000), no pagination.

4. Set in 1970s Hong Kong, *Duidao* tells the parallel stories of Chunyu Bai, an old reporter from Shanghai who fled to Hong Kong in the 1940s to escape the

Japanese Occupation, and Ah Xing, a young single woman who lives with her parents. Bai is nostalgic, fuelled by his memories of Shanghai, his youthful liaisons with dancehall girls and his failed marriage. Ah Xing is forward-looking. Always day-dreaming about herself as a famous singer or a movie star, she longs to find love and marry a handsome husband, someone 'a bit like Ke Junxiong, a bit like Deng Guangrong, a bit like Bruce Lee, and a bit like Alain Delon' (Liu, 'Intersections', 92). Triggered by songs, old photographs, and magazine covers and posters of movie stars, the two characters' temporalities are retrospective and projective. In the story, they only meet once sitting next to each other in a crowded cinema. Everyday practices like walking, commuting, listening to music, watching television and going to the movies highlight their close encounters. These practices construct Hong Kong, already a Chinese migrant enclave and a metropolis dizzy with escalating property prices and swirling in the popular media mix of Taiwanese Mandarin pop songs, Filipino renditions of American Top Ten hits, Hollywood cinema and French film icons. The oft-repeated phrase, 'a bit like Ke Junxiong, a bit like Deng Guangrong, a bit like Bruce Lee, and a bit like Alain Delon', epitomises the cultural mix. As this essay will show, these practices are also significant to *IMFL*, because they function as the film's historical and cultural mode of production.

5. Audrey Yue, 'Preposterous Horror: On *Rouge*, *A Chinese Ghost Story* and Nostalgia', in *The Horror Reader*, ed. Ken Gelder (New York: Routledge, 2000), 365–399; 'Transition Culture in Clara Law's *Autumn Moon*: Refiguring the Migrant and the Foreigner', *Intersections*: <wwwsshe.murdoch.edu.au/intersections> no. 4 (2000) (20 September 2000); and 'What's so queer about *Happy Together*? aka Queer (N)Asian: Interface, Mobility, Belonging', *Inter-Asia Cultural Studies Journal*, 1, no. 2 (2000): 251–263.

6. Wong Kar-wai, 'From *Summer in Beijing* to *In the Mood for Love*', in *Tony Leung: In the Mood for Love* (Taiwan: Block 2 Music Co. & Universal Music Ltd, 2000), no pagination.

7. For example, David Ansen, 'Ansen's Top 15: Our Critics Pick his Best and Brightest from the Pack', *Newsweek*, 14 January 2000: 58; Richard Corliss, 'Cinema (Arts and Media/The Best and Worst of 2001', *Time International*, 24 December 2001: 78; and Anthony D'Alessandro, 'Top Grossing Pics of 2001', *Variety*, 7–13 January 2002: 38.

8. Stephen Teo, 'Wong Kar-wai's *In the Mood for Love*: Like a Ritual in Transfigured Time', *Senses of Cinema*: <www.sensesofcinema.com/contents/01/13/mood.html> (10 April 2001).

9. See for examples: Kent Jones, '*In the Mood for Love* (Review)', *Film Comment*, 37, no. 1 (2001): 22. Teo refers to *IMFL* reflecting 'an ideal dreamtime of Hong Kong' (ibid.). Abbas suggests that the city functions as 'leitmotif of a space that enforces physical proximity but forbids intimacy', and has become a protagonist that is only perceptible in 'fragments, metonymies, displacements', in 'Dialectic of Deception', *Public Culture*, 11, no. 2 (1999): 362–363. Marc Siegel extends this to show that it produces 'new kinds of intimacy' that exist 'outside in the public sexual world', in 'The Intimate Spaces of Wong Kar-wai', in *At Full Speed: Hong Kong Cinema in a Borderless World*, ed. Esther C. M. Yau (Minneapolis: University of Minnesota Press, 2001), 290, 285.

10. See Jones, '*In the Mood for Love* (Review)'. See also Jean-Marc Lalanne, 'Images from the Inside', trans. Stephen Wright, in Jean-Marc Lalanne, David Martinez, Ackbar Abbas, Jimmy Ngai, *Wong Kar-wai* (Paris: Editions Dis Voir, 1997), 9–28; Ewa Mazierska and Laura Rascaroli, 'Trapped in the Present: Time in the Films of Wong Kar-wai', *Film Criticism*, 25, no. 2 (2000): 2–20.

11. Teo, 'Wong Kar-wai's *In the Mood for Love*'.

12. Paul Gilroy, *The Black Atlantic: Modernity and Double Consciousness* (London: Verso, 1993), 37; emphasis in original. Gilroy's counter-modernity relates to Hong Kong modernity as forms of alternative modernity. On alternative modernities, see also Dilip P. Goankar, 'On Alternative Modernities', *Public Culture*, 11, no. 1 (1999): 1–18.

13. Hamid Naficy, 'Phobic Spaces and Liminal Panics: Independent Transnational Film Genre', in *Global/Local: Cultural Production and the Transnational Imaginary*, ed. Rob Wilson and Wimal Dissanayake (Durham: Duke University Press, 1996), 130.

14. Abbas, 'Dialectic of Deception'; Siegel, 'The Intimate Spaces'.

15. Jeffrey Ressner, 'Asia Scores: The Region's Movies Come of Age at the Cannes Festival, with Four Big Awards – and, in Ang Lee's Martial-arts Fantasy, One Peerless Triumph', *Time International*, 115, no. 22 (2000): 54.

16. On 'Asia' as a discourse of regionality, see: Rob Wilson and Wimal Dissanayake, ed., *Asia/Pacific as Space of Cultural Production* (Durham: Duke University Press, 1995); Chen Kuan-Hsing, ed., *Trajectories: Inter-Asia Cultural Studies* (London: Routledge, 1998); Aihwa Ong and Donald Nonini, ed., *Ungrounded Empires: The Cultural Politics of Modern Chinese Transnationalism* (London: Routledge, 1997); Tu Wei-ming, ed., *Confucian Traditions in East Asian Modernity* (Cambridge, MA: Harvard University Press, 1996); Arif Dirlik, ed., *What is a Rim?* (Boulder: Westview Press, 1993); Ron Martin, ed., *Money and the Space Economy* (Chichester: John Wiley & Sons, 1999); Kris Olds et al., ed., *Globalisation and the Asia Pacific: Contested Territories* (London: Routledge, 1999); Myong-gon Chu, *The New Asia in Global Perspective* (New York: St Martin's Press, 2000); and Leo Ching, 'Globalizing the Regional, Regionalizing the Global: Mass Culture and Asianism in the Age of Late Capital', *Public Culture*, 12, no. 1 (2000): 233–257.

17. Appadurai's disjunctive scapes point to the production of the image as a practice of transnational imagination, in 'Disjuncture and Difference in the Global Cultural Economy', *Public Culture*, 2, no. 2 (1990): 1–24. An example of this image in Asia is evident in Leo Ching's writings on mass Asianism.

18. Ackbar Abbas, 'Cosmopolitan De-scriptions: Shanghai and Hong Kong', *Public Culture*, 12, no. 3 (2000): 778.

19. Ibid., 775.

20. Frank Welsh, *A History of Hong Kong* (London: HarperCollins, 1994), 458, 461.

21. Jonathan Stock, 'Zhou Xuan: Early Twentieth-century Chinese Popular Music', *Asian Music*, 26, no. 2 (1995): 123.

22. Andreas Steen, 'Tradition, Politics and Meaning in 20th Century China's Popular Music. Zhou Xuan: "When will the Gentleman Come Back Again?"' *Chime*, 14–15 (1999–2000): 150.

23. Margaret Kartomi, 'The Pan-East/Southeast Asian and National Indonesian Song Bengawan Solo and its Javanese Composer', *Yearbook for Traditional Music* (1998), 97–98.

24. On *Centre Stage*, see Brett Farmer, 'Mémoire en Abîme: Remembering (through) *Centre Stage*' (review essay), *Intersections: Gender, History and Culture in the Asian Context*, 4: (September 2000): <wwwshe.murdoch.edu.au/intersections/issue4/centre_review.html> (10 October 2000); and Shuqin Cui, 'Stanley Kwan's *Center Stage*: The (Im)possible

Engagement between Feminism and Postmodernism',
Cinema Journal, 39, no. 4: (Summer 2000): 61–76; as
well as Bérénice Reynaud's essay in this volume.

25. Olivia Khoo, ' "Anagrammatical Translations": Latex
Performance and Asian femininity unbounded in
Olivier Assayas's *Irma Vep*', *Continuum*, 13, no. 3
(November 1999): 383–395.

26. Ding-Tzann Lii, 'A Colonized Empire: Reflections
on the Expansion of Hong Kong Films in Asian
Countries', in Chen, *Trajectories*, 122–141.

27. On the nature of commodity consumption in Wong
Kar-wai's other films, see Gina Marchetti, 'Buying
American, Consuming Hong Kong: Cultural
Commerce, Fantasies of Identity, and the Cinema', in
The Cinema of Hong Kong: History, Arts, Identity, ed.
Poshek Fu and David Desser (Cambridge,
Cambridge University Press, 2000), 289–313.

17　*Love Eterne*: Almost a (Heterosexual) Love Story

Tan See Kam and Annette Aw

In *Farewell My Concubine* (Chen Kaige, 1993), Leslie Cheung and Zhang Fengyi play two opera stars best known for their rendition of the concubine and the Emperor in the eponymous Beijing opera. On the opera stage, they epitomise an ideal heterosexual couple. Off-stage, the two stage-brothers are as close as men can be; the former wishes for greater intimacy, but the latter is avowedly heterosexual. Cheng's intense but unrequited love for Duan – along with his cross-sex acts in *Farewell My Concubine* – open a window to the queer sexual potential of Chinese film and film-opera culture for international film audiences of the early 1990s. For audiences well acquainted with this culture, the history is far longer. Between 1948 and 1964, at least eight film versions of the Liang Shanbo and Zhu Yingtai legend circulated in the diasporic Chinese film circuits of East and South-east Asia. They were all opera films, made in various Chinese languages. The story is typically about Zhu's quest for a formal education, and her subsequent love affair with her classmate, Liang. It starts as a comedy based on mistaken identities and cross-dressing masquerades, before turning into a fully fledged tragedy about love that transgresses class boundaries, so shoring up a critique of Confucian patriarchy and oppression. The star-crossed lovers finally find eternal bliss as immortal butterflies. Shaw Brothers' production, whose English title is *Love Eterne* (Li Han-Hsiang, 1963), was the best known.[1]

Love Eterne is a *Huangmei diao pian*, or *Huangmei* opera film. *Huangmei* opera films are Mandarin productions that overlay traditional Chinese narratives, be they oral, folk, literary or theatrical, with the technology of film-making. They primarily draw on *Huangmei* opera from the Anhui Province of China, which itself has a history of creatively blending different Chinese folk arts, such as tea-picking music and peasant folk dance, and regional theatrical reper-

toires and traditions, such as Anhui and Shanghai opera.[2] They feature gentle and melodic orchestral music and natural singing. Though defunct now, they were all the rage from the late 1950s until the late 1960s. They were high-budget productions with star-studded casts, extravagant sets and lavish costumes.

Love Eterne was no exception. Shot on Shawscope and in Technicolor, it recounted the familiar legend in seven chronological acts.[3] It boasted a record thirty-four songs, variously inspired by three librettos from the Republican China period: *The Willow Shade Account* (Sichuan opera), *Liang Zhu* (Shanghai opera) and *Butterflies on a Skirt Hem* (Cantonese opera).[4] Its ingenious camera movements and shot framings had the effect of turning the *mise en scène* into an imaginative dance of images that moved with the pace and rhythm of the singing. Occasional dialogue was interspersed amongst the songs, while stylised acting added to the film's appeal.

Upheld as a 'screen miracle' of its time,[5] *Love Eterne* was a box-office sensation and a multi-award-winning film.[6] It affirmed Li Han-Hsiang's status as the foremost director of *Huangmei diao pian* and catapulted actress Ivy Ling Po, who played the male protagonist Liang, to stardom. The film's success in turn helped Shaw Brothers secure its growing reputation and prestige as the major studio for Mandarin film-making.

Writings on the film are largely restricted to anecdotes in film-related literature (newspapers, magazines and books), reminiscences of film directors and stars in their autobiographies or biographies, and website postings of archival material by fans and commercial enterprises. The lack of any sustained study on the film can be attributed to the fact that scholarly interest in Hong Kong cinema is a recent phenomenon, resulting in research that has tended to focus on its cinematic practices and phenomena of the last two decades. In the last few years, however, there appears to be a more concerted effort to study Hong Kong cinema, prior to the 1970s, which our present study joins.

Our essay is also partly triggered by an interview which Chinese/transnational film-maker Ang Lee granted Rick Lyman of the *New York Times* in 2001. Lee's interview is noteworthy on two counts. First, it draws timely attention to the relatively neglected *Love Eterne*. Second, it attests to the film's enduring impression on people who saw it as a child. For Lee, *Love Eterne* 'reminds me always of my innocence … [I]n every movie I make, I always try to duplicate [and recapture] that feeling of purity and innocence that I got when I saw this movie' at the age of nine.[7]

Lee's take on 'audiences at the time' with regards to *Love Eterne* is insightful at times, but leaves something to be desired. As Lee suggests, it is plausible that some people were oblivious to the 'kinky' and 'very sexy' facets of the film manifested in the love story and the casting. But his assumption of a universe of prudish viewers is at issue. Lee claims that the film's 'pure' and 'sexless' love story conveys 'no sense of lust for the audience', and that the performance has the innocence of 'an all-boys choir' because it has two actresses (Ivy Ling Po and Betty Loh Ti) in the lead roles. These claims reach ridiculous heights when he asserts that the sight of 'a real man expressing romantic feelings for a woman on the screen … would have been too strong for the audiences then', and adds, 'China was a very repressed society'.[8] This explanation smacks of (self)-Orientalism. Its first part is also erroneous. The romantic couples in Li Han-Hsiang's earlier *Huangmei* opera films *Tiau Charn* (1958) and *The Kingdom and the Beauty* (1959) were all performed by actors whose on- and off-screen genders corresponded.

Lee's insistence that two actresses playing a chaste heterosexual couple could not generate sexualised identification for the viewers also belies a latent homophobia. His insistence accords with Judith Butler's 'heterosexual matrix', which contructs heteronormativity and the heterosexist logic that identification and desires must be mutually exclusive: 'if one identifies as a given gender, one must desire a different gender.'[9] The cross-dressing themes in *Love Eterne* challenge Lee's viewpoint. The corresponding narrative and performance mechanisms through which these themes find articulation can generate

fantasies of gender crossings and passings, fantasies which drive the queer gaze where 'multiple, contradictory, shifting, oscillating, inconsistent and fluid' identifications and desires are found.[10] In other words, Lee's take on the audience in regards to the love story and cross-sex acts amounts to a denial of the queer gaze.

Of course, the queer gaze as an academic model for conceptualising the spectatorial process finds more critical and cultural leverage now than during the era of *Love Eterne*. However, while we are reluctant to force the model of queer spectatorship retroactively, we are also hesitant to block out the possibility of queer identification by film audiences of some forty years ago, for several reasons. First, reports exist that men perceived Ling as a woman while women perceived her as a man after watching her performance as Liang Shanbo.[11] Second, cross-sex acting where an actress appeared in a male role, or a female role included cross-dressing as male was common in *Huangmei* and other opera films. This shows that viewers at the time accepted cross-sex acting in films. Furthermore becoming a *fanchuan*er[12] – an actor who specialises in cross-gender acting – was a career option at the time.

Ling's case demonstrates that this career choice was a rewarding one. The extent to which cross-sex identification was socially acceptable can be further glimpsed in the way Ling's public embraced her as 'Liang Xiong', or Elder Brother Liang – the pet name Zhu uses to address Liang in the film. This public declaration of adoration, reverence and worship for the actress has endured to the present-day, especially in Taiwan where the 'screen miracle' first appeared in 1963. 2002 saw a Taiwan-wide commemoration of the fortieth anniversary of the *Love Eterne* phenomenon. It included a stage production of *Love Eterne*, featuring surviving members of the Shaw Brothers cast, Ling included, in their original roles. The poster for the stage production includes a still of Ling as Liang Xiong. Beneath it is Ling's signature. On the top left-hand corner is an extract from a duet in *Love Eterne* consisting of Liang's pledge to Zhu: 'In life or death, I want to be with you.'

Ling capitalised on the allure of her gender malleability. It allowed her to build up an impressive repertoire of both female and male leads. Shaw Brothers also milked that allure for all it was worth.

Love Eterne: Betty Loh Ti and Ivy Ling Po, both dressed as young men.

This manifested most blatantly in its production of *The Perfumed Arrow* (Kao Li, 1965), not just because Ling was cast in the role of the occasionally cross-dressing female lead, but more because Shaw Brothers' execution of this *Huangmei* opera film rested on the decision to give viewers '*equal* excitement and enjoyment'.[13] As a result, Ling's character underwent frequent cross-gender make-overs, and variously found her/himself the amorous focus of three other 'straight-playing' characters: two men and one woman. This production clearly recognised the marketability of cross-gender fun predicated on multiple spectatorial positions, and Ling's diverse repertoire enhanced rather than negated her polymorphous appeal.

With respect to *Love Eterne*, the narrative traditions of the *caizi-jiaren* or scholar–beauty romance and the performance conventions of traditional Chinese opera, from which the film derives its style, form and content, can give further insights into the film's shifting spectatorial positions. A leitmotif of

popular folklores, vernacular period novels, traditional opera and opera films, *caizi-jiaren* romances typically tell a highly romanticised love story between a scholar (*caizi*) and a beauty (*jiaren*), hinted at in Liang's pledge. Their stories characteristically unfurl in a Confucian setting in traditional China, and have a strong populist orientation that has the characteristics of the Bakhtinian carnivalesque: ridicule of officialdom, inversion of hierarchy, violations of decorum and proportion, and celebration of bodily excess.[14] In *Love Eterne*, the carnivalesque defies Confucian authority and articulates an intricate interplay of youthful rebellion, young love, same-sex conspiracy and cross-sex masquerades, producing subtexts that append a queer dimension to the film's heterosexual love story. This dimension dovetails well with, and lends itself to, contemporary queer scholarship.

In *caizi-jiaren* romances, the lovers are usually matched in terms of intelligence, moral fibre and appearance. They both seek love and romance, and above all, marriage to a partner of their choice. However, while pursuing affairs of the heart, they are mindful of their status as Confucian subjects, and act in accordance with the compulsory morality of legalised Confucianism.[15] Legalised Confucianism stringently upholds patriarchal familism, and endorses gender segregation, arranged marriage and female chastity. In *caizi-jiaren* narratives, these Confucian practices engender conflicts along as well as across class, gender, generational and other social lines, generating conflict-driven resolutions based on the playful breaching and restoring of Confucian norms. As such, the queer possibilities generated by themes of Confucian contestation and containment are generic. The resultant tension forges a plurality of Confucian subjectivities. In *Love Eterne*, these include a conservative patriarch (Zhu's father), a loving mother figure (Zhu's mother), a liberal scholar with a conservative streak (Liang), a rebellious but chaste daughter who is also a brilliant scholar (Zhu), and a silent observer of Confucian familism and its attendant conflicts (Zhu's maid). These subjects are in turn multi-dimensional. For example, Zhu is variously an anti-Confucian rebel, a dutiful daughter, a cheeky male physician, a clever male student, a martyr of love, her own ambitious younger sister and the Goddess of Mercy incarnate. These personae allow her to wield carnivalesque power at will, but within the constraints of Confucian strictures.

More often than not, it is the *jiaren* who is the most rebellious. She has good reasons to be so since she has more to gain than lose from struggling against a world where masculinist Confucianism holds sway. Here, Zhu is an archetype. She embodies the quintessential *jiaren*: she is young, beautiful, intelligent and resourceful. Above all, she has ambition. If the beauty's motto in *caizi-jiaren* romances is 'Though in body I am a woman, in ambition I surpass men',[16] then the cross-dressed 'male' Zhu's self-referential description of 'his' imaginary sister to Liang in a song alludes to this 'ambition':

My younger sister has high aspirations.
She strives to be equal or superior to men.
She has no need for rouge, only ink and brush.
She does not like jewellery, only literature.

Zhu's quest for equal opportunity, self-fulfilment and self-determination spurs her journey into the male world. It rests on her overwhelming desire to com-

pete with men, morally and intellectually. These themes are common in *caizi-jiaren* romances, and visible in the scene where Zhu has a debate with Liang over the Confucian dogma that 'Women are the source of all troubles.' Bursting into song, Liang argues in support of this dogma, citing the historical figures of Daji and Baosi, whom he says caused the respective downfalls of Kings Zhou and You.[17] In retort, Zhu sings: 'My dear elder brother, you are not critical of the books you read ... Those tyrannical emperors ruined themselves/[But Confucian historiography] puts the blame on women.' Finally, 'he' offers a list of counter-examples: Nüwa, Luo Zhu, and Mengmu.[18] All are 'intelligent and virtuous women' from ancient times, but forgotten by Confucian historians. This list taps a different epistemological genealogy, producing alternative models of subjectivity, variously noted for female resourcefulness, resolution, enterprise and courage. Awed by Zhu's scholastic brilliance, Liang promises to learn to be critical of the books he reads. In this way, Zhu proves herself intellectually superior to Liang.

A condition for Zhu's entry in the man's world, paradoxically, is that she cross-dresses as a male. Sartorial disguise grants Zhu privileges otherwise exclusively enjoyed by men – autonomy, mobility and education. To achieve these by recourse to sartorial disguise highlights female marginalisation within the Confucian society at large. This marginalisation is not equivalent to hopelessness. Instead it points out an aspect of social injustice that needs addressing, including gender discrimination. At the same time, it also points to the possibility of alternatives. Borrowing Butler's words, the significance of the 'man' Zhu occasionally performs can be understood as 'a crucial part not only of subject *formation*, but of the ongoing contestation and reformulation of the subject as well. The performative ... is one of the influential rituals by which subjects are formed and reformulated ... [It] can work in ... counter-hegemonic ways.'[19] In other words, Zhu's efficacious performance of what it might mean to be a man, or what it takes to be one, also grants her the carnivalesque power a woman-man can wield.

Conventionally, the *jiaren*'s final goal is no more than marriage, which is a narrative constraint on her development into a revolutionary heroine who breaks all restrictions. However, Zhu's insistence that marriage be based on love and mutual consent does demonstrate an active struggle for self-determi-nation. 'I will marry the man of your choice,' she sings to her father curtly, 'only if the sun rises from the West!' Her eventual decision to choose death over a marriage not of her choice manifests similar defiance of Confucian patriarchal power and confirms her virtue, in that she remains true to herself and faithful to Liang to the end. In these ways, Zhu counters the hegemonic Confucian dogma that *nüzi wu cai shi de*, 'a virtuous woman is one without literary abilities or literacy'.

In addition to feminist potential, *Huangmei* opera films such as *Love Eterne* have narrative mechanisms for enabling multiple points of identification. Two interrelated performance techniques commonly employed by opera/opera film actors to effect cross-sex transformations are pertinent to our present task. One is what we would call female maling.[20] The other is called *kaiguang*.[21] These techniques are also central to the performance of subject-constitution (in the Butlerian sense) in opera and opera films.

In *Love Eterne*, the transformation of Zhu into an occasional cross-dresser and actress Ling into Liang is achieved through female maling, while *kaiguang* sustains their cross-sex acts. The *kaiguang* technique separates the host body (that of the actor/actress) and the role body (that of the character) by dismantling the former to allow the latter to 'shine' through. The female maling technique is chiefly concerned with wrapping the role body over the host body so that the two become enshrouded in an aura of maleness and masculinity

Female maling involves body, gender and erotic maling. Body maling gives the host body a physical make-over, using codified make-up and costumes, and the mimicry of movements, gestures and mannerisms typically associated with the *xiaosheng* (young man) prototype in opera and opera films, including his distinctive speaking and singing style. In short, it is most concerned with appearance. Zhu the scholar is thus different from Zhu the daughter in looks: the former has the appearance of a *xiaosheng*, while the latter that of a *dan* (young woman). As male, 'he' wears a hat and sports eyebrows shaped like a pair of willow leaves. As female, she has arched eyebrows and neatly combed hair, adorned with bejewelled hairpieces. The two also have different foot movements. For instance, Zhu the scholar walks with exuberant masculinity like a

xiaosheng, rather than shuffling gracefully. The latter is the footwork for a *dan*, which Zhu the daughter adopts.

Gender maling overlaps with body maling, but mainly concerns the many ways malers assume the behaviour and emotions associated with being male, or those of the *xiaosheng* type. For example, when sorrowful, Zhu the scholar would shed a quiet tear, whereas Zhu the daughter would bawl her eyes out. In sum, both body and gender maling endow the host/role body with male and masculine characteristics. Together they produce erotic maling as an after-effect. Charged with a sexual energy, erotic maling arouses the spectators' erotic desires because it holds out the promise of (cross-)sexual pleasure. The tripartite process of body, gender and erotic maling thus helps bring to presence the performance or *biaoyan* – *biao* (express) and *yan* (act out) – of a sexed, gendered and sexualised entity that is connected to yet distinct from the host body's.

This *biaoyan* therefore turns on a performance that helps bring about the (cross-)gender transform-ation of the performer. Rather than becoming a bio-logical man *per se*, s/he carries the aura of one. It is this aura that enables her/him to pass as a 'man'. In short, s/he is a 'make-believe' man. A 'make-believe' man embodies camp: as androgynous figures, they concurrently encapsulate the beauty of the feminine and femininity in masculine men, and the masculine and masculinity in feminine women.[22] In a sense, 'he' is *feinan feinü* (non-man, non-woman). Yet 'he' is not a transvestite, even though 'he' is a cross-sex cross-dresser of sorts. Nor is 'he' a female transsexual, for there exist scenarios in *caizi-jiaren* romances in which 'he' is endowed with procreative capability. Here *The Mermaid* (Kao Li, 1965) is an example: scholar Chang Cheng (also played by actress Ling in a male role) impregnates a beauty who is a carp incarnated in human form (played by actress Lee Ching). Finally, 'he' may be androgynous, but is not an androgyne. The gender identity of a female maler is therefore – as Butler might put it – 'performatively constituted by the very 'expressions' that are said to be results' of the performance.[23] That is to say, gender is a performance: it is what the character *biaoyan*s at particular times. Hence the maler may stand for any of those entities (man, woman, trans-sexual, transvestite, androgyne, non-man and non-woman), or various composites of them, at any given time, but is ultimately irreducible to any one of them. The challenge for the performer then is to call forth the appropriate entity or composition, as and when required by the plot.

If female maling simultaneously wraps the host and role bodies with the male aura, then the performative art of *kaiguang* would tie that aura more firmly to the role body than the host body. As mentioned, *kaiguang* subjects the latter to an 'opening process'. It cuts it up into separate units of articulation, and replaces it, part by part – the eyes, hands, fingers and feet – with those of the role body. It necessitates 'emptying' the performer's body of 'its personal or individual essence (soul)' so as to allow for the *qi* (presence, life, energy) of the performed body to emerge, or to 'shine' through.[24] The process of simultaneously dissecting the host body, hollowing it out and reassembling it into another harmonious whole is the crucial technique by which the role body becomes both narrator and subject. Meanwhile the *qi* that maintains and dissolves both distance and proximity between the two bodies bring to the fore the personae as required by the plot. Not only that, it also throws a *kaiguang*-feel on the spatial-temporality of the fictive world, much as the female maling aura affects the actions, events and objects, in addition to the performer (body, self and identity). The fictive world, now belonging more to the role body or bodies than the host body or bodies, in turn connects with the many gazes of the viewers, enticing them to enter into the performance space. The audience in turn makes the entry, not as passive observers, but as interested parties who would read that space, connecting layers of meaning the performed bodies throw up and out, in relation to the situations and contexts of the performance. This form of participation inevitably demands the suspension of disbelief.

The presence of female malers in *Love Eterne*, be it actress Ling in a male role or actress Loh in a female role who periodically cross-dresses as a male, does not necessarily cancel out viewers' prior knowledge of their host body. Nor would they be overwhelmed by the spectacle of their role body to the point of becoming stunned by it: the sight of the carnivalesque is all too familiar in opera/opera films. Nonetheless, the resultant discordance between prior knowledge and the spectacle opens up a space for negotiation. In this space is room for anyone who

wants, or dares, to indulge in polymorphous desires and identification to do just that, with respect to the films' narrative and performance of cross-sex masquerades. In so doing, such viewers would imbue the film's themes of compulsory heterosexuality with a polymorphous appeal. This is not to repudiate the fact that *Love Eterne* features a narrative progression favouring a heterosexual closure, but to point out that the films' gender-bending activities can generate subject-positions other than heteronormative ones. Nuances of performance become especially pertinent for viewers seeking alternative, even oppositional, modes of identification. The narrative interstices simultaneously opened up and covered over by cross-gender *biaoyan*s allow for this. They also permit all sorts of readings, including against-the-grain ones. The love story's overtly heterosexual slant therefore cannot foreclose on alternative or oppositional readings. At face value, the love story may well accede to compulsory heterosexuality, but its narrativisation and performance can produce (unintended) subtexts. In *Love Eterne*, carnivalesque comedy is in the air most when actresses Ling and Loh are concurrently male on screen. The double entendres that Zhu the cross-dressed scholar uses to convey 'his' desire for Liang have the effect of confusing Liang. Bursting into an angry song, Liang (played by a woman) scolds Zhu, 'I am not a female!' *Love Eterne* is therefore at most almost a heterosexual love story.

NOTES

1. In this essay, we exclusively refer to the videocassette disc (VCD) version of the film.
2. See Wang-Ngai Siu, *Chinese Opera: Images and Stories* (Vancouver: University of British Columbia Press, 1997), 22–23.
3. According to the film's production notes, the legend originated in folklores around the time of the Eastern Jin Dynasty (317–420). It first appeared in print during the Song Dynasty (960–1279), while theatrical adaptations appeared only during the Yuan Dynasty (1271–1368). By the time of the Republic (founded in 1911), there were some twenty to thirty opera librettos based on the legend in circulation. *Nanguo*, no. 59 (1963): <66.216.18.55/%7Elingboh/web/ drama/ Eterne/Eterne01.htm> (25 December 2002). *Nanguo* was Shaw Brothers' in-house film journal. It carried information on Shaw Brothers productions in Mandarin and English. Its English title is *Southern Screen*.

4. Ibid.

5. *Nanguo*, no. 65 (1963): <66.216.18.55/%7Elingboh/ web/drama/Eterne/Eterne07.htm> (25 December 2002).

6. See *Nanguo*, no. 63 (1963): <66.216.18.55/ %7Elingboh/ web/drama/ Eterne/Eterne06.htm> (25 December 2002); *Nanguo*, no. 68 (1963): <66.216.18.55/%7Elingboh/web/info/shaw shaw01.htm> (25 December 2002); and *Nanguo*, no. 72 (1964): <66.216.18.55/%7Elingboh/ web/drama/ Eterne/Eterne10.htm > (25 December 2002).

7. Rick Lyman, 'Watching Movies with Ang Lee: Crouching Memory, Hidden Heart', *New York Times*, 9 March 2001: <nytimes.qpass.com> (6 January 2002). In this feature article, Lyman gives the film's English title as *Love Eternal*. This title differs from that in the film's opening credit: *The Love Eterne*. The film's Chinese title is *Liang Shanbo Yu Zhu Yingtai*, not *Qi Cai Hu Bu Gui*, as reported by Lyman. *Qi Cai Hu Bu Gui* (known in English as *Eternal Love*) is the Chinese title of a Cantonese opera film, directed in 1966 by Li Tie and starring Josephine Xiao Fangfang and Chen Baozhu. The story for that film is not based on the Liang-Zhu legend.

8. Ibid.

9. Judith Butler, *Bodies that Matter: On the Discursive Limits of 'Sex'* (London: Routledge, 1993), 239.

10. Caroline Evans and Lorraine Gamman, 'The Gaze Revisited, or Reviewing Queer Viewing', in *A Queer Romance: Lesbians, Gay Men and Popular Culture*, ed. Paul Burston and Colin Richardson (London: Routledge, 1995), 46.

11. See, for example, '1963 belongs to Ling Boh!' (25 October 1963; source of original publication and author unknown): <66.216.18.55/%7Elingboh/web/ lingpo/lingpo631025_2.htm> (25 December 2002).

12. See Tan See Kam , 'The Cross-gender Performances of Yam Kim-Fei, or the Queer Factor in Postwar Hong Kong Cantonese Opera/Opera Films', in *Queer Asian Cinema: Shadows in the Shade*, ed. Andrew Grossman (New York: Harrington Park Press, 2000), 201–212.

13. *Nanguo*, no. 92 (1965): <66.216.18.55/ %7Elingboh/ web/drama/perfumed/perfumed01.htm> (25 December 2002).

14. Mikhail Bakhtin, *Rabelais and His World*, trans. Hélène Iswolsky (Cambridge: MIT Press, 1973).

15. John C. H. Wu, J., 'The Individual in Political and Legal Traditions', in *The Chinese Mind: Essentials of Chinese Philosophy and Culture*, ed. Charles A. Moore (Honolulu: University of Hawaii Press, 1968), 340–364. See also Tani Barlow, 'Theorizing Woman: *Funü, Guojia, Jiating* (Chinese woman, Chinese state, Chinese family)', in *Body, Subject and Power in China*, ed. Angela Zito and Tani Barlow (Chicago: University of Chicago Press, 1994), 253–289.

16. Keith McMahon, 'The Classic "Beauty–Scholar" Romance and the Superiority of the Talented Woman', in Zito and Barlow, *Body, Subject and Power*, 227–252.

17. See Lu Yanguang, *100 Celebrated Chinese Women* (Singapore: Asiapac Publication, 2001), 21 and 25.

18. Ibid., 1, 11 and 55.

19. Judith Butler, *Excitable Speech: A Politics of the Performative* (New York: Routledge, 1997), 160.

20. Richard Ekins, 'The Career Path of the Male Femaler', in *Blending Genders: Social Aspects of Cross-dressing and Sex-changing*, ed. Richard Ekins and Dave King (London: Routledge, 1996), 39–47.

21. Jo Riley, *Chinese Theater and the Actor in Performance* (Cambridge: Cambridge University Press, 1997), 117.

22. Susan Sontag, 'Notes on Camp,' in *A Susan Sontag Reader* (London: Penguin, 1983), 108.

23. Judith Butler, *Gender Trouble: Feminism and the Subversion of Identity* (London: Routledge, 1990) 25.

24. Riley, *Chinese Theater*, 115.

18   *Not One Less*: The Fable of a Migration

Rey Chow

In one of his more recent films, *Happy Time* (1999), Zhang Yimou has inserted a remarkable scene that may be cited as a summation of his consistently dialectical treatment of visuality. At the home of the fat lady who just received a marriage proposal from her suitor, Lao Zhao, we encounter the blind girl, left in her care by her previous husband, who has moved to Shenzhen. In order to impress her suitor, the fat lady, who normally treats this stepdaughter rather cruelly, serves the latter some ice cream. But this gesture of kindness lasts only as long as the brief duration of the suitor's visit. Once he has left, the fat lady snatches the cup of ice cream from the blind girl and, scolding her as someone not worthy of such a luxury item, puts it back in the refrigerator.

Although it is possible to derive a moral lesson from this scene (for instance, by seeing it as yet another illustration of the lamentable condition of human hypocrisy), what is much more interesting is the suggestive reading it offers of the semiotics and politics of seeing – indeed, of sight itself as a kind of material sign around which specific values are implicitly enacted and negotiated. The fat lady's opportunistic manner of handling the ice cream indicates that sight, as what renders the world accessible, is not a natural but an artificial phenomenon, one that is, moreover, eminently subject to manipulation. The fat lady consciously performs to Lao Zhao's sight by making an appearance of her own generosity; yet once that sight is no longer around, there is no need for this performance to continue. Sight, in other words, is not a medium of transparency or a means of understanding, as we commonly think; rather, it is a surveillance mechanism installed on (other) human bodies, which means that one must behave appropriately when someone else is watching, but that otherwise there is no intrinsic reason to do so. What Lao Zhao 'sees' is actually the opposite of what he thinks he has obviously seen or understood. The fat lady's

behaviour is disturbing because, contrary to what most people believe, she has not internalised or naturalised the function of sight in such a way as to make it her own conscience, her *automatised self-surveillance*. Sight remains for her something of an arbitrary and external function, a device to be exploited for her own benefit. As the film goes on to show, with the events that unfold around the blind girl, sight can also be a disability, an elaborate network of mendacity devised to fool others that ends up, ironically, trapping oneself more and more deeply. Having sight is not necessarily the opposite of being blind but may under some circumstances become an extension of blindness, a kind of handicap that distorts or obstructs reality as much as the physical inability to see.

This distinctive grasp of the materiality of a medium that has traditionally been associated with clarity, wisdom and transcendental vision continues to mark Zhang Yimou's films of the mid- to late 1990s and early 2000s, despite the rather misleading critical consensus that his recent films depart sharply from the early ones – *Red Sorghum* (1988), *Judou* (1990), and *Raise the Red Lantern* (1991) – that made him internationally famous.[1] It is now often suggested that Zhang has more or less abandoned the orientalist styles of the early classics, which portray a mythified timeless China in order to pander to the tastes of foreign devils, for a realist cinematic style that depicts simple people's lives in contemporary Chinese society. The well-known cultural critic Zhang Yiwu, for instance, has argued that this stylistic change, observed in films such as *The Story of Qiu Ju* (1993), *Keep Cool* (1997) and *The Road Home* (1999-2000), as well as *Not One Less* (1999–2000) and *Happy Time*, may be traceable to the changing trends in the mainland Chinese film industry, which has been compelled by the pressures of globalisation to produce a more inward-looking approach, centred on China's internal problems and aimed at a pre-dominantly Chinese audience.[2] Having allegedly made such a change, Zhang Yimou has, it seems, finally been accepted and endorsed even by the Chinese authorities, once his most hostile critics, who not only consented to having him serve as the director of the unprecedented, internationally collaborative performance of Puccini's opera *Turandot* in Beijing in September 1998 (with Zubin Mehta as the conductor), but also appointed Zhang to film the official documentary showcasing Beijing in China's competition for hosting the 2008 Olympics. While this saga of how a native son who was first accused of selling out to the West is subsequently fully co-opted by his critics for purposes that are, strictly speaking, no less orientalist, no less opportunistic and no less commodification driven, has to be dealt with in detail elsewhere, my point in bringing it up is simply to emphasise how the story of alternating rebuke and embrace that has followed Zhang's career, too, may itself be taken as an example of the power struggle over seeing and visuality in post-colonial post-modernity, a power struggle of which Zhang's work to date has provided some of the most provocative demonstrations.[3]

My aim, then, is to argue, in part through a reading of *Not One Less*, that the warm reception of Zhang's more realist films is perhaps as problematic as the hostile reactions to his early ones.

While the early films are consistently accused of orientalist tendencies involving ungrounded fantasies, the realist ones are generally considered as a return to more authentic subject matter and a faithful documentary style. But as one critic, Shi Wen-hong, points out in relation to *Not One Less*, the subject matter of present-day poverty, too, can be exotic in the eyes of some (Western) audiences.[4] The valorisation of realism as an ethnographically more authentic/faithful representation of a culture remains, strictly speaking, part and parcel of an ideological legacy, in particular that accompanying the treatment of non-Western peoples. (One need only think of *National Geographic* to see my point.[5]) Indeed, the study of modern and contemporary China is so dominated by so-called realism that even the most imaginative writings and art works, however avant-garde they might be, have tended to be read largely for factographic value, for making contributions to the production of empirical knowledge about China.

This critical proclivity towards realism in the institution of area studies is inseparable from the strategic targeting of non-Western political regimes during the Cold War, and the representational politics surrounding China remain tightly in its grip. If the preference for realist depictions belongs to a thoroughly politicised history of reading and viewing China (one in which the aesthetic qualities of works tend to be sidestepped or dismissed in order to legitimate the dogged attempts at information retrieval), then the critical, indeed laudatory, revaluation of a director such as Zhang in the form of 'Ah, he is finally becoming more realist!' must itself be subjected to rethinking.

As I will argue in the following reading of *Not One Less*, what is intriguing about Zhang's work is the possibility it offers for a critique of the historical import of the mediatised image, a critique that may have little to do with Zhang's personal intention *per se* but that nevertheless takes shape through the semiotic movement discernible in his handling of visuality. If Zhang has chosen more realist-looking locales, characters and happenings in comparison with the mythical stories of his early films,[6] his recent work nevertheless continues to deliver shrewd reflections on the politics of visuality and cultural identity, and their imbrications with the massively uneven effects of globalisation.

Such shrewd reflections have to do with Zhang's grasp of visuality as a second-order labour – labour not in the physical sense but in the form of cinematic and mediatised signification. Hence, strictly speaking, the early films displaying China's decrepitude were not only about poor peasants struggling against the injustice of life in the countryside but also about a process in which such struggles are transformed, through the film apparatus, into signs for a certain encounter, signs that convey the cross-cultural imaginary, 'Chineseness', to those watching it from the outside. Making these signs, building entertaining stories around them and rendering them visually appealing are for Zhang never a matter of realist reflectionism but always a matter of the specificities of film-making, of experimenting with colour, sound, time control and narrative. His critics, by contrast, have repeatedly ignored the materiality of this film-making process and insisted on the reality that is somehow always lying beyond it. For the latter, that reality is, of course, always China and its people, a

Not One Less.

reality that 1) must, it is implied, direct and dictate how films should be made; 2) will always escape such framing; yet 3) must nonetheless continue to be used as a criterion for judging a film's merits.

In light of the hegemony of realist reflectionism in the field of China studies and of the obdurate moralism of his critics, it is interesting to consider the tactical adaptations Zhang makes in his evolving work.[7] As a way perhaps to distract and elude his critics' sight, he has been, over the past several years, making films that indeed seem more documentary-like in their contents and settings. Often, these films are about poor rural folk or *xiao shimin* (ordinary citizens) in big cities, whose lives are unglamorous but filled with hardships. Like *Red Sorghum*, *Ju Dou* and *Raise the Red Lantern*, these films are marked by Zhang's characteristic fascination with human endurance: the female characters in *Qiu Ju*, *The Road Home* and *Happy Time*, like those in the early films, stubbornly persist in their pursuit of a specific goal. But whereas Jiu'er, Judou, Songlian and Yan'er (the servant girl in *Raise the Red Lantern*) pay for their strength of character with their own lives or their sanity, the more contemporary female characters tend

to be successful in getting what they want. Similarly, in *Not One Less*, we witness a young girl's struggle against systemic indifference that ends happily. Whereas the earlier films seem to be exhibits of a bygone cultural system, sealed off with an exotic allure, a film such as *Not One Less* seems to offer hope. Is this indeed so?

The story of *Not One Less* is briefly as follows. At the primary school of an impoverished northern Chinese village (Shuiquan Village), a group of pupils are learning under difficult conditions. Their teacher, Mr Gao, has to go home to tend to his sick mother, and a thirteen-year-old girl from a neighbouring village, Wei Minzhi, is hired as his substitute for one month. Before leaving, Mr Gao advises Wei that quite a number of the pupils have been dropping out and instructs her to make sure that the remaining twenty-eight stay until he returns – 'not one less'. For her substitute teaching, Wei is promised fifty *yuan*. As she starts teaching, the pupils are not exactly co-operative, and Wei is confronted with various obstacles, including the relative lack of chalk, which she must use sparingly. One day, a boy named Zhang Huike fails to show up: his mother is ill and in debt, and can no longer afford his school fees, so the boy has been sent off to the city to look for work. Wei is determined to bring this pupil back. After a series of failed efforts at locating him, she succeeds in getting the attention of the manager of the city's television station, who arranges for her to make an appeal on a programme called 'Today in China'. Zhang Huike, who is washing dishes at a restaurant and sees Wei on TV, is moved to tears by Wei's appeal and turns himself in. Teacher and pupil return to the village with a crowd of reporters as well as a large supply of classroom materials and gift donations to the village from audiences who have watched the programme.

If stubbornness, persistence and endurance are human qualities that recur in Zhang's films, in *Not One Less* they take on the additional significance of being constituents of a humanism *vis-à-vis* an impersonal and inefficient official system, which is impotent in remedying the disastrous conditions of the village school. But how does this humanism express itself? Ironically, it does so through the very spirit of *productionism* that is, arguably, left over from official socialist propaganda, a productionism most clearly evident in the form of quantifiable accumulation (we recall the slogans of the Great Leap Forward period, for instance, during which the campaign for national well-being was promoted in terms of measurable units – so many tons of steel, so many tons of iron, so many tons of agricultural produce, etc.). As critics have reminded us, Wei Minzhi has come to Shuiquan Village to work for fifty *yuan*. Money, however, is only part of the issue. As the film progresses, we are made increasingly aware of the ideological as well as economic problem of how *resources* (of which money is an important though not the exclusive component) are (supposed) to be garnered and produced.

The clearest example of such productionism is the elementary method of counting and permuting adopted by Wei and her pupils to collect her bus fare for the city. Moving one brick (in a nearby factory), they discover, will earn them fifteen cents, so to make fifteen *yuan*, they should move one hundred bricks. Although this method of making money is based on a basic exchange principle – X units of labour x Y units of cash – its anachronism is apparent precisely in the mechanical correspondence established between two different kinds of values involved – concrete muscular/manual labour, on the one hand, and the abstract, general equivalent of money, on the other. Sustained by the belief that if they contribute their labour they will indeed get the proper remuneration, the girl teacher and her pupils put themselves to work. At Zhang's hands, this simple event, what appears at first to be a mere narrative detail, turns out to be the manifestation of an entire economic rationale. As is demonstrated by the numerical calculations Wei and her pupils perform on the blackboard, this rationale is based not only on manual labour but also on the mathematics of simple addition, multiplication and division. At the heart of this rationale is an attributed continuum, or balance, between the two sides of the equation – a continuum whereby effort logically and proportionally translates into reward.

The tension and, ultimately, incompatibility between this earnest, one-on-one method of accounting, on the one hand, and the increasingly technologised, corporatised and abstract (that is, Enron-esque) method of value generation, on the other, is staged in a series of frustrations encountered by Wei, who is confronted each time with the futility of her own calculations. First, having earned 15 *yuan* for moving 100 bricks, she and her pupils discover that the bus fare is actually 20.50 *yuan* each way. She attempts to solve this problem with her physical body, first by trying to get on the bus illegally and then, reluctantly, by walking. She is finally able to get a ride with a truck driver. On arriving in the city with 9 *yuan* (having already spent 6 *yuan* on two cans of Coca-Cola for her pupils), she has to agree to pay 2.50 *yuan* to the girl who was last with Zhang Huike before this girl will take her to the train station to look for him. The two girls end up paging him with a loudspeaker announcement around the station – to no avail. Wei spends the remainder of her money, 6.50 *yuan*, on ink, paper and a brush in order to write out her notices one by one, only to be told by a passer-by that such notices are useless and then to have them blown all over by the wind and swept away by the morning street-cleaners. By this time Wei has, at the passer-by's suggestion, made her way to the television station. After a long and stubborn wait, she finally succeeds in getting the attention of the manager.

Unlike her counterparts in Zhang's early films, women who have become immobilised in their rural positions or household status, Wei is the heroine of a migration, the migration from the countryside to the city. Even the countryside, however, is not the pure, original, primitive locale it is often imagined to be: the bus fare and the price of a can of Coke are but two examples of how a remote poor village, too, is part of the global capitalist circuit premised on commodified exchanges. If there is a residual primitivism here, it is, I'd contend, the ideology of accounting that Wei embodies, an ideology that has her believe that the expenditure of physical efforts will somehow be balanced off by due compensation and that, if she would try just a little harder, an equivalence can somehow be found between the two. To this extent, the film's title, *Yige dou bu neng shao* – literally, 'not even one can be allowed to be missing' – foregrounds this ideology of accounting in an unexpected manner: the ostensible goal of bringing back the missing child becomes simultaneously the epistemological frame over which a residual and familiar kind of passion unfurls – one that is organised around actual, countable bodies, in an economy in which resources are still imagined as successive, iterative units that can be physically stockpiled, expended or retrieved at will.[8] Wei's migration to the city is thus really a migration to a drastically different mode of value production, a mode in which, instead of the exertions of the physical body, it is the mediatised image that arbitrates, that not only achieves her goal for her but also has the ability to make resources proliferate beyond her wildest imagination.

Despite her strenuous physical efforts (moving bricks, walking, writing out notices longhand, sleeping on the street, starving, waiting for hours), it is when Wei transforms herself into an image on metropolitan television that she finally and effortlessly accomplishes her mission. As Wang Yichuan comments, there are two stories in Zhang's film: one is about 'human struggle'; the other has to do with the importance of money and television, and the emergence of the mediatised sign:

Money has been playing a fundamental role throughout the entire film: it is closely linked to Wei Minzhi's job as a substitute teacher, her attempt to save chalk, the collective moving of bricks, her ride to the city, and her search [for the missing pupil] through television; what's more, money controls it all .... My sense is that the narrative structure of the entire film contains two stories: underneath the story about a girl as a substitute teacher lurks another story – the story about the magic of television or money ....

When the bumpkin-ish and flustered Wei Minzhi is brought before the TV screen by the program anchor as the interviewee making her appeal to the public, her bumpkin-ness and simplicity are no longer just bumpkin-ness and simplicity but instead turned into a powerful and conquering sign.[9]

The return to Shuiquan Village must therefore be understood as a post-migration event, when the system of value making has been fundamentally altered, when the fatigued, confused and powerless figure of the girl herself has been transformed into an image signifying 'the rural population'. Recall how Wei's appeal is dramatised on television: she is featured on the programme 'Today in China', aimed explicitly at educating the metropolitan audiences about China's rural areas. As the anchor introduces the objectives of the programme, in the background appears a bucolic, bright-green lawn with pretty bluish hills in the distance and a clean white tricycle with flowers in front. This fantastical landscape, in stark contrast to the landscape of Shuiquan Village we have already seen, conjures the national imaginary by drawing attention to the plight of the countryside as an urgent social problem. Anonymous and unrelated TV consumers are thus interpellated as 'the Chinese people' and, although they have never met the villagers in the flesh – how materially deprived they are, how hard they must work to keep surviving, and so forth – the effect of Wei-the-image is such that it forges 'meaningful links' among this network of strangers at the speed of virtuality.

Once the rural population has been disseminated as a televised image, charitable donations pour in, and the return of Wei and Zhang to the village is accompanied by a plenitude of supplies, including especially colour chalk of various kinds, which allow the students to practise writing a character each on the blackboard. As well, this return is accompanied by eager reporters with cameras, intent on 'documenting' the village and its inhabitants with a relentless, henceforth infinitely reproducible gaze. In a public sphere made up of electronically transmitted signals, virtuality transforms exponentially into cash, in ways that would never have been achievable by the earnest logic of calculating resources on which Wei and her students had sought to rely. The closing credits offer a glimpse of the positive outcomes of this migration towards the image: Zhang Huike's family debt is paid off; Wei is able to return to her own village; the girl pupil who is a fast runner has gone on to join the county's track meet, and the village is now renamed Shuiquan Village of Hope. Finally, we read this important message: 'One million children drop out of school because of poverty in China every year. With financial assistance from various sources, about fifteen percent of them are able to return to school.'[10]

If what Zhang has provided with his early films is an imaginary ethnographic treatment of China – as a decrepit primitive culture – what he accomplishes in *Not One Less* is, to my mind, a similar kind of ethnographic experiment, albeit *within* Chinese society itself. What is often criticised as the orientalist gaze in Zhang's early films, a gaze that produces China as exotic, erotic, corrupt, patriarchally repressive and so forth for the pleasurable consumption of Western audiences, is here given a thought-provoking twist to become none other than the national gaze. Whereas the object of the orientalist gaze in the early films is arguably an ahistorical 'China', in *Not One Less* that object is more specifically China's 'rural population' living in wretched conditions, especially children deprived of education. In the latter case, the similarly fetishising and exploitative tendency of the media is underwritten not by the discourse of orientalism (read: depraved Western imperialist practice) but instead by the oft-repeated and clichéd discourse of national self-strengthening and concern for future generations ('Save the children!').[11] These two seemingly opposed discourses are affined paradoxically through the magic of the image, which not only supersedes older notions of the exchange value of labour but eradicates the validity of manual labour and production altogether. The image asserts itself now as the indomitable way of creating resources, displacing an obsolete method such as moving one brick x fifteen cents to the abject peripheries of contemporary Chinese society.

This migration towards the dominance of the image, which Zhang explores through an apparently more realist contemporary story is, therefore, in tandem with the experimental attitude expressed towards visuality in his early films. The humanistic impulses that guide the narrative, leading it towards the telos of collective good, are at the same time punctured by a firm refusal on Zhang's part to idealise or eulogise the image, including especially that

of Wei making her sentimental plea. Instead, the latter is consciously presented as a media event in the new information economy. The image *works*, as it were, by deflating the currency of (human) work. Seen in this light, *Not One Less* rejoins the explorations of the non-urban others in the Chinese films of the 1980s (*Yellow Earth* (Chen Kaige, 1984), *On the Hunting Ground* (Tian Zhuangzhuang, 1985), *Sacrificed Youth* (Zhang Nuanxin, 1985), *Horse Thief* (Tian Zhuangzhuang, 1986), *A Good Woman* (Huang Jianzhong, 1986), *King of the Children* (Chen Kaige, 1987), just to mention a handful), albeit with a different emphasis. In the 1980s, when cultural introspection took shape in the aftermath of the Cultural Revolution, film offered the Fifth Generation directors and their contemporaries the exciting possibility of experimenting with technological reproducibility and artful defamiliarisation. As China becomes globalised at the turn of the twenty-first century, the anthropological impulses of the 1980s films have given way to a sociological one. From an investment in, or a fascination with, China's otherness, filmmaking at the hands of Zhang has shifted to a seasoned and cautionary approach to visuality as social regimentation, discipline and surveillance, but above all as *benevolence-driven coercion*.

In dramatising this trans-valuation of the labour performed over quantifiable, slowly cumulative time (bricks, hours, days, dollars, written notices) into an instantaneous spectacle, *Not One Less* stages a schism between two irreconcilable kinds of philosophical trajectories. There is, on the one hand, the trajectory opened in accordance with a pro-Enlightenment telos of a better and brighter future, towards which human will power and media capability inadvertently join forces. On the other hand, as is demonstrated by the usurpatory nature of the mediatised image and its tendency to cannibalise human labour, we are confronted with an aggressive radicalisation of the terms of communication, communal relations and, increasingly in the case of the People's Republic of China, communism's own political agenda. The image's limitless potential, in this regard, cannot be seen naively as an ally to human will power or simply as its latest instrument. Rather, its smooth and speedy superficiality announces a new collective reality to which human will power is likely to find itself increasingly subordinated, and to which human beings, especially those struggling against any kind of social inequity, will need to resort just to be recognised. As the ending of the film shows, it is to the image that people will give their concern and compassion, and it is the image, rather than the actual suffering human body, that now generates capital and, with it, social influence and political power. Instead of propelling us towards the telos of an improved future, then, this other philosophical trajectory lays bare the expanse and intensity of a new kind of oppression.

This dialectical narrative method, which is as astute in its cynicism (in the etymological sense of scepticism) towards the mediatised image as it is skilled in conveying a warm, sentimental story, remains Zhang's unique contribution. His work is about the relationship between labour and the image, about the transit from an economy in which humans can still make the world with their physical bodies to one in which the image has taken over that function, leaving those bodies in an exotic but also superfluous condition (a condition in which being 'real' simply means being stuck, that is, unable to trans-valuate into cash).

As in *Happy Time*, the ability to see, the availability of sight and the possibility of becoming a spectacle that are made such palpable events in contemporary Chinese life are turned by Zhang into the ingredients of a fable with a certain moral. But the notion of fable is rooted in the process of fabulation, and the moral at stake in Zhang's work is often elsewhere from the place at which his critics try to see it. However artificial, being and becoming imaged is, his recent work says, something no one can afford not to desire; yet the ever-expanding capacities for seeing and, with them, the infinite transmigrations of cultures – national, ethnic, rural – into commodified electronic images are part and parcel of an emergent regime of value making that is as utterly ruthless as it is utterly creative. With the harsh *and* flexible materiality of this regime, critics of contemporary Chinese cinema have yet, seriously, to come to terms.

ACKNOWLEDGMENTS
Thanks to Chris Berry, Yomi Braester and Yvonne Leung for their assistance with this essay.

NOTES

1. See, for instance, the discussions of Zhang's evolving work in the special issue devoted to *Not One Less* entitled *Yige Dou Buneng Shao Yingpian Gean Fenxi*, in *Aesthetics of Chinese Film: 1999* (*Zhongguo Dianying Meixue: 1999*) (Beijing: Beijing Guangbo Xueyuan, 2000), and various discussions of the film in *Film Art* (*Dianying Yishu*), nos 1, 3 and 5 (2000).

2. See Zhang Yiwu, 'Once Again Imagining China: the Challenge of Globalization and the New "Inward-Looking Tendency" ' ('Zaidu Xiangxiang Zhongguo: Quanqiuhua de Tiaozhan yu Xin de "Neixianghua"'), *Film Art* (*Dianying Yishu*), no. 1 (2001): 16–21.

3. For a discussion of the implications of orientalism raised by Zhang's early work, see Rey Chow, *Primitive Passions: Visuality, Sexuality, Ethnography, and Contemporary Chinese Cinema* (New York: Columbia University Press, 1995), Part 2, Chapter 4, and Part 3. For related discussions, including Zhang's responses to some of his critics, see the interviews with Zhang regarding the making of *Not One Less* in the following: *Aesthetics of Chinese Film: 1999* (*Zhongguo Dianying Meixue: 1999*), 29–35; *The Fifth Generation of Chinese Filmmakers in the 1990s* (*Jiushi Niandai de Diwudai*), ed. Yang Yuanying, Pan Hua and Zhang Zhuan (Beijing: *Beijing Guangbo Xueyuan Chubanshe*, 2000), 121–127. For general interest, see also *Zhang Yimou: Interviews*, ed. Frances Gateward (Jackson: University of Mississippi Press, 2001).

4. See Shi Wenhong, 'The Sadness of *Not One Less*' ('Yige Dou Buneng Shao de Aichou'), *Film Critics Quarterly* (*Yingpingren Jikan*), nos. 6, 7 (2000).

5. For a sustained critique of the magazine's politics of representing non-Western cultures, see Catherine A. Lutz and Jane L. Collins, *Reading National Geographic* (Chicago: University of Chicago Press, 1993).

6. The cast of *Not One Less*, for instance, was made up of amateur actors, many of whom were actual villagers from the film's location. However, as Xiaoling Zhang points out, 'the whole suggestion of reality is entirely artificial: the school was chosen from a few dozen schools in that area, the eighteen pupils were selected from among thousands of pupils, and the girl playing Wei Minzhi was picked from twenty thousand girls, in an auditioning process which lasted more than half a month'. See Zhang, 'A Film Director's Criticism of Reform China: A Close Reading of Zhang Yimou's *Not One Less*', *China Information*, XV, no. 2 (2001): 138.

7. As one critic, Zeng Guang, writes:

Under the current political system, he [Zhang Yimou] feels that the biggest difference between himself and directors from foreign countries, Hong Kong, and

Taiwan lies in the fact that 'when I receive a film script, the first thing I think about is not whether there will be an investor for the film, but how I can make the kind of film I want with the approval of the authorities. This passage is cited as the epigraph in Sheldon H. Lu, 'Understanding Chinese Film Culture at the End of the Twentieth Century: the Case of *Not One Less* by Zhang Yimou', *Journal of Modern Literature in Chinese*, 4, no. 2 (2001): 123–142.

8. Note that although the film was adopted from Shi Xiangsheng's story 'A Sun in the Sky' ('Tian Shang You ge Taiyang'), *Feitian*, no. 6 (1997), Zhang changed the title to one that highlights the act of counting (bodies).

9. Wang Yichuan, 'Civilization and Civilized Barbarity' ('Wenming yu Wenming de Yeman'), *Aesthetics of Chinese Film: 1999* (*Zhongguo Dianying Meixue, 1999*), 67–75; the cited passages are on pages 71 and 73; loose translation from the Chinese is mine. This is the only reading I have come across that identifies money and the media as the decisive issues of the film.

10. Hu Ke writes that Zhang's narrative method is like an 'ad for charity'. See his 'Documentary Record and Fictional Construct' ('Jishi yu Xugou'), *Aesthetics of Chinese Film: 1999* (*Zhongguo Dianying Meixue: 1999*), 41–49; the point about 'ad for charity' is on page 42. This view is shared by other critics: see, for instance, Wang Ailing, 'Obedient Children' ('Tinghua de Haizi'), in *A Look Back at Hong Kong Cinema of 1999* (*1999 Xianggang Dianying Huigu*), ed. Wang Ailing (Hong Kong: *Xianggang Dianying Pinglun Xuehui*, 2000), 301–302; Valerie Wong, '*Not One Less*', *Cinemaya*, no. 45 (1999): 20–21. This type of reading is not incorrect, but the main problem I have with it is that these critics tend to read Zhang's film as a completed realist *message* rather than as a process and a structure in which a dialectical understanding (of the changes brought to Chinese society by the new media) is being actively produced. For an opposite type of reading that sees Zhang's film not as propaganda but as a laudable piece of social criticism, see Zhang, 'A Film Director's Criticism of Reform China'.

11. For the latter point, as well as an informative discussion of Zhang's film in relation to recent conditions of film production and reception in mainland China, see Lu, 'Understanding Chinese Film Culture at the End of the Twentieth Century'.

19 *The Red Detachment of Women*: Resenting, Regendering, Remembering

Robert Chi

INTRODUCTION

Given the recent resurgence of People's Republic of China (PRC) nationalism, the increased willingness within China to re-examine the Maoist period (roughly 1949–1979) in both academic and non-academic discourses, and the increasingly varied and sophisticated ways in which cultural theory has informed Asian studies, it has become both possible and necessary to fit the Maoist period back into China's long twentieth century. The most promising recent scholarship has proposed two strategies: first, crossing the period's beginning and ending markers (especially 1949);[1] and second, focusing on the psychic, aesthetic, affective and everyday dimensions of experience during the Maoist period.[2] With respect to cinema, we are faced here with two questions. First, how might we reconsider the functioning of culture and the arts under Maoism? Second, how are we to think of cinema as both a public art and a site for mass experience? To these more obvious questions I would like to add a third: what aesthetic and political operations take place in the name of memory? These questions are intimately connected in the many films of the Maoist period that combine revolutionary history with the coming-to-consciousness of a single representative character. One of the best and most influential of these is *The Red Detachment of Women* (Xie Jin, 1960).

Red Detachment is set on Hainan Island, off the south coast of China, and begins in 1930. In the first part of the film, a Communist cadre disguised as a rich merchant encounters the local landlord, Nan Batian. By chance an intractable maidservant has run away only to be recaptured and flogged. When the cadre leaves, Nan Batian gives the maid, Wu Qionghua, to the cadre. As they pass Boundary Hill, the cadre frees Qionghua and directs her to a Communist women's militia – a red detachment of women – that is forming nearby. Along the way

Qionghua meets another embittered woman, Fu Honglian, and the two of them follow the newly formed militia. Qionghua pleads with the (female) company commander to let them enlist. Now in uniform, the cadre, Hong Changqing, arrives with the local (male) division commander, and the two men allow the two women to enlist.

In the second part of the film, Qionghua and Honglian are sent to spy on Nan Batian. Hungry for personal revenge, Qionghua violates the rules of discipline and fires at him. Nan Batian is wounded in the left shoulder, and the women retreat. Back at the base Hong Changqing confines Qionghua to quarters. A few days later the cadre dons his rich merchant disguise again and takes Qionghua and several others to trap Nan Batian. They capture the landlord and parade him through the village. The landlord, however, escapes; giving chase, Qionghua is shot in the left shoulder. After recuperating at a field hospital, she returns to the red detachment. Along the way, she encounters Hong Changqing; passing by Boundary Hill again, they have not a love scene but a scene of instruction. For Qionghua

Qionghua enlists in the red detachment of women.

proposes to go undercover to kill Nan Batian, whereupon Hong Changqing takes her back to base to show her a map of China. The point is that Hainan Island is only one tiny part of China, and so only collective struggle, not individual vendettas, can liberate the whole country. Qionghua applies for Party membership, and later Honglian marries a fellow Communist soldier.

In the third part of the film, the KMT Nationalist government sends an expeditionary force to Hainan Island to fight the Communists. The Kuomintang (KMT) army and Nan Batian's militia defeat the red detachment at Boundary Hill. Qionghua and the other women soldiers retreat, but Hong Changqing is captured and then burned alive in front of the villagers. The KMT commander refuses to pursue the red detachment, which he considers a negligible threat, but Nan Batian – now bent on personal revenge – wants to attack. The red detachment captures the landlord, and the rest of the Communist forces defeat the KMT troops. Qionghua finally kills Nan Batian, ostensibly in self-defence. The film closes with Qionghua taking Hong Changqing's place as Party cadre for a second red detachment of women.

Previous analyses of *Red Detachment* have usually focused on its questionable vision of women's liberation, given the way that Hong Changqing dominates Qionghua's trajectory as saviour, teacher, disciplinarian, forbidden lover and symbolic creditor.[3] This is not to discount its affective appeal. But recognition of the latter usually turns on a gendered notion of melodrama as excess. This tends to reduce the film to a Rorschach test: it gives women the illusion of freedom only within an essentially patriarchal system, or it belies a patriarchal panic at the figure of woman as other, or it allows women a spectatorial room of their own. The notion of melodrama as excessive can also combine with a scepticism towards socialist realism, resulting in the dismissal of the film as exaggerated and unrealistic (as well as exoticist, being set on a tropical island) and hence ultimately ineffectual to all. My analysis is based on a re-evaluation of melodrama, namely that the latter is neither strictly gendered nor strictly a genre, which is why the film is able to fold women into a masculinist vision of women's liberation. More importantly, melodrama here shares a common genealogy and articulation with non-cinematic practices under Maoism, all of which place memory-work at the centre of the struggle for liberation.

MEMORY-WORK

Four theoretical contributions to the critical discourse on memory are particularly useful here. First, Maurice Halbwachs argues that memory is always essentially social: specific memories are always associated with, tagged according to and triggered by social contexts.[4] Second, Paul Connerton looks more closely at just 'how societies remember', drawing attention to bodily practices in particular.[5] These include periodic commemorative rituals where the anamnestic function is overt and conscious, as well as pedagogical activities that unconsciously convey and condition subjects as followers in a long tradition such as that of a particular writing system. Third, Pierre Nora suggests that one can speak of memory only when there is an effort to remember.[6] That effort might not appear to be conscious or overt or intentional; it may work out in unexpected ways; and it may fail as well. Nevertheless, Nora's distinction is useful because it implies agency and hence the motivating anxiety of *not* remembering. For memory is often thought of as an effort against negation: 'never forget', 'we will/must always remember', and so on. Fourth, Ian Hacking has proposed the notion of 'memoro-politics' as a science of the soul.[7] It complements Michel Foucault's anatomo-politics of the body and bio-politics of populations. All three are sciences of power/knowledge that construct a normative model of the subject. Memoro-politics in particular has to do with the notion that subjects have interiority, dimensionality and depth, as well as the notion that absence – what is forgotten, not what is remembered – determines us. Thus for Hacking memory operates through a productive repression, just as for Foucault sex does. Moreover, both memory and sex operate specifically on the body, and they may even be interconnected via an erotics of memory. Such an erotics would not just be represented in a film through, for example, character sexuality. More importantly it would be felt through spectatorial engagement grounded in the body, such as through intense emotions and their somatic correlates. It would be a question of desire, love and pleasure – even the pleasure of suffering, violence and death.

Memory is often contrasted with history on the grounds that the latter is a selective and repressive official narrative and hence the former is a site for political resistance. But this is a misleading contrast, since the state itself often openly engages in mnemonics. Obvious examples of this include monuments and memorials, as well as museums, textbooks, holidays, currency, postage stamps, and the naming of public spaces and architecture. During the Maoist period culture played a crucial role in the overall effort to narrate the origins of the People, the Chinese Communist Party (CCP) and the PRC. Privileged topics included the organisational efforts of the leftists and the Communists during the 1920s through the 1940s, as well as the armed conflict against the KMT and the Japanese. Such narratives appeared in a variety of forms and genres. For example, fictional and semi-fictional narratives appeared in literature and drama, while non-fictional narratives included reportage, interviews and memoirs.

To be sure, for cinema historians the Maoist period is quite heterogeneous, mainly because the Cultural Revolution (1966–1976) saw very few new films produced – or old films screened. In contrast what in Chinese is referred to as the Seventeen Years (1949–1966) was a period of abundant production, wholesale expansion and reconfiguration of the film industry, and numerous overlapping sub-periods marked out by the interactions among politics, economics and culture. The Seventeen Years saw over one hundred feature films about the revolutionary wars or revolutionary history in general, as well as many documentary films on similar subjects. In the decade after its release, *Red Detachment* itself was turned into a revolutionary ballet, then a revolutionary model opera and then finally into filmed versions of both of those, in 1970 and 1972, respectively. Even today revolutionary history films continue to be central to what in the post-Cultural Revolution years have been dubbed 'main melody' (*zhu xuan lü*) works – witness the parade of often two- or three-part films since the 1980s recounting major battles, campaigns and CCP leaders.

At the same time, PRC history has seen a whole procession of anniversary observances. Throughout the Seventeen Years there were many anniversaries, holidays and commemorations of revolutionary events. Moreover, they usually involved generically heterogeneous memory-texts, making such memory-work what textual studies calls simply intertextuality, allusion, reference, tradition. For example, the original film version of *Red Detachment* was released on 1 July 1961 as part of a week-long series of new films

– the series itself being only one of a range of works and events – celebrating the fortieth anniversary of the founding of the CCP. The films included feature films, children's films, documentaries and educational films.[8] As one might expect from a commemoration of the CCP at that point, more than half of the films (among the fifteen advertised in the *People's Daily*) – including both fiction and documentary films – are about revolutionary history. Similar events take place today as well, such as the various film series, theatrical performances and museum exhibits in Shanghai during the summer of 2001 that celebrated the eightieth anniversary of the founding of the CCP.

Besides these reproducible and transportable works, live public acts of storytelling have been crucial to the formation of revolutionary subjects. Before 1949 one of the most significant symbolic devices and social practices under the CCP had been the public airing of grievances or *suku*, the recounting of suffering under China's 'feudal' conditions. It is important to note that imagining and expressing interiority in this way – as in, for example, judicial proceedings – long predated the CCP. But during its years of revolutionary struggle the latter turned it into a means of publicity, recruitment, motivation, training and organisation. Even after the establishment of the PRC in 1949, such narrative recollection continued to integrate the recollection of past suffering, the revolutionary struggle for liberation and the imperative not to let the 'feudal' past repeat itself. Such public airings of grievances were institutionalised in the form of mass rallies and public denunciations. They included visual-somatic elements such as the baring of scars and the shedding of tears, both of which figure prominently in *Red Detachment*. This served to focus particular attention on the body as the site of both memory (as suffering, as an effort against negation) and sociality – this latter being in fact the interface between individual and collective, or simply the mass public experience. The public airing of grievances continued to be a crucial technique for the formation of revolutionary subjects, as shown by the far-reaching land reform and anti-counterrevolutionary, anti-corruption and anti-capitalist campaigns of 1950–1952, as well as the all-too-common denunciations of the Cultural Revolution.[9]

Ci Jiwei has analysed the Party's memory-work in terms of a 'calculus of debts'.[10] *Red Detachment*

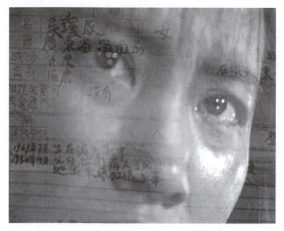

Qionghua and her application to join the Party.

thematises this on screen and diegetically through the circulation of coins, as do other films of the Seventeen Years such as *Daughter of the Party* (Lin Nong, 1958).[11] In *Red Detachment*, when Hong Changqing grants Qionghua her freedom at Boundary Hill he immediately monetises that debt by giving her four silver coins to buy food on her journey to the red detachment base. Later, as Qionghua and the other women soldiers are preparing to retreat from the battle at Boundary Hill, Hong Changqing tells her that her Party membership application has been approved. She gives him the four coins as payment of her Party dues. After witnessing Hong Changqing's execution Qionghua recovers the cadre's bag, which contains her now-approved Party application form and the four coins. This last sequence is the emotional climax of the film and provides little

plot-related action. Instead it is dominated by close-up reaction shots of Qionghua witnessing the execution and then walking home benumbed. This culminates in the prolonged series of close-ups of Hong Changqing's bag, the four coins in Qionghua's hand, and a remarkable montage of dissolves and superimposed images of Qionghua in tight close-up and her Party application, which she is ostensibly reading. Amidst this is a barely diegetic monumental close-up of her clenched fist, in which she has just grasped the four coins, held aloft in the Communist salute. The repeated swelling of the Internationale on the soundtrack holds the whole three-minute sequence together.

By working through memory, the calculus of debt ensures the interiorisation, the *making one's own*, of that indebtedness to the Party. The Communist salute clenching the four coins serves to transvalue the latter from money to *memento mori*, and even more important than the Communist oath, the gesture's unspoken verbal component is 'I shall never forget'. As Wang Hui argues in one of the best Chinese-language commentaries on the film's director Xie Jin, what is at stake is not compliance but a willingness to comply, not just control but a belief in the legitimacy of that control.[12] Thus when Qionghua is confined to quarters after breaking the rules of discipline, she has a heart-to-heart talk with Honglian. While fingering the four silver coins, Qionghua marvels: '[Hong Changqing] lectures you, he disciplines you, and even as he is disciplining you, he makes you [want to] comply wholeheartedly [*jiao ni kou fu xin fu*, literally 'makes your mouth and heart submit'].' If *Red Detachment* mobilises memory in the service of the Party, just how does it turn audiovisual images from mechanically reproducible and publicly circulating tokens to iconic talismans with inestimable sentimental value?

THE RED ATTACHMENTS OF WOMEN

The director of *Red Detachment*, Xie Jin, is perhaps the single most important film-maker during the first half-century of the PRC. Born in 1923, Xie Jin began working in the film industry in Shanghai in 1948, on the eve of the establishment of the new China. After several years as assistant director, he made his first film as director in 1951. Among his pre-Cultural Revolution films, *Woman Basketball*

Body, image, monument: Qionghua enters the Party.

Player No. 5 (1957), *The Red Detachment of Women* and *Stage Sisters* (1964) are especially notable. Xie Jin's films continued to be popular and critical successes after the Cultural Revolution; examples include *The Legend of Tianyun Mountain* (1980), *The Shepherd* (1981), *Garlands at the Foot of the Mountain* (1984) and *Hibiscus Town* (1986). These later films in particular played a crucial role in the negotiation of the state's 'main melody' in the reform era. Even after 1989 Xie Jin's films continued to be noteworthy if only for the way that they stubbornly hewed to the 'main melody' – witness *The Opium War* (1997) commemorating the return of Hong Kong, as well as *Woman Soccer Player No. 9* (2000), an undisguised feature-length advertisement for the PRC women's national soccer team that doubled as a remake of *Woman Basketball Player No. 5*.

Xie Jin's major films both before and after the Cultural Revolution all engage in one way or another with the problem of the individual experience of history, a history that in the PRC is always writ large as a story whose protagonist is a collective one – the People. More specifically, the embodiment of that individual experience is usually a woman, and the mode of experience is melodrama. The vexed notion of 'Asian melodrama' is outside the scope of the present essay, and certainly any notion of a 'Chinese melodrama' can find local or 'traditional' sources and conditions that account for Xie Jin's privileged mode. However, it is useful to note that recent re-evaluations of melodrama see it as neither a genre nor a deviation or excess with respect to the norm of classical or mainstream cinema. For example, both Linda Williams and Christine Gledhill contend that melodrama is a fundamental mode (if not *the* fundamental mode) of mainstream cinema.[13] Melodrama negotiates between morality and feeling, between realism as a mode and modernity as contemporary lived experience, and between fictional and real worlds. This revised notion of melodrama is not in itself gendered as feminine, since it also accounts for masculine genres like Westerns and action films. An apparent hybrid like *Red Detachment*, a women's war film, thus confirms the underlying identity of the two, just as the Maoist practice of the public airing of grievances, itself traceable to pre-Communist antecedents in China, can be seen as a kind of melodramatic theatre.

In both cases that melodrama is figured in terms of memory. Melodrama's aims of stirring spectators to pathos as well as the recognition of moral virtue and innocent victimhood are precisely the aims of the Maoist practice of publicly airing grievances. What the latter specifies is that they are based on historical experience, so the pathos and sympathy of spectators spring from their recognition of common experiences in their own pasts – in other words, identification under the sign of memory. *Red Detachment* foregrounds this by presenting not one but a series of scenes of such grievance airing. In fact, there are three key scenes in which Qionghua announces her bitter personal memories, and these scenes serve to punctuate her trajectory from slavery to liberation, from personal revenge to collective class struggle and from taking orders to giving them. The three scenes consist of the first passage across Boundary Hill, the enlistment scene and the public parading of the captured Nan Batian. Together the three scenes form a developmental sequence on several levels. In all three Qionghua's speech is interrupted: first by herself, then by the arrival and mere presence of Hong Changqing and finally by Honglian's admonition which results in a redirection of Qionghua's *j'accuse* to praise of the Communist revolution. It takes an increasingly active and external intervention to interrupt Qionghua, which means that she herself is becoming increasingly active in both expression and action. Likewise, the diegetic audiences of the three scenes go from Hong Changqing to the assembled women's detachment to the people of the village. This sequence traces a progression in number as well as an ideological progression from the Party as specular leader to the People themselves.

There are also several supplementary and countering moments that serve to highlight Qionghua's trajectory. First, other characters confess their own personal bitter memories, too. Not surprisingly the two major characters to do so are Honglian and Hong Changqing. They are Qionghua's symbolic partial doubles in that the former remains within the family structure and hence becomes both wife and mother, while the latter is the mentor whose place Qionghua ultimately occupies instead. Hong Changqing in particular teaches Qionghua and the film's audiences about the emotive or 'melodramatic' basis of revolution: when he chastises her for violating discipline and firing at Nan Batian during the scouting mission, the Party secretary asks her rhetorically, 'Do you think that only you feel such resentment [*yuan chou*]? What proletarian's heart is not steeped in tears?' Later, as part of the map-lesson about the priority of collective struggle over personal vendettas, the secretary tells Qionghua of his own background, his own bitter past. Here Hong Changqing is pointedly engaged in a bit of stage business, namely chopping open a very large coconut. Besides adding a bit of exotic local colour or realism, this somatic correlate to the bitter recollection serves to express the secretary's own pent-up resentment as he grips the knife and coconut and delivers the final, violent blow to the latter. But the business ends up being channelled into the productive, positive, nourishing action of pouring and drinking the coconut's milk. Grasping the lesson, Qionghua responds, 'In other words, every proletarian's heart is steeped in tears!' Second, Qionghua has another partial double whose trajectory is the mirror image of hers: Nan Batian. He reflects not alternatives but opposites, his story moving from the pinnacle of power at the beginning of the film to a bullet wound in the left shoulder, escape from his captors and finally a desire for revenge over strategy that proves to be his undoing. Thus the symmetrical contrast between Qionghua and the retrograde Nan Batian further suggests the structural necessity of suffering and the bitter past as the threat of negation that motivates the utopian remembering of Maoism.

The most emblematic of Qionghua's three scenes of grievance-airing is the enlistment scene, when Qionghua and Honglian ask to join the red detachment. When the company commander tells them to submit a formal application explaining why they have come, Qionghua impetuously tears open her blouse to reveal the scars she has suffered under Nan Batian's whip. She shouts that she wants revenge: 'What for? You want to know what for? For this! Revolt! Revenge! Kill the officials! Cannibals! Skin them alive! I … I …' It is at this moment that the film cuts to a counter-shot of Hong Changqing and the division commander entering – and it is this which silences Qionghua's outburst. While the uncovering of scars accompanied by passionate denunciation perfectly combines the public airing of grievances with the iconic low-angle close-up that Stephanie Donald calls the 'socialist-realist gaze',[14] what is most revealing about this scene is its possible alternatives. After making the film Xie Jin wrote his

'Director's Notes on *The Red Detachment of Women*'. There he laments that the scar scene does not express Qionghua's class identity clearly enough. He writes that upon finally seeing a sympathetic audience of fellow proletarians, Qionghua should have been overflowing with things to say. She should have struggled to find the right words first, before revealing her scars and shouting – instead of doing so right away, without missing a beat.[15] In contrast, the model opera version filmed in 1972 (dir. Cheng Yin) has Hong Changqing and the red-detachment commander welcoming Qionghua immediately and without doubt. They do not ask her what she came for; instead, noticing her scars, Hong Changqing simply invites her to air her grievances before her comrades. This turns into a lengthy (i.e. verbose) aria. The two alternatives bracket the melodramatic aspect of the scene. The former opts for a classical cinematic naturalism of character motivations and behaviour, which moreover should have been indicated precisely by the inability to make oneself understood that is a key trope of melodrama. The latter, coming at the more radically utopian moment of the Cultural Revolution, dispenses with such blockage and deferral, resolving the dilemma through the immediate embrace of the Party.

In his 'Director's Notes' Xie Jin also presents three simple but crucial ideas that summarise how cinema of the Seventeen Years operates as a form of memoro-politics. First, Xie Jin recounts actual responses to a preview screening to show that different viewers indeed interpret the main idea of a film differently: in this case, different audience glosses include 'Chinese women took up arms, the greatest suffering did not deter them, and the Chinese people are invincible'; 'Resistance that springs from the individual is limited, it is necessary to act collectively in order to generate great strength and in order to defeat all enemies'; and 'Dare to struggle, dare to win'. Second, he attributes this difference to the fact that each reader or spectator of a work associates the latter with his or her own experience.[16] Finally, he insists throughout that the measure of a film is to what extent it moves its audience as if in a 'mutual cry' or reverberation [*gong ming*] with its characters.[17] Spectatorship as reverberation here resides at the intersection among affect, cognition, soma and memory, and it is figured specifically as an oral-aural experience. Given the real past experiences of individual spectators – which in turn form their interests, tastes and concerns in the present – a film aims to foreground characters as sites for identification and hence education. Cognitive self-reflection on that education, here expressible in the form of summaries of the main idea of the film, can vary widely. But what is ultimately at stake for Xie Jin is the affective-somatic aspect of identification. In other words, the revolutionary call to action consists not only of ideological education but of moving the spectatorial body – moving both as somatic gesture and as emotional stimulation.

The abundance of narratives and commemorations of revolutionary history in the PRC reminds us of just how important it was – and still is – to popularise and multiply memory-images of the struggle for liberation. The further fact that relatively little critical attention has been focused on this unmistakeable link between pre-1949 China and post-1949 China confirms that memory is a supplement, without necessarily being a site of resistance, to the master narrative of dramatic leaps and breaks in the course of inexorable forward progress away from the past – the temporality of revolution or historical abjection. Cinema under Mao was part of this attempt to radically restructure subjectivity – a wholesale 'cultural revolution' – and in films such as *The Red Detachment of Women* that revolution takes place 'where the heart is'.

NOTES

1. For example, see Tang Xiaobing, ed., *Rereading: Mass Culture and Ideology* (*Zai jiedu: dazhong wenyi yu yishixingtai*) (Hong Kong: Oxford University Press, 1993); and Peng Hsiao-yen, ed., *Literary and Art Theory and Popular Culture* (*Wenyi lilun yu tongsu wenhua*), 2 vols (Taibei: Zhongyang yanjiu yuan Zhongguo wen zhe yanjiu suo choubei chu, 1999).

2. For example, see Ban Wang, *The Sublime Figure of History: Aesthetics and Politics in Twentieth-century China* (Stanford: Stanford University Press, 1997). In fact, the Cultural Revolution in particular did inspire many attempts at psychological analysis of Mao Zedong and of the Red Guards. These were sometimes combined with historical analysis under the rubric of 'psychohistory'. See, for example, Robert Jay Lifton's remarkable studies *Thought Reform and the Psychology of Totalism: A Study of 'Brainwashing' in China* (New York: Norton, 1961) and *Revolutionary*

Immortality: Mao Tse-tung and the Chinese Cultural Revolution (New York: Random House, 1968). Such psycho-historical studies do take the realms of the psychic and the everyday seriously, but they do not offer much specific analysis of cultural forms such as literature, cinema, theatre and the fine arts.

3. *The Red Detachment of Women* has been the subject of much passing commentary in English-language scholarship, but there have been no published attempts to analyse it at length. For example, the two earliest English-language monographs that address cinema under Maoism mention it briefly: Jay Leyda, *Dianying: An Account of Films and the Film Audience in China* (Cambridge: MIT Press, 1972), 303; and Paul Clark, *Chinese Cinema: Culture and Politics Since 1949* (Cambridge: Cambridge University Press, 1987), 102–103. A more recent work that again mentions the film several times but only in passing is Stephanie Hemelryk Donald, *Public Secrets, Public Spaces: Cinema and Civility in China* (Lanham: Rowman and Littlefield, 2000), 1, 41, 65, 76, 116. The most sustained analysis of the film that I have seen in English is Esther Ching-mei Yau, 'Filmic Discourse on Women in Chinese Cinema (1949–65): Art, Ideology and Social Relations', unpublished dissertation, UCLA, 1990, 256–259.

4. Maurice Halbwachs, *The Collective Memory*, trans. Francis J. Ditter, Jr. and Vida Yazdi Ditter (New York: Harper & Row, 1980).

5. Paul Connerton, *How Societies Remember* (Cambridge: Cambridge University Press, 1989).

6. Pierre Nora, ed., *Realms of Memory*, English edition ed. Lawrence D. Kritzman, trans. Arthur Goldhammer, 3 vols (New York: Columbia University Press, 1996–1998).

7. Ian Hacking, *Rewriting the Soul* (Princeton: Princeton University Press, 1995) and 'Memory Sciences, Memory Politics', in *Tense Past: Cultural Essays in Trauma and Memory*, ed. Paul Antze and Michael Lambek (New York: Routledge, 1996), 67–87.

8. See advertisements published around this time in the *Renmin ribao* (Beijing) and the *Wen Hui Bao* (Shanghai).

9. For more on the public airing of grievances and the psychic significance of such narrative practices, see David E. Apter and Tony Saich, *Revolutionary Discourse in Mao's Republic* (Cambridge: Harvard University Press, 1994); and Ann Anagnost, *National Past-Times: Narrative, Representation, and Power in*

Modern China (Durham: Duke University Press, 1997), esp. Chapter 1.

10. Jiwei Ci, *Dialectic of the Chinese Revolution: From Utopianism to Hedonism* (Stanford: Stanford University Press, 1994), 82–85.

11. The film *Daughter of the Party* is based on the 1954 short story 'Party Dues' by Wang Yuanjian, and there are also various stage versions of *Daughter of the Party* – all of which confirm the centrality of the premise of indebtedness to the Party.

12. Wang Hui, 'Politics, Morality, and the Secret of their Displacement: An Analysis of Xie Jin's Films' ('Zhengzhi yu daode ji qi zhihuan de mimi – Xie Jin dianying fenxi'), *Film Art (Dianying yishu)*, no. 2 (1990): 23–45.

13. Linda Williams, 'Melodrama Revised', in *Refiguring American Film Genres*, ed. Nick Browne (Berkeley: University of California Press, 1998), 42–88; and Christine Gledhill, 'Rethinking Genre', in *Reinventing Film Studies*, ed. Christine Gledhill and Linda Williams (London: Arnold, 2000), 221–243.

14. Stephanie Hemelryk Donald, *Public Secrets*, 59–64.

15. Xie Jin, 'Director's Notes on *The Red Detachment of Women*' [*Hongse niangzi jun* daoyan zhaji], in *The Red Detachment of Women: From Screenplay to Film* (*Hongse niangzi jun: cong juben dao dianying*) (Beijing: Zhongguo dianying chubanshe, 1962), 278.

16. Ibid., 271–272.

17. Ibid., 291–292.

20 *A Time to Live, A Time to Die*: A Time to Grow

Corrado Neri

A Time to Live, A Time to Die (1985) is an autobiographical film by Hou Hsiao-hsien, in which the director, who was born in China in 1947 but grew up in Taiwan, recalls his youth and adolescence. The movie is part of a 'biographical trilogy', through which the director reconstructs the memories of his generation. Hou had a solid technical background, because in the early part of the 1980s he directed three successful musical comedies. The turning point was *The Sandwich Man* (1983), a portmanteau feature film that marks the birth of the movement of the New Taiwan Cinema and for which he directed one part. Then came *Boys from Fenggui* (1983), a partly autobiographical film, in which Hou, still hovering between commercial film-making and personal expression, started investigating the themes that remained the focus of his later work – growing up, the generation gap, sexuality, Taiwan's economical and political problems, and the rural–urban dichotomy. He also started investigating a new language to express these themes, by experimenting with non-professional actors, long takes, still camera shots and elliptic editing. *Boys from Fenggui* is still experimental, but the biographical trilogy demonstrates maturity. The first chapter is *Summer at Grandpa's* (1984), based on the memories of the writer Zhu Tianwen. The second is *A Time To Live, A Time to Die*, which is autobiographical (the screenplay was co-written by Zhu Tianwen, as all other Hou movies have been). The third is entitled *Dust in the Wind* (1986), and it is based on the experiences of Wu Nianzhen, the famous Taiwanese screenwriter, actor and director.[1]

The very first film of the Taiwan New Cinema, *In Our Time* (Edward Yang, Ke Yizheng, Zhang Yi and Tao Dechen, 1982), also deals with memory, as the directors were asked to work on an episode taken from their youth. The New Cinema opposed artistic movies to commercial comedies, realism to studio-made films, non-professional actors to the star-system, and reflection on society and human lives to pure escapism. The directors, and in particular Hou, started describing their own experiences, trying to put reality back on the screen by dealing with the familiar landscapes of memory. Hou, with his Taiwan trilogy of *A City of Sadness* (1989), *The Puppetmaster* (1993) and *Good Men, Good Women* (1995), Yang Dechang, Wu Nianzhen and the other Taiwan New Cinema directors undertook a very precise process moving first to deal with autobiography, and then with history *tout-court*. Because of the socio-political commitment of Chinese artists, the investigation of the past cannot stop at personal feelings and nostalgia; it also has to deal with the nation itself, society, and cultural identity.[2] *A Time* is consistent with the Chinese tradition of placing the personal story within the greater context of history, and Hou's cinematic style is consistent with the Confucian vision of a committed artist. As I shall note later, it should be emphasised that some stylistic procedures also express the director's deepest feelings, even if in an implicit and poetic manner.

Biography and particularly autobiography, is traditionally a literary genre that links back to history as its original source. As Nienhauser reminds us, 'The principal aim of autobiography was to celebrate one's name and make known one's parents.'[3] The first autobiography in China is usually identified as the *Lisao*, a famous poetic composition by Qu Yuan, which starts with a description of the poet's genealogy.[4] The autobiographical notes by Sima Qian in the conclusion of his historical *opus magnum*, the *Shiji*, are also noteworthy.[5] Here the presentation of the author's life is justified and takes on significance owing to and through the text itself. The inter-textual references form a network from the past to the present, inscribing the writer in a rich and noble tradition that gives order to the world. The identity of the individual man is to be found and understood in this semantic context, thanks to his being part of a larger scheme. The historian finds his place in society and the meaning of his life by defining himself as the one who hands down and keeps the memories of past events alive. He finds a way to be remembered by remembering.[6]

Autobiography (*zizhuan*) is far from the modern Western tradition of autobiography, characterised by romanticism and psychology.[7] It is more a matter of finding a place in society (and nature) that can provide a sense of harmony in existence. It is also a way to pay respect to the memory of parents and family, which is, together with society, the greater context of human existence.

In accordance with Chinese cultural tradition, Hou speaks of himself in an indirect manner. (It is significant that nothing in the film suggests the fact that Hou will become an artist.)[8] He evokes the most personal memories and recreates images of his youth on screen. These were the strongest images that had marked his imagination and have gone on to become obsessions in later years. However, this procedure is carried out through a de-personalisation of the narration, putting his intimate feelings at a distance and choosing a detached perspective, as if he were merely a spectator of his own story and not the protagonist. The real protagonists are his family and his country. The scholar Ni Zhen writes:

Hou Hsiao-hsien's systematic and highly stylized cinematic prose expresses very incisively and vividly the ethical spirit of Confucian culture and the emotional attachment to the native land typical of the Orient. The family is a cohesive, highly symbolic unit of Confucian culture, the fundamental space within which to view and examine the psychological world of the Chinese.[9]

The movie also features some cultural traits that emerge indirectly: Hou seems to revitalise the *biji* tradition. The *biji* is a literary genre dating back to the Song Dynasty. It is a diary form in prose, a miscellany made up of annotations, which are often very refined and poetic.[10] The most remarkable example is Shen Fu's eighteenth-century *Fusheng liuji* (*Six Chapters from a Floating Life*). 'This work, now consisting of four chapters … amounts to a systematically arranged autobiographical review of the author's life; within the Chinese tradition it is unusual for its detail and candor.'[11] It is difficult to classify the *Six*

Chapters among the literary genres. It anticipates some features of the modern novel (*xiaoshuo*), because it contains an atypical expression of the self as well as a self-conscious pleasure in pure writing that is neither socially nor politically engaged. The latter is a characteristic that Lu Xun ascribes to the novel.[12] However, we do not find classical narration with a beginning and an end, but a juxtaposition of impressions and strong images, characters and landscapes. Therefore, the *biji* is a mix of a very traditional sensitivity, as well as an innovative and modern way of dealing with memories. It refuses exposition according to the logic of cause and effect, preferring an impressionistic approach and refusing to write a *Bildungsroman* in which the characters are exemplars. We will not find catharsis, redemption or a climax, but the placid rhythm of life floating along. Another important characteristic of the autobiographical *biji* narrative is that it has an episodic structure, and does not follow chronological criteria. Hou's films do follow a chronological line, but like the *biji* form they accumulate their details according to atmospheric affinities and the similarity of various visual impressions. So, like this typical Chinese form and unlike the Western tradition of autobiography, Hou's films are repetitive and apparently not demonstrative, and proceed by accumulation and not by synthesis. Certain scenes repeat like a hypnotic rhythm through the film: the women of the family talking while they sit on the wooden floor in a medium-long shot; the eldest son working at the father's desk in a medium shot with the camera placed outside the room; the grandmother sleeping on the floor in a medium shot, and so on. Hou uses autobiography as a means to express personal feelings and to develop a unique style of his own in an episodic manner that recalls the *biji* tradition, as well as to describe and hand down the experiences of his family and country in the *xiaoshuo* tradition.[13]

As concerns his visual approach, it is interesting that Hou does not admit any direct inspiration, but cites only the 'panoramic vision' of Shen Congwen (1902–1988).[14] The writer's influence on Hou could only be indirect. Shen's autobiography[15] starts with a wide perspective on the writer's hometown, the houses and the people, and only later is his character introduced. This is exactly what happens in Hou's movies, which also follow this descriptive technique of proceeding by successive reduction. This is how

Hou introduces himself into the narrative of *A Time*. After the description of the house in Hou's own voice-over over a few still shots, the grandmother goes to the village looking for her grandson. There is a wide pan shot of the little town, then a cut to a medium shot that focuses slowly in on a group of children playing. Hou must be among them, but which one is he? This is a very elegant and discreet way of introducing himself into the story. The beginning of the film already introduces the poetics of the contemplative slow rhythm, the aesthetics of the long take and the composition of long shots including blank spaces.[16] Unlike other writers of the period, Shen Congwen had only been negligibly influenced by Western literature (as Hou is not ostensibly influenced by Western cinema). Their approaches to creation are very instinctive and unmediated. Both are strongly attached to the soil of their motherland and celebrate it in their works, and both rejected formal schooling to learn from real life. Their attitude is somehow similar, and quite atypical in the Chinese context. Furthermore, as in Shen Fu's memories, Hou Hsiao-hsien and Shen Congwen's works both display an alternation between an intimate description of the author's inner feelings that is doubly striking given their position as distant observers and a detached description of their backgrounds, often made up of an enumeration of family names, place names and visual details, transferred in Hou's case into cinematic language by the use of the long-take description of village life and geometric compositions that inscribe the characters in their family and social context.

Made up of very long takes, elliptical narrative, an aesthetics of stasis and elaborate geometric compositions, Hou's mature aesthetic reached complete harmony in *A Time*. This aesthetic claims the status of art for film-making, and imposes a distinctive authorial gaze and the patient habit of careful observation. The long shot is used with a full understanding of its possibilities: every frame is divided into multiple frames made up of windows, doors and mirrors. The frame is balanced and in perfect stillness, the movements of the characters providing an internal rhythm. Once again, this is a stylistic strategy, but it also corresponds to the way things were perceived at that time, when all doors and windows were always open, when people were used to talking for hours sitting on the doorsteps of their houses,

before skyscrapers, tiles, pollution and the urbanisation of Taiwan. Thanks to these techniques, the spectator feels as if he were an intimate witness, just like little Hou.[17]

Hou works on reality, flirting with documentary film – almost all his actors are non-professionals. He tries to revive old pictures of his family, re-creating the exact conditions of the past for new people. One sequence shows his sister's class, all in a line in a medium shot, and a photographer taking a picture. The students are still but moving; they comb their hair and arrange their clothes. The image cuts to an old black-and-white picture of a class. With this editing, like a poetic juxtaposition placing the real picture against the fictional shot, Hou signals one sense of the movie; it is a new form of archaeology, an attempt to re-create the past by restoring movement back to a still image and bringing the subjects back to life.

This attitude also confirms a deep interest in memory and historical reconstruction. 'It can be argued that this desire to (re)construct a family or regional history is in itself the result of an obsession with history, which is certainly a dominant Chinese cultural trait', argues Leo Ou-fan Lee.[18] Memory is fragmented, and Hou, free from any demonstrative project or a romantic representation of the self, creates particles that can be inscribed in history.

One of the indirect ways to introduce history in narration is to use the eyes of witnesses as a filter, especially the bewilderment in the eyes of children. Another formal strategy (frequent in *A City of Sadness*) is to utilise news from the radio to let the historical context filter into the private lives of the family. Hou's family, following his father, moved to Taiwan only two years before the separation from the mainland. As suggested in the film, Hou feels the island is his homeland because he lived there all his life; but his parents cannot help feeling they are exiles. They cannot find their place in the new country where they were supposed to live only a few months, but where they find themselves obliged to stay forever. The strongest symbol of this situation is undoubtedly the character of the grandmother. The old lady disappears from time to time and is found walking lost in the neighbourhood. She is looking for a mythical bridge that can take her back home, because she cannot stand to be far from the graves of her ancestors. With this significant character, Hou

A Time to Live, A Time to Die.

creates both a touching figure of a 'time to die' and the unstoppable decay of body and mind, as well as a metaphor of exile. Bai Xianyong argues in some of his best short stories that the Chinese in general are parricidal because they 'killed' the legacy of Confucius in the first decades of the century, denying the importance of tradition while worshipping the idea of an imported modernity.[19] If this is true, the Chinese-Taiwanese must be even guiltier, having severed the ties with their motherland. Another important symbol of the father's generation's sense of exile is provided by the father's chair – the same metaphor as used in *Boys from Fenggui*. It is made, as is the rest of the furniture, of bamboo. As the sister discovers by reading her father's journal after his death, this was not an aesthetic choice but a practical need. Bamboo is cheap, flexible and light. The father did not want to settle down in Taiwan and was always ready to return to the continent as soon as the KMT Nationalist army took it back. The Hou family's bamboo furniture becomes both a sign of the premature death of the father and subsequent economic difficulties and a metonymy of Taiwan, an empire

born from exile, from retreat, loss and emptiness. There are other elliptical strategies indicating the tense situation of the times. For example, one morning after a sleepless night for Hou's father, the people of the village find huge tank tracks in the mud outside their poor houses. War is thundering just outside the door, with its fearful rumble. Tension is created, and a sensation of malaise and threat filters into the film in a very subtle way. This visual procedure also corresponds to Hou's real experience, as he was just a child in the early 1950s and only became aware of the situation and drama of his relatives by small clues and brief intuitions in exactly this manner. The spectator never sees the threat waiting off-screen, only its shadow drawing over the serenity of daily life. Last but not least, this is also an expressive example of how a low-budget movie can resolve problems without sacrificing strong meaning and deep impact.

It is significant that after the most dramatic sequences, which imply time to be linear, there is a shot focused on clusters of trees and the sky, suggesting a circular idea of time. Historical or private tragedies are to be reconstructed and re-created in front of the camera, but the sky is always the same, the same blue now as when Hou was a child. The episode thus preserves its significance, engraved forever in memory, but is also seen as inscribed in the serene circularity of nature.

Could this mean that there is no lesson for the young Hou to learn? Perhaps it is useful to return to the idea of the *biji* form and the English title of the film.[20] The structure of the film, though apparently very simple and linear, is punctuated by key images that create an echo, linked together by the artist's retrospective eye. It is possible to classify life experiences according to various inventories. As Shen Fu catalogues his experiences under titles like *Of Small Delights in Idleness* and so on, Hou lists the peaceful moments and the pleasures, and the violence and the mourning under the categories of 'a time to live' and 'a time to die', respectively. The time to live includes the nostalgic description of his youth, childhood games, first loves, lost sensations of summer smells, long talks around a table and the anticipation typical of every adolescence, as well as the feeling of loss (conveyed by the long, still takes). In these moments, the movie seems free, spontaneous and almost random.

The time to die is the hidden structure of the movie, the trace of signification. Even if these tragic events seem to flow with the natural movements of the seasons, they are actually symbols of crucial moments in Hou's life. They are different stages, each of them bringing a different awareness.

The first death is the father's. In Hou's process of growing up this signifies lack, an awakening and awareness of emptiness, and rupture. (It is possible to use the same terms for the Taiwan nation, as well.) The father's death occurs during a blackout; his passing away is not shown, but the screen remains black for several seconds. After a few scenes, there is another powerful ellipsis, the most significant temporal ellipsis of the film. After long scenes of mourning, there is a medium shot of young Hou going to the bathroom. Hearing a cry, he turns his head. There is a close-up of the young Hou, his eyes wide open with fear. The next cut to a medium shot shows that it is his mother who cried out. Then there is another close-up on Hou, who is now a teenager. Something like ten years have passed. This is an efficient and surprising stylistic choice, made even more notable because close-ups are so rare in the film. This

cut occurs after one hour, almost mid-way through the movie. Significantly, Hou decides to avoid representation of the mourning period and the difficult years without his father, so that these dramatic and painful events remain off-screen. They are not seen, but their presence casts a shadow on the rest of the movie, implicit, but strong nonetheless. The boy's existence is built on emptiness, on a sense of loss. In this way it is exactly like the film, for Hou's voice-over at the beginning of the film states, 'this film is about my father'. However, the father passes away very soon, so more precisely, it is a film about the absence of the father. This absence had profound consequences for Hou, the most direct being loss of respect for authority and lack of respect and projects for the future, which his gang of friends shares and expresses in pointless violence and rebellion against authority.[21]

Childhood ends, in Hou's experience, with death and pain; ellipsis itself is a loss, things missing. Furthermore, the cut is on a pair of eyes: the first express the terror of a child who sees his family broken; the second just give the lazy glance of an annoyed teenager. But can the audience not see in that gaze the shadow of a past tragedy? It is an invisible reflex, a faded trace, but by approaching the two dimensions of his character in this manner, Hou suggests a dark continuity. This continuity is the impotence that exists when faced with loss. Hou manages to describe the more imperceptible consequences of drama (and of history), like the trace of infinite sadness in the eyes of his characters, and he entrusts the unspoken, the suggestion and minimal description of small details to mirror ineffable feelings.

The death of the mother is also treated with a particular stylistic strategy that creates the invisible architecture of the film. It underlines the peculiar structure of echoes and repetitions, and establishes a connection between sexuality (the son's puberty and first sexual experience) and death (the mother's illness).

I do not think this reveals a vision of sexuality as sin or implies an oedipal relationship, but rather it underscores the cycle of the seasons, and of life and death. Perhaps, by dealing with such delicate and difficult themes together, there is also an attempt to accept them as complementary and inscribe them in the natural flow of events. Besides that, the sequence of the mother's agony is similar to that of the father's.

This gives a sense of the creeping circularity of time, like nature always repeating its own fearful symmetry. These must have been terribly strong images that the young Hou could not elaborate until the making of the film, and they remain identical and obsessive. They filter experiences, while also lending poetic unity to the film as leitmotifs. In this sense, I believe that behind the veil of the interest in history and society, it is possible to glimpse traces of deep reflection, and the author's feelings and obsessions. Hou gives flesh and blood to the ghosts imprinted on his retina, crucial points where everything dropped away and then all resumed. The long takes and the other formal features discussed above allow these images to penetrate into the eyes of the spectator as they penetrated Hou's eyes, like ink absorbed by paper.

The last strong image is the death of the grandmother, an image that gives Hou the possibility to state indirectly what he will be. She dies in her sleep. The nephews find her when some ants are already walking over her body. First we see a close-up of the young Hou writing, then a long shot of the house from outside as the voice-over starts again, followed by a medium shot of the grandmother lying on the floor (possibly sleeping, as usual). Then there is a close-up of her hands, with ants running over her fingers, a medium shot of the woman in which it is evident her face is white, and then a long-take long shot as the nephews arrive. This end is lyrical (the quiet silence of the image, the sweet death of the woman) and prosaic (the voice-over speaks with apparent detachment), violent (the clotted blood, the neighbourhood reproaching the three nephews because they did not discover the body earlier) and tender (the three hovering close to each other). The film ends with Hou's voice-over as we see a medium shot of the nephews looking at their grandmother's body. He says, 'I remember', and it is as if he were taking over his mother's role, for she was always remembering family histories and refused to let the doctor operate on her because she would not have been able to speak, and that is what she needed to do. Now she is dead, and the role of the person who speaks and remembers and tells the stories must be filled again.

Tied with love and modesty to his recollections and to his lost adolescence, Hou, who comes together as both character and director only at the end of the film, is a sweet murmur of memory. He is the one who is not going to forget, who is going from one village to another to remember his people, the way it was in the lost time of their youth. This voice cries on a chaotic island, in a city of sadness, in a country rocked by the post-economic boom and by forced Westernisation, and from an alien country repudiated by his own native land, seeking success and modernisation with dangerous enthusiasm. Hou murmurs about time lost and time found, using cinema not as an amazing machine but as art; a potential *madeleine* both personal and social. The hiatus between a time to live and a time to die must be filled (or, it is full to the brim) with other times, especially a time for reflection and a time for memory, and this movie represents them softly, with a gaze full of affection. Hou, the character, facing his dead grandmother, does not think, but remembers. In this way, he grows.[22]

NOTES

1. See Bérénice Reynaud, 'Taiwanese Cinema: from the Occupation to Today' ('Cinema di Taiwan: Dall'Occupazione Giapponese a Oggi'), in *The History of World Cinema* (*Storia del Cinema Mondiale*), vol. 4, ed. Gian Piero Brunetta (Turin: Einaudi, 2001), 857–877; Peggy Chiao (Jiao Xiongping), *New Taiwan Cinema* (Taiwan Xin Dianying) (Taipei: Shibao Wenhua Chuban Qiye Youxian Gongsi, 1988); Marco Müller, ed., *Taiwan: New Electric Shadows* (Taiwan: nuove ombre elettriche) (Venice: Marsilio, 1985); Yingjin Zhang and Zhiwei Xiao, *Encyclopaedia of Chinese Film* (New York: Routledge, 1998).

2. See Robert Hegel, ed., *Expression of Self in Chinese Literature* (New York: Columbia University Press, 1985); Wendy Larson, ed., *Literary Authority and the Modern Chinese Writer; Ambivalence and Autobiography* (Durham: Duke University Press, 1991).

3. William H. Nienhauser cites the Confucian scholar Liu Chih-chi in *The Indiana Companion to Traditional Chinese Literature* (Bloomington: Indiana University Press, 1986), 842.

4. 'Descendant of the ancestor Kao-Yang,/ Po-yung was my honoured father's name./When the constellation She-t'i pointed the first month,/on the day *keng-yin* I was born.' In Burton Watson, trans. and ed., *The Columbia Book of Chinese Poetry* (New York: Columbia University Press, 1984), 54.

5. The Grand Historian [the author's father] grasped

my hand and said, weeping, 'Our ancestors were Grand Historians for the house of Zhou … will this tradition end with me? If you in turn become Grand Historian, you must continue the work of our ancestors. … Now, filial piety begins with the serving of our parents; next, you must serve your sovereign; and, finally, you must make something of yourself, that your name may go down through the ages to the glory of your father and mother.

In Theodore de Bary and Irene Bloom, *Sources of Chinese Tradition*, vol. 1 (New York: Columbia University Press, 1999), 370.

6. See Stephen Owen, *Remembrances: The Experience of the Past in Classical Chinese Literature* (London: Harvard University Press, 1986), 136–137.

7. C. T. Hsia, *The Classical Chinese Novel* (New York: Columbia University Press, 1968), 312.

8. Hou says: 'I have always been searching for a particular Chinese style and method of expressing feeling. The Chinese people have always gone about a tortuous and roundabout route in expressing emotions.' Peggy Chiao, 'History's Subtle Shadows', *Cinemaya*, no. 21, (1993): 8.

9. Ni Zhen, 'Classical Chinese Painting and Cinematographic Signification', in *Cinematic Landscapes: Observations on the Visual Arts and Cinema of China and Japan*, ed. Linda C. Ehrlich and David Desser (Austin: University of Texas Press, 1994), 75.

10. Wilt Idema and Lloyd Haft, *A Guide to Chinese Literature* (Ann Arbor: Centre for Chinese Studies, University of Michigan, 1997), 58–59, 161–162.

11. Ibid., 188.

12. Lu Xun, *A Brief History of Chinese Fiction* (Beijing: Foreign Languages Press, 1976), 80–81.

13. Lu Xun cites the *Han Dynasty History*: 'Xiaoshuo were the talk on the streets … All the talk of the streets and highways was recorded.' And then, citing the scholar Chi Yun: '… the *xiaoshuo* writers were successors of the Zhou dynasty officers who collected information … the task of these officers was to help the ruler to understand country ways and morals.' Lu, *A Brief History*, 4, 6. The word *xiaoshuo* is now used to indicate the novel.

14. In Michel Frodon, ed., *Hou Hsiao Hsien* (Paris: Cahiers du Cinéma, 1999), 73.

15. Shen Congwen, *Recollection of West Hunan*, trans. Gladys Yang (Beijing: Foreign Languages Press, 1982).

16. For discussions on the 'Chineseness' of this style, see (among others) Lin Niantong, 'A Study of the Theories of Chinese Cinema in Their Relationship to Classical Aesthetics', *Modern Chinese Literature*, 1, no. 2 (1985): 185–198; Yeh Yueh-yu, 'Politics and Poetics of Hou Hsiao-hsien's Films', in *Postscript*, 20, no. 2/3 (2001): 61–76. Note also that there are at least two versions of the film in circulation, one of which does not begin with the voice-over.

17. In Stanley Kwan's 1996 documentary, *Yang + Yin: Gender in Chinese Cinema*, Hou says he feels a strong sense of nostalgia for a time when life was lived in a community. Now, he complains, everyone is hidden behind thick walls of concrete. This sensation is transmitted in his movies.

18. Leo Ou-fan Lee, 'Afterword: Reflections on Change and Continuity in Modern Chinese Fiction', in *From May Fourth to June Fourth*, ed. Ellen Widmer and David Der-Wei Wang (Cambridge: Harvard University Press, 1993), 378. The author refers to Lao Shi, Ba Jin, Shen Congwen, Mo Yan and others.

19. See Bai Xianyong, 'Winter Nights', in Joseph Lau, ed., *Chinese Stories from Taiwan: 1960–1970* (New York: Columbia University Press, 1976), 337–354.

20. I am aware that the original title conveys a different meaning (*Tongnian Wangshi* means 'the past things of youth'). Still, as in every Taiwanese production, the original title is accompanied by an English title, directly chosen by the director himself.

21. It is possible to make a comparison with the gangs in Tsai Ming-liang's films, especially *Rebels of the Neon God*. These latter are much more nihilistic and desperate; they live in a modern city. If the young Lee Kang-sheng in *The River* is a kind of Oedipus, the strangers in *A Time …* are like his daughter, Medea, forced into exile. As Lee does not blind himself, but sees everything and goes on living, indifferent, here the Medeas, with the natural indifference of time and the seasons, simply get used to the new place. If still some contrasts exist with the generation of Hou's parents, his generation is like a river that creates its new bed, with time and patience, and without tragedy.

22. In *Yang + Yin*, Hou says that he wants to teach his children two values: respect for themselves and the ability to adapt.

A Touch of Zen: Action in Martial Arts Movies

Mary Farquhar

This essay is about action in *A Touch of Zen* (Parts 1 and 2, King Hu, 1971). Action – or combat – is the essence of the film and of the martial arts genre, known in Chinese as *wuxiapian, wudapian* and *gongfupian* (*gongfu/kung-fu* movies are the southern sub-genre). *A Touch of Zen* is acknowledged as a pioneering martial arts film in the northern swordplay subgenre, containing some of the best-known action sequences in the Chinese cinema.

Released after three years of production, *A Touch of Zen* won prizes in Taiwan and at Cannes in 1975. *A Touch of Zen* is part of a body of work by King Hu in the 1960s and early 1970s that reshaped martial arts action into a mainstay of the Hong Kong and Taiwanese film industries, influencing subsequent action film-makers such as Tsui Hark, John Woo, Jackie Chan, Ang Lee and, now, Zhang Yimou.

In much writing on martial arts film, action is treated in isolation as a purely formal delight. Here, *A Touch of Zen*'s action is analysed as narrative, as spectacle and as morality play under the rubric of a cinema of spectacle-attractions. The approach extends the Western framework to non-Western cinemas, building on my earlier work on Chinese cinematic modes.[1] Overt theatricality is a feature of early cinematic spectacle in the West. In the earliest Chinese cinema, this spectacle is operatic, recasting martial arts movies as contemporary 'shadow opera' and a mode of Chinese film-making developed out of indigenous literary tradition and in operatic performance. King Hu's films best illustrate this point. They are feature films. But their theatricality was so obvious that a contemporary reviewer described them as a 'cinematisation of Beijing opera' (*pingjude dianyinghua*).[2] Another wrote that both story and form emerged from 'the womb' of opera.[3] Stephen Teo later called King Hu's films 'cinema opera' (*xiqu fengwei dianying*).[4]

The concept of cinema opera is a starting point for analysing action in *A Touch of Zen*. Action cannot be considered in isolation. Its meaning is related to its location in the text on two levels. First, action is integrated into narrative, not isolated from it. This is generally the case in the martial arts genre. Second, action is not purely abstract, but culturally overcoded. The essay outlines an interrelated aesthetic *and* ethic of action in *A Touch of Zen* that propelled King Hu's work in 'the martial arts genre into the ninth heaven of cinema abstraction'.[5]

ACTION AS PART OF NARRATIVE

While combat is the core attraction of the martial arts genre, the plot usually triggers action sequences. Otherwise, action would be pure display. Furthermore, action does not suspend so-called realist storytelling. Even the most extraordinary martial arts combat scenes contain drama as counterpoint and continuation of the story-line. Hence action is enmeshed in the narrative as both spectacle and storytelling device.

Nevertheless, everyone knows that martial arts movies are about action as novel display in its own right. Hence twentieth-century martial arts movies – whether swordplay such as *A Touch of Zen* or *gongfu* – provide spectacular action as the novel attraction. Novelty ranges across the surreal in the 'ghost-and-demon' film *fantastique* of the early twentieth century; the highly physical in the *gongfu* subgenre from the 1970s; and the dream-like ballet atop the bamboo in Ang Lee's *Crouching Tiger, Hidden Dragon* at the turn of a new century. The dance, the physicality and the *fantastique* are all present in diverse action sequences of *A Touch of Zen*.

The story provides this action with its moral framework. It is adapted from a famous Qing dynasty short-story collection. Yang Huizhen is the warrior-daughter of an upright Ming dynasty minister, who is executed when he offends the Chief Eunuch. Her father's powerful enemies – the Chief Eunuch's palace guard – now hunt her and her father's friends in forbidding landscapes on the edge of empire. There are three cumulative movements to the narrative: the personal, the political and the spiritual.[6] The personal is a romance between Yang and the scholar, Gu Shengzhai. The film's first combat scene ends this movement. The second movement is the political combat between Yang's group and her enemies. It contains the bamboo-forest fight sequence, one of the most famous in the genre. The third movement shifts to the spiritual, ending with a cosmic combat involving this world and beyond. The fight sequences are therefore vital narrative elements in the story's suspense, building towards an extraordinary climax in which a mysterious monk with supernatural martial powers hovers between humanity and Buddhahood – between life and death, earth and sky, real and surreal, matter and void, victory and defeat. The monk gives the film its English title, *A Touch of Zen*. Its Chinese title, *Xianü* or *Lady Knight Errant*, focuses on the warrior heroine rather than on the magical monk who comes to her aid.

Narrative therefore supports action in the martial arts genre. Christian Metz has argued that the merger of cinema and narrativity is 'a great fact, which was by no means predestined'.[7] It follows that the Chinese merger may diverge from Western models. We have already demonstrated that, unlike the West, complex narrative and visual display were concurrent elements in China's earliest films and the merger continues in such contemporary films as *Farewell My Concubine* (Chen Kaige, 1993). King Hu developed the narrative format of martial arts movies, minimising plot to focus pleasure on combat spectaculars.[8] So action or at least the expectation of action dominates the form.

The pleasure of action may be postponed to heighten the effect. The first combat scene in *A Touch of Zen* comes almost an hour into the film. Before this, there is growing tension as Scholar Gu meets strangers in the village, including the beautiful Yang Huizhen with whom he falls in love. But who are these strangers? Like Hitchcock, King Hu builds suspense through point-of-view shots, off-screen looks and restricted knowledge, primarily attached to Scholar Gu. Yang Huizhen refuses his marriage proposal but invites Scholar Gu to her house one night.

Part of the novelty is the film's delicious shift away from Confucian domestic propriety and female subordination to warrior virtues and gender equality. It begins as Gu arrives to find Yang Huizhen playing a lute under the moon, singing a poem by Li Bai as he moves towards her. She is caught in his gaze but the audience knows that she has contrived his gaze and the moonlit setting. Her song ends:

> The moon sways with my song,
> My shadow moves with the dance,
> After we've drunk, we part
> But we cherish our feeling
> Until we meet – if ever we meet – again.

She now looks back at him, he smiles and she beckons him inside. Images and sounds of nature suggest love-making and birdsong suggests dawn. Then, to the sound of cymbals, the door is pushed open by unknown hands. Yang awakes and tickles the sleeping Gu with a strand of grass. Commander Ouyang Nian, a spy for the evil palace guard, then enters the room and orders Yang home. The fight begins suddenly. Gu sees his lover change from feline softness to deadly swordswoman, from *wen* arts (poetry, wine, lute and love) to combat (*wu*), from graceful singer to acrobatic swordfighter, and from bedroom seductress to family avenger, fighting through grasses, trees, forest, rocks, battlements and turrets. Ma Guoguang describes the film as 'blood draining into poetry'.[9] David Bordwell analyses Hu's action technique in this and other scenes as 'the aesthetic of the glimpse'.[10] In part, the glimpse aligns with Gu who runs outside to follow the fight, falls, and looks up at the sun in a shot reminiscent of Kurosawa's famous sun-shot in *Rashomon*. He faints. The action ends. The film then cuts to the second movement. Scholar Gu is summoned to the magistrate's to learn of the Yang family's outlaw status. The first combat scene and its surrounding narrative therefore resolve the mystery about the strangers who come to town. The battle is no longer secretive; Yang Huizhen and Generals Lu and Shi are no longer in hiding; and Scholar Gu is now drawn into the political intrigue, the moral dilemma and therefore the physical combat. In the second movement, Gu's point-of-view remains the storytelling thread that binds the private to the now public domain.

The first hour of *A Touch of Zen* shows the extent to which action is empowered by a classical narrative format. The audience is not directly addressed as in early cinema but absorbed into the story as in so-called 'realist' cinema. Martial arts movies therefore mix cinematic modes – the aesthetic of attractions and the classical – to great effect. In the literature on a cinema of attractions, scholars note that the star system, music and techniques such as extreme close-ups in contemporary Western cinema are all continuations of early film spectacle. These elements support both the action-attraction and the storytelling in *A Touch of Zen*. For example, extreme close-ups of Scholar Gu and Ouyang Nian, as they look off-screen, suggest that there is a dark reality beneath the ordinary small-town façade that fills the film's first movement. This façade is peeled back at the first movement's end and in the subsequent narrative. Action provides the first climax. It rips apart the illusion of everyday life to reveal realities behind realities until the final combat ends in a landscape reduced to colour and form. The film's *finale* suggests a central tenet of Buddhist philosophy: the illusion (*maya*) that is the phenomenal world. Thus, the martial arts genre in King Hu's hands operates in merged mode. It is a narrative cinema that foregrounds action-attraction, pushing visual symbolism and bodily action to the limits of credibility. Here, action starts slowly. In other works, martial arts combat explodes on the screen much earlier. Either way, the audience expects it.

AESTHETICS: THE *YIN-YANG* OF ACTION (AND INACTION)

There is therefore an aesthetic of action at work in *A Touch of Zen*. King Hu choreographed combat. His innovation was to conceptualise martial arts action as operatic dance. The dance is a rhythmic interplay around the two poles of *qi* or cosmic energy: a dance of *yang* (movement) and *yin* (stillness).

While martial arts movies are classed as a genre of 'action movies' (*dongzuopian*) in which 'fast, rhythmic action constitutes the film's main interest',[11] the term *dongzuo* does not capture the aesthetic complexity of the dance. Luo Bu writes of the genre:

Yes, film is a 'moving' (*dong*) art but the word *dong* should not be narrowed to actual 'movement' or 'action' in *dongzuo*; it should involve such alternative meanings as the *dong* in *liudong* (to float), *yuedong* (to leap) and *sheng-dong* (vibrant, alive). Fierce movements (*dongzuo*) are of

course *dong* but a vital rhythm and dance of *qi* (*qiyun*), a coming alive of characters, and the narrative flow are also *dong*.[12]

One term for martial arts movies, *wudapian*, captures this variety in that *wuda* refers to acrobatic fighting in dance/opera/film. Simply stated, *wuda* is rhythmic fighting akin to dance. King Hu is quite explicit on this point. He said that his combat moves do not come from *gongfu* or martial arts techniques (*wushu*); they come from Beijing opera, which he constantly watched as a young boy in Beijing. He said, 'In fact, all the action scenes come from fighting in Beijing opera, that is, they are a kind of dance.'[13]

Action choreography is now considered crucial to the genre. Since King Hu, this is the province of the martial arts choreographer. Indeed, King Hu credited the success of his ground-breaking martial arts style to his own director/choreographer, Han Yingjie. Hu said:

That [the martial arts in my films are so new] has a direct link with my martial arts director Han Yingjie. The term 'martial arts director' (*wushu zhedao*) actually started with me using Han Yingjie. It has a lot to do with his ideas. During the making of *Come Drink with Me* it was quite difficult for me to handle the action. I had no problems with handling the story because I had read many martial arts stories. I have never had any training in the martial arts and I don't know how to fight, so I called in Han Yingjie, a Beijing opera actor, to help me out. I studied his martial arts moves and selected the best.[14]

How does this work? What is meant by action as dance? How does film technology transform the action into a *yin-yang* rhythm, the music of *qi*? Han Yingjie has partly explained this in relation to the famous bamboo fight scene midway through *A Touch of Zen*. Yang Huizhen, her two generals and Scholar Gu ambush Ouyang Nian and two others on Green Bamboo Mountain to prevent them reporting to the fearsome Commander Men Da, newly arrived at the frontier. Han Yingjie attributes the stunning effects of such combat scenes first to performance – specifically, to revitalised martial arts styles, well-researched costumes and realistic acting – and second to film editing (*jianjie*).[15]

According to Han Yingjie, action movements were designed according to King Hu's requirements. Most shots were improvised on the set but climactic action was storyboarded beforehand. One such climax is the bamboo-forest fight scene.[16] The most spectacular move in this sequence (and perhaps in the Chinese movies) is Yang's free-fall from the top of the bamboo to pierce one of the two bodyguards below. This move is a highly physical merger of warrior and sword and it ends the battle, apart from a short coda when General Shi kills the second bodyguard. The acting is realistic in a comparative sense. The bare operatic stage is replaced by real film locations (such as the bamboo forest) and symbolic operatic gestures are replaced by realistic action (such as the enemy meeting in the forest on horseback). The superhuman action – leaps, somersaults and flying – are achieved with wires, trampolines and stunt[wo]men in the film whereas they are suggested by acrobatic movements in opera. The on-screen performance gains further credibility through meticulously researched historical background and period costumes. In the bamboo forest sequence, the red enemy costumes are glimpsed through the mist in the first long shot, distinguishing them from the plain costumes of the heroes when the action turns to fast, close combat. The real

bamboo forest, the stylised acting, the operatic percussive beat and the period costumes all enhance the spectacle. Hence the overall effect of the action choreography is towards realism (*xieshi*) and away from operatic symbolism (*xieyi*).

For example, the *fantastique* effect of Yang Huizhen's dive in the bamboo forest scene comes from editing but its visual basis is an actual dive. Han Yingjie said:

> The bamboo forest was located in Taiwan in a place that only had sunshine during noontime. The temperature inside the forest was lower by twelve degrees and the trees were so tall that we couldn't use trampolines or wires. In the end we put the camera in the middle of a lake next to a cliff, and took shots of the stuntmen diving into the lake, then cut back to the forest.[17]

The dive is rendered realistic on-screen through rapid cutting, shot juxtapositions and discontinuous movement so that the stunt dive is broken up and barely discernible within the frame. King Hu calls this the aesthetic of 'crookedness' (*quzhe*), 'a twisting and turning that cannot be grasped in a single glance'.[18] But the action also relies on frozen

A Touch of Zen: Yang Huizhen, the lady knight errant.

moments for miraculous effect. For example, Yang's frenetic dive is interspersed with still shots of sunlight and bamboo and extended close-ups of the astonished onlookers, including the enemy just before he is pierced from above. Thus, action choreography is a rhythmic flow between movement (*yang*) and stillness (*yin*), without resorting to obvious trickery and special effects. This is *qi* in Chinese aesthetics, an invisible force that animates voids and phenomena so that the still frames become active intervals in action choreography. Movement emerges out of stillness. Indeed, this scene begins with a slow long shot of shadowy enemy shapes in the bamboo forest and ends with the two exhausted victors, Yang Huizhen at rest and General Shi sheathing his sword. Ouyang Nian escapes. The enemy's martial prowess increases in the second and third movements, moving from Ouyang Nian to Commander Men Da and finally to the Commander-in-Chief, Xu Xianchun, played by Han Yingjie.

Han's pioneering action choreography is now a staple of the genre. Jet Li said that he only signs a film contract once he knows the choreographer's name.[19] Similarly, the action in *Crouching Tiger, Hidden Dragon* (Ang Lee, 2000) is the work of Yuen Wo Ping, who helped establish heroes such as Jackie Chan and Jet Li. Ang Lee said, 'in Yuen's choreography, the martial art becomes a performing art'.[20] Elsewhere, he likens the combat to dance or ballet. Zhang Yimou's foray into martial arts film, *Hero,* also features an established Hong Kong choreographer. The film's breathtaking Mongolian fight is again likened to ballet, not to battle.[21] This is the legacy of King Hu and his action director, Han Yingjie.

ACTION ETHICS: THE COMBAT BETWEEN GOOD AND EVIL

The opening shots of *A Touch of Zen* are justly famous. They are a metaphor for evil that ensnares the world. Nine shots of spiders weaving webs at night to trap victims fill the frame in the first sequence. Panoramic shots of misty mountains at dawn follow, almost inviting the viewer into a tranquil Chinese landscape painting. But evil stalks this vista. Like the spider, it exists, it hunts, and it is a force of nature. Evil requires action, which is understood in relation to non-action (*wuwei*) in Chinese philosophy. Action is variously validated in the film's three worlds: the hierarchical Confucian society of

the border town, the brotherhood of the martial arts world (*jianghu*), and finally the Buddhist world of transcendence. We look at each in turn. The common denominator is that evildoers precipitate the violence. Heroes re-act.

The action poetry of *A Touch of Zen* unravels a moral universe that seeks to restore order in disorder through the heroic *wuxia* or lady knight-errant. *Wuxiapian* or martial arts film translates as 'knight-errant movies' so the principle of heroic action against overwhelming evil is fundamental to King Hu's films, which clearly distinguish good and evil. Indeed, good (*Dao* or The Way) and evil (*Mo* or monsters) are in mortal, political and eventually cosmic combat. Confucian rites (*li*), such as filial piety, female submission, marriage and civil service examinations, dominate the first movement until dispatched with wondrous irony in the first fight. Such rites were considered essential to Confucian civilisation, which relies on hierarchies of patriarchal virtue descending from Heaven through the Emperor to clan and family. The social hierarchy is doubly subverted in the film. First, the good Minister Yang is tortured and killed by the evil eunuchs who block his memorandum to the Emperor/Father. Thus imperial order is perverted, not rejected. Second, the father of the Yang family is dead and his lineage threatened in the hunt for his daughter. Yang Huizhen's fight is legitimised by a Confucian system that demands vengeance for the father and declares lack of sons the ultimate unfilial act. She not only fights. She also bears Gu a son and literally leaves him holding the baby in the final act while she retires to a monastery. Hence her martial persona is an extension of the Confucian moral order in times of dire peril. Yang Huizhen acts as a filial daughter in the long tradition of women-warriors.

The Yang family remnants become outlaws with warrants issued for their capture and execution. They escape to a mythic Chinese underworld called *jianghu* (literally 'rivers and lakes') on the frontier, leaving the dangerous spider spaces of city, town and village. Ng Ho has reconstructed *jianghu* as both a real criminal underworld and a mythic realm in Chinese fiction. He writes:

Jianghu was an anarchic, reckless world with no appreciable demarcations between good and evil. It was a martial (*wu*) world unsupported by valour (*xia*). Chivalrous heroes [*wuxia*] were merely icons conjured by man's desire for an ethical order, answering their need for moral arbitrators in this undisciplined realm. For this reason, chivalrous figures only appear in fiction [and film], seldom in history.[22]

The fictional *jianghu* is not a self-sufficient world. It operates as the mirror image of Confucian society and its virtues are also the opposite of the Confucian order. Warriors *(wu)* displace literati *(wen)* at the top of the hierarchy. Gu Shengzhai personifies this displacement, moving from scholar to military strategist and from law-abiding citizen to outlaw in the second movement.

A Touch of Zen constructs its own version of this world. Yang Huizhen – the chivalrous *xianü* – epitomises military prowess, although her chivalry is discriminating. At one point, she hesitates as an enemy begs for mercy. Gu intervenes, repeating the Confucian dictum that female benevolence always causes trouble. So she plunges the sword into the enemy's belly in full close-up. In *jianghu*, inaction against an enemy is death; chivalry is reserved for the 'brotherhood' of heroes, the righteous and the oppressed. The sword is more than a means of survival. Its supreme mastery by the heroine symbolises a deep desire for moral order that can only come about by the violent overthrow of evil. Hence, combat is more than necessary. It is the central poetry of the martial arts world.

The violence legitimised in these two worlds is rejected in the third world of Buddhist transcendence. This third world shifts *A Touch of Zen* into the 'ghost and Zen' subgenre (*guichanpian, chan* being the Chinese term for Zen), which showed King Hu's art at its peak. Huang Ren claims that:

These films [of King Hu] transcend the forms of this world, entering a space where ghostly and human compassion and revenge meet, and where personal grievances are usually abandoned through enlightenment. An example is [the glimpse of] nirvana in *A Touch of Zen*, an elevated conceptualisation of the martial arts film.[23]

The central motif in this third world is compassion (*en*) rather than revenge. *A Touch of Zen* ends with a meditation on action itself in which compassion is concentrated in the Zen master, Hui Yuan, and his acolyte monks. Hui Yuan appears twice in the second movement as the incarnation of stillness and non-violence, despite his (almost) invincible martial powers. This stillness dominates the film's third movement when Hui Yuan confronts the epitome of evil, the weaver of webs, the great exponent of martial arts – Commander-in-Chief Xu Xianchun.

The combat between Hui Yuan and Xu is the clash of good and evil, compassion and revenge, set up in the preceding narrative. The sequence is imbued with mystic symbolism, unearthly power and visual beauty. The third movement reaches its final crescendo as Gu seeks Yang, finds the baby but is then betrayed to Commander-in-Chief Xu. Hui Yuan sends Yang and General Shi to save him but the combat proves Xu to be more powerful. So the monks intervene, defeating Xu but letting him live after unsuccessfully trying to dissuade him from a life of evil. They leave. Ma Guoguang claims that this Xu-Hui Yuan sequence alone is worth the price of the ticket.[24] But Xu is not finished. He waylays Hui Yuan, begs for mercy and then stabs him. This leads to the extraordinary finale as Xu looks up, hallucinates, shakes his head and sees the monk against a cosmic skyscape washed in light. Hui Yuan turns, pulls out the dagger and bleeds gold to the chant of a full male choir. The sky dissolves into greens and reds. Xu leaps, falls to his death, followed by alternating shots of his corpse on the ground and encircling birds of prey in the sky.

The closing minute of this sequence is shot-reverse shots of the three main characters looking at a transfigured Hui Yuan *always* still and *always* at the centre of a panoramic frame.

Medium close-up	A wounded Yang looks up from the desert
Extreme long shot (1)	Hui Yuan is a vague shape suffused with light and centred high in the frame between a shadowy crest of rock and a golden sky
Close-up	Shi falls, looking up in amazement
Extreme long shot	As in (1) but shadowy robes flutter
Long shot	Gu, holding the baby, falls to his knees as he looks up
Extreme long shot	As in (1)

Close-up	Yang rises
Extreme long shot	As in (1) but now a shadowy arm rises, and a sleeve flutters
Close-up	Yang continues to look up
Extreme long shot	As in (1)
Close-up	Yang looks up
Extreme long shot	A silhouette of Hui Yuan's monastery is shown on a dark mountainside against a golden sky
Extreme long shot	The frame then serially dissolves into its negative of red and white, into a silhouette of Hui Yuan (with halo), bathed in light, and into a core of light that irradiates the frame. Then the shadowy figure stands and finally becomes a clear silhouette of Hui Yuan as Buddha with a golden halo. THE END

The final shots alternate between images of the real and of the surreal, between Buddhist redemption and earthly suffering. The soundtrack is now a full female choir. Throughout, Hui Yuan calls the monastic life *kongmen*, the gate to the void. But the image of the void is not empty; it is light, infinite space and changing colour with Hui Yuan – a Buddha – at its centre. It is as if the film-maker is standing in the gateway and showing us two worlds as alternative human options that relate directly to the characters' actions: earthly suffering and the sky of nirvana. Violent action kills enemies so *jianghu* heroes can survive for the next combat. Non-violence cherishes life, kills no-one and defeats death itself through karmic transfiguration beyond 'the endless sea of suffering', to use Hui Yuan's own words. Thus, non-action as the choice *not* to kill defeats martial arts action, the art of killing.

The changed ethic is matched by a changed aesthetic that forgoes King Hu's earlier 'twisting and turning' aesthetic of 'crookedness'. Stillness overcomes movement and is presented visually in two ways at the end of the film. Repeated glimpses of Hui Yuan against the sky show a centred, serene, 'enlightened' core of being high in the frame. Hui Yuan's centrality is reinforced by the onlookers' gaze upward and always

at him from different vantage points on the ground. He is encircled by looks of enlightenment, the opposite of earthly desire. King Hu's feat was to visually incorporate this abstract complexity and transcendent world into *A Touch of Zen*.

This discussion on action in *A Touch of Zen* has led us to King Hu's own meditation on (non)action in the martial arts genre.

NOTES

1. Mary Farquhar and Chris Berry, 'Shadow Opera: Towards a New Archaeology of the Chinese Cinema', *Postscript*, 20, nos 1, 2 and 3 (2001): 25–42.
2. Liu Chenghan, 'Auteur Theory and King Hu' ('Zuozhelun he Hu Jinquan'), 1975, cited without full publishing details in Fu Shizhuan, 'Visual and Auditory elements in King Hu's Martial Arts World' ('Hu Jinquan wuxia shijielide sheting yuansu'), in *The World of King Hu* (*Hu Jinquan de shijie*), ed. Huang Ren (Taipei: Taipeishi Zhongguo dianyingziliao yanjiuhui, 1999), 235.
3. Luo Bu, 'Hu Jinquan', in Luo Bu, Wu Hao and Zhuo Baitang, *Genre Theory in Hong Kong Cinema* (*Xianggang dianying leixinglun*) (Hong Kong: Oxford University Press, 1997), 41.
4. Stephen Teo, 'Only the Valiant: King Hu and His Cinema Opera', in *Transcending the Times: King Hu and Eileen Chang*, ed. Provisional Urban Council (Hong Kong: Provisional Urban Council, 1998), 19–24.
5. Teo, 'Only the Valiant', 24.
6. Tony Rayns, 'King Hu: Shall We Dance', in *A Study of the Hong Kong Martial Arts Film*, ed. Provisional Urban Council (Hong Kong: Urban Council, 1980), 103.
7. Christian Metz, *Film Language: A Semiotics of the Cinema*, trans. Michael Taylor (New York: Oxford University Press, 1967), 93.
8. Stephen Teo, 'Love and Swords: The Dialectics of the Martial Arts Romance, A Review of *Crouching Tiger, Hidden Dragon*', *Senses of Cinema*, no. 11, (2000): www.sensesofcinema.com/contents/00/11/crouching.html (9 January 2001).
9. Ma Guoguang, '*A Touch of Zen*: Blood Draining into Poetry', in Provisional Urban Council, *Transcending the Times*, 65–67.
10. David Bordwell, 'Richness through Imperfection: King Hu and the Glimpse', in Provisional Urban Council, *Transcending the Times*, 33–34.

11. Wang Jie'an, chief ed., *Film Dictionary* (*Dianying Cidian*) (Taibei: Dianying Ziliaoguan, 1999), 11.

12. Luo Bu, 'The Beginnings of Mandarin Martial Arts Film' ('Wuxia guoyupiande qianlu'), in Luo et al., *Genre Theory*, 21.

13. Huang Ren, 'A Path of Creative Variety' ('Duocai duozide chuangzuo zhi lu'), in Huang, *The World of King Hu*, 115.

14. Hirokazu Yamada and Koyo Udagawa, 'King Hu's Last Interview', in Provisional Urban Council, *Transcending the Times*, 75.

15. Han Yingjie, 'Remembering King Hu', in Provisional Urban Council, *Transcending the Times*, 83.

16. See a shot-by-shot analysis in Cheuk Pak Tong, 'A Pioneer in Film Language: On King Hu's Style of Editing', in Provisional Urban Council, *Transcending the Times*, 60–61. Also see Chris Berry and Mary Farquhar, *Cinema and Nation: China on Screen* (New York: Cambridge University Press, forthcoming).

17. Han, 'Remembering King Hu', 83.

18. Hu Jinquan cited in Fu Shizhuan, 'Visual and Auditory Elements', 245–246.

19. Stephen Short and Susan Jakes, 'Violence Doesn't Solve Anything, *Time* talks exclusively to martial-arts master Jet Li', *Timeasia.com*, 2001: www.time.com/time/asia/features/hero/int_jet_li.html (18 January 2002).

20. Ang Lee, 'Working with Fight Choreographer Yuen Wo Ping', in *Crouching Tiger, Hidden Dragon*, ed. Linda Sunshine (New York: New Market Press, 2000), 95.

21. Stephen Short and Susan Jakes, 'Making of a Hero', *Timeasia.com*, 2002: www.time.com/time/asia/features/hero/story2.html (18 January 2002).

22. Ng Ho, 'Jianghu Revisited: Towards a Reconstruction of the Martial Arts World', in *A Study of the Hong Kong Swordplay Film* (1945–1980), ed. Provisional Urban Council (Hong Kong: Urban Council, 1981), 84.

23. Huang, 'A Path of Creative Variety', 118.

24. Ma Guoguang, '*A Touch of Zen*', 67.

22 *Vive L'Amour*: Eloquent Emptiness

Fran Martin

Vive L'Amour (Tsai Ming-liang, 1994), winner of the Golden Lion at the 1994 Venice International Film Festival, is the second part in a three-part film-cycle by Tsai Ming-liang, the Malaysian-born art-house director working from Taiwan. Following *Rebels of the Neon God* (Tsai Ming-liang, 1992) and preceding *The River* (Tsai Ming-liang, 1996), *Amour* contributes to Tsai's ongoing filmic exploration of the conditions of human subsistence in millennial Taipei.[1] His films' settings amid the city's dismal concrete and neon streetscapes, their minimalist stories of the aimless days and nights of drifting, marginal characters and their austere cinematic style have earned Tsai his name as filmic philosopher of existential anxiety in post-'economic miracle' Taiwan.[2]

Tsai's films have been discussed by critics within Taiwan and internationally mainly in relation to their distinctive cinematic style and their thematic explorations of post-modern alienation.[3] But within Taiwan's local lesbian and gay (*tongzhi*) communities Tsai's film-cycle is frequently analysed in relation to its representations of homosexuality, a topic less often foregrounded in existing English-language scholarship.[4] Taiwan's *tongzhi* movement, encompassing activist and social groups as well as *tongzhi*-directed cultural production and consumption (including film-making, film-going and film criticism), emerged during the 1990s as part of the series of popular movements proliferating in the wake of the Kuomintang government's lifting of martial law in 1987.[5] In what follows, I assume the context of *Vive L'Amour*'s production in 1990s Taiwan, in the same cultural moment that saw the emergence of the *tongzhi* movement. Bearing in mind Tsai's films' popularity with *tongzhi* audiences, I consider how *Vive L'Amour* indexes current transformations in constructions of sexuality and family. My approach to Tsai's film thus differs from much existing work less in its methodology than in its thematic focus and its

emphasis on the film's social context. Rather than reading the film as an expression of a generalised, global post-modern malaise, on the one hand, or of nostalgia for a mythic, lost 'Chinese family', on the other, I will suggest that *Amour* indexes a particular moment in the transformation of available discourses on sexuality in 1990s Taiwan. I will analyse the film's representation of *tongxinglian* (homosexuality) through its organisation of space and through the characterisation of Xiao Kang (Lee Kang-sheng), the central character who has appeared in a lead role in all of Tsai's films to date.

With its principal cast carried over from *Rebels* (Lee Kang-sheng as Xiao Kang, and Chen Zhao-rong, who played A'Ze in *Rebels*, as A'Rong), *Amour*'s plot concerns the ephemerally intertwined lives of three characters, A'Rong, Mei-mei and Xiao Kang, as they cross paths in a vacant luxury apartment awaiting sale. Mei-mei (Yang Kuei-mei) is an estate agent who spends her days driving between apartment and empty apartment, making calls on her mobile phone in the hope that someone will turn up to view the properties. Taking a break for a cigarette and a drink in a crowded coffee shop in the Hsi-menting entertainment district, she encounters A'Rong, an itinerant salesman who peddles women's clothing illegally on the street outside a department store. After a protracted exchange of glances, A'Rong follows Mei-mei from the coffee shop to a vacant luxury apartment Mei-mei handles, and the two have sex. Unbeknownst to either one, a spare key to the same apartment has been swiped by the third character, Xiao Kang, who makes his living pre-selling funerary niches in a crematorium. At a measured pace, the film explores each character's relationship with the others as they return to the apartment at various times and for various purposes over the days that follow. Mei-mei goes to the apartment in order to show the property to potential buyers (and also to eat her lunch from polystyrene *biandang* lunchboxes, and to take an occasional nap). A'Rong goes there to have sex with Mei-mei (also to masturbate with a porn magazine, sleep, take a bath in the jacuzzi and eat hotpot with Xiao Kang). Xiao Kang goes there initially to attempt suicide (and, later, to stage a one-man bowling game with a watermelon, model a little black dress, feather boa and heels from A'Rong's merchandise bag, and hide under the bed where A'Rong and Mei-mei have sex, then emerge to kiss the sleeping A'Rong's face).

As the Taiwanese critic Jiang Xun notes, each of the character's occupations represents an aspect of the underside of Taiwan's 'economic miracle'. Mei-mei is a middle-person in the property boom, but cannot legitimately share in the luxury lifestyles she sells – her working-class accent makes a stark contrast with her expensive-looking outfits, and her own apartment is decrepit by comparison with the five-star properties she handles.[6] A'Rong possesses heightened mobility in two opposite senses: he earns enough for regular trips to Hong Kong to buy merchandise; yet at the same time, selling his wares in the informal street economy, he is forced into an uneasy state of perpetual motion by regular police raids on the floating market that hovers at the doorstep of the high-end department store. Xiao Kang, meanwhile, letterboxes ads for the tiny funerary niches that are often the only viable option on a small island where skyrocketing land values have put a grave site in a traditional cemetery outside most people's reach.

Along with Taiwan's rapid industrialisation and urbanisation, the structure and practice of the family (or *jia*, a term meaning both 'family' and 'home') has also transformed over the past three to four decades. Post-1960s generations have abandoned the villages for the big cities of Taipei and Kaohsiung, and the agricultural basis of village economies has been rapidly eroded with the expansion of first the manufacturing and more recently the service sectors. As many commentators have observed, Tsai's film-cycle foregrounds the resultant crisis and reconfiguration of the *jia* in turn-of-the-century Taiwan.[7] While *Rebels* and *River* both deal directly with *jia* at the level of the story by foregrounding Xiao Kang's relationship with his father (played in both films by Miao Tien), it is in *Amour* that the idea of *jia* and its apparent absence is most arrestingly present at a symbolic

level, in the metaphor of the empty apartment. Taiwanese feminist scholar Chang Hsiao-hung argues convincingly that what we see in *Amour* is not so much a dramatisation of the tragic breakdown of some mythic 'traditional Chinese family', as has been suggested by some, but rather an 'emptying out' of the *jia* itself that compels a fundamental re-thinking of its significance in relation to current transformations in Taiwan's society and culture.[8] In what follows, I will consider how Chang's notion of the emptied-out *jia* can help us think through other, related interpretations of the film's various figurations of 'emptiness'. In particular, I will suggest a possible correlation between the film's representation of 'emptiness' and its figuration of *tongxinglian*.

Like *Rebels, Amour* and *River*, and other Taiwanese films including *The Wedding Banquet* (Ang Lee, 1993), the independent film *The Love of Three Oranges* (Hung Hung, 1998) frames the subject of homosexuality in relation to the *jia*.[9] Also like *Amour*, this quirky first-time feature from Hung Hung examines a complex interplay between three characters: young lesbian lovers Star (also called Pony) and Mimi, and Star's high-school boyfriend who has reappeared after two years away on military service. Near the beginning of the film, Star has a conversation with her ex-boyfriend in which she tells him that she and Mimi plan to have a baby and raise the child together. When he asks how she means to do this, Star implies that she's prepared to have sex with a man in order to get pregnant. Shortly thereafter, she begins to have regular sex with the ex-boyfriend. Mimi grows jealous, and a love triangle is formed that resolves, at the close of the film, with Mimi's marriage to Star's ex-boyfriend/lover.

At one point, the ex-boyfriend secretly reads Mimi's diary. Mimi has written: 'Star's high-school boyfriend showed up. Star says she can't forget him, because she was once pregnant with his child. If what is between [Star and me] cannot produce a real child, then do our kisses count as real?' In this question, the lesbian love between Mimi and Star is constructed by Mimi as 'false' because it does not promise the presumed 'realness' of reproductive heterosexuality. Mimi's question crystallises the tension between homosexual love and the reproductive demands and desires of the *jia* that suffuses and organises the film as a whole. In Ang Lee's *Wedding Banquet*, the reconciliation of the desires of a gay son with the demands of his family that he enable his ageing father to 'hold his grandson' (*bao sunzi*) is achieved by the creation of a situation in which the son becomes able to produce an heir, as it were, *despite* being gay. Indeed, the tension between patrilineal heredity and homosexual desire is a central theme of Tsai's film-cycle as well, and comes to a climax in *River*.[10] All these films suggest that in the context of contemporary Taiwan, where the requirements of the *jia* are socially and psychically entrenched in the lives of individual sons and daughters, the imperative to familial reproduction remains a force to be reckoned with in the elaboration of liveable ways of being for *tongzhi* subjects.

It is for this reason that Mimi asks herself whether lesbian kisses can be considered 'real' if they cannot produce children. In asking this question, Mimi follows the lead of a dominant culture that has tended to construct *tongxinglian* as an unreal, empty, or ghostly counterpart to reproductive heterosexuality. As Naifei Ding observes, in the 1990s literary movement of *tongzhi wenxue* (queer literature), *tongxinglian* was frequently aligned with ghostly or cipher-like non-human (*feiren*) forms. Ding interprets this tropology as demonstrative of the fact that *tongxinglian* transgresses the rules of the 'human' when the human is defined by its relationship of interiority to the heterocentric *jia*.[11] For example, the popular *tongzhi* author Hsu Yoshen begins his first novel, *Man Betrother, Man Betrothed* (*Nanhun Nanjia*), a semi-autobiographical coming of age story, with the following words, figuring the narrator's gay life as a posthumous state: 'The year I turned thirteen, my queue stood on end – you know what I mean: I died. Because that year, I realised I was an incurable homosexual.'[12] Similarly, Chen Xue's lesbian short story, 'Searching for the Lost Wings of the Angel' commences with the protagonist's description of herself and her lover as insubstantial beings suspended between worlds, wingless 'angels': 'We're both angels who have lost our wings. Our eyes are fixed on a height attainable only in flight; our bare feet stand on the searing, obdurate earth, and yet we have lost the direction mankind ought to have.'[13] Qiu Miaojin, author of the now-classic lesbian novel *The Crocodile's Journal* (*Eyu Shouji*) parallels her lesbian protagonist's story with that of an anomalous urban crocodile which lives invisibly among the people of Taipei yet at a distance

from them, due to its inability to disclose its true identity.[14] Meanwhile, the queer Gothic fiction of Lucifer Hung (Hong Ling) is peopled by vampires, werewolves, demons and other such unquiet spirits.[15] Following Foucault, this figuration of *tongxinglian* by *tongzhi* authors through cipher-like, non-human figures can be interpreted as a reverse-discourse: a form of resistance to the dominant discourse that would place *tongxinglian* beyond the bounds of the human due to its perceived threat to the reproductive, heterosexual *jia*.[16] In the light of this conceptual linkage between *tongxinglian* and the cipher, in what follows I want to read *Amour*'s often noted foregrounding of emptiness alongside its representation of *tongxinglian* in the character of Xiao Kang.

Vive l'Amour reveals an obsession with emptiness on several levels. First, at the level of the graphic space of the screen itself, many shots appear empty by virtue of the harsh composition with simple blocks of flat colour dissected by stark lines produced by architectural frames like balustrades, window frames and doorways. This composition is seen in the first shot, a close-up of a key hanging from a lock in a deserted corridor, ultimately grabbed by an out-of-focus Xiao Kang. The shot is dominated by the vertical lines of the walls and doors in the corridor, and the camera remains fixed on these solid architectural forms before and after the blurry human forms enter and exit the frame, giving an impression of the ephemerality of this human movement against the stolid substantiality of the concrete artifice. Similar shots, with flat screen space dissected by harsh framing devices that seem both to circumscribe and render trivial the movements of the characters, proliferate throughout the film.

The film's soundtrack, too, is characterised by an uncomfortable emptiness. There is a brutal refusal of dialogue and extra-diegetic music; we hear instead the inconsequential sounds of everyday life: traffic, other people's half-heard conversations, footsteps, the characters' breathing, the sounds of Mei-mei and A'Rong having sex, construction racket, Buddhist muzak in the crematorium, the ringing of cash registers in convenience stores and supermarkets, dogs barking in the distance, the calls of street vendors, sirens, Mei-mei's mobile phone's ring-tone.

The film's most concrete representation of emptiness is of course its depiction of the three-dimensional architectural spaces of the apartment. This

Vive L'amore: A'Rong and Mei-mei cruise each other.

apartment in which the three characters uneasily cohabit is conspicuously devoid of settlement: it is minimally furnished, but lacks the comforting detritus of everyday life. The bedroom in which Mei-mei and A'Rong first have sex, for example, has a double bed but no bed-linen, and is otherwise unfurnished except for a lone pot plant and a bedside rug. The other apartments Mei-mei handles are just as cavernous and impersonal, if not more so. The second apartment where we see Mei-mei, squatting in the foreground dwarfed by the desolate vacancy of the space, is a huge void made by two units knocked into one. Given the depressingly useless expansiveness of this space, in which surely no-one could imagine actually living, Mei-mei's cheery greeting to prospective buyers rings with a certain irony: 'Come in, come in – the place is pretty big!' It is these most thematically and diegetically central representations of emptiness that occasion Chang's argument on the key significance of the emptied-out *jia*.

All this emptiness contributes to the sense of an existential vacuum that commentators have frequently noted in Tsai's films, a sense that concretises for many in this film's closing scene, in which Mei-mei weeps inconsolably for a full four minutes in the muddy construction-site void of what is to become Da'An Forest Park.[17] And yet, in the light of the film's parallel thematisation of *tongxinglian*, this emptiness may turn out to signify something in excess of the existential ennui so routinely attributed to Tsai's films. When contextualised in relation to the prevalent cultural logic that links *tongxinglian* with notions of emptiness, *Amour*'s parallel thematisation of these two subjects seems quite clearly overdetermined. The metaphorics of emptiness, and the emptied-out *jia* in particular, can be interpreted as encoding an implicit reference to *tongxinglian*, associated as that subject is with cultural anxieties over a *jia* 'emptied out' from within through a failure of heterosexual reproduction. In this sense, the film's paralleling of the homosexual theme with its obsessive focus on graphic, architectural, aural and metaphysical emptiness rehearses the familiar cultural logic that makes *tongxinglian* merely the cipher of heterosexual plenitude. To consider what the film does with this idea, having raised it at a connotative level, necessitates a closer analysis of the film's denotative representation of *tongxinglian*.

Underpinning *Amour*'s subtextual reference to *tongxinglian* through its foregrounding of emptiness and the emptied-out *jia* is its explicit representation of *tongxinglian* through the character of Xiao Kang. As Chris Berry observes:

> We are given plenty of material enabling us to interpret Hsiao Kang [Xiao Kang] as a young man gradually coming to terms with his homosexuality: the attempted suicide is followed by a growing interest in Ah Jung [A'Rong]; a scene in which he tries on some of the women's clothes Ah Jung is selling; and finally, the morning after he has hidden under the bed on which Ah Jung and Mei-Mei are having sex, a scene in which he tentatively kisses the sleeping Ah Jung.[18]

In addition, Xiao Kang's character can be read as conforming to the representational convention that links *tongxinglian* with the realm of the ghost and the cipher. Jiang Xun remarks:

> If Yang Kuei-mei is a salesperson of homes for the living, then Lee Kang-sheng is a salesperson of homes for the dead. An atmosphere of death saturates the ghoulish presence of the Lee Kang-sheng character: he seldom speaks; tries again and again to kill himself; and lives a hermit-like existence in the apartment awaiting sale whose key he has stolen.[19]

Drifting about the city on his scooter peddling funerary niches, with his characteristically expressionless demeanour, Xiao Kang indeed appears rather ghostly. His ghoulish air is particularly intense in the scene in which he wears a somewhat formal and old-fashioned black suit and tie, and sits in a dimly lit café solemnly stapling his name-card to his niche ads that urge potential customers: 'Be together with your ancestors.' This written exhortation, on which the camera lingers, explicitly cites the ideology of the continuing family line while also elliptically intimating the 'death' of this model – since the precondition for getting together with your ancestors in a funerary niche is that all of you are dead. This linkage of familial ideology and death in Xiao Kang's advertising material reinforces the triangulation between *jia*, ghosts and *tongxinglian*, according to the central logic in which *tongxinglian*'s perceived threat to terminate the family line and effectively kill off the *jia* is deflected defensively back onto *tongxinglian* itself,

which is then, in place of the *jia*, made to appear 'dead' and ghostly. This scene, where a spectral and (it will emerge) probably homosexual Xiao Kang quietly prepares his ads for final resting places for dead families represents a key point in the film's interrogation of the homophobic syllogism that opposes 'human', '*jia*' and 'life' to 'non-human,' '*tongxinglian*' and 'death'.

Elaborating on the same theme is the scene in which Xiao Kang watches a group of office workers play a corporate bonding-style game similar to musical chairs. In the game, the odd one out calls out a rhyme answered by all the other players, who are organised into three-person make-believe family units: 'I want to move house (*ban jia*)!' 'Who wants to move house?' '[Mothers/fathers/sons/everyone] move house!' Following this, there is a general upheaval as the 'families' rearrange themselves in a new configuration. Throughout the game Xiao Kang, again wearing the black suit, watches silently from the sidelines, utterly separate and apparently unseen by anyone including one man who has to pass directly by him to enter the office where the game takes place. Xiao Kang's invisibility and insignificance to the players in the 'family game' again aligns his character with the extra-familial ghost or cipher.

Further associating Xiao Kang with the ghostly, Xiao Kang's growing interest in A'Rong in *Amour* parallels Xiao Kang's 'haunting' of the Chen Zhaorong character, A'Ze, in *Rebels*. In that film, Xiao Kang's haunting of A'Ze as the incarnation of the rebellious boy-god Nuozha is foreshadowed and paralleled by the 'haunted' lift in A'Ze's government apartment building. The lift always stops unbidden on the fourth floor (*si* meaning 'four' being a homophone for *si* meaning 'death') because, as the girl A'Gui remarks just before A'Ze and Xiao Kang cross paths and Xiao Kang begins obsessively to shadow the other boy, 'There's a ghost on the fourth floor, isn't there?' The fourth-floor ghost in A'Ze's building is soon joined by the spirit of Nuozha in Xiao Kang, who haunts A'Ze throughout the days that follow. In *Amour*, Xiao Kang again haunts the Chen Zhaorong character, A'Rong.

But while Xiao Kang exemplifies the ambivalent metaphor linking *tongxinglian* with the ghost and the cipher, the kiss scene between him and A'Rong reworks the film's paralleling of *tongxinglian* with emptiness in a new way, and to different effect. This scene, in which Xiao Kang emerges from under the bed where A'Rong and Meimei have had sex, to lie down with A'Rong then kiss him, represents a key turning point for the film both formally and thematically. After Xiao Kang appears from under the bed where A'Rong sleeps following Mei-mei's departure, the camera follows Xiao Kang as he creeps around the bed and enters the dark alcove that leads to the door. But after hesitating a while, Xiao Kang – once again, with a certain spectral air – soundlessly re-emerges from the darkness of the alcove into the light of the room and stands immobile for several moments, still framed by the dark rectangle of the door alcove, gazing at the slumbering A'Rong. Finally, he walks out of this dark frame towards the bed. The next shot is a high-angle mid-shot of the two men lying on the bed, with Xiao Kang, like some shy novice vampire, gathering his courage and drawing slowly towards A'Rong's inert form, lips parted. Interestingly, during Xiao Kang's lengthy approach, a series of (perhaps incidental) children's shouts is faintly audible in the background, as though somewhere in another part of the building a child were perhaps waking and getting ready for school. The cries of the invisible child are too faint to make out with certainty, but in the clearest of them, the child seems to call urgently: 'Baba!' ('Daddy!'). At the moment when the film's most direct depiction of homosexual desire is taking place on screen, such a desperate plea to the father from a unseen child fits aptly into the cultural scheme that I've argued this film, like the others in Tsai's film-cycle, addresses: the crisis of the patrilineal *jia* that *tongxinglian* is presumed to occasion.

From the mid-shot of Xiao Kang's approach to A'Rong, the film cuts to its only extreme close-up: of A'Rong's out-of-focus face across the lower foreground of the shot as Xiao Kang approaches from over his shoulder. With this unprecedented filling of the screen by a human face, the alienating distance of the previous scenes, dominated by medium and long shots, is challenged for the first time. This shot is also conspicuous as the only close-up with two faces in frame: the sex scenes have been mainly mid-shots, often with only A'Rong's or only Mei-mei's face in frame at one time. In this sense, too, the kiss scene breaks the formal rules that have governed the film up to now and replaces emptiness, distance and solitude with fullness, proximity and union. Follow-

ing the shot with A'Rong's face in the foreground is a close-up from above with the two men's heads against the background of the white bed, now facing each other as A'Rong rolls over in his sleep and throws an arm about Xiao Kang. The shot is graphically arresting in its contrasting of the pale background with the darker tones of men's faces. As Xiao Kang draws slowly nearer to A'Rong, the empty white space separating the two men is bridged and finally overcome by Xiao Kang, when he gently kisses the other man's lips and their heads fill the screen to the all but total exclusion of the white background.

In some ways, the kiss scene looks forward to the conclusion of *The River*. In particular, the soft, blue dawn light that illuminates this scene adumbrates the dawn that greets Xiao Kang and his father in the Taichung hotel at the conclusion of the later film. In *River*'s final scene, Xiao Kang walks out onto the balcony and wanders off-screen for a moment, then returns, looking about him in the light of the new day in what Tsai has interpreted as a gesture of hope.[20] Even more specifically, the close-ups of Xiao Kang and A'Rong's faces as they lie in bed foreshadow another scene with two men in bed: Xiao Kang and his father in *River*, after they return from the sauna where they have unwittingly had sex together. In *River*, as in *Amour*, the scenes of Xiao Kang in bed with another man are remarkable for their use of close-ups and the absence of the harsh architectural framing devices that have created the sense of claustrophobia in each film up to that point. In both films, Xiao Kang's sexual connection with another man marks a crucial shift in the film's formal composition, suggesting the defeat of distance by closeness, and the overpowering of emptiness by the plenitude of a different kind of love. In one sense, the queer plenitude of these films seems the opposite of the existential emptiness critics frequently read in Tsai's oeuvre; yet this plenitude is also fixed in a dialectical relationship with emptiness insofar as it is the unravelling of older social systems that at once occasions existential crisis and creates space for new ways of being.[21]

In the ways outlined above, *Vive L'Amour* references the homophobic cultural logic that opposes *jia* to *tongxinglian* and relegates the latter to the realm of ghostliness, emptiness and unreality. But it cites that system only to destabilise it by suggesting, at the last moment, that love between men might, on the contrary, occasion a hitherto unimagined fullness and connection. Additionally, in direct contradiction of the system that opposes *jia* to *tongxinglian*, of the three main characters it is Xiao Kang, ghostly as he may be, who seems most eager to turn the eerie apartment into a kind of alternative *jia*.[22] As Chang observes, it is he who devises a scheme to make a washing machine of the jacuzzi by adding detergent and dirty laundry, and he also goes food shopping and prepares a hotpot meal to share with A'Rong. Appropriated and re-imagined in these ways by Xiao Kang, the space of the apartment becomes a liminal one, somewhere in between the familial *jia* and a new kind of 'post-*jia*' social space that is as yet in the process of being imagined: a space, perhaps, where non-traditional forms of love and intimacy might be more fully elaborated.[23]

Thinking of the empty apartment, in the way Chang suggests, as a liminal space that indexes the need for a new kind of social space makes it possible to rethink the figures of ghost and cipher along similar lines. Ghosts, too, are liminal figures, hovering unquietly between the world of the living and the world of the dead. Equally, the cipher-like beings such as angels, crocodiles and vampires associated with *tongxinglian* in fiction and film could be interpreted as liminal figures caught between humanity as it is currently imagined, and something new, and emerging at a time when, as Taiwan's *tongzhi* groups insist, what is urgently required is a collective imagining of new ways of being human – new ways of thinking and practising culture and sexuality in social contexts so thoroughly transmuted. In this sense, *Vive L'Amour* contributes to the 1990s wave of *tongzhi* cultural production that re-works *tongxinglian*'s association with emptiness and ghostliness to figure a nascent sexual subjectivity, struggling to emerge into the anxious spaces excavated by cultural transformation.

NOTES

1. Tsai's films, *The Hole* (Tsai Ming-liang, 1998) and *What Time is it Over There?* (Tsai Ming-liang, 2001) utilise the same pool of actors once again (Lee Kang-sheng, Yang Kuei-mei, Miao Tien, Chen Zhaorong and Lu Yi-ching (formerly known as Lu Hsiao-ling)) and extend the general theme of urban alienation. However, the use of song-and-dance sequences in *Hole* sets this film apart stylistically from the first three, to a certain degree, and it is questionable whether the story traceable in the first three films is continued in *Hole*. Miao Tien plays Xiao Kang's father again in *Time*, but again the transnational setting (Paris and Taipei) sets this film apart to a certain degree from Tsai's first three features.

2. Jiang Xun, 'Body Heat and Salvation' ('Tiwen yu jiuduxin'), *Vive L'Amour* (screenplay) (*Aiqing Wansui*), Tsai Ming-liang et al. (Taipei: Wanxiang, 1994) 144–151.

3. Chuck Stephens, 'Intersection: Tsai Ming-liang's Yearning Bike Boys and Heartsick Heroines', *Film Comment*, 32 (Sept.–Oct. 1996): 20–23; Tony Rayns, 'Confrontations', *Sight & Sound*, 7 (March 1997): 14–18; Richard Read, 'Alienation, Aesthetic Distance and Absorption in Tsai Ming-liang's *Vive L'Amour*', *New Formations*, 40 (Spring 2000): 102–112.

4. But see Chris Berry, 'Where is the Love? The Paradox of Performing Loneliness in Ts'ai Ming-Liang's *Vive L'Amour*', *Falling For You: Essays in Cinema and Performance*, eds Lesley Stern and George Kouvaros (Sydney: Power Publications, 1999), 147–175. For Chinese-language discussion of Tsai Ming-liang's films in relation to *tongzhi*, see Ke Jiazhi, 'A River Flowing Toward the Dawn: Tsai Ming-liang's Films and My World' ('Wang liming liutangde he – Cai Mingliangde dianying yu wode shijie'), *Isotope Electronic Bulletin* (Tongweisu Dianzibao), 28 April 1998: <www.south.nsysu.edu.tw/sccid/today/isotope/98/04/isotope980428.html> (15 November 2001); Chang Hsiao-hung, 'An Erotic Map of Taipei' (*Taibei qingyu dijing*), *Queer Desire: Gender and Sexuality* (Yuwang Xin Ditu: Xingbie, Tongzhixue) (Taipei: Lianhe Wenxue, 1996), 78–107; and Chang Hsiao-hung, 'A Queer Family Romance: *The River*'s Mise-en-scene of Desire' ('Guaitai jiating luomanshi: *Heliu* zhongde yuwang changjing'), *Queer Family Romance* (Guaitai Jiating Luomanshi) (Taipei: Shibao, 2000), 111–141.

5. For more detail on this history, see Fran Martin, 'Queer Comrades: The Emergence of Taiwan's Literature of Transgressive Sexuality', *Angelwings: Contemporary Queer Fiction from Taiwan*, trans. and ed. Fran Martin (University of Hawaii Press, forthcoming).

6. Jiang, 'Body Heat and Salvation', 148.

7. See, for example, Berry, 'Where is the Love?'; Chang, 'Erotic Map'; and Chiao Hsiung-ping, 'Lonely Taipei People' ('Gujide Taibeiren'), in Tsai *et al.*, *Vive L'Amour*, 152–156.

8. For an example of a nostalgic reading of the breakdown of the *jia* in Tsai's cinema, see Chiao, 'Lonely Taipei People'; Chang, 'Erotic Map', 96–97.

9. Chris Berry has written at length on the tendency in East Asian film to represent homosexuality in relation to blood family. See for example Chris Berry, 'Asian Values, Family Values: Film, Video and Lesbian and Gay Identities', *The Journal of Homosexuality*, 40, nos 3/4 (2000): 211–232.

10. For an extended discussion of this question, see Fran Martin, 'Perverse Utopia: Reading *The River*', *Situating Sexualities: Queer Narratives in 1990s Taiwanese Fiction and Film* (Hong Kong University Press, forthcoming).

11. Ding Naifei in discussion in 'Homosexual Politics' ('Tongxingliande Zhengzhi'), *Visionary Essays in Sexuality/Gender Studies* (*Xing/Bie Yanjiude Xin Shiye*), vol. 1, ed. He Chunrui (Taipei: Yuanzun, 1997), 189–229.

12. Hsu Yoshen, *Man Betrother, Man Betrothed* (*Nanhun Nanjia*) (Taipei: Kaixin Yangguang, 1996), 8 (my translation).

13. Chen Xue, 'Searching for the Lost Wings of the Angel' ('Xunzhao Tianshi Yishide Chibang'), trans. Fran Martin, *Positions: East Asia Cultures Critique*, 7, no. 1 (1999): 51–69 (51).

14. Qiu Miaojin, *The Crocodile's Journal* (*Eyu Shouji*) (Taipei: Shibao, 1994).

15. For a detailed account of the *tongzhi wenxue* movement, see Martin, 'Queer Comrades'.

16. I find the idea of the cipher particularly suggestive due to its double meaning: both 'non-entity' and 'code'.

17. But Chang interprets the construction site as an optimistic metaphor, and actress Yang Kuei-mei understood this scene to represent hope, since as she cries her face is illuminated by a ray of sun. Chang, 'Erotic Map', 102–105; Tsai Ming-liang interviewed by Shelly Kraicer, *Positions: East Asia Cultures Critique*, 8, no. 2 (2000): 579–588 (582).

18. Berry, 'Asian Values', 170.

19. Jiang, 'Body Heat and Salvation', 149.

20. Tsai Ming-liang, 'A Life of Desire, Repression, and Fragmentation' ('Yuwang, Yapo, Bengjiede Shengming'), interview with Chen Baoxu, *The River* (screenplay) (*Heliu*), ed. Chiao Hsiung-ping (Taipei: Huangguan, 1997), 52–76 (59); see also Martin, 'Perverse Utopia'.

21. Cf. Chang, 'Erotic Map', 104–105.

22. On this point, see ibid., 100.

23. Ibid., 103.

23   *Wedding Banquet:* A Family (Melodrama) Affair

Chris Berry

Most existing critical discussion of Ang Lee's *Wedding Banquet* (1993) focuses on issues of identity politics. However, this short analysis considers the film in the context of its genre – the family melodrama. When scholars talk about the family melodrama, in fact they usually mean the American or Hollywood family melodrama. A genre analysis of *Wedding Banquet* challenges this presumption that the Hollywood form is universal or a default category. In many ways, the story of *Wedding Banquet* is similar to those found in typical Hollywood family melodramas. However, I argue here that while audiences used to Hollywood films may see *Wedding Banquet* as a variation on a familiar pattern, that 'variation' is in fact the trace of a different category of family melodrama – the Chinese family melodrama. *Wedding Banquet* returns to and rejuvenates both the Hollywood and the Chinese family melodrama, which focuses less on the individual in conflict with the family and more on the family as a collectivity in crisis. In *Wedding Banquet*, this manifests itself in both the narrative conventions and in the tropes and patterns of filmic discourse, promoting audience empathy and identification not with any one individual but with the Confucian family unit as it negotiates the interface with globally hegemonic American culture. With this understanding, we can not only begin to insist that scholars specify melodrama historically and socially, but also begin to grasp the specificity of the Chinese genre and the ideological terrain it negotiates.

Perhaps it is not surprising that identity has captured the attention of most critics writing about *Wedding Banquet*, because it can claim to be the first mainstream Taiwanese and possibly even the first Chinese-language film to portray homosexuality seriously and sympathetically. In the film, Taiwanese migrant landlord Wai-Tung lives happily in New York with his Anglo boyfriend Simon. Their bliss is interrupted only by the long-distance efforts of his Taiwanese parents to find him a bride. Simon suggests a marriage of convenience to Wei-Wei, a mainland Chinese tenant in need of a green card. However, the comedy really gets under way when Wai-Tung's parents, the Gaos, insist on visiting and throwing a lavish wedding banquet. Simon and Wai-Tung 'de-gay' the house, move Wei-Wei in and have Simon pose as 'landlord and friend'. On the night of the banquet, Wei-Wei 'liberates' Wai-Tung and gets pregnant. The Gaos' departure is delayed by Mr Gao's ill-health, which provokes Wai-Tung to come out to his mother. She makes him swear never to tell his father. However, Mr Gao reveals to Simon that he has already figured the situation out, and swears him to secrecy, too. Asked why he is maintaining the charade Mr Gao explains, 'Otherwise, how would I have got my grandson?'

Most responses to *Wedding Banquet* judge it according to hopes and expectations for the representation of various identities, including not only gay Chinese men, but also Asian-Americans and Chinese women. For example, Gina Marchetti quotes a variety of contrasting audience reactions, from disappointment that 'gay relationships must compromise themselves and bow to traditional, straight values and family structures' to praise for the film's demonstration that 'family relationships actually do mean something to us'.[1] Sheng-mei Ma believes *Wedding Banquet* and other Ang Lee films challenge stereotypes by 'undermining fixed categories in racial, cultural, and sexual identities'.[2] Along similar lines, Cynthia Liu notes that the film challenges the gay stereotypes of the 'rice queen' and 'potato queen' as young effeminate Asian man and older white man, a point also discussed in detail by Marchetti.[3] But Liu's main argument is about gender, and she notes that, 'under the guise of "cultural difference", the narratives of Lee's trilogy exhibit a punitive tendency in his constructions of the feminine'.[4] Given that Mrs Gao is portrayed as little more than a sweet but stupid wife and mother and that Wei-Wei sacrifices her independence and rebellion to take on the most stereotypically conformist of female roles, her claims are persuasive.[5]

Some writers on these questions of identity are confident they can discern a clear message in the film. Cynthia Liu's article is based on her conviction that 'the patriarch [is] the character through which film viewer's [sic] sympathies are so inexorably channeled'.[6] Shu-mei Shih agrees that 'the patriarch always wins', even though she notes the 'flexibility' of Lee's films as they play differently to Taiwanese and American audiences.[7] Gina Marchetti places her main emphasis on this latter aspect, concluding that '[P]roduced, distributed, and marketed within a transnational matrix of economic, political, cultural, ethnic, and linguistic relationships, The Wedding Banquet does not posit a singular position for an abstract, "ideal" viewer'. Although she also notes that the need to play to different audiences limits the degree to which the film can be ideologically challenging, this suggests a more open text.[8]

In her essay on Crouching Tiger, Hidden Dragon in this volume, Felicia Chan argues that ambiguity and ambivalence are hallmarks of Ang Lee's films produced by the mixing of different genres. Taking this lead, I examine the generic genealogy and hybridisation of Wedding Banquet in order to address the question of how the text works on spectators, as well as to delineate the cultural and historical specificity of different kinds of melodrama. Is there a clear message or is it an open text? I argue that playing on different versions of the family drama genre is both part of and enhances the openness that Marchetti notes. But I also argue that although the viewer is not placed to identify with the individual patriarch (Mr Gao), openness is limited by an overall perspective that takes certain values for granted.

Although farce is clearly one of the genres that Wedding Banquet draws on, its main genre is the family melodrama.[9] The film matches the primary characteristics of the Hollywood family melodrama, and in particular the coming-out story subgenre. In this subgenre, an individual discovers a personality trait (homosexuality) in dramatic conflict with the values of his family and strives to express that trait, often leaving the blood family and seeking out a chosen family in the gay, lesbian or transgender community.[10] Wedding Banquet seems to tell the story of a man who has done just that, but has omitted the crucial stage of telling his family, which the film addresses.

Thomas Schatz notes that in Hollywood, the general term '"melodrama" was applied to popular romances that depicted a virtuous individual (usually a woman) or couple (usually lovers) victimised by repressive and inequitable social circumstances, particularly those involving marriage, occupation and the nuclear family.'[11] Wai-Tung appears as a virtuous character according to conventional Chinese or American middle-class virtues. In the opening scenes, he is shown to be concerned about his parents and also so hard-working that his partner Simon is resentful they have been unable to take a planned vacation together. But he is also so caring that, over a romantic dinner for two, he promises to make up for this by taking Simon to Paris. Although he is a slum landlord, he is concerned enough about his tenant Wei-Wei to take one of her paintings in lieu of rent and buy her an air conditioner. The pressure from his parents to marry presents itself as Schatz's 'inequitable social circumstances' concerning marriage. In so far as homophobia and misogyny in both Chinese and American cultures link gay men and women, he is even edged towards the conventional focus of the Hollywood melodrama on women.

Schatz also argues that generic elements of the Hollywood family drama include 'The aging patriarch ... the search for the father/lover/husband ... the male intruder-redeemer who regenerates and stabilizes the family, the household itself as locus of social interaction, and the ambiguous function of the marital embrace as both sexually liberating and socially restricting ...'[12] Mr Gao, who has already had one stroke in Taiwan and is concerned about getting his only son to continue the family line, represents the aging patriarch perfectly. And by having the Gaos and Wei-Wei move into Simon and Wai-Tung's New York brownstone, Wedding Banquet not only creates the pressure cooker of confinement that helps to generate frantic farce but also fulfils 'the household itself as locus of social interaction' requirement. The gay 'twist' in this version of archetype generates some interesting complications concerning the redeemer/intruder. Is it Simon or Wei-Wei, or maybe both, who fits this part of the model? Certainly, given that Wai-Tung is gay but that Wei-Wei's pregnancy liberates him from his parents' pressures, the marriage and formation of the couple – or is it a *ménage à trois*? – at the end of the film fits the ambiguous formation of the couple.

In Schatz's analysis of the genre, implausibility can prompt questioning on the part of the audience and therefore create an ironic and critical dimension. For example, he cites 1950s melodrama director Douglas Sirk's comment that 'there is no real solution of the predicament the people in the play are in, just the *deus ex machina*, which is now called "the happy end" '.[13] Certainly the miracle of a woman made pregnant by a gay man and agreeing to marriage and motherhood despite her previous commitment to independence strains credulity, not to mention the willingness of his parents to accept the complicated domestic arrangements that appear inevitable. However, it also true that *Wedding Banquet* is shot in a conventionally realist fashion, featuring none of the mannered play with colours, lighting and framing that critics like Schatz associate with a self-reflexive subversion in Sirk.

Given the many Americans involved in making Ang Lee's films and his own many years in the United States, it is not surprising that *Wedding Banquet* follows the pattern of the Hollywood melodrama in many ways. But what about the Chinese family melodrama? The term 'melodrama' is commonly used in the discussion of Asian cinemas in general and Chinese cinema in particular.[14] Yet all the existing accounts of the development of Hollywood melodrama trace complicated genealogies through many different branches of stage productions, literature and popular cultural forms – all of them exclusively European and American.[15] Such considerations lead Nick Browne to ask, 'On what basis can an aesthetic ideology so embedded in the popular entertainment forms of Western culture – Christian and capitalist – be treated as significant, culturally speaking, to the form and meaning of contemporary Chinese film?'[16]

An attempt to trace a genealogy of the Chinese family melodrama in general is beyond the scope of this article. However, two basic factors should be noted. First, Western stage forms were introduced into China in the early part of the twentieth century, meaning that Chinese dramatists and film-makers are familiar with Western melodrama. On the other hand, although popularisation of Western stage forms like melodrama in China coincides with the advent of modernity, as Peter Brooks has noted is also the case in Europe,[17] this was not part of a transition to secularity, because dominant Confucian ideology was already secular in focus. What, then, do Chinese scholars and critics mean when they use the term 'melodrama'?

Wimal Dissanayake has noted that none of the Asian languages has a synonym for 'melodrama',[18] and this is also true in Chinese. In 1986, the Hong Kong International Film Festival's annual retrospective was on 'Cantonese Melodrama 1950–1969'. The Chinese title of the catalogue and all the essays in it use 'melodrama' as a translation of *'wenyipian'*. This term literally means 'literature and art film'. But as Li Cheuk-to notes, although it is different from the European melodrama because the *wenyipian* is defined more by subject matter than mode, it has many dramaturgical characteristics in common with the European melodrama: 'highly schematic characters, plots punctuated by fortuities and coincidences, extreme emotions and conflicts …'[19] Taiwanese critic Cai Guorong traces the general form and history of the *wenyipian* to the 1920s and defines it by theme, setting and tone as films about family and romance, set in modern times, and with a lyrical focus on emotion.[20]

However, when we turn to the family melodrama, it is notable that the Chinese term translated in this way is not 'family *wenyipian*' but instead 'family ethics film' (*jiating lunlipian*).[21] This is significant, for *lunli* is a specifically Confucian term for ethics, referring to the Confucian code of reciprocal ethical obligations. These are the five relationships (*wulun*): emperor–subject, father–son, husband–wife, elder brother– younger brother, friend–friend. As Ma Ning notes, 'although the *wulun* relationships are asymmetical and structured as patron–client relations, they are naturalized in ethical terms'.[22] This emphasis on ethical expectations based on hierarchically defined social and kinship position leads Ma to add that 'the Chinese melodramatic narrative facilitates the construction of a subjectivity that can be best described as intersubjectivity'.[23] This understanding of selfhood has grounded narratives in China for many centuries, as contradictions between different obligations or between obligation and personal desires can motor all manner of stories.[24] In contrast to this relationally defined 'intersubjectivity', a hallmark of the transition to secularity in Europe discussed by Brooks as grounding the emergence of European melodrama is the emphasis on the individual 'personality' understood as a unique and natural individual psychology.[25] The resultant emphasis is not on ethics (behaviour) but on morality (good or bad character).

In these circumstances, the distinction between the European family melodrama and the Chinese family *lunlipian* produces a tension between two different models of secular subjectivity, one based on psychology and its expression and the other based on ethically defined social and kinship roles. In so far as the emergence of the modern Chinese melodrama is coincident with the Chinese experience of modernity as a European import, we may therefore hypothesise that the Chinese family *lunlipian* is itself a modern and hybrid form that stages the tension between 'tradition' and 'modernity' as a tension between different models of subjectivity, with competing value systems for judging behaviour. In the remainder of this essay, I would like to examine how *Wedding Banquet* can be read as a *lunlipian* as well as a Hollywood-style family melodrama, and how this is manifested not only in narrative but also in *mise en scène* and editing to create ambiguity around the message of the film and ambivalent audience engagement.

Homosexuality is ripe for melodramatisation in the Western tradition as a personality trait in conflict with dominant social values. It is also ripe for narrativisation in the tradition of the *lunlipian*. Here, however, the drama is driven by the potential ethical difficulty of being unable to fulfil one of the most fundamental obligations expected of a son: the production of a grandson to continue the family line.[26] Wai-Tung's discussions with Simon early in the film concern homosexuality as personality – he is lying about who he is and should he just come out to his parents? However, when a potential match sent from Taiwan tells Wai-Tung about his father's stroke, she also tells him that his father has said his greatest wish is to see his grandson before he dies – emphasising the Confucian ethical dimension of the situation.

These tensions between what can be seen as ethical practice or oppression and self-expression or selfishness animate the rest of the film. They extend beyond Wai-Tung and are often made explicit in heart-to-heart conversations. Wai-Tung's father is a retired career army officer who everyone refers to as 'the commander'. But soon after arriving in New York, he tells his son he joined up to escape an arranged marriage. Indeed, he only got married at all after learning that his family in the mainland had died, leaving the responsibility of continuing the family line to him. Since Wai-Tung is an only son, the ethical parallels are clear. But it is also clear that Mr Gao's own experiences include the negotiation of parallel tensions.

After the truth has come out about both Wai-Tung's sexuality and Wei-Wei's pregnancy, Wei-Wei feels obliged to return the Gaos' wedding presents to Mrs Gao. Mrs Gao refuses, insisting that she wants her grandson. Wei-Wei responds, 'What about my future?' But after this stand-off between ethical kinship obligation and self-realisation, Mrs Gao tells Wei-Wei she envies younger women and their independence and education, and Wei-Wei responds that she came to regard the Gaos as her own parents because she is so alone in America. Again, both women live the struggle between different ideological systems and corresponding modes of subjectivity.

Even Simon is unconsciously caught up in these tensions. He tries hard to fulfil the ethical obligations of a traditional daughter-in-law, cooking and cleaning diligently for Wai-Tung and his parents. Although his motivation for suggesting marriage to Wei-Wei is selfish – getting Wai-Tung's parents off their backs – this act mimics the ideal behaviour of a barren daughter-in-law in suggesting a second wife to enable her husband to produce an heir. However, when things go wrong, Simon starts going out with friends and tells Wai-Tung he plans to leave, presumably because the complex situation is not satisfying his needs. Towards the end of the film, Wai-Tung and Wei-Wei decide to keep the baby and ask him to co-parent. When he nods, Wai-Tung asks tentatively, 'So you'll stay?' But the ironic clincher is Wei-Wei's invocation of the Western equivalent of kinship obligations: 'You must, for the sake of the child.'

This double thematic focus on mutual obligations and self-expression certainly helps audiences of different backgrounds to engage with *Wedding Banquet*. But the moral ambivalence produced by mixing the two sets of values is a distinctly new feature of the film. Both the Hollywood and Chinese family melodrama had a very clear sense of right and

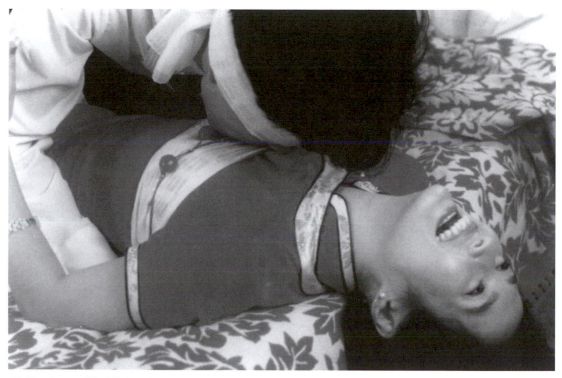

Wedding Banquet: Wei-Wei's wedding night.

wrong. Indeed, they functioned to rehearse and affirm well-known values. But so much of the drama in *Wedding Banquet* is produced not only by the clash between values but also the acknowledgment of both sets of values by the central characters that the result is a new characteristic for the genre – deep-seated moral and ethical ambivalence.

This ambivalence makes it less easy to determine how the film works to position audiences. Is it organised to promote a primary identification with any one particular character? In the opening credits sequence, only Wai-Tung appears, working out at the gym. This might seem to indicate that this is his story. His mother's voice on the audiotape letter pressuring him to marry might be taken to promote further sympathy and identification with him, especially for audiences already favourable to the idea of self-expression and steeped in Hollywood melodrama.

But in the scenes that follow, other characters are introduced. Although Simon and Wei-Wei's relationships to Wai-Tung are quickly established, in each case we are first given a sense of their lives beyond him. In Simon's case, we see him at work as a physiotherapist before the sequence continues into

a dinner date with Wai-Tung. The next morning, we see Simon running into a gay friend outside the house he shares with Wai-Tung and they touch upon HIV-AIDS activism briefly, a theme that will be picked up again later in the film. In Wei-Wei's case, she is first shown alone in her overheated basement studio in Wai-Tung's building, sweating, drinking, listening to loud music and working on her abstract paintings. Only then does Wai-Tung arrive. Although it is unlikely anyone could claim that *Wedding Banquet* is primarily Simon's or Wei-Wei's story, these scenes make it harder to see it as Wai-Tung's alone.

Furthermore, these narrative techniques are complemented by camerawork and editing enabling the audience to perceive how different characters feel, rather than tying them into seeing things from one character's point of view only. Some of the most often cited work on Hollywood film has emphasised the potential for ideological persuasion through the use of point-of-view shots and other techniques that align the audience with the perspective of a particular character.[27] Setting aside for the moment at least thirty years of argument about how true this might be in Hollywood studio-era cinema, it is important to note that this is not the technique deployed in *Wedding Banquet*.

First, *Wedding Banquet* does not align audience perspectives with the literal point of view of any one character. Although point of view shots are used, in particular as a way of heightening dramatic tension in scenes where people argue, I cannot discover any privileging of one character's point of view. Indeed, the film does not privilege the point of view shot as an identification device at all. Instead, in many scenes, the dominant device is the arrangement of the characters in the *mise en scène* and the editing so as to give the audience access to the different reactions and ideas of all the main characters. This is mainly produced by keeping everyone in the same frame with their faces visible to the camera, as for example in the scene where Wei-Wei returns the gifts to Mrs Gao. But it may be produced by editing. For example, prior to the wedding banquet Wei-Wei and Wai-Tung kneel before Mr and Mrs Gao. It is not possible to view all of the characters' faces at once. The camera cuts back and forth so that we can see Mr and Mrs Gao getting happier as he makes his long paternal blessings speech, but also Wei-Wei and Wai-Tung getting more uncomfortable.

This example brings up a second important point about audience perspective. This scene depends for its effect on our superior narrative knowledge. At this stage of the film, we know more about each character's background and feelings than any one character does, and we are moved because the clash of emotions is invisible until, much to Mr and Mrs Gao's surprise, Wei-Wei breaks down in tears. I have referred to this device elsewhere as a kind of spectatorial 'third place', but I would further specify that we can call the pleasure of superior knowledge 'epistemophilia'.[28]

Nick Browne notes in his article on *Stagecoach* that superior knowledge can override the identification potential of the point-of-view shot. He analyses a scene where point-of-view shots align the audience physically with disapproving gazes upon the character of Dallas, a prostitute. However, prior knowledge has established audience sympathy with her, which overrides this alignment and makes its use only a way of poignantly underlining prejudice.[29]

Just prior to telling Wai-tung why he joined the army, Mr Gao has a point-of-view shot that is strongly marked, both because such shots are unusual in the film and it is not motivated by a movement or sound drawing his attention. He (and we) look at the two empty chairs in the garden of the house. Does this mean the audience is aligned with the patriarch, Mr Gao? First, the film gives us no idea what he is thinking about these two chairs, although if Simon is the live-in landlord and Wai-Tung and Wei-Wei are his tenants – as he has been told – the arrangement may seem odd. And second, we already know far more than he does, meaning that we certainly do understand the significance of the chairs. Therefore, the use of the shot is deeply ambivalent.

Similarly, at the end of the wedding banquet itself, Wei-Wei and Wai-Tung watch Simon lead Mr and Mrs Gao off. Are we to understand our perspective as anchored in either Wei-Wei or Wai-Tung's vision or both? And what emotions are we to attach to this view? Nothing in the text prompts a definitive answer. We may look at it from either character's perspective, or our own. We cannot be sure if Wai-Tung and Wei-Wei are happy or feel manipulated. This ambivalence is even more heightened in the final scene of the film, where Wei-Wei, Wai-Tung and Simon see off Mr and Mrs Gao at the airport. Prior to the notoriously ambivalent final shot where the film freezes on Mr Gao raising his arms in what could be interpreted as surrender or as triumph, the family looks at the wedding-photograph album. The scene seems like a self-referential retrospect. We cut back and forth between shots of their facial reactions and their point of view of the pictures in the album. Should we identify with one character's point view? Do we need to identify with any individual perspective? The text seems more open.

However, although these techniques produce considerable flexibility and ambivalence the film is not completely open. Rather, it produces its ideological effect through a different set of devices than point-of-view shots. The combination of narrative knowledge and camerawork offers the audience access to the feelings of all the central characters and enables knowledge that exceeds that of any one character, enabling different audience members to work through the film with different trajectories. However, the text itself forecloses upon certain crucial narrative possibilities. All the characters strive hard to understand and satisfy the needs of the other characters, whether based on individual self-expression or the fulfilment of social and kinship roles. At no point is any serious criticism of either set of values voiced within the film itself. Nobody denounces Mr Gao's obsession with the family line, and nobody denounces Wai-Tung and Simon's sexuality as immoral or selfish. Of course, a real audience member may always bring their own ideas from outside the film to bear upon their interpretation of it. But the film's ambivalence is itself an ideological move appropriate to the sustenance of globalised liberal capitalism, for it enables that system by finding a way to maintain simultaneously two otherwise incompatible value systems that it brings into proximity. In this way, it produces a new melodramatic hybrid appropriate to the negotiation of the 'moral occult' of globalism.

NOTES

1. Gina Marchetti, '*The Wedding Banquet*: Global Chinese Cinema and Asian American Experience', in *Countervisions: Asian-American Film Criticism*, ed. Sandra Liu and Darrell Y. Hamamoto (Philadelphia: Temple University Press, 2000), 281.

2. Sheng-mei Ma, 'Ang Lee's Domestic Tragicomedy: Immigrant Nostalgia, Exotic/Ethnic Tour, Global Market', *Journal of Popular Culture*, 30, no. 1 (1996): 191.

3. Cynthia W. Liu, ' "To Love, Honor and Dismay": Subverting the Feminine in Ang Lee's Trilogy of Resuscitated Patriarchs', *Hitting Critical Mass: A Journal of Asian American Cultural Criticism*, 3, no. 1 (1995): 37–40; Marchetti, '*The Wedding Banquet*', 285–288.

4. Liu, ' "To Love, Honor and Dismay" ', 9.

5. However, one largely overlooked identity dimension of the film in all the critical discussion is ethnicity. For further analysis see Chris Berry and Mary Farquhar, 'Where Do You Draw the Line? Ethnicity in Chinese Cinemas', in *Cinema and Nation: China on Screen* (New York: Cambridge University Press, forthcoming).

6. Liu, '"To Love, Honor and Dismay"', 14.

7. Shu-mei Shih, 'Globalisation and Minoritisation: Ang Lee and the Politics of Flexibility', *New Formations*, no. 40 (2000): 92–93.

8. Marchetti, '*The Wedding Banquet*', 292–293.

9. Scholarship over the last twenty years or so has challenged the idea that melodrama is a generic type, and argued instead that it is a mode of cinematic narration that can be found in all manner of genres including the Western and the gangster film. Crucial though this argument is, it does not undermine the status of the family melodrama as a distinct genre deploying the melodramatic mode. The key essay on this topic is Christine Gledhill's 'The Melodramatic Field: An Investigation', in *Home Is Where the Heart Is: Studies in Melodrama and the Woman's Film*, ed. Christine Gledhill (London: British Film Institute, 1987), 5–39. Gledhill makes it clear she believes the effort to confine the melodramatic mode to the Hollywood genres of the woman's film and the family melodrama are motivated by misogynistic prejudice against emotion and excess. Linda Williams extends the argument to revise our understanding of classical Hollywood cinema as a whole and attack the common division between realist cinema and melodrama in 'Melodrama Revised', in *Refiguring American Film Genres: History and Theory*, ed. Nick Browne (Berkeley: University of California Press, 1998), 42–88.

10. Ken Plummer, *Telling Sexual Stories: Power, Change and Social Worlds* (London: Routledge, 1995), 83.

11. Thomas Schatz, 'The Family Melodrama', in *Hollywood Genres: Formulas, Filmmaking, and the Studio System* (Philadelphia: Temple University Press, 1981), 222.

12. Ibid., 229–230.

13. Ibid., 244.

14. See, for example, the essays collected in Wimal Dissanayake, ed., *Melodrama and Asian Cinema* (New York: Cambridge University Press, 1993).

15. In addition to accounts in Gledhill, Schatz and Williams, see Thomas Elsaesser, 'Tales of Sound and Fury: Observations of the Family Melodrama', in Gledhill, *Home Is Where the Heart Is*, 43–69.

16. Nick Browne, 'Society and Subjectivity: On the Political Economy of Chinese Melodrama', in *New Chinese Cinemas: Forms, Identities, Politics*, ed. Nick Browne, Paul G. Pickowicz, Vivian Sobchak and Esther Yau (New York: Cambridge University Press, 1994), 42.

17. Peter Brooks, *The Melodramatic Imagination: Balzac, Henry James, Melodrama and the Mode of Excess* (New Haven: Yale University Press, 1976), 15–18.

18. Wimal Dissanayake, 'Introduction', in Dissanayake, *Melodrama*, 3.

19. Li Cheuk-to, 'Introduction', in *Cantonese Melodrama 1950–1969 (Aoyu Wenyipian Miangu 1950-1959)*, ed. Li Cheuk-to (Hong Kong: The Urban Council, 1986), 9.

20. Cai Guorong, *A Study of the Modern Chinese Melodrama* (*Zhongguo Jindai Wenyi Dianying Yanjiu*) (Taipei: Taiwan Film Archive, 1985), 3–7. For further discussion in English, see Law Kar, 'Archetype and Variations', in Li Cheuk-to, *Cantonese Melodrama*, 15.

21. This Chinese term appears as the original on page 8 translated into English as 'family melodrama' on page 9 in Li Cheuk-to's introduction, for example. The same translation can be found comparing the Chinese original and the English original of Stephen Teo's 'The Father–Son Cycle' ('Fu yu Zi–Aoyupian Zhuti de Yanxu'), in Li Cheuk-to, *Cantonese Melodrama*, 42–47 and 37–41 respectively. This essay forms the foundation for Chapter 4 of Teo's own book, Stephen Teo, *Hong Kong Cinema : The Extra Dimensions* (London: BFI, 1997), 61–72. Cai Guorong also uses the term in his book on the general category of the *wenyipian*.

22. Ma Ning, 'Spatiality and Subjectivity in Xie Jin's Film Melodrama of the New Period', in Nick Browne et al., *New Chinese Cinemas*, 18.

23. Ibid., 23. For further discussion of the early origins of these and related concepts, see Donald J. Munro, *The Concept of Man in Early China* (Stanford: Stanford University Press, 1969).

24. Andrew H. Plaks, 'Towards a Critical Theory of Chinese Narrative', in *Chinese Narrative: Critical and Theoretical Essays*, ed. Andrew H. Plaks (Princeton: Princeton University Press, 1977), 343–345.

25. Brooks, *The Melodramatic Imagination*, 42.

26. These questions of homosexuality and the space and ideology of the family are discussed further by Fran Martin in this volume. I have also considered the question at greater length in various essays, including 'Asian Values, Family Values: Film, Video, and Lesbian and Gay Identities', in *Gay and Lesbian Asia: Culture, Identity, Community*, ed. Gerard Sullivan and Peter A. Jackson (New York: Harrington Park Press, 2001), 211–233.

27. The two most famous examples are probably Daniel Dayan, 'The Tutor-Code of Classical Cinema', in *Movies and Methods*, ed. Bill Nichols (Berkeley: University of California Press, 1976), 438–451; and Laura Mulvey, 'Visual Pleasure and Narrative Cinema', *Screen*, 16, no. 3 (1975): 6–19. The second article works on the gendered quality of these structures.

28. Chris Berry, 'Sexual Difference and the Viewing Subject in *Li Shuangshuang* and *The In-Laws*', in *Perspectives on Chinese Cinema*, ed. Chris Berry (London: BFI, 1991), 30–39.

29. Nick Browne, 'The Spectator-in-the-Text: The Rhetoric of *Stagecoach*', in *Film Theory and Criticism: Introductory Readings*, ed. Leo Braudy and Marshall Cohen, 5th edn (New York: Oxford University Press, 1999), 148–163.

24 *Yellow Earth*: Hesitant Apprenticeship and Bitter Agency

Helen Hok-Sze Leung

Writers and artists concentrate everyday phenomena, typify the contradictions and struggles within them and produce works which awaken the masses, fire them with enthusiasm and impel them to unite and struggle to transform their own situation … To sum up, the creative labour of revolutionary cultural workers transforms the raw material of everyday life into literature and art that serve the people.

> Mao Zedong, 'Talks at the Yan'an Forum on
> Art and Literature' (1942)

The sun has gone down behind the clouds,
My mouth says nothing but my heart is grieving.
Green grass and cow stool cannot put out a fire,
So these mountain songs cannot save Cuiqiao.
Me, Cuiqiao! Ah, the lot of a woman!

> Folk song in *Yellow Earth*
> (Chen Kaige, 1984)

If Mao were to have his cultural workers 'transform' Cuiqiao's song, the bitter assertion that 'these mountain songs cannot save Cuiqiao' would probably be the first line to attract their editorial attention. The suggestion that folk songs may be useless for the improvement of one's material situation is surely not the best way to 'awaken the masses, fire them with enthusiasm and impel them to unite and struggle to transform their own situation'.[1] Yet, the very 'uselessness' of Cuiqiao's song, which calls attention to the limits of the singer's agency, offers other kinds of transformative possibilities. Chen Kaige's remarkable first film tells the story of an encounter between Gu Qing, a cultural worker from the Eighth Route Army, and the peasants whose songs he is supposed to collect and transform. The film is at once a critique of Mao's dysfunctional political project and an embodiment of the desire such a project inspires but is unable to fulfil.

Since its controversial release in 1984, followed by a critically acclaimed reception at the Hong Kong International Film Festival in 1985, *Yellow Earth* has sparked a number of important debates, not only in the study of Chinese cinema, but more generally in the consideration of Chinese culture, nationalism and the ambivalent legacy of the Communist Revolution. The initial critical reaction to the film in China largely comprises of literal interpretations that focus on questions of historical accuracy and the image of the peasantry.[2] By contrast, critics in the West seem much more interested in the film's figurative aspects, which appear to conceal far more than they reveal. For many critics, the elusive character of the film's symbolism creates a rupture in the text: a dimension of otherness that resists the film's dominant structure and ideology. Esther Yau locates this otherness in the 'non-perspectival presentation of landscapes' which decentres the gaze and instigates a Daoist aesthetic contemplation that undercuts the narrative strands of the text and resists her own 'Western analysis'.[3] Mary Ann Farquhar develops this argument further and argues that the film's 'blank' shots of nature and sounds of silence are figures for the repressed and ignored Daoist principle of *yin*, the dearth of which results in a cosmic and seasonal disorder.[4] Wary of attributing too hastily a 'Chinese difference' to the film, Rey Chow calls attention to the scene of the film's own dilemma: how to represent China through the arguably non-Chinese technology of the cinema.[5] Chow suggests that the film stages conflicting notions of reform: the filmic image is aligned with a politics of identity while music, which 'empties out' rather than anchors the image's signification, alludes to a politics of difference.[6] In a more recent article, Stephanie Donald also seeks to locate 'points of disruption' in *Yellow Earth* by analysing the film's landscape as a 'demon lover' that devours 'the object of its passion and the agency of its rivals'.[7]

These figures of otherness, whether interpreted as blank spaces, silence, music, or the landscape, are pitched against the ideological rigidity of the Maoist project, apparently signified by Gu Qing. Chow characterises the soldier's presence in the village as symbolic of a 'politics of record' that 'signifies the thorough nature of political intervention in civilian life'.[8]

Donald also understands Gu Qing to be an 'agent of the Party' whose agency disappears as he becomes integrated into nature, because he 'cannot move forward as a successful agent of the Party' when he 'occupies a harmonious position in the circulation of the natural world'.[9] The Maoist project is thus perceived to be absolutely incompatible with the film's trope of alterity: an outmoded historical moment that is superseded and displaced by the film's new aesthetic.

While my reading of *Yellow Earth* owes a great deal to these insightful analyses, I wish to address the relative inattention they pay to the proximity between the desire of the Maoist project and that of the film itself. Chen Kaige, like most of the intellectuals, writers and artists of his generation, had spent parts of his early adulthood in the countryside as a sent-down youth. Mao's injunction in this campaign to 'apprentice' urban youths to the peasantry was driven by ideological assumptions very similar to those behind Gu Qing's assignment. Like many of his contemporary film-makers and writers, Chen often returns to the scene of this early 'class apprenticeship' in his works, most explicitly in *King of the Children* (1987). In fact, Chen's description of how he and his cinematographer Zhang Yimou prepared for the filming of *Yellow Earth* is curiously reminiscent of Gu Qing's sojourn in the village: 'We went to the area where we were going to shoot for a month. We stayed with the peasants, lived with them, ate with them. We didn't have a car or a bus. We walked.'[10] The actual practice of making *Yellow Earth*, which involves the film-maker's apprenticeship to his film's subjects, thus *repeats* the soldier's narrative. Like Gu Qing, the film-maker wrestles with the problematic but utopian desire to undo the fixity of one's class origins through a radical cultural practice. Throughout the history of Communist China, such desire has haunted the lives of many intellectuals (who in the Party's eyes are as likely to hold on to their class privilege as they are to 'defect'

to the side of the masses) as they struggle to live up to the demands of the revolution. Yet, the film neither documents nor instantiates the fulfilment of this desire for what Gayatri Spivak has, in another context, provocatively termed 'class deconstruction'.[11] Rather, the film's elusive tropes of otherness, i.e. of what remains *persistently* desired, marks the impossibility of fulfilment. I will show that the failure of both Gu Qing's and the film's enterprise is a necessary corollary – and precisely the radical implication – of the logic of the enterprise itself.

MUTUAL APPRENTICESHIP AND THE MASS LINE

Yellow Earth begins with an encounter between sound and image. We hear a short folk tune, followed by the sound of wind blowing, as a short description of the film's setting scrolls down the screen. The archaic script of the text recalls the immense historical significance of the Shaan-Gan-Ning border region as the cradle of early Chinese civilisation and, subsequently, the heartland of an imperial culture. While this 'four-thousand-year-old culture' provides a powerful ideological symbol for a 'national culture', the resolute iconoclasm in Chinese nationalism also condemns it as a burden of tradition that stands in the way of modernity. The very incongruity of an archaic calligraphy scripting a story about the Communist Revolution ironically recalls the charge Chen Duxiu levied on the ideographic script as a 'home of rotten and poisonous thought' which is incapable of communicating modern ideas.'[12] In this opening scene, folk culture (the musical tune) is associated with nature (the sound of wind) and orality. It remains marginal to the image of the written text and functions as a possible resolution to the contradiction exemplified by the image.

Gu Qing's assignment is an example of Mao's attempt to create a national and modern culture that is at the same time revolutionary in character. Mao does not advocate the abandonment of all traditions, but rather an 'assimilation' of the 'democratic' aspect of traditional culture:

A splendid old culture was created during the long period of Chinese feudal society. To study the development of this old culture, to reject its feudal dross and assimilate its democratic essence is a necessary condition for developing our new national culture and increasing our national self-confidence, but we should never swallow anything and everything uncritically. It is imperative to separate the fine old culture of the people which had a more or less democratic and revolutionary character from all the decadence of the old feudal ruling class.[13]

The injunction to separate the 'fine old culture of the people' from the 'decadence of the old feudal ruling class' would privilege Shaanbei folk songs over Tang poetry (which is arguably also 'indigenous' to the region) as the defining ingredient of a national culture. Unlike Tang poetry, which is the fruit of imperial glory, this 'fine old culture of the people' has in fact been nurtured by adversity and oppression. When Gu Qing naively asks the old peasant how it is possible for people to remember so many folk songs, the peasant replies that one remembers 'when life is hard'. The unique character and the most dynamic radicalism of the Communist Revolution was also fostered in dire material conditions, exemplifying Mao's belief that backwardness is an asset, rather than an obstacle, to the building of socialism. Yan'an politics, which deviated from more orthodox Comintern principles, was characterised by an emphasis on the revolutionary potential of the spontaneous consciousness of the masses and a deep suspicion of the rigid organisational structure of the Leninist vanguard party. The notion of the 'mass line' – which provides the motive for the Gu Qing's assignment in the film – was developed at this time. Mark Selden describes the 'mass line' in these terms:

Mass line conceptions of leadership brought honour and status within the grasp of every youth or adult who was prepared to devote himself wholeheartedly to the revolutionary cause, regardless of his class, formal training, or family background. If peasants could 'rise' to leadership through struggle and self-education, students, bureaucrats, and traditional elite elements could 'descend' by means of 'to the village' and production campaigns to unite with and lead the people within the confines of the village. In either case, leadership implied a break with the elitism of the past and the acceptance of a multiplicity of roles which traditionally had been separate and distinct.[14]

Gu Qing's assignment is thus supposed to serve a double purpose: to create a new national culture by 'assimilating' the 'democratic essence' of the culture of the region, as well as to foster the 'mass line'

through cultural workers' efforts to 'unite with and lead' the peasants. The collection of folk songs is important both in and of itself, and as a process through which a community may be built on 'the acceptance of a multiplicity of roles which traditionally had been separate and distinct'.

The insistence on *mutuality* presents some suggestive problems. In a talk delivered to the cultural workers of the Shaan-Gan-Ning region in 1944, Mao refers to a dilemma Gu faces in the film:

Our culture is a people's culture; our cultural workers … must act in accordance with the needs and wishes of the masses. All work done for the masses must start from their needs and not from the desire of any individual, however well-intentioned. It often happens that objectively the masses need a certain change, but subjectively they are not yet conscious of the need, not yet willing or determined to make the change. In such cases, we should wait patiently. We should not make the change until, through our work, most of the masses have become conscious of the need and are willing and determined to carry it out.[15]

For Mao, consciousness-raising is necessary because class location and class identification do not necessarily – or even usually – coincide. The Party collects and transforms folk songs as a means to instil a 'subjective consciousness' in the peasantry. At the same time, Mao realises that class identification cannot be imposed from without, least of all by members of another class.

In the film, Gu Qing follows this demand faithfully as he constantly engages the peasant on issues of revolution and women's emancipation, but refrains from actively intervening in Cuiqiao's situation. Gu is committed to learning from the peasants at the same time that he tries to educate them. The most provocative lesson arises, however, when what Gu learns actually disproves the fundamental assumptions of his enterprise. What if the peasants are 'subjectively' thoroughly conscious of their 'objective' needs but are still not impelled to follow the 'objective' solutions prescribed by the Party? What if the Party's solutions do not always satisfy the masses' needs, but merely instigate their desire to find other solutions? What if the truly radical implication of a 'mutual apprenticeship' between the Party and the masses demands that the Party relinquish its own authority as a representative of the masses?

BITTERNESS AND AGENCY

These questions are most clearly raised by the following scene, which takes place when Gu eats with the peasant's family after ploughing the fields together:

> Peasant: Young officer, what was it you said last night that you came here to collect?
> Gu: I'm collecting folk songs [*min'ge*] from Shaanbei.
> Peasant: (laughs) What folk songs, they're just bitter tunes [*suan qu'er*]!
> Gu: Do you know how to sing them, Uncle?
> Peasant: I'm neither happy nor sad, what's the point of singing?
> Gu: There are so many folk songs in the region. Tell me, how do people remember them all?
> Peasant: When life is difficult, you'd remember … Why are you collecting bitter tunes?
> Gu: To put new words to them, so that soldiers of Cuiqiao's age can sing them. When people hear them, they'll know why they're suffering, why women are beaten, why workers and peasants should rise up. When our army hears them, they'll fight the rich and the Japanese even more bravely. Chairman Mao and Commander Zhu both love listening to folk songs. Chairman Mao doesn't just want us to learn how to sing, but also to learn to read and write. He wants all the people of China to eat properly.

The ordering of Gu's wants implies that consciousness-raising (through singing, reading and writing) is the precondition for material well being (eating properly). This belief assumes that when people's consciousness is raised, agency follows. It is, however, a 'directed' agency. The songs should spur people's will to participate in a political movement organised by the Party, which would, in turn, ensure the material well-being of the people it represents. The insistence on such 'direction' means that any undirected (i.e. unintended and unforeseen) consequences of the consciousness-raising project must be eradicated at all costs.

The peasant's response to Gu's questions illustrates a different understanding of the relation between consciousness and agency. He does not understand why the soldier is so interested in folk songs, which to him are 'just bitter tunes'. The soldier uses the term *min'ge*, which refers to 'folk songs' or 'songs of the people'. By contrast, the peasant refers to the songs as *suan qu'er*: bitter tunes. This term drops out any mention of the 'folk', privileges the songs' melody over their lyric, and draws attention to the element of lament (bitterness). To the peasant, these songs are not important as part of a folk tradition or as raw material to be revolutionised by the party. They are simply to be sung spontaneously, when one is happy or sad, and are remembered when 'life is difficult'. Folk songs are, according to the peasant's understanding, affective responses to one's lived experience. They exist solely within, and not a moment beyond, the immediate context of their spontaneous production. It would thus make no sense to 'collect' them. The film presents many moments of folk singing to illustrate this understanding of 'bitter tunes' and its critical implications for the soldier's project.

Worried that the soldier may be reprimanded by his leaders for not having collected enough folk songs, the peasant sings for him for the first and only time. This compassionate 'performance' on the eve of the soldier's departure suggests, in two distinct ways, that the peasant's understanding of the world far exceeds the assumptions behind the soldier's project. First, the composition of the shot that shows this

Yellow Earth: Cuiqiao.

performance draws attention to the peasant's 'bitter' compassion for his daughter. A close-up of the peasant's face is juxtaposed with a blurred image of Cuiqiao in the background, listening while she works. The song is a lament for the suicide of a young widow. Prior to this scene, we have learnt that the peasant has arranged a marriage for Cuiqiao to a much older man. Between her mother's funeral and savings for his little brother's future bride-price, there is little money left for a dowry and hence the prospect of a good match. In Gu Qing's eyes, the peasant is an unenlightened patriarch who does not understand his daughter's oppression. Yet, this song, ostensibly a performance for the soldier, also functions as a lament for his daughter, whose future is likely to be similarly tragic. It shows that, contrary to the soldier's belief, the peasant is neither unconscious of nor unsympathetic to his daughter's situation, even though such awareness and empathy do not in themselves lead to any action or change. The 'bitterness' of these songs thus derives not only from the sentimental music or the tragic scenario depicted by the lyric, but more fundamentally from an awareness of a discontinuity between subjective awareness and objective change. Second, the peasant sings for the soldier even though, as the scene discussed above clearly shows, he does not believe in the soldier's project. In fact, it is because the peasant does not believe that the collection of folk songs for revolutionary use is tenable that he stages this performance for the soldier. The peasant understands with insight that the project will fail. Out of empathy and compassion, he sings for the soldier so that he would have something in his 'collection' and not be reprimanded by his superiors. The actual moment of 'collection' thus belies the logic of the project. Yet, it should be valued precisely because it could facilitate the 'mutual apprenticeship' Mao envisions.

Cuiqiao's songs also question the relation between consciousness and agency. Her songs depict the condition of her oppression, yet they fail to articulate any possibility for change. Bitterness in song is not even considered an articulation in and of itself: thus Cuiqiao sings, 'I wish to speak my mind but I don't know how', even when she has just spoken her mind in a song. However, Cuiqiao's desire to sing prompts her to search for something beyond both the songs and the soldier's promise. Gu Qing's political ideals initially appeal to Cuiqiao because they propose equality for women. Gu argues with her father that women shouldn't be forced into arranged marriages and should be given educational opportunities. He 'shows off' his sewing skill to Cuiqiao to demonstrate that men in the Communist Party share responsibilities that are traditionally designated to be women's concerns. However, these apparently feminist principles actually marginalise Cuiqiao in their own ways. The rhetoric of equality is underwritten by a process of masculinisation that inscribes the ideology of masculinity as the norm in which everyone may 'equally' participate. The film illustrates this process by contrasting the cinematic representation of Cuiqiao's singing with that of the waist-drum dance at Yan'an. Cuiqiao's songs—as yet 'unassimilated' by the revolution—are sung to sentimental orchestral accompaniment and linked, by means of parallel editing, to images of nature which are filmed in natural lighting and extreme long shots, minimally edited in slow panning long takes. Combined with the shadowy images of Cuiqiao's solitary figure and markers of her feminised labour (a water-bucket, a spinning-wheel, a bellows), these sequences reinforce the association of 'pre-revolutionary' folk culture with femininity, which is in turn associated with emotions and nature. By contrast, the waist-drum dance is filmed in a well-lit open space, edited at a frenzied pace, and foregrounds the male dancers' expressionless faces and highly co-ordinated movement. The image of disciplined and masculine collectivity bears a resemblance to the rain dance performed by male peasants at the end of the film. The parallel suggests that the 'revolutionary transformation' of folk songs marginalises feminine 'bitterness' in the same way that the rural patriarchal order, in a desperate bid for survival (during a famine), also substitutes 'bitterness' with collective discipline. The particular feminist rhetoric of Gu Qing's assignment is thus unwittingly complicit with a suppression of femininity in the interest of organisational discipline and ideological certainty.

There is, however, one very important and suggestive difference between the two scenes I compared above. In contrast to the high-angled long shots which film the rain dance as a spectacular upsurge of mass energy, the waist-drum dance is filmed in the style of hand-held motion photography. The systematic and co-ordinated movement of the dancers is incongruously represented in erratic and jerky shots.

A shot/counter-shot links this agitated perspective to a close-up of the hesitant and anxious expression of Gu Qing watching as an onlooker. When the waist-drum dance becomes the object of Gu Qing's gaze – in short, the gaze of someone who has submitted himself to the Maoist pursuit of the 'mass line' – its status as 'revolutionary culture' becomes extremely unstable. Uncertainty and anxiety lurk beneath revolutionary ardour and discipline. What has the soldier learnt from (the failure of) his assignment that produces this moment of anxiety? What is the relation between his lesson and Cuiqiao's? I shall consider this question by discussing the most prominent figure of elusiveness in the film: nature.

RESPECT

Images of nature abound not only in the film, but also in Cuiqiao's folk songs, the aesthetic of which is related to the film's cinematography. Cuiqiao's songs always juxtapose a natural imagery (the frozen yellow river in June) with a social situation (being forced by one's father to get married). There is, however, no semantic link that would compel the listener to make a specific correspondence between the two. It is thus impossible to establish whether the frozen river resembles the situation of forced marriage or the girl's sorrow, or whether it is simply the scenery in front of her eyes when she sings. Similarly, the film's cinematography uses jump cuts to juxtapose images of Cuiqiao's singing to that of the natural landscape, without diegetically connecting the two. Images of nature are thus not exhaustively assimilated to the narrative movement of both Cuiqiao's songs and the film's plot.

The film thus suggests that nature cannot be assimilated to the soldier's assignment and, by extension, the revolutionary project of the Chinese Communist Party that, like all other great revolutions of its time, is tied to the ideology of modernisation. One of the soldier's biggest blunders during his visit is his failure to understand the peasant's reverence for the natural landscape. In response to Gu's disrespectful laughter when he ritually sprinkles grains onto the ground before eating, the peasant says: 'You young people would not understand. This piece of yellow earth – you tread on it, step after step; you plough it, mile after mile. How can you not respect it?' What appears to the soldier to be merely a superstitious ritual signifies the peasant's particular lived

relation to the land. Unlike the soldier's 'revolutionary' attitude towards rural life, the peasant does not regard nature simply as raw material. The yellow earth enables his livelihood but is not reducible to that function. The 'respect' it demands from him is a marker of this irreducibility.

The film also pays respect to nature precisely by its refusal to assimilate it, visually or diegetically, to an exhaustive signifying function. The dramatic sequence of Cuiqiao's departure illustrates the critical import of this gesture of respect. The camera cuts from a long shot of Cuiqiao rowing her little boat into the Yellow River to extreme long shots of the natural landscape wherein the human figure has disappeared from sight. The significance of the editing remains unclear. Has nature 'swallowed' her boat, thus rendering her desire and agency irrelevant? Or has it carried her to the other side, thus providing a bridge between her desire and concrete changes? There is nothing in the cinematography or the subsequent narrative to supply the link between these images. The fate of Cuiqiao – as well as the role nature plays in it – remains ambiguous. As Cuiqiao sets out into the river, we hear her sing the revolutionary song that the soldier taught her brother. The last line of the song is, however, not completed: 'The salvation of the people/ Depends on (the) Communist –.' Curiously overlooked by many critics, it is only the word 'Party' and not the word 'Communist' that has been silenced by the sounds of wind and water. Just as Cuiqiao may have survived, so the salvation of the people may depend, not on the Party – which is shown to have failed to live up to its promise, a failure ironically caused by its own ideological rigidity – but the utopian ideal (communism) it claims to serve. In contrast to the project of the Party, which seeks to suppress feminised figures of uncertainty, the film respectfully gives in to the irreducibility of nature. Images of nature are irreducible to the limits of signification imposed by the act of filming/reading, in the same way that folk songs are not reducible to their function as raw material in the service of the revolution.

This strategy of editing is used again at the very end of the film, in a similarly respectful act of refusal to assimilate the figure of the peasantry. This sequence shows the soldier's return to the village. It is unclear if he has come to continue his unfinished project, to (belatedly) fulfil his promise to Cuiqiao, or to start something new. The film cross-cuts between shots showing the soldier walking away from the horizon, and that of the peasants performing the rain dance. Hanhan stands out amongst the peasants as he waves to the soldier and desperately tries to run against the crowd to meet him. At the end of the sequence, the soldier has disappeared from view and the final shot simply shows an image of the infertile earth. Does the soldier finally meet up with Hanhan or does the frenzied crowd keep them separate? Echoing the uncertainty of Cuiqiao's fate, the film again refuses to supply the answer. This closing image of the earth is accompanied by Cuiqiao's voice singing the words of the revolutionary song, not to the original melody, but to the melody of her bitter tune. This song does not belong to the scene of that frame because Cuiqiao is either dead or has joined the army and is nowhere near the village during the drought. The song signifies the fulfilment of the soldier's assignment: a harmonious and mutual assimilation between the folk and the revolutionary. It remains an impossible utterance under the circumstances presented to us in the film, and thus exists in this last shot only as a ghostly echo, recalling the truncated song (and the as yet undelivered promise of communism) that circulates over the natural landscape after Cuiqiao has disappeared from the scene.

These ambiguous 'openings' in the film – Cuiqiao's departure and the soldier's questioning gaze and return to the village – are products of the Party's initial project, even though they are not its intended results. They are accidental corollaries of the revolutionary project, unaccounted for by its projections and subversive of its authority. Historically, such openings were consistently and ruthlessly shut down so that the authority and ideological certitude of the Party could be maintained.[16] The film poses the challenging question: What if these openings were pursued rather than suppressed? It critiques the revolutionary history of the People's Republic of China on its own terms, while revealing the unrealised utopian potential of that history. What is impossible to articulate, and remains ambiguous within the diegetic logic of the film, becomes figures for what may be possible elsewhere, outside the medium of film and under different historical conditions.

NOTES

1. Mao Zedong, 'Zai Yan'an wenyi zuotanhui shan de jianghua' ('Talk at the Yan'an Forum on Literature and Art'), in Mao Zedong Xuanji (Selected Works of Mao Zedong), vol. 3 (Beijing: Renmin chubanshe, 1991), 866. English translation in Mao Zedong On Art and Literature (Beijing: Foreign Language Press, 1960), 19.

2. For a summary of the film's critical reception at the time of its release, see Geremie Barmé and John Milford, ed., Seeds of Fire: Chinese Voices of Conscience (New York: Hill and Wang, 1988), 251–269.

3. Esther Yau, 'Yellow Earth: Western Analysis and a Non-western Text', Wide Angle, 11, no. 2 (1989): 22–33.

4. Mary Ann Farquhar, 'The "Hidden" Gender in Yellow Earth', Screen, 33, no. 2 (1992): 154–164.

5. Rey Chow, 'Silent is the Ancient Plain: Music, Filmmaking and the Conception of Reform in China's New Cinema', Discourse, 12, no. 2 (1990): 87–89.

6. Ibid., 96–99.

7. Stephanie Donald, 'Landscape and Agency: Yellow Earth and Demon Lover', Theory, Culture and Society, 14, no. 1 (1997): 97–112.

8. Chow, 'Silent is the Ancient Plain', 94.

9. Donald, 'Landscape and Agency', 110–111.

10. Chen Kaige, 'Breaking the Circle: the Cinema and Cultural Change in China', Cineaste, 17, no. 3 (1990): 29.

11. Gayatri Spivak, In Other Worlds (New York: Routledge, 1988), 182.

12. Cited in Lin Yu-Sheng, Crisis of Chinese Consciousness (Madison: University of Wisconsin Press, 1979), 77.

13. Mao, 'Xin minzu zhuyi de wenhua' ('The Culture of New Democracy'), Xuanji, 2 (January 1940): 707–708; Mao, On Art and Literature, 75.

14. Mark Selden, The Yenan Way in Revolutionary China (Cambridge: Harvard University Press, 1971), 276.

15. Mao, 'Yan'an zuotanhui' ('Yan'an forum'), Xuanji, 1012; Mao, On Art and Literature, 117.

16. See Merle Goldman, Literary Dissent in Communist China (Cambridge: Harvard University Press, 1967) for an account of the consequence of dissent within the Chinese Communist Party (especially from cultural workers) during the revolutionary period; and her China's Intellectuals: Advise and Dissent (Cambridge: Harvard University Press, 1981) for the post-revolutionary period under Mao's regime.

25   *Yi Yi*: Reflections on Reflexive Modernity in Taiwan

David Leiwei Li

If Fredric Jameson's well-known treatise in *The Geopolitical Aesthetic* put Edward Yang (Yang Dechang) on the map of Anglo-American academic criticism, the director's cinematic mapping of Taipei over the decades has culminated most masterfully in *Yi Yi* (2000). The film won the Best Director prize at Cannes, garnering long overdue popular renown for a serious artist, whose oeuvre articulates the local condition of transnational capitalism in manners 'more deeply symptomatic and meaningful than anything the enfeebled centre still finds itself able to say'.[1] While Yang's thematic elaboration of originality and copy in *Yi Yi* is, following Jameson's suggestive judgment on *Terrorizer*, 'archaically modern', the film's treatment of men mired in money and mobility is exemplary of a 'post-modern' 'proliferation of the urban fabric that one finds in the First and Third Worlds alike'.[2] Jameson's brilliant take on Yang dismantles the conceptual binary of East and West as tradition versus modernity, enabling readings that recognise both the border-transcending flow of global commerce and the reflexive capacity of residual local cultures.

It is in this interpretive promise, ironically, that Jameson's generous inclusion of Yang within the post-modern sentiment of the deceased subject and displaced morality seems to come short. For him, Yang's Taipei becomes synonymous with any 'international urban society of late capitalism' where 'moral judgements are irrelevant'.[3] While the disintegration of extended and nuclear family forms and the decentring of the self are everywhere evident in *Yi Yi*, Yang does not seem to subscribe to the inevitability of a post-modern planetary amorality or the demise of artistic agency. It may be helpful if we break the stranglehold of the modern and post-modern debate to situate Yang's work – and by extension, artistic productions from all societies whose historical experience of capitalism is both relatively recent and radically condensed – in the framework of 'reflexive modernity'.

Developed by Ulrich Beck, Anthony Giddens and Scott Lash, 'reflexive modernity' shares with 'post-modernity' the recognition that the organised capitalism of earlier industrialisation is over. However, contrary to post-modern dystopic resignation to the impossibility of truth claims, proponents of reflexive modernity seize the tumultuous global transition to disorganised capitalism as a moment of reflection and reorganisation. Since this phase of modernity has set free individuals from such collective structures as 'class, nation, [and] the nuclear family', they argue, it must be viewed 'with the decline of influence on agents of class structures', 'with the crisis of the nuclear family and the concomitant self-organization of life narratives'. Reflexivity is thus at once structural and subjective, in which agents are called upon to reflect on the 'rules' and 'resources' of dysfunctional structures and to institute self-regulation against the 'heteronomous monitoring' or externally imposed governance of the previous era.[4] *Yi Yi*'s representation of the Taiwanese family in 'Wei Ji' or 'crisis' stands as Yang's most illuminating reflection to date on the 'jeopardy' and 'opportunity' of reflexive modernity. (The Chinese word 'Wei Ji' or 'crisis' is made of two characters that, read independently, mean 'jeopardy' and 'opportunity'.) The film reveals that Taiwan's transition to satellite state in the late capitalist universe and 'silicon island' in the information age has heralded a fundamentally new experience of time and space, which in turn demands an appropriate ethical imperative.[5]

1.

The film opens with a wedding, sandwiches a birth in the middle and ends with a funeral. Beyond its focus on the multi-generational family, it also includes its members' interactions with neighbours, friends, schools, businesses, the local city space, and the global sphere of media and commerce. If the cradle to grave story suggests a traditional narrative linearity, the imaging of radiating global city space reminds one of the 'concentric circles' that inform both Tu Weiming's neo-Confucian revival and Martha Nussbaum's working of the Stoics.[6] Both posit an ideal of social affinity that extends from the individual self, to the immediate family, to the local community, and onwards to national and global societies. The problem, however, is that the sense of beginning and ending requisite for any narrative and the solidity of a centre, necessary for the sustenance of the ever-extending circles, are not at all self evident. For in reflexive, late or post-modernity, individuals are no longer significantly or singularly interpellated into the biological family, or for that matter, into the biological destiny.

Yang frames this difficulty earlier on with the wedding pictures. First is the ideal composition of the big family photo: families and friends saunter over and gather under the lush canopy for a group picture that symbolises the vitality of 'the living tree' and its ever-expanding roots and branches.[7] The serenity of nature's green, however, is followed by the crimson red of the banquet hall that suggests less festivity than the intense heat of contention. The groom's old flame, Yunyun, literally bursts into the wedding party, vociferously accusing the bride of hijacking her man while frantically apologising to the groom's mother for failing to become her daughter-in-law. Amid the commotion and confusion, the gigantic photo blow-up of the newlyweds, Adi and Xiaoyan, is misplaced. Heads down towards the floor, smiles turned into grimaces, it reverses optical logic just as the obvious pregnancy of the bride disrupts the old social sequence of marriage and child bearing. No wonder Popo, the grandmother of the family, withdraws from the ceremony and suffers shortly afterwards a stroke that puts her into a coma.

The doctor prescribes that the family 'talk with' grandma to stimulate her brain and enhance her chances of revival. What is meant as therapy for the ancestor on life support, however, turns out to be torture for the progeny. Son and groom Adi, the self-proclaimed champion talker, assures his mom that he is out of his money trouble but soon runs out of words to say. Daughter Minmin gets so depressed by the poverty of her daily routine and the perfunctory minutes by Popo's side she cannot help but weep. A sagacious matriarch of a bygone age and a retired teacher who cannot talk, let alone instruct, Popo is Edward Yang's object-correlative for the newly built-in obsolescence of the old filial authority while the breakdown of generational interlocution is his overall figure of familial disintegration.

What Yang cinematically exposes in terms of 'the great transformation' in Taiwan, or historically mixed and compressed modernity in East Asia, coincides with what Alisdair MacIntyre engages in his philosophical critique of the Enlightenment Project.[8] Both seem preoccupied with the consequences of the disappearance of both the density of social fibre and the teleological understanding of individual destiny. Though unquestionably liberating, the kind of instrumental rationality underlying the formation of the sovereign modern individual is for MacIntyre ultimately unsatisfactory, because it is devoid of significant societal dimensions and detached from a 'narrative' and thus a social conception of the good:

> The key question for men is not about their own authorship; I can only answer the question 'What am I to do?' if I can answer the prior question 'Of what story or stories do I find myself a part?' We enter human society, that is, with one or more imputed characters – roles into which we have been drafted – and we have to learn what we are in order to be able to understand how others respond to us and how our responses to them are apt to be construed.[9]

While sharing MacIntyre's insistence on the ascriptive or given condition of the self and its necessary imbrication with the discursive and the historical, Yang is hardly as prepared as MacIntyre to evoke the construction of traditions and 'local forms of community' that are pre-modern in historical origin and relatively enclosed socially.[10] The director of *Yi Yi* is not 'after virtue' in the abstract; he is more interested in revealing how the 'imputed characters' or given roles of individuals have necessarily become more complex after modernity and how under conditions of globality the 'local forms of community' are no longer bounded by its own centripetal energy.

2.

The attenuation of filial linearity as the central motif of self-actualisation coincides with the everyday dispersion of activities: individuals in reflexive modernity are living on multiple planes with ever-expanding social horizons. Yang figures this world of layered complexity and blurring boundaries with his ingenious use of abundant glass in metropolitan architecture, which, whether in Tokyo or in Taipei, is the transnational space his characters traverse. Unlike masonry walls, glass panes mark space without total delimitation, suggesting permeability, liquidity and flexibility, typical of the age of transnational capitalism or reflexive modernity. Yang foregrounds the visual prominence of the glass immediately before the presentation of Ota (the Japanese computer legend) when NJ and his colleagues ride in Dada's car, debating rescue plans and exit strategies. One suggests searching for a copycat Ota in Taipei while another banters about Dada's retirement to San Francisco. The characters appear one moment through the windshield and disappear the next in the curve of the auto-glass, as the reflection of office buildings in the uniform international box style rolls over, engulfing their visage. Yang conveys through the medium of glass the intertwined connectivity and intricate fluidity between global capital flow and the motion of business and people. But this double play of transparency and reflexivity also becomes a larger metaphor for the collapse of the older binaries that Jameson describes as the 'depth model', such as 'essence and appearance', 'latent and the manifest', and 'authenticity and inauthenticity'.[11]

Although implicitly privileging the depth and composure of character more favoured in the earlier modernity and capital of 'inner direction', Yang shows that the 'other direction' of reflexive subjectivity is more symptomatic of the material abundance of a consumer society. Yang shares David Riesman's analysis that yesterday's telos-driven self-discipline of 'inner direction' is yielding to a peer prompted and mass communication mediated 'other direction' of today.[12] And he is especially sensitive to the sway of that 'other direction' on his characters when Taiwanese society swings far more suddenly than American society did towards a post-industrial information economy. Minmin's anguish about life's monotony is a case in point. After an extraordinarily long take, the camera steers away from the sobbing

Minmin, the mirror image of her back and the semi-open venetian blinds filtering the intermittent light of car traffic below. Her husband NJ pauses, looking at his wife pensively, and turns his back to close their bedroom door and shield the children from the sorrow. The camera cuts to a long shot outside the apartment, with street lamps in the distance, headlights rushing towards us and the reflection of the house lights mixed together on the same plane of vision. The apartment next door is then illuminated at the upper-left corner of the screen, showing the silhouettes of lovers in a bitter squabble against the indifference of nocturnal city motion. The camera pans in towards the domestic sphere of Minmin as NJ paces towards the window, and slowly closes the venetian blinds as though to contain the troubles. We can no longer see the inside but we are overwhelmed by the outside: the windowpane-reflected urban panorama of pitch darkness is broken by dotted white lights, the neighbours' bickering now commingling with Minmin's whimpering.

Glass as a visual trope of dimensions that one can see through or dimensions that are overlaid with reflection and refraction thereby comes to denote horizontal 'other direction' in reflexive modernity, a dialogical formation of subjectivity that displaces the centrality of the linear 'inner direction' of old. Glass also figures the growing indistinguishability of the inside and outside that Michael Hardt and Antonio Negri describe as characterising the generation of 'imperial subjectivity'. 'The enclosures that used to define the limited space of the institutions have broken down,' they argue in *Empire*, 'so that the logic that once functioned primarily within the institutional walls now spreads across the entire social terrain.'[13] The sequence on Minmin we have followed amply illustrates the invasion of the outside, or the internalisation of the external, that engenders much psychological and social instability. Husband and wife are not the principal agents of their own ennui but subjects in conversation with other social forces in a much larger nexus of economic and emotional exchange. The transparency and reflexivity of the glass enables the camera's panning to establish visual simultaneity and spatial complementarity not only between the two apartments but also their relation to the city as an engine of social as well as individual change. Although the residents may entertain the illusion of their sovereign existence in separate units, Yang convinces us that they actually inhabit the same condominium of 'the lonely crowd' and without optimal escape routes.[14]

To drive this point home, the director frames Minmin before a mammoth window again, this time at her office. We see her at the beginning of the shot almost completely immersed in the gloom, standing motionless and staring blankly at the void, which as we recognise all too quickly is the reflection of the city below. In the distance is the reflection of the steady flash of a stop signal positioned precisely where Minmin's heart would be if we had X-ray vision. The audience is absorbed in the rhythmic beat of the red light at the intersection of a far away surface street, the perpetual swishing of the tires on the nearby freeway the only sound audible. The heart is where the light is, their separate pulses regulated by a parallel surge of synergy and a parallel arrest of stagnation. The human–machine interface is figured in this over-layering, a breathtaking image of the total interpenetration and interpellation of society and subjectivity, and of exteriority and interiority. 'Haven't you gone back yet?' inquires Nancy after she steps into the office. After a long-drawn-out moment, Minmin replies, 'I have nowhere to go.'

3.

The sense everywhere of having nowhere to go is surely symptomatic of reflexive modernity, a global risk society whose predicament is defined by Ulrich Beck as 'unintentional self-dissolution or self-endangerment'.[15] As NJ puts it to the comatose Popo after Minmin has left home, 'I am not sure about anything these days. Every morning, I wake up feeling uncertain.' 'If you were me,' he asks Popo, 'would you like to wake up?' The vanishing certainty about old social structures and systems of knowledge entails the use of a new decentralised expert system, according to Anthony Giddens, wherein the reflexivity and circularity of social know-how can help the subject change her condition of action.[16] Minmin's retreat to the Buddhist temple, a Chinese equivalent of the therapist's couch in the West, certainly indicates how the traditional folk or new age spirituality can reclaim authority alongside other burgeoning expert systems in late modernity. But this does not hide director Edward Yang's distrust of the expert: the master monk is later shown to be a travelling priest, coming down the mountains apparently to recruit NJ but returning happily with his fat cheque. For Yang finally, self-reflexivity will have to involve self-reflection, not reflection as the bouncing back and forth of images or the superficial suturing of subjectivity but as the possession of knowledge and the apprehension of totality.

This reflective search for knowledge is also couched in the film as a cinematic dialectic of vision. As the boy protagonist Yangyang puts it to his father NJ, 'I can only see what it is in front of me and not what's behind. Does it mean that we can only see half of the world?' Yangyang is evidently a junior alter ego of Director Yang. With all his intellectual precocity, Yangyang is concerned about vision and cognition in at least two different senses. One is the urge to transcend partial and peripheral for holistic vision, an attempt at grasping social and spatial interdependency and integrity. The other is the desire to recognise a temporality of sight, to couple the forward-looking eye/I with the history of its own immanence and the origin of its imminent becoming. If Yangyang pictures the rear of people's heads to enable their self-perception, the director of *Yi Yi* wants to locate the failure of constructing totality in the post-modern fracturing of time and space and at the same time recuperate its possibility.

Ironically, the loss of holistic vision results from a contemporary saturation of vision – a vision of life burdened with sensorial overload and its absolute satisfaction. 'Fatty' tells Tingting after their trip to the movies that the invention of cinema has extended human life: 'the experience we get through the movies at least doubles what we experience in real life.' To illustrate, he cites the movie as a manual for murder. Only when Fatty is arrested for that crime does the audience realise the importance of cinematic foreshadowing. The boundary between fantasy and reality has been abolished while the pursuit of intensified virtual experience in actuality becomes Yang's apt allegory of moral collapse. Not rejecting modern technologies and the enrichment of life movies and video games can bring, Yang encourages his audience to keep sight of the life narrative.

If the audience has so far been frustrated by the random dispersal of families and friends, they are illuminated by the sequence of frames that inter-cut NJ and 'Sherry' with Tingting and Fatty. On learning of NJ's business visit to Ota, his now married first love

Sherry flies from Chicago to Tokyo to meet him. The camera captures both waiting at a Japanese commuter train station, catching up on old times and new stories. 'I get jealous as my daughter is growing into a woman,' NJ says, 'knowing that she'll eventually be with someone else.' Before his voice tails off, a passing train obscures NJ and Sherry, and the film cuts to Tingting standing at the corner of a Taipei theatre. As Fatty slowly walks into view the clucking of the train fades into the din of city traffic. Tingting asks, 'What's the time?' 'Nine', replies Fatty. 'It's almost ten now. Eight a.m. Chicago time', Sherry's voice jumps in, just before the film cuts back to her. 'Nine p.m. in Taipei', murmurs NJ as they saunter towards a railroad crossing. Time and space of transnational proportions are radically compressed into living immediacy to exemplify the arrival for some of the condition of a global village. Sherry remarks on the crossing's resemblance to the one near their school, harking back in late modern Japan to a modernising Taiwan three decades ago. 'That's long gone,' NJ updates her, 'but I remember the first time I held your hand there, before our going to the movies.' We hear this as the camera cuts from the quiet night of the Japanese town to the hustle and bustle of the Taipei street crossing, where Tingting and Fatty are waiting for the pedestrian light, silently holding hands. 'I'm holding your hand once again,' continues NJ's voice, speaking to Sherry off screen, 'only at a different place, at a different time, at a different age.' The lens closes in on Tingting and Fatty, hands clasped together, crossing the street, as Sherry's voice finishes NJ's sentence, 'but the same sweaty palm'.

In his cinematic correlation of romance across separate international time zones, different generations and varied speeds of motion, Yang signifies both generational distinctions and identity. The remarkable simultaneity of overlapping concentric circles that exemplifies reflexive modernity is set against the unchanging cycle of the generations, of human procreation, of economic production and of the origination of subjectivity that defies the immediacy of time. The contemporary dispersion of subjectivity in the multiple spheres of work and leisure should not distract us either from an awareness of our origins or an anticipation of our demise. While global capital's perpetual manufacturing of difference and engineering of sensation threatens to compact our sense of time into ephemeral pleasures, we ought

The same sweaty palm across generations and geopolitical time zones.

not to lose sight of such simple beauty as the generational repetition and duration of locked hands and hearts. *Yi Yi* is not content with merely stating the finitude of human life; it wants the recognition of this finitude to effectively counter a normative conception of time in late modernity as instantaneously self-fulfilling.

Fatty's formula of experiential expansionism in the episodic mode thus provides the backdrop against which NJ's deliberation resolutely rails. Indeed, NJ's interlude with Sherry in Japan is not fundamentally different from the flights of fancy that plague Fatty or his in-laws, neighbours and friends, who all wish for the thrill of novel experience. There are no impeccable characters on Yang's late modern landscape immune to the passage from industrialising society to a consumer one with their respective cultural logics, the 'delay of gratification' for one and the 'delay of payment' for the other.[17] However, some are less vulnerable and more capable than others to recall Yangyang's dialectical tale of hindsight and foresight, to weigh the excitement of the moment with the progression of a chosen trajectory.

After considerable reflection – in postures evocative of Auguste Rodin's 'The Thinker', one in a silhouette behind a Japanese screen and another on an embankment stretching out to the ocean – NJ turns down Sherry's proposal to start their life anew, and goes back to his Taipei family and company. With Popo's death and Minmin's return, Yang has finally brought the couple together in the same frame for the first time in the film, reminiscing about their absence from each other:

> NJ: How was it up in the mountains?
> Minmin: It was OK. In fact, it was not that different. It was as if they [the monks] were talking to Mom, except our roles were reversed. They were like me and I was like my mother. They took turns talking to me about the same things, repeating them several times a day. I've come to realise that so much is in fact not complicated. But why did they ever appear so?
> NJ: Right. Can I say this? While you were away I had a chance to relive part of my youth. I thought that if I had had the opportunity to do it again, things would have turned out differently. They turned out pretty much the same. I suddenly realised that even given a second chance, I would not really need it. It is quite unnecessary.

If Minmin has emerged from the confusing complexity of reflexive modernity by grasping the kernel of simplicity underneath, NJ has refrained from the tantalising prospect of a fresh start and an apparent alternative to his perceived rut. Having wandered lonely as a cloud in the lonely crowd, husband and wife have literally landed on their bed, an image of re-embedding after their disembedding ventures into the exhilarating unknown.[18]

The reconciliation of the couple hinges on a shared refusal of endless experiential experiments, and a restoration of binaries, boundaries and brakes (traffic lights and slow or stop signs abound in the film as cautions against reckless movements and unbridled mobility). For Minmin, the recognition that appearance can be deceiving leads to her conviction of an inarticulate essence. For NJ, that essence is

defined by his reconceived needs and obligations as opposed to his equally reticent and ultimately repressed wants. Both have embraced, through their individual routes of discovery, a generational cycle of perpetuity that entails a limitation of individual gratification. The centrifugal forces of reflexive modernity that engender much confusion for Yang's characters have finally occasioned the reflection necessary for self-regulation and re-organisation to occur.

Although the site of the biological family appears the cinematic centre of this recuperation from and within radiating reflexive modernity, the film is not endorsing a model of traditional patrilineal governance. An earlier coupling of Popo and Tingting's hands, the symbolic gesture of affection and affinity between maternal grandma and granddaughter, for instance, receives its visual encore in Tingting and NJ towards the movie's closing, suggesting a disruption of paternal heritage as well as the preservation of kindred sentiments.[19] A similar logic of the visual duet is at work in the film's successive frontal framing of Tingting and NJ, Yangyang and NJ, and Ota and NJ together behind the windshield, intimating a transgender, transgenerational and transnational solidarity of spirit, at once locally embedded and embodied yet befitting contemporary globality. By contrast, Adi's ride with NJ is shot from behind just as NJ is put in the passenger seat when Dada drives: neither seems NJ's true fellow traveller nor shares with him his ideal universe. If Adi's crass materialism is condemned in the rapid boom and bust of his fortune, Dada's chase of Ato, the copycat of Ota that cannot deliver, is a lesson against instant profits. The kind of instrumental reason or rational choice that matches means to ends economically turns out neither ethical nor efficient. Whether it is in the arena of emotional or economic transaction, those who seek short-term interests fare much worse through Yang's lens than those who are committed to the durability of reciprocal benefits.

Such mild melodramatic manichaeism is reminiscent of Henry James and Balzac's unveiling of the 'moral occult', a 'domain of spiritual forces and imperatives that is not clearly visible' but 'believe[d] to be operative' in a 'desacralised' post-Enlightenment world.[20] An exemplary film at the turn of a new millennium, *Yi Yi* provides a similar yet more radical dramatisation of Taiwan's passage into another world of risk-ridden modernity. There, the providential is no longer viable, the filial and the local no longer stable, yet rediscovery of the ethical imperatives that used to depend on them remains vital. Edward Yang seems to have possessed an identical urge as the masters of early modernity to register into consciousness the power of the residual, to recover a weakened sense of historicity, a narrative conception of the self and a teleology of the human species. Cultural capital properly belonging to a previous era yet not entirely eradicated in the mixed and compressed modernity of Taiwan seems to hold promise: Tingting, Yangyang, NJ and Ota are emblems not of the past but of the potential of our planet where 'the end of history' is yet the indeterminate future.[21]

'I'm sorry, Popo. It wasn't that I didn't want to talk to you. I thought whatever I told you, you would have already known', Yangyang says in tribute to Popo at her funeral. 'I know so little, Popo. But you know what I'll do when I grow up? I will tell people what they do not know and show them what they cannot see.' Reflexive modernity finally requires that social 'knowledge spiral in and out of the universe of social life, reconstructing both itself and that universe as an integral part of that process'.[22] The film has shown us a world of jet travel, bullet trains and instant electronic transfer of money, image and information. But it has also illuminated the incontrovertible limits of nature on human life, Popo's death being the most striking sign, despite the scientific overcoming of space and time. Yangyang's remark thus implies that the ever-expanding circles of social knowledge, enabled by the liberating technologies of global modernity, must be appropriated with full recognition of nature's limits and the cycle of the species.

'Throughout human history,' argues Zygmunt Bauman, 'the work of culture consisted in sifting and sedimenting hard kernels of perpetuity out of transient human lives [and] actions, in conjuring up duration out of transience', and in 'transcending thereby the limits imposed by human mortality by deploying mortal men and women in the service of the immortal human species'. It is not incidental that Bauman deploys the past tense in his summary of that history, for 'demand for this kind of work is', as he puts it, 'shrinking'.[23] Bauman's concern with the waning of such demand and the devaluation of immortality is Edward Yang's as well, for both are

preoccupied with the decisive turning point in human history when the sovereign individual – the figure of 'Yi', 'the One' – is becoming the figure of hegemony in global modernity. No one can fully anticipate the consequences of globalisation as a radical individualisation of culture, but it may not be premature to recall a cultural outlook that has sustained the divergent groups of humanity thus far. 'I miss you, Popo, especially when I see my still nameless newborn cousin. I remember that you always say that you feel old. I'd like to tell my cousin,' the boy Yangyang declares, 'I feel old too.' Childhood and age, and innocence and experience finally converge in this articulation of a continuous life narrative, and with it, a reiteration of an ethical imperative so often submerged in the fragments of late modernity. Unlike the pre-modern resignation to fate and or a postmodern deferral of death in instant consumption, Yangyang's signification on Popo's silence suggests a collective triumph over atomic mortality, a cultural transcendence of the individual earthly sojourn. The film Yi Yi has come to affirm a sense of purposeful time in order to embody a notion of spatial and social relatedness, a version of neo-Confucianism perhaps, or the tenets of a planetary communitarianism regardless of civilisational origins.[24]

NOTES

1. Fredric Jameson, *The Geopolitical Aesthetic: Cinema and Space in the World System* (Bloomington: Indiana University Press, 1995), 155.
2. Ibid., 121, 117. For an informative Chinese language study of Yang's film career up to *A Confucian Confusion*, see Huang Jianye, *A Study of Yang Dechang's Films (Yang Dechang Dianying Yanjiu*: Taipei: Yuanliu, 1995).
3. Ibid., 128.
4. Ulrich Beck, Anthony Giddens and Scott Lash, *Reflexive Modernization: Politics, Tradition and Aesthetics in the Modern Social Order* (Stanford: Stanford University Press, 1994), 115–116.
5. 'Silicon island' is Yang's reference to Taiwan in his comments on the DVD version of *Yi Yi* (New York, Windstar TV and Video, 2001). All English dialogue in the text is based on this edition's subtitles and my own translation.
6. See Tu Weiming, 'Human Rights as a Confucian Moral Discourse', in *Confucianism and Human Rights*, ed. Wm. Theodore de Bary and Tu Weiming (New

York: Columbia University Press, 1998), 297–307; and Martha C. Nussbaum, 'Patriotism and Cosmopolitanism', in *For the Love of Country*, ed. Joshua Cohen (Boston: Beacon, 1996), 2–17.

7. See Tu Weiming, *Dædalus*, 120, no. 2 (1991): *The Living Tree: The Changing Meaning of Being Chinese Today*.

8. See Robert M. Marsh, *The Great Transformation: Social Change in Taipei. Taiwan Since the 1960s* (Armonk: M. E. Sharpe, 1996); and Alisdair MacIntyre, *After Virtue: A Study in Moral Theory* (Notre Dame: Univesrity of Notre Dame Press, 1984).

9. Ibid., 216.

10. Ibid., 263. See also John Haldane, 'Maclntyre's Thomist Revival: What Next?', in *After MacIntyre: Critical Perspectives on the Work of Alisdair MacIntyre*, ed. John Horton and Susan Mendus (Notre Dame: University of Notre Dame Press, 1994), 91–107.

11. Fredric Jameson, *Postmodernism, or, The Cultural Logic of Late Capitalism* (Durham: Duke University Press, 1992): 12.

12. David Riesman, *The Lonely Crowd: A Study of the Changing American Character* (New Haven: Yale University Press, 1961), 14–25.

13. Michael Hardt and Antonio Negri, *Empire* (Cambridge: Harvard University Press, 2000): 196.

14. Riesman, *The Lonely Crowd*.

15. Beck et al, *Reflexive Modernization*, 176.

16. Ibid., 187.

17. Zygmunt Bauman, *Life in Fragments: Essays in Postmodern Morality* (Oxford: Polity Press, 1995), 5.

18. This resembles the denouement of Zhou Xiaowen's *Ermo*, as I analyse in my essay, 'What Will Become of Us if We Don't Stop? *Ermo*'s China and the End of Globalization', *Comparative Literature*, 53, no. 4 (2001): 442–461.

19. NJ is practically married into Minmin's family since Popo is his mother-in-law. The scenario of Tinging and Nainai, or her paternal grandma, holding hands would suggest some sort of straight patrilineal descent.

20. See Peter Brooks, *The Melodramatic Imagination: Balzac, Henry James, Melodrama, and the Mode of Excess* (New Haven: Yale University Press, 1976; 1995), 15, 20–21.

21. Francis Fukuyama, 'The End of History?', in *Globalization and the Challenges of a New Century*, Patrick O'Meara, Howard A Mehlinger and Matthew Klein (Bloomington: Indiana University Press, 2000), 161–180.

22. Anthony Giddens, *The Consequences of Modernity* (Stanford: Stanford University Press, 1990), 15–16.

23. Zygmunt Bauman, *Liquid Modernity* (Cambridge, Polity University Press, 2000), 126.

24. See Tu, 'Human Rights', 299, and also Daniel Bell, *Communitarianism and its Critics* (New York: Clarendon Press, 1993).

Chinese Names

Compiled by Wang Dun

This list consists of characters for Chinese names that appear in the essays in this volume. The names included are personal names for filmmakers, actors, and characters, as well as those of authors of Chinese-language publications. The list is organised alphabetically according to family name. However, the names are given as they appear in the essays. For example, 'Maggie Cheung' is listed under 'C' for 'Cheung'. Because there are no standard translations or transcriptions for Chinese names, different translations of the same name may appear in different essays. In these cases, each translation receives a separate entry.

A Cheng	阿城	Chen Duxiu	陈独秀	Fei Mu	费穆
A Gui	阿贵	Chen Gongbo	陈公博	Fleur	如花
A Ying	阿英	Chen Kaige	陈凯歌	Fu Honglian	符红莲
A'Gui	阿桂	Chen Kengran	陈铿然	Fu Shizhuan	符诗专
A'Rong	阿荣	Chen Mo	陈墨		
A'Ze	阿泽	Chen Shui-bian	陈水扁	Mr. Gao	高先生
Adi	阿弟	Chen Wu	尘无	Mrs. Gao	高太太
Ah Cheng	阿城	Chen Xue	陈雪	Ge You	葛优
Ah Mei	阿梅	Chen Yanyan	陈燕燕	General Lu	鲁将军
Ah Wah	阿花	Chen Zhaorong	陈昭荣	General Shi	石将军
Ann Hui	许鞍华	Cheng Dieyi	程蝶衣	Gong Li	巩俐
Aunt Yee	珊三仪	Cheng Pei Pei	郑珮珮	Gu Hua	古华
Ba Jin	巴金	Maggie Cheung Man-yuk	張曼玉	Gu Qing	顾青
Bai Xianyong	白先勇	Cheung Po-tsai	張保仔	Gu Shengzhai	顾省斋
Baosi	褒姒	Jacky Cheung	张学友	Guan Jinpeng	关锦鹏
Bei Cun	北村	Leslie Cheung	张国荣	Guigui	桂桂
Bi Yan Hu Li	碧眼狐狸	Maggie Cheung	張曼玉	Guo Moruo	郭沫若
Black Monster	黑山老魔	Chiao Hsiung-ping	焦雄屏		
Bu Wancang	卜万苍	Ching Siu-tung	程小东	Han Bangqing	韩邦庆
		Chow Mo-wan	周慕云	Han Yingjie	韩英杰
Cai Chusheng	蔡楚生	Chow Yun Fat	周润发	Hanhan	憨憨
Cai Guorong	蔡国荣	Chow Yun-fat	周润发	He Chunrui	何春蕤
Chai Xiaofeng	柴效锋	Stephen Chow	周星驰	He Qiwu	何奇武
Anthony Chan Yau	陈友	Cuiqiao	翠巧	He Yi	何一
Jackie Chan	成龙			He Zhuoxian	何焯贤
Chang Che	张徹	Dada	大大	Hong Changqing	洪常青
Chang Chen	张震	Dai Jinhua	戴锦华	Hong Ling	洪凌
Chang Cheng	張珍	Daji	妲己	Hong Shanqing	洪善卿
Chang Chung-hsiung	張俊雄	Dame Huang	黄二姐	Hou Hsiao-hsien	侯孝贤
Chang Hsiao-hung	张小虹	Deng Guangrong	邓光荣	Hou Xiaoxian	侯孝贤
William Chang Suk-ping	张叔平	Deng Xiaoping	邓小平	Hsu Yoshen	许佑生
Eileen Chang	张爱玲	Ding Naifei	丁乃非	Hu Jinquan	胡金铨
Terence Chang	張家振	Director Gu	谷燕山	Hu Ke	胡克
William Chang	张叔平	Douzi	豆子	Hu Yuyin	胡玉音
Chen Baoxu	陈宝旭	Duan Xiaolou	段小楼	King Hu	胡金铨
Chen Baozhu	陈宝珠			Hua Mulan	花木兰
Chen Chuhui	陈楚惠	Ermo	二嫫	Huang Ailing	黄爱玲

Huang Cuifeng	黄翠凤	Li Pingqian	李萍倩
Huang Jianxin	黄建新	Li Tie	李铁
Huang Jianye	黄建业	Jet Li	李连杰
Huang Ren	黄仁	Liang Qichao	梁启超
Hui Yuan	慧圆	Liang Shanbo	梁山伯
Hung Hung	鸿鸿	Liang Xin	梁信
Sammo Hung	洪金宝	Lin Niantong	林年同
		Lin Nong	林农
Jade Fox	碧眼狐狸	Brigitte Lin	林青霞
Jiang Wen	姜文	Ivy Ling Boh	凌波
Jiang Xun	蒋勋	Little Broadcast	小广播
Jiaorui	娇蕊	Liu Chenghan	刘成汉
Jiu'er	九儿	Liu Huiqin	刘惠琴
Judou	菊豆	Liu Jinxuan	刘晋喧
Juxian	菊仙	Liu Wendian	刘文典
		Liu Yanyun	柳艳云
Kao Li	高立	Liu Yichang	刘以鬯
Ke Jiazhi	柯嘉智	Lo	罗小虎
Ke Junxiong	柯俊雄	Loh Tih, Betty	乐蒂
Ke Yizheng	柯一正	Lu Buwei	吕布韦
King You	(周) 幽王	Lu Guozhu	陆国柱
King Zhou	(商) 纣王	Lu Hao-tung	陆皓东
Stanley Kwan	关锦鹏	Lu Jue	卢珏
		Lu Xun	鲁迅
George Lam Chi-Cheung	林子祥	Lu Yi-ching	陆弈静
Edward Lam	林弈华	Lu Yukun	吕玉堃
Ringo Lam	林岭东	Luo Bu	罗补
Lao Lao	姥姥	Luo Mingyou	罗明佑
Lao She	老舍	Luo Xiaohu	罗小虎
Lao Zhao	老赵	Luo Zaier	罗载而
Andy Lau Tak-Wah	刘德华	Luo Zhuoyao	罗卓瑶
Carina Lau	刘嘉玲	Luo Zifu	罗子富
Law Kar	罗卡		
Clara Law	罗卓瑶	Ma Guoguang	马国光
Lee Ching	李菁	Season Ma Si-San	马斯晨
Lee Kang-sheng	李康生	Mao Zedong	毛泽东
Ang Lee	李安	Mei-mei	美美
Bruce Lee	李小龙	Men Da	门达
Leo Ou-fan Lee	李欧梵	Mencius	孟子
Lillian Lee	李碧华	Mengmu	孟母
Waise Lee	李子雄	Mengzi	孟子
Lei Zu	嫘祖	Miao Miao	缪淼
Tony Leung Chiu-wai	梁朝伟	Miao Tien	苗天
Leung Foon	梁欢	Minmin	明明
Tony Leung Kar-fei	梁家辉	Mo Yan	莫言
Tony Leung	梁朝伟	Anita Mui	梅艳芳
Li Bai	李白		
Li Bihua	李碧华	Nan Batian	南霸天
Li Cheuk-to	李焯桃	Naribilige	纳日碧力戈
Li Guoxiang	李国香	Ng Ho	吴昊
Li Han-Hsiang	李翰祥	Nie Er	聂耳
Li Hung-chang	李鸿章	Nie Xiaoqian	聂小倩
Li Lili	黎莉莉	Ning Caichen	宁采臣
Li Mangeng	黎滿庚	Nuozha	哪吒
Li Mu Bai	李慕白	Nüwa	女娲
Mark Li Ping-Bin	李屏宾		
Ouyang Nian	欧阳年		
Rebecca Pan	潘迪华		
Peter Pau	鲍德熹		
Peng Hsiao-yen	彭小妍		
Peng Xiaolian	彭小莲		
Popo	婆婆		
Pu Songling	蒲松龄		
Qin Shutian	秦书田		
Qiu Miaojin	邱妙津		
Qu Yuan	屈原		
Rong Weijing	荣韦菁		
Ruan Lingyu	阮玲玉		
Shaw Brothers	邵氏兄弟		
Shaw Runme	邵仁逸		
Shen Congwen	沈从文		
Shen Fu	沈浮		
Shen Fu	沈复		
Shen Xiaohong	沈小红		
Shen Xiaoyin	沈晓茵		
Shi Wenhong	史文鸿		
Shi Xiangsheng	施祥生		
Shitou	石头		
Shu Lien	俞秀莲		
Sima Qian	司马迁		
Sima Xiaojia	司马小加		
Songlian	颂莲		
Su Li-zhen	嚟丽珍		
Sun Yat-sen	孙中山 (孙逸仙)		
Sun Yu	孙瑜		
Tang Jishan	唐季珊		
Tan Xinpei	谭鑫培		
Tang Xiaobing	唐小兵		
Tao Dechen	陶德辰		
Tao Yufu	陶玉甫		
Stephen Teo	张建德		
Tian Han	田汉		
Tian Zhuangzhuang	田壮壮		
Tingting	婷婷		
Tsai Ming-liang	蔡明亮		
Tsui Hark	徐克		
Tu Wei-ming	杜维明		
Wai-Tung	伟同		
Wang Chenwu	王尘无		
Wang Dehou	王得后		
Wang Fengkui	王凤奎		
Wang Jie'an	王介安		
Wang Liansheng	王莲生		
Wang Qiushe	王秋赦		
Wang Shuo	王朔		

Wang Xiaoshuai	王小帅	Xie Jin	谢晋	Zhang Junzhao	张军钊
Wang Xifeng	王熙凤	Xie Tieli	谢铁骊	Zhang Liang	张良
Wang Yichuan	王一川	Xu Baoqi	徐宝琦	Zhang Nuanxin	张暖忻
Wang Yunman	王云缦	Xu Xianchun	许显纯	Zhang Shichuan	张石川
Wang Zuxian	王祖贤	Xu Xingzhi	许幸之	Zhang Xuan	张煊
Wei Ming	韦明			Zhang Yi	张毅
Wei Minzhi	魏敏芝	Yam Kim-fei	任钊辉	Zhang Yimou	张艺谋
Wei Yu	魏育	Simon Yam	任达华	Zhang Yiwu	张颐武
Wei, Vicky	魏莜惠	Yan	燕大侠	Zhang Yuan	张元
Wei-Wei	威威	Yan'er	雁儿	Zhang Zhen	张震
Wong Ching-chin	黄程展	Yang Dechang	杨德昌	Zhang Ziyi	章子怡
Wong Fei-hung	黄飞鸿	Yang Huizhen	杨慧贞	Zhao Dan	赵丹
Wong Kar-wai	王家卫	Yang Kuei-mei	杨贵媚	Zhao Shuxin	赵书信
Butterfly Woo	胡蝶	Edward Yang	杨德昌	Zhenbao	振保
John Woo	吴宇森	Yangyang	洋洋	Zheng Junli	郑君里
Wu Hao	吴昊	Yanli	烟鹂	Zheng Xiaoqiu	郑小秋
Wu Nianzhen	吴念真	Herman Yau	邱礼涛	Zheng Yunbo	郑云波
Wu Qionghua	吴琼花	Michelle Yeoh	杨紫琼	Zheng Zhengqiu	郑正秋
Wu Tian	吴天	Yu Dafu	郁达夫	Zhou Changmin	周昌民
Wu Yonggang	吴永刚	Yu Jiaolong (Jen)	玉娇龙	Zhou Shuangyu	周双玉
Wu Ziniu	吴子牛	Yu Min	于敏	Zhou Shuangzhu	周双珠
		Yu Xiulian	俞秀莲	Zhou Xiaowen	周晓文
Xia Yan	夏衍	Yuan Shaolou	袁少楼	Zhou Xuan	周璇
Xiao Fangfang, Josephine	萧芳芳	Yuen wo-ping	袁和平	Zhu Jian	朱剑
Xiao Guangbo	小广播	Yunyun	云云	Zhu Shilin	朱石麟
Xiao Kang	小康			Zhu Shuren	朱淑人
Xiaosi'r	小四儿	Zhang Che	张徹	Zhu Tianwen	朱天文
Xiaoyan	小燕	Zhang Damin	张大民	Zhu Wenshun	朱文顺
Xiaoyu	小玉	Zhang Fengyi	张丰毅	Zhu Xijuan	祝希娟
Xiazi	瞎子	Zhang Huike	张慧科	Zhu Yingtai	祝英台
Xie Fei	解飞	Zhang Huizhen	张惠贞	Zhuangzi	庄子

Chinese Film Titles

Compiled by Wang Dun

This list includes all the characters for the titles of Chinese films as they appear in the essays in this volume. The list is organised alphabetically according to the English translations of the titles. Because there are no absolutely standard translations of film titles, different translations of the same Chinese title are used in some essays. In these cases, each English translation receives a separate entry.

The Actress	阮玲玉	*Flowers of Shanghai*	海上花	*National Hero Zheng Chenggong*	英雄郑成功
After Separation	大撒把	*Flowers Reborn*	再生花	*New Camille*	新茶花
As Tears Go By	旺角卡門	*Flying Dragon, Leaping Tiger*	龍騰虎躍	*The New Woman*	新女性
Ashes of Time	东邪西毒			*New Women*	新女性
Au Revoir Shanghai!	再会吧，上海	*Garlands at the Foot of the Mountain*	高山下的花环	*No Regrets About Youth*	青春无悔
Autumn Moon	秋月	*Gen Y Cops*	特警新人類 2	*Not One Less*	一个都不能少
		Girls of a Special Economic Zone	特区打工妹		
A Better Tomorrow	英雄本色	*The Goddess*	神女	*On the Hunting Ground*	猎场扎杀
Between Life and Death	阴阳界	*Good Men Good Women*	好男好女	*One and Eight*	一个和八个
The Big Mill	大磨坊	*A Good Woman*	良家妇女	*Opera Heroes*	梨园英烈
Black Cannon Incident	黑炮事件			*The Opium War*	鸦片战争
Boat People	投奔怒海	*Happy Time*	幸福时光	*Orchid in the Ravine*	空谷兰
The Boy From Vietnam	来客	*Happy Together*	春光乍泄		
Boys from Fenggui	风柜来的人	*The Harbour*	海港	*Peach Blossom Weeps Tears of Blood*	桃花泣血记
The Boys from Fengkuei	风柜来的人	*Hero*	英雄	*The Peach Girl*	桃花泣血记
Bullet in the Head	喋血街头	*Hibiscus Town*	芙蓉镇	*A Personal Memoir of Hong Kong*	念你如昔
		Hold You Tight	愈快乐愈堕落	*Plunder of Peach and Plum*	桃李劫戏梦人生
Camel Xiangzi	骆驼祥子	*The Hole*	洞	*Puppetmaster*	倩女幽魂
Centre Stage	阮玲玉	*Home, Sweet home*	我想有个家		
Children of the Storm	风云儿女	*Horse Thief*	盗马贼	*Raise the Red Lantern*	大红灯笼高高挂
Children of Troubled Times	风云儿女			*Rebels of the Neon God*	青少年哪吒
A Chinese Ghost Story	倩女幽魂	*In Our Time*	光阴的故事	*The Red Detachment of Women*	红色娘子军
Chungking Express	重庆森林	*In the Mood for Love*	花样年华	*Red Firecracker, Green Firecracker*	炮打双灯
A City of Sadness	悲情城市	*Island Tales*	有时跳舞	*Red Rose, White Rose*	红玫瑰与白玫瑰
Classic for Girls	女儿经			*Red Sorghum*	红高粱
Come Drink with Me	大醉侠	*Joyous Heroes*	欢乐英雄	*Remarriage*	重婚
Coming Back	归来	*Judou*	菊豆	*Return*	归来
A Confucian Confusion	独立时代			*The River*	河流
Conned Once	上一当	*Keep Cool*	有话好好说	*The Road Home*	我的父亲母亲
Crouching Tiger, Hidden Dragon	卧虎藏龙	*The Killer*	喋血双雄	*Rouge*	胭脂扣
Crows and Sparrows	乌鸦与麻雀	*King of Children*	孩子王	*Rouge Tears*	胭脂泪
		King of the Children	孩子王		
Dawn Over the Metropolis	都会的早晨			*Sacrificed Youth*	青春祭
Days of Being Wild	阿飞正传	*A Lady of Shanghai*	上海一夫人	*The Sandwich Man*	儿子的大玩偶
Declawing the Devils	斩断魔爪	*Lan Yu*	蓝宇	*Sea of Fragrant Snow*	香雪海
Devils on the Doorstep	鬼子来了	*The Legend of Tianyun Mountain*	天云山传奇	*The Sea of Fragrant Snow*	香雪海
Ding Jun Shan	定军山	*Li Shuangshuang*	李双双	*Secret Guards in Canton*	羊城暗哨
The Dove Tree	鸽子树	*Liang Zhu*	梁祝	*Shaolin Soccer*	少林足球
Dust in the Wind	恋恋风尘	*Life*	人生	*The Shepherd*	牧马人
		Lin Family Shop	林家铺子	*Sister Flowers*	姊妹花
The Emperor and the Assassin	荆柯刺秦王	*Little Toys*	小玩意	*Sketch of a Fool's Life*	二百五小传
The Enchanting Shadow	倩女幽魂	*Love Eternal*	七彩胡不归	*Song of the States*	国风
Enemy of Women	女性的仇敌	*Love Eterne*	梁山伯与祝英台	*Sparkling Fox*	火狐
Ermo	二嫫	*The Love of Three Oranges*	三桔之恋	*Stage Sisters*	舞台姐妹
Evening Bell	晚钟			*The Story of Qiuju*	秋菊打官司
		Maternal Radiance	母性之光	*The Story of Woo Viet*	胡越的故事
Fallen Angels	堕落天使	*The Mermaid*	鱼美人	*Summer at Grandpa's*	冬冬的假期
Farewell China	爱在他乡的季节	*My Memories of Old Beijing*	城南旧事		
Farewell My Concubine	霸王别姬	*Mysterious Travelling Companions*	神秘的旅伴	*Temptation of a Monk*	诱僧
Fate in Tears and Laughter	啼笑姻缘			*Ten O'clock on the National Holiday*	国庆十点钟
A Fishy Story	不脱林的人	*Nanjing Massacre*	南京大屠杀	*Terrorizer*	恐怖分子
Floating Life	浮生	*The National Anthem*	国歌		

A Time to Live, a Time to Die	童年往事	*Wayside Flowers*	野草闲花	*Woman Soccer Player No.9*	女足九号
The Troubleshooters	顽主	*Wedding Banquet*	喜宴	*Women's Story*	女人的故事
Three Modern Women	三个摩登的女性	*The Wedding Banquet*	喜宴		
A Touch of Zen	侠女	*What Time Is It Over There?*	你那边几点?	*Yang + Yin: Gender in Chinese Cinema*	男生女相
Two Stage Sisters	舞台姐妹	*White Haired Girl*	白毛女	*Yanzhi Kou*	胭脂扣
		The Willow Shade Account	柳荫记	*Yellow Earth*	黄土地
The Untold Story	八仙饭店之人肉烧包	*Woman*	女人	*Yi Yi*	一一
		Woman Basketball Player No.5	女篮五号		
Vive L'Amour	爱情万岁				

LIST OF ILLUSTRATIONS

Whilst considerable effort has been made to correctly identify the copyright holders, this has not been possible in all cases. We apologise for any apparent negligence and any omissions or corrections brought to our attention will be remedied in any future editions.

Black Cannon Incident (*Hei pao shi jian*), 1986, Xi'an Film Studio/Manfred Durniok Film- und Fernsehpr; *Boat People* (*Tou bun no hoi*), 1982, Bluebird Movie Enterprises; *Bullet in the Head* (*Die xue jie tou*), 1990, John Woo Film/Golden Princess Film Productions; *Centre Stage* (*Ruan Ling-yu*), 1992, Canal +/Golden Way/Paragon Films/Golden Harvest; *A Chinese Ghost Story* (*Sinnui yauman*), 1987, Cinema City Co./ Film Workshop Co. Ltd; *Chungking Express* (*Chong qing sen lin*), 1994, Jet Tone Production; *Crouching Tiger, Hidden Dragon* (*Wo hu zang long*), 2000, United China Vision Incorporated/UCV LLC/Edko Films/Zoom Hunt International/Columbia Pictures/Sony Pictures/Golden Harvest; *Crows and Sparrows* (*Wuya yu maque*), 1949, Kunlun Film Company; *Ermo*, 1994, Shanghai Film Studio/ Ocean Film Company; *Evening Bell* (*Wan zhong*), 1989, China Film/August First Studio; *Farewell My Concubine* (*Ba wang bie ji*), 1993, Tomson Films/China Film Co-production Corp./ Beijing Film Studio; *Floating Life*, 1996, Hibiscus Films; *Flowers of Shanghai* (*Hai shang hua*), 1998, Shochiku Co. Ltd/3H Films; *The Goddess* (*Shennu*). 1934, Lianhua Film Company; *Hibiscus Town* (*Fu rong zhen*), 1986, Shanghai Film Studio/China Film Corporation; *In the Mood for Love* (*Fa yeung nin wa*), 2000, Jet Tone Production/ Block 2 Pictures/Paradis Films/Orly Films; *Love Eterne* (*Liang Shan Ba yu Zhu Ying Tai*), 1963, Run Run Shaw; *Not One Less* (*Yi ge dou bu neng shao*), 1999, Guangxi Film Studio/Beijing New Picture Distribution Co.; *The Red Detachment of Women* (*Hong se niang zijun*), 1961, Tianma Film Studio; *A Time to Live, A Time to Die* (*Tong nien wang shi*), 1985, Central Motion Picture Corporation; *A Touch of Zen* (*Xai Nu*), 1969, International/Union Film Company; *Vive L'Amour* (*Aiqing wansui*), 1994, Central Motion Picture Corp./ Sunny Overseas Corp./Shiung Fa Corporation; *Wedding Banquet* (*Hsi yen*), 1993, Central Motion Picture Corp./Good Machine; *Yellow Earth* (*Huang tu di*), 1984, Guangxi Film Studio; *Yi Yi*, 2000, Atom Films/1+2 Seisaku Iinkai/Pony Canyon/Omega Project/Hakuhodo.

Index

2001: A Space Odyssey, 13

Abbas, Ackbar, 25–6, 29n16, 38n19, n28, 49–50, 52, 54n4, n12, n16, 128, 131, 132, 134n1, 135n9, n10, n14, n18
Adams, Eddie, 29n10
Ah Cheng, 107
Agamben, Giorgio, 28, 30n31
American Beauty, 98
An American in Paris, 124
Anagnost, Ann, 127n20, 158n9
Ansen, David, 134n7
Antze, Paul, 158n8
Aoyama, Shinji, 131
Apollon, Willy, 14n13
Appadurai, Arjun, 135n17
Apter, David E., 158n9
Arendt, Hannah, 45n1, 87n15
As Tears Go By, 128
Ashbrook, John, 54n19
Ashes of Time, vi, 48, 128, 132
Assayas, Olivier, 135n25
Augustin, roi du Kung Fu, 134
Autumn Moon, 98, 101, 134n5
Aw, Annette, vi, 2, 5, 137

Ba Jin, 166n18
Bai Xianyong, 163, 166n19
Bakhtin, Mikhail, 143n14
Baldwin, James, 37
Balzac, 126n5, 189n17, 203, 205n20
Bardem, Javier, 56
Barker, Michael, 56
Barlow, Tani E., 79n1, 95n8, 143n15
Barmé, Geremie R., 126n3, 197n2
Barrymore, Lionel, 112
Battsek, Daniel, 57
Bauman, Zygmunt, 204, 205n17, n23
Bazin, André, 87
Beck, Ulrich, 198, 201, 204n4, 205n15
Bei Cun, 81, 82, 87n10
Bell, Daniel, 205n24
Benjamin, Walter, 39, 45, 45n1, 70–1, 72n24, n25, n27, 76, 79, 80n8, n13, 84, 87n15
Bernard, Tom, 57

Berry, Chris, vi, vii, 1, 8, 14n2, n4, n9, 64n37, n44, 71n3, 95n5, 110n12, 150, 173n1, 174n16, 179, 181n4, 182n7, n9, n18, 183, 189n5, 190n28
Bersani, Leo, 33, 38n17
A Better Tomorrow, 131
Between Life and Death, 83, 84, 88n18
Bhabha, Homi, 45, 46n14, 100
Biers, Dan, 63n3, n7
The Big Mill, 83, 84
Binetti, Vincenzo, 30n31
Binoche, Juliette, 56
Black Cannon Incident, 5, 8–14
Blonde Venus, 112, 113
Bloom, Irene, 167n5
Blue Kite, 122
Boat People, 7, 15–22
Bodman, R.W., 127n16
The Boy from Vietnam, 15
The Boys from Fengkuei, 105, 109, 160, 163
Bordwell, David, 1, 2, 7n3, 25, 26, 28n11, 29n6, n9, n17, 45n2, 52, 55n26, 169, 173n10
Bori, Alessandro, 37n4
Braester, Yomi, vi, 4, 5, 89, 150
Braudy, Leo, 191n29
Brewster, Ben, 29n22
Britten, Andrew, 41
Britton, Celia, 30n22
Brooks, Peter, 126n5, 185, 186, 189n17, 190n25, 205n20
Browne, Nick, 14n1, 22n4, 120, 126n2, n7, n8, 159n13, 185, 188, 189n9, n16, 190n22, n29
Brunetta, Gian Piero, 165n1
Bu Wancang, 32, 34, 36, 115
Buck, Pearl, 121
Buck-Morss, Susan, 76, 80n8
Bullet in the Head, 5–6, 23–30
Burgwinkle, William, 14n8
Burston, Paul, 143n10
Butler, Judith, 38n11, 45, 46n15, 138, 143n9, n19, n23

Cai Chusheng, 33, 34, 36
Cai Guorong, 185, 190n20, n21

Carson, Diane, 38n35
Caruth, Cathy, 30n32
Casablanca, 120
Casarino, Cesare, 30n31
Centre Stage, 2, 6, 31–8, 119n33, 134, 135n24
Chai Xiaofeng, 79n6
Chambers, Simone, 127n22
Chan, Anthony, 22n12
Chan, Felicia, vi, 1, 4, 56, 184
Chan, Natalia Shui Hung, 37n4
Chan, Jackie, 3, 57, 62, 103n4, 130, 134, 167, 171
Chang Che, 36
Chang Chen, 58, 62
Chang Chung-hsiung, 58
Chang, Eileen, 34, 173n4
Chang Hsiao-hung, 176, 181n4
Chang, Jung, 121
Chang, Michael G., 38n13, n24, n29, n33, n36
Chang, William, 48, 130
Charles, John, 16, 17, 22n4
Chen Baichen, 65, 71n2
Chen Baoxu, 182n20
Chen Baozhu, 143n7
Chen Bo, 118n2
Chen Duxiu, 192
Chen Gongbo, 114
Chen Huaikai, 92–3, 95
Chen Kaige, 4, 30n32, 36, 61, 74, 81, 82, 86, 87n4, n10, 89, 90, 92, 95n6, 96n12, n14, 97, 137, 149, 168, 191, 192, 197n10
Chen Kuan-Hsing, 135n16
Chen Mei, 14n4
Chen Mo, 85–6, 87n10, 88n21, n22, n23, n30
Chen Wu, see Wang Chenwu
Chen Yanyan, 33, 34, 36
Chen Zhao-rong, 175
Cheng Jihua, 71n1, n2, 118n23, 119n39
Cheng Pei Pei, 58, 62
Cheng, Scarlet, 58, 63n21, 64n27
Chen Xue, 177, 182n13
Cheng Yin, 157
Cheuk Pak Tong, 173n16

Cheung, Jacky, 24
Cheung, Joe, 59
Cheung, Leslie, 40, 41, 42, 43, 45, 91, 92, 100, 137
Cheung, Maggie Man-yuk, 31, 32, 34, 35, 37, 128, 130, 134
Chi, Robert, vi, 5, 152
Chi Yun, 167n13
Chiang Kai-shek, 17, 65, 69
Chiang Su-hui, 103n20
Chiao Hsiung-Ping Peggy, 64n44, 165n1, 166n8, 182n7, n8, n20
Children of Troubled Time, 88n26
Chinatown, 97
A Chinese Ghost Story, 2, 6, 39–46, 134n5
Ching, Leo, 135n16, n17
Chion, Michel, 69, 72n21
Chow, Rey, vi, 1, 2, 6, 29n4, 30n32, 38n20, 46n7, 63, 64n45, 79, 79n2, 81n23, 108, 110n6, n13, n15, 113, 118n17, 144, 150n3, 191, 197n5
Chow, Stephen, 59
Chow Yun-fat, 62, 103n4, 131
Chu, Henry, 63n16, n18
Chu, Myong-gon, 135n16
Chung, Thomas, 59
Chungking Express, 3, 6, 47–55, 128, 130
Ci Jiwei, 154, 159n10
Ciecko, Anne T., 79n1
Cimino, Michael, 25, 29n8
City of Sadness, vii, 7n1, 108, 110n1, 160, 162
Clark, Paul, 158n3
Clover, Carol, 6, 39, 40, 41, 42, 46n3, n5
Cohen, Marshall, 30n25, 190n29
Cohen, Myron, 126n10
Cole, Nat King, 133
Collins, Jane L., 150n5
Come Drink with Me, 169
Conned Once, 94
Connerton, Paul, 153, 158n5
Conrad, Joseph, 44, 46n13
Corliss, Richard, 134n7
The Corruptor, 97
Cowie, Peter, 22n3, n8, n15
Cox, Jeffrey, 126n12
Creed, Barbara, 46n12
Crouching Tiger, Hidden Dragon 1–2, 4, 5, 56–64, 129, 131, 167, 171, 173n8, 174n20, 184,
Crowe, Russell, 56
Crows and Sparrows 1, 6, 65–72
Cui Shuqin, 37n4, 135n24

Dai Jinhua, 9, 10, 14n5, 79n6, 81, 87n3, n4, 92, 95n8
Dai Limin, 63n15
D'Allesandro, Anthony, 134n7
Dayan, Daniel, 30n23, 110n14, 190n27
Days of Being Wild, 129, 133

Dannen, Frederic, 29n20
Daughter of the Party, 155, 159n11
Davis, Bette, 37
Davis, Darrell W., 30n29
De Bary, Theodore, 167n5, 204n6
De Gaulle, Charles, 128
De Niro, Robert, 52
Debord, Guy, 30n31, 76, 79, 80n9
Declawing the Devils, 9, 10, 11, 12, 13
The Deer Hunter, 25, 27–8, 29n9
Delon, Alain, 134n4
Deleuze, Gilles, 51–4, 54n22, 55n28, n29, n30, n32
Dench, Judi, 56
Deng Guangrong, 134n4
Dergarabedian, Paul, 56
Desser, David, 2, 7n3, 14n2, 103n12, 136n27, 166n9
Devils on the Doorstep, 131
Dietrich, Marlene, 36, 111
Dikötter, Frank, 38n33, n26
Ding Jun Shan, 132
Ding, Naifei, 177, 182n11
Dirlik, Arif, 135n17
Dittmar, Linda, 38n35
Dissanayake, Wimal, 118n16, 135n13, n16, 185, 189n14, n18
Doane, Mary Ann, 32, 33, 38n8, n14
Donald, Stephanie Hemelryk, 157, 158n3, 159n14, 191, 197n7, n9
The Dove Tree, 83, 84, 87n13
Doyle, Christopher, 48, 54n20, 130
Dust in the Wind, 160
Dyer, Richard, 38n10, n18, n34

Eastman, Lloyd E., 118n25
Ehrlich, Linda C., 14n2, 166n9
Ekins, Richard, 143n20
Elley, Derek, 15, 22n3
Ellickson, Lee, 54n7
Elsaesser, Thomas, 189n15
The Enchanting Shadow, 46n4
Enns, Anthony, 30n24
Erens, Patricia Brett, 16, 17, 22n4, n5, n9
Ermo, 2, 4, 73–80, 205n18
Escher, M.C., 13, 14n11
Eternal Love, 143n7
Eureka, 131
Evans, Caroline, 143n10
Evening Bell, 2, 81–8

Fallen Angels, 54n5, 100, 128, 130
Farewell China, 98, 99, 101
Farewell My Concubine 4, 5, 36, 81, 89–96, 122, 137, 168
Farquhar, Judith, 79
Farquhar, Mary, vi, 1, 2, 5, 7n2, 8, 14n2, n9, 87, 167, 173n1, 174n16, 189n5, 191, 197n4

Farmer, Brett, 135n24
Fate in Tears and Laughter, 95
Fei Mu, 115
Feldstein, Richard, 14n13
Felman, Shoshana, 30n32
Fingarette, Herbert, 126n9
Fischer, Lucy, 118n9
First Strike, 97
A Fishy Story, 22n12
Floating Life, 2, 4, 97–103
Flowers of Shanghai, 2, 7, 104–10
Flying Dragon, Leaping Tiger, 59
Ford, John, 120
Foster, Hal, 103n6
Foucault, Michel, 31, 37n5, 73, 79, 79n3, 110, 153, 177
The Four Hundred Blows, 20
Freud, Sigmund, 6, 27, 28, 30n27, 32, 37n7, 38n41, 77, 80n15
Friedberg, Anne, 77, 80n12
Friedman, Lester D., 22n10
Frodon, Michel, 167n14
Fu, Ping, vi, 2, 4, 73
Fu Poshek, 2, 7n3, 103n12, 136n27
Fu Shizhuan, 173n2, 174n18
Fukuyama, Francis, 205n21
Fuss, Diana, 38n24

Gamman, Lorraine, 143n10
Garland, Judy, 33, 36
Garlands at the Foot of the Mountain, 87n11, 156
Galeta, Robert, 54n22
Gao Yuan, 121
Gateward, Frances, 150n3
Ge You, 94
Gelder, Ken, 134n5
Gen-Y Cops, 59
Gibson, Mel, 19
Giddens, Anthony, 198, 201, 204n4, 205n22
Giese, Diana, 103n8, n16
Gilbert, Helen, 103n14
Gilda, 32, 38n8
Giles, Herbert A., 46n4
Gillett, John, 20, 22n13
Gilloch, Graeme, 72n25, n27, n28
Gilroy, Paul, 135n12
Girls from the Special Economic Zone, 73
Gish, Lillian, 112
Gledhill, Christine, 119n13, 156, 159n13, 189n9, n15
Glissant, Édouard, 23, 28
Goankar, Dilip P., 135n12
Godard, Jean-Luc, 47
The Goddess, 2, 3, 4, 32, 34, 111–19
Goldhammer, Arthur, 158n6
Goldman, Merle, 197n16
Gong Li, 91, 94

Good Men, Good Women, 160
A Good Woman, 149
Gorbman, Claudia, 72n21
Gough, Jamie, 38n39
Gould, Stephen J., 79n1
Grammaticas, Damian, 53
Grant, Barry Keith, 64n39
Griffith, D.W., 112, 118n6
Grossman, Andrew, 143n12
Gu Changwei, 91
Gu Hua, 120, 122, 125, 126n1
Guzzetti, Alfred, 29n22

Hacking, Ian, 153, 158n7
Hada Michiko, 105, 107
Haft, Lloyd, 167n10
Halbwachs, Maurice, 153, 158n4
Haldane, John, 205n10
Hall, Kenneth E., 29n8
Hammond, Stefan, 29n2, n18
Han Bangqing, 104, 105, 107, 108, 109, 110n10, n11
Han Yingjie, 169–70, 171, 174n15
Hansen, Jeremy, 64n34
Hansen, Miriam, 118n7
Happy Time, 144, 146, 150
Happy Together, 128, 130, 134n5
Hardt, Michael, 30n31, 200, 205n13
Harris, Kristine, vii, 3, 4, 38n20, n31, 111, 119n33
Hayford, Charles, vii, 4, 120, 126n10, 126n12
Hayles, N. Katherine, 29n15
He Ping, 87n5
He Yi, 87n6
Heath, Stephen, 30n23, 110n14
Hegel, Robert, 165n2
Herman, Judith, 30n30
Hershatter, Gail, 118n10
Hibiscus Town, 4, 5, 120–7, 156
Hinsch, Bret, 38n22
Hitchcock, Alfred, 168
Ho, Elaine Yee-lin, 16, 22n5
Hofstadter, Douglas R., 13, 14n11
Hold You Tight, 31
The Hole, 181n1
Hoover, Michael, 2, 7n3, 29n5, n9, n17, 45n2
Horton, John, 205n10
Hou Hsiao-hsien, vii, 5, 7, 49, 54n7, 104–10, 160–6
Hou Jianping, 64n30
Hsia, C.T., 167n7
Hsu Yoshen, 177, 183n12
Hu Die, see Butterfly Woo
Hu Jingquan, see King Hu
Hu Ke, 14n4, 151n10
Hu, King 1, 9, 167–74
Hu Ying, 95n8

Hua, Shiping, 103n20
Huang Ren, 172, 173n2, 174n13
Huang Jianxin, 8, 13, 14n1, 126n7
Huang Jianye, 204n2
Huang Jianzhong, 149
Hui, Ann, 7, 15–22
Hung Hung, 176
Hung, Lucifer, 177
Hung, Sammo, 59
Hunt, Linda, 19
Hunter, Lauren, 56, 63n2

Idema, Wilt, 167n10
In the Mood for Love, 4, 128–36
Irma Vep, 134, 135n25
Island Tales, 31
Iswolsky, Hélène, 143n14

Jackson, Peter A., 190n26
Jacobs, Lea, 118n27
Jakes, Susan, 174n19, n21
James, Henry, 126n5, 189n17, 203, 205n20
Jameson, Fredric, 46n6, 54n11, 66–7, 71n7, n8, 72n30, 79, 97, 103n6, 198, 200, 204n1, 205n11
Jephcott, Edmund, 72n27
Jia Leilei, 88n29, n33
Jiang Hao, 87n10
Jiang Wen, 131
Jiang Xun, 176, 179, 181n2, n6, 182n19
Jin C, 132
Joffe, Roland, 18
Jones, Kent, 135n9, n10
Joyous Heroes, 83, 84, 88n18
Judou, 144
Julien, Isaac, 38n37

Kaldis, Nicholas, 109, 110n16
Kao Li, 139, 141
Kaplan, E.Ann, 118n13, 119n41
Kartomi, Margaret, 133, 135n23
Ke Jiazhi, 181n4
Ke Junxiong, 134n4
Ke Yizheng, 160
Keep Cool, 144
Kelly, Gene, 124
Kennedy, Harlan, 17, 22n9
Keough, Peter, 110n1
Kieslowski, Krzystof, 47
Khoo, Olivia, 136n25
Khoo, Tseen, 103n14
The Killing Fields, 18,
King of the Children, 81, 87n4, 89, 107, 110n6, 149, 192
King, Dave, 143n20
King, Henry, 112
The Kingdom and the Beauty, 138
Kipnis, Andrew, 127n21
Klein, Matthew, 205n21

Klinger, Barbara, 15, 16, 22n2, n6
Koehler, Robert, 63n6
Kouvaros, George, 181n4
Kristeva, Julia, 30n28, 42, 46n11
Kritzman, Lawrence D., 158n6
Kubrick, Stanley, 13
Kung Fu Soccer, 59
Kurosawa, Akira, 54, 57, 61, 168,
Kwan, Stanley, 6, 31–8, 119n33, 135n24, 166n17
Kymlicka, Will, 127n22

Lacan, Jacques, 13, 14n13, 30n28, 37, 38n15, 39, 42, 44, 46n10
The Lady from Shanghai, 87n1
A Lady of Shanghai, 112
Lalanne, Jean-Marc, 38n30, 51, 55n25, 135n10
Lam, Edward, 34
Lam, George, 15, 19, 22n11
Lam, Ringo, 34
Lambek, Michael, 158n7
Lan Yu, 31
Lang, Fritz, 13
Lang, Robert, 118n9
Lao Shi, 166n18
Larson, Wendy, 165n2
Lash, Scott, 198, 204n4
Last Plane Out, 18
Last Year at Marienbad, 48
Lau, Andy, 15
Lau, Carina, 105
Lau, Jenny Kwok Wah, 95n2
Lau, Joseph, 167n19
Law, Clara, 2, 97, 98, 101, 102, 103n17, 134n5
Law Kar, 15, 22n5, 36, 190n20
Lee, Ang, vi, 1, 5, 56–64, 97, 127n18, 138, 143n7, 130, 131, 135n15, 167, 171, 174n20, 176, 183, 184, 185, 189n2, n3, n7
Lee, Bruce, 62, 134n4
Lee Ching, 142
Lee Kang-sheng, 166n21, 175, 179
Lee, Leo Ou-fan, 38n20, 65, 71n3, 162, 166n18
Lee, Lillian, see Li Bihua
Lee, Waise, 24
The Legend of Tianyun Mountain, 156
Leung, Helen Hok-Sze, vii, 4, 37n4, 191
Leung Ping-kwan, 16, 22n4
Leung, Tony Chiu-wai, 24, 105, 107, 128, 130, 133, 134n6
Leung, Tony Ka Fai, 36
Leung, Yvonne, 150
Levie, Matthew, 60–1, 64n36
Leyda, Jay, 158n3
Li Bai, 168
Li Bihua, 93, 96n13

Li Cheuk-to, 16, 19, 22n4, 185, 189n19, 190n20, n21
Li, David Leiwei, 1, 2, 79n1, 198
Li, Han-Hsiang, see Li Hanxiang
Li Hanxiang, 46n4, 137
Li, Jet, 171, 174n19
Li Lili, 34, 36
Li, Mark Ping-Bin, 130
Li, Nancy, 134n2
Li Pingqian, 112
Li Shaobai, 71n1, n2, 118n23
Li Suyuan, 71n14
Li Tie, 143n7
Li Tuo, 58, 63n30
Li Xun, 57
Li Zhenya, 110
Liang Heng, 121, 126n13
Liang Qichao, 109, 110n17
Liao Binghui, 95n2
Lieberman, Sally Taylor, 118n14, 119n36
Life, 115
Lifton, Robert Jay, 158n2
Lii, Ding-Tzann, 136n26
Lin, Brigitte, 36, 49, 54n14
Lin Niantong, 166n16
Lin Nong, 9, 155
Lin Wenqi, 110n5, n18
Lin Wenji, 95n2
Lin Yu-Sheng, 197n12
Ling, Ivy Po, 137, 138–9, 141, 142
Lippman, John, 63n8, n11
Little Toys, 36, 115
Liu Chenghan, 173n2
Liu, Cynthia W., 183, 184, 189n3, n4
Liu Huiqin, 119n40
Liu Weihong, 87n12
Liu Yichang, 128, 132, 134n2
Lo, Jacqueline, 103n14
Lo, Kwai-cheung, 14n8
Loh, Betty Ti, 138, 142
Logan, Bey, 29n21
Long, Barry, 29n20
Loren, Sophia, 54
Lotringer, Sylvere, 50, 54n3, n21
Lou Mingyou, 114
Louie, Kam, vii, 2, 4, 97, 103n4, n7, n20, n23
Love Eterne, 2, 5, 137–143
The Love of Three Oranges, 176
Lu Fei-I, 7n3
Lu Guozhu, 84
Lu Jue, 9
Lu, Sheldon Hsiao-peng, 38n20, 79n1, 92, 95n9, 98, 103n12, 119n33, 151n7, n11
Lu, Tonglin, 122, 126n15
Lu Xun, 161, 166n12, n13
Lu Yanguang, 143n17
Luo Bu, 169, 173n3, 174n12
Luo Zaier, 105

Lutz, Catherine A., 150n5
Lyman, Rick, 138, 143n7
Lynch, David, 47, 48

Ma Guoguang, 168, 172, 173n9, 174n24
Ma, Lili, 103n17
Ma Ning, 126n2, 185, 190n22
Ma, Season, 15
Ma, Sheng-mei, 183, 189n2
MacIntyre, Alistair, 199, 205n8, n10
Madame X, 112
Madsen, Richard, 127n22
The Magnificent Seven, 57, 61
Mamoulian, Rouben, 34
Man, Glenn, 14n8
Mao Zedong, vi, 4, 8, 9, 10, 11, 12, 14n6, 93, 94, 121, 123, 124, 125, 126, 127n17, n19, 158, 191, 192, 193, 194, 195, 197n1, n13, n15, n16
Marchetti, Gina, viii, 97, 103n3, 136n27, 183, 184, 189n1, n3, n8
Marcus, George E., 16, 22n7
Marsh, Robert M., 205n8
Martin, Fran, vii, 2, 7, 175, 181n5, 182n10, n13, 190n26,
Martin, Ron, 135n16
Martinez, David, 135n10
Marx, Karl, 29, 77, 80n15
Mast, Gerald, 30n25
The Matrix, 57
Mazierska, Ewa, 49, 54n6, n8, n10, n11, 135n10
McGrath, Jason, vii, 5, 8
McLuhan, Marshall, 80n11
Mehlinger, Howard A., 205n21
Mehta, Zubin, 145
Mencius, 112
Mendus, Susan, 205n10
The Mermaid, 141
Metropolis, 13
Metz, Christian, 29n22, 168, 174n7
Mercer, Kobena, 38n37
Miao, Cora, 18
Miao Tien, 176, 181n1
Milford, John, 197n2
Miller, Jacques-Alain, 26
Miller, Toby, 3, 7n4
Mitchell, Elvis, 61, 64n38
Mitchell, Juliet, 38n15
Mo Yan, 166n18
Modleski, Tania, 31, 37n6
Möller, Olaf, 37n4
Moore, Charles A., 143n15
Mu Miao, 118n2, 119n37
Mui, Anita, 34
Mulholland Drive, 48
Müller, Marco, 165n1
Munro, Donald J., 190n23
Mulvey, Laura, 26–7, 30n24, n25, 190n27

Murnau, F.W., 42
Murphy, Kathleen, 98, 103n13
My Memories of Old Beijing, 91, 94
Myers, Fred R., 16, 22n7
Mysterious Travelling Companions, 9, 10

Naficy, Hamid, 135n13
Nanjing Massacre, 83, 84, 86
Natale, Richard, 63n1
The National Anthem, 86, 88n25, n31
National Hero Zheng Chenggong, 87
Neale, Stephen, 3, 7n5, 61, 64n39
Negri, Antonio, 200, 205n13
Nelson, David, 18
Neri, Corrado, vii, 5, 160
New Camille, 112
New Women, 34
Ng Ho, 171, 174n22
Ngai, Jimmy, 54n5, 135n10
Ni Zhen, vi, 95n5, 161, 166n9
Nichols, Bill, 30n23, 66, 71n5, 190n27
Nicholson-Smith, Donald, 80n9
Nie Er, 88n26
Nienhauser, William H., 160, 165n3
No Regrets about Youth, 94
Nolte, Nick, 18
Nonini, Donald, 135n16
Nora, Pierre, 153, 158n6
Nornes, Mark Abe, 2, 7n1
Nosferatu, 42
Not One Less, 1, 2, 6, 144–51
Notar, Beth, 79n1
Nussbaum, Martha C., 199, 205n6

Olivier, Laurence, 56
Olds, Kris, 135n16
O'Meara, Patrick, 205n21
Ommundsen, Wenche, 103n17
On the Hunting Ground, 149
One and Eight, 81, 82
Ong, Aihwa, 79, 80n22, 135n16
Opera Heroes, 94–5
The Opium War, 156
O'Regan, Tom, 98, 103n10
Oudart, Jean-Pierre, 108, 110n14
Owen, Stephen, 167n6

Pan Hua, 150n3
Pan, Rebecca, 133
Pappas, Charles, 63n8, n9
Passek, Jean Loup, 38n32, 118n7
Pau, Peter, 58
Peach Blossom Weeps Tears of Blood, 115
The Peach Girl, 32
Peckinpah, Sam, 25, 29n8, n9
Peng Hsiao-yen, 158n1
Peng Xiaolian, 73
The Perfumed Arrow, 139
A Personal Memoir of Hong Kong, 31

Peterson, Margaret, 79n4
Petro, Patrice, 119n30
Pettman, Dominic, 100, 103n15,
Pickowicz, Paul G., 8, 14n1, 22n4, 120,
   126n2, n6, n7, 189n16
Plaks, Andrew H., 190n24
Plummer, Kenneth, 189n10
Plunder of Peach and Plum, 118n4
Polanski, Roman, 97
Polizotti, Mark, 54n3
Power, Bruce, 80n11
Pratt, Leonard, 103n22
Propp, Vladimir, 40, 46n6
Pu Songling, 46n4
Puccini, 145
The Puppetmaster, 95n2, 105, 160
Pym, John, 22n11

Qiu Miaojin, 177, 182n14
Qu Yuan, 160
Les Quatre Cents Coups, 20
Queen Christina, 34
Quiquemelle, Marie Claire, 38n32, 118n7

Rascaroli, Laura, 49, 54n6, n8, n10, n11,
   135n10
Rashomon, 168
Raise the Red Lantern, 87n5, 89, 144, 146
Rayns, Tony, 15, 18, 22n3, n11, 48, 54n2,
   n13, n15, 79n1, n5, 173n6, 181n3
Read, Richard, 181n3
Rebels of the Neon God, 166n21, 175, 176,
   179
The Red Detachment of Women, 5, 152–9
Red Firecracker, Green Firecracker, 87n5
Red Rose White Rose, 34
Red Sorghum, 81, 84, 120, 122, 125, 144,
   146
Rennie, David, 63n13
Resnais, Alain, 47, 48
Ressner, Jeffrey, 131, 135n15
Return, 115
Reynaud, Bérénice, vii, 2, 6, 29n3, n17, 3,
   136n24, 165n1
Richardson, Colin, 143n10
Riesman, David, 200, 205n12, n14
Riley, Jo, 143n21, n24
The River, 166n21, 175, 176, 177, 180,
   181n4, 185n10, n20
Rivière, Danièle, 54n5
Riviere, Joan, 33, 38n12
The Road Home, 144, 146
Robbins, Jerome, 23
Rodin, Auguste, 203
Rofel, Lisa, 95n8
Rolf, Tom, 52
Rong Weijing, 80n19
Rose, Jacqueline, 38n15
Rose, Steve, 63n5

Rothman, William, 113, 115, 116, 118n16,
   119n29, n35, n38
Roudiez, Leon R., 46n11
Rouge, 34, 41, 134n5
Rouge Tears, 117, 119n40, n41
Ruan Lingyu, 31–8, 111, 115, 119n33, 134
Ruiz, Raul, 47, 48
Russo, Vito, 34, 38n9, n21

Sacrificed Youth, 149
Saich, Tony, 158n9
Saith, Ashwani, 80n16
Salvador, 18
The Sandwich Man, 160
Sassen, Saskia, 77, 78, 80n17, n18
Saunders, David, 57, 63n10
Sawada, Kenji, 132
Secret Guards in Canton, 9, 10, 11, 189n11,
   n15
Seven Samurai, 57
Schatz, Thomas, 184–5, 189n11, n12, n13,
   n15
Scorsese, Martin, 52
Scott, L., 46n6
Selden, Mark, 193, 197n14
Selwyn, Edgar, 112
Semsel, George S., 64n30
Sengupta, Somini, 97, 103n2
Sennett, Richard, 80n14
Seno, Alexandra A., 64n34
Shaheen, Jack G., 103n5
Shaolin Soccer, 59
Shapiro, Judith, 121, 126n13
Shen Congwen, 161–2, 166n15, n18
Shen Fu, 9
Shen Fu, 102, 103n22, 161, 162, 164
Shen Xiaoyin, 110n5
The Shepherd, 156
Shepherd, Simon, 38n39
Shi Wenhong, 145, 150n4
Shi Xiangsheng, 151n8
Shih, Shu-mei, 184, 189n7
Short, John Revne, 78, 80n20
Short, Stephen, 174n19, n21
Shorter, Kingsley, 72n27
Shu Kei, 38n32
Siegel, Marc, 132, 135n9, n14
Silbergeld, Jerome, 8,   14n3, n9, 123,
   126n2
Silverman, Kaja, 37, 38n38, n40, 41, 46n10
Sima Qian, 160
Sima Xiaojia, 86
Simmel, Georg, 80n14
The Sin of Madelon Claudet, 112, 117
Sirk, Douglas, 185
Siu, Wang-Ngai, 142n2
Smith, Gary, 72n24
Sobchack, Vivian, 14n1, 22n4, 126n2
Sontag, Susan, 143n22

Spagnoletti, Giovanni, 37n4
Sparkling Fox, 86
Spivak, Gayatri, 192, 197n11
Spottiswoode, Roger, 18
Springer, Claudia, 18–19, 22n10
Spryer, Patricia, 80n7
Stage Sisters, 94–5, 156
Stagecoach, 188
Stanwyck, Barbara, 111
Steen, Andreas, 133, 135n22
Steintrager, John, vii, 5–6, 23
Stella Dallas, 112, 117, 119n41
Stephens, Chuck, 181n3
Stern, Lesley, 181n4
Stock, Jonathan, 133, 135n21
Stokes, Lisa Odham, 2, 7n3, 29n5, n9, n17,
   45n2
Stone, Oliver, 18
The Story of Qiu Ju, 121, 144, 146
The Story of Woo Viet, 15
Straayer, Chris, 38n35
Strachey, James, 30n27
Stringer, Julian, vii, 7, 15, 22n1, 30n24,
   n32, 37n4
Stromquist, Shelton, 126n12
Su Xiaokang, 127n16
Sullivan, Gerard, 190n26
Summer at Grandpa's, 160
Sun Yu, 32, 36, 115
Suzuki Seijun, 132

Tam, King-far, 126n11
Tan, Jessica, 63n14, n18, n19
Tan, See Kam, viii, 2, 5, 137, 143n12
Tan Xin Pei, 132
Tang Jishan, 31, 33
Tang, Xiaobing, 110n17, 158n1
Tao Dechen, 160
Tarantino, Quentin, 47–8, 129–30
Tatara, Paul, 56, 63n4
Taussig, Michael, 80n13
Taylor, Michael, 173n7
Temptation of a Monk, 98
Ten O'Clock on the National Holiday, 10, 11
Teo, Larry, 62, 64n25, n40
Teo, Stephen, 2, 7n3, 16, 22n4, 29n17,
   45n2, 54n9, 62, 64n41, 98, 103n11,
   130, 135n8, n9, n11, 167, 173n4, n5,
   n8, 190n21
Thorpe, Vanessa, 63n12
Tian Han, 86, 88n26,
Tian Zhuangzhuang, 81, 149
Tiau Charn, 138
A Time to Live, A Time to Die, 5, 110,
   160–6
Time Regained, 48
Tinkcom, Matthew, 7n4
To Live, 122
Tobias, Mel, 17, 22n8

Toffler, Alvin, 54n10
Tomlinson, Hugh, 54n22
Tong, Janice, viii, 2–3, 6, 47
The Touch, 59
A Touch of Zen 1, 5, 9, 17, 167–74
The Troubleshooters, 94
Truffaut, François, 20
Tsai Ming-Liang, 47, 166n21, 175–82
Tsui Hark, 34, 57, 134, 167
Tu Wei-ming, 102, 103n19, 135n16, 199, 204n6, n7, n24
Tung, Donna, 58

Udagawa, Koyo, 174n14
Umebayashi, Shigero, 131
Under Fire, 18
The Untold Story, 28

Vidor, Charles, 32
Vidor, King, 112, 117, 118n9, 119n41
Villarejo, Amy, 7n4,
Virilio, Paul, 48, 50, 54n3, n21
Vive L'Amour, 2, 7, 175–82
Viviani, Christian, 118n13
Von Sternberg, Josef, 112

Wallis, Mike, 38n39
Wan, P.P., 127n16
Wang, Ban, 158n2
Wang Ailing, 151n10
Wang Chenwu, 113, 118n4
Wang, David Der-wei, 126n6, 166n18
Wang Dehou, 79n6,
Wang Gungwu, 103n18
Wang Hui, 155, 159n12
Wang Jie'an, 174n11
Wang, Jing, 95n8
Wang, Joey, 40
Wang Ling-chi, 102, 103n18
Wang Luxiang, 127n16
Wang Shuo, 94
Wang Xiaoshuai, 87n6
Wang Yichuan, 79n6, 148, 151n9
Wang Yiman, viii, 1, 6, 65
Wang Yuanjian, 159n11
Wang Yunman, 119n40
Waterston, Sam, 18
Watson, Burton, 165n4
Way Down East, 112, 118n9
Wayne, Valerie, 14n8
Wayside Flowers, 32
Weaver, Sigourney, 19
Wedding Banquet, 2, 5, 176, 183–90
Wei, Vicky, 105
Wei Yu, 118n4, n20
Weir, Peter, 18, 56
Weisser, Tom, 25
Welles, Orson, 87n1
Welsch, Janice R., 38n35

Welsh, Frank, 135n20
West Side Story, 23, 29n9
Widmer, Ellen, 126n6, 166n18
The Wild Bunch, 25, 27–8
Wilkins, Mike, 29n2, n18
Williams, Annwyl, 29n22
Williams, Linda, 119n41, 156, 159n13, 189n9,
Williams, Raymond, 71, 72n29, 78, 80n21
Williams, Tony, 29n7
Wilson, Rob, 135n13, n16
Wing, Betsy, 29n1
Winston, Brian, 67, 71n13
Wise, Robert, 23
Woman Basketball Player No.5, 155–6
Woman Soccer Player No.9, 156
Women's Story, 73
Wong, Nancy Y.C., 79n1
Wong, Valerie, 151n10
Woo, Butterfly, 117, 119n40
Woo, John, 5, 23–30, 57, 167
Woods, James, 18
Woods, Stephen, 55n25
Wright, Stephen, 135n10
Wu Hao, 173n3
Wu, John C.H., 143n15
Wu Nianzhen, 160
Wu Tian, 10
Wu Yonggang, 32, 111–19
Wu Ziniu, 81–8

Xia Hong, 64n30
Josephine Xiao Fangfang, 143n7
Xiao, Zhiwei, viii, 22n1, 118n22, n24, 165n1
Xie Fei, 57
Xie Jin 4, 5, 36, 87n11, 94, 96, 120–2, 125, 126n2, 152, 155, 157, 158, 159n12, n15, 190n22
Xing Zuwen, 71n1, n2, 118n23
Xu Baoqi, 73
Xu, Gang Gary, viii, 2, 7, 104
Xu Xingzhi, 88n26

Yam, Kim-fei, 143n12
Yam, Simon, 24
Yamada, Hirozaku, 174n14
Yang + Yin: Gender in Chinese Cinema, 31, 32, 33, 34, 166n19, 166n22
Yang, Edward Dechang, 1, 131, 160, 198–205
Yang, Gladys, 126n1, 166n15
Yang Kuei-mei, 175, 179, 181n1, 182n17
Yang Yuanying, 150n3
Yar See, 89, 95n3
Yau Ching, 37n4
Yau, Esther C.M., 2, 7n3, 14n1, 22n4, n5, 126n2, 135n9, 158n3, 189n16, 191, 197n3

Yau, Herman, 28
The Year of Living Dangerously, 18, 19
Yeh Yueh-Yu, 2, 7n1, 30n29, 166n16
Yellow Earth, 4, 14n2, 61, 64n37, 82, 79n7, 89, 120, 122, 126, 149, 191–7
Yeoh, Michelle, 59, 62
Yi Yi, 1, 2, 131, 198–205
Yu Min, 84–6, 88n19, n20
Yue, Audrey, vii, viii, 4, 103n14, 128, 135n5
Yuen Wo-ping, 57, 172, 174n20
Yumeji, 132
Yumeji, Takehisa, 132

Zanasi, Margherita, 117
Zarrow, Peter, 121, 126n11, n14
Zeitlin, Judith, 46n4
Zeng Guang, 150n7
Zha, Jianying, 95n1
Zhang, Benzi, 95n4
Zhang Damin, 31, 33, 36
Zhang Fengyi, 91, 94, 137
Zhang Junxiang, 119n39
Zhang Junzhao, 81
Zhang Liang, 73
Zhang Nuanxin, 58, 64n30, 149
Zhang Shichuan, 95, 112
Zhang Xiaoling, 150n6
Zhang Xuan, 86, 87n1, n8, n9, n13, n14, 88n17, n24, n32
Zhang Xudong, 120, 126n4
Zhang Yi, 160
Zhang Yimou, 1, 22n32, 74, 75, 81, 84, 87n5, n10, 89, 95n9, 144, 145, 150n3, n6, n7, 167, 171, 192
Zhang Yingjin, viii, 2, 5, 22n1, 81, 87n5, n11, 88n35, 113, 115, 117, 118n10
Zhang Yiwu, 150n2
Zhang Yuan, 87n6
Zhang Zhuan, 151n3
Zheng Xiaoqiu, 94
Zhao Dan, 68, 72n15
Zheng Junli, 1, 65, 66, 68, 71n9, n10, n11, 72n17, n20, n23
Zhou, Kate, 80n16
Zhou Xiaowen, 4, 73, 75, 78, 79n1, n6, 80n19, 205n18
Zhou Xuan, 72n14, 133, 135n21, n22
Zhu Dake, 122n3
Zhu Jian, 119n40
Zhu Shilin, 115
Zhu Tianwen, 104, 107, 110n2, n7, n8, n9, 160
Zhu Wenshun, 9
Zhuangzi, 102, 103n21
Zhuo Baitang, 173n3
Zizek, Slavoj, 14, 14n10, n13, 30n28
Zito, Angela, 143n15, n16
Zohn, Harry, 45n1, 87n15
Zou, John, viii, 2, 6, 3